Brilliant Microsoft® Excel 2007

Steve Johnson

Perspection, Inc.

PEARSON
Prentice
Hall

Harlow, England • London • New York • Boston • San Francisco • Toronto
Sydney • Tokyo • Singapore • Hong Kong • Seoul • Taipei • New Delhi
Cape Town • Madrid • Mexico City • Amsterdam • Munich • Paris • Milan

Pearson Education Limited
Edinburgh Gate
Harlow
Essex CM20 2JE
England

and Associated Companies throughout the world

Visit us on the World Wide Web at:
www.pearsoned.co.uk

Original edition, entitled MICROSOFT OFFICE EXCEL ON DEMAND, 1st edition, 078973642X by
JOHNSON, STEVE; PERSPECTION, INC., published by Pearson Education, Inc, publishing as
Que/Sams, Copyright © 2007 Perspection, Inc.

This UK edition published by PEARSON EDUCATION LTD, Copyright © 2007

This edition is manufactured in the USA and available for sale only in the United Kingdom, Europe,
the Middle East and Africa

The right of Steve Johnson to be identified as author of this work has been asserted
by him in accordance with the Copyright, Designs and Patents Act 1988.

ISBN: 978-0-132-05890-2

British Library Cataloguing-in-Publication Data
A catalogue record for this book is available from the British Library

10 9 8 7 6 5 4 3 2 1
10 09 08 07 06

Printed and bound in the United States of America

The publisher's policy is to use paper manufactured from sustainable forests.

Brilliant Guides

What you need to know and how to do it

When you're working on your PC and come up against a problem that you're unsure how to solve, or want to accomplish something in an application that you aren't sure how to do, where do you look?? Manuals and traditional training guides are usually too big and unwieldy and are intended to be used as an end-to-end training resource, making it hard to get to the info you need right away without having to wade through pages of background information that you just don't need at that moment – and helplines are rarely that helpful!

Brilliant guides have been developed to allow you to find the info you need easily and without fuss and guide you through the task using a highly visual, step-by-step approach – providing exactly what you need to know when you need it!!

Brilliant guides provide the quick easy-to-access information that you need, using a detailed index and troubleshooting guide to help you find exactly what you need to know, and then presenting each task on one or two pages. Numbered steps then guide you through each task or problem, using numerous screenshots to illustrate each step. Added features include "See Also ..." boxes that point you to related tasks and information in the book, whilst "Did you know?..." sections alert you to relevant expert tips, tricks and advice to further expand your skills and knowledge.

In addition to covering all major office PC applications, and related computing subjects, the *Brilliant* series also contains titles that will help you in every aspect of your working life, such as writing the perfect CV, answering the toughest interview questions and moving on in your career.

Brilliant guides are the light at the end of the tunnel when you are faced with any minor or major task!

a

Acknowledgements

Perspection, Inc.

Brilliant Microsoft Excel 2007 has been created by the professional trainers and writers at Perspection, Inc.

Perspection, Inc. is a software training company committed to providing information and training to help people use software more effectively in order to communicate, make decisions, and solve problems. Perspection writes and produces software training books, and develops multimedia and Web-based training. Since 1991, we have written more than 80 computer books, with several bestsellers to our credit, and sold over 5 million books.

This book incorporates Perspection's training expertise to ensure that you'll receive the maximum return on your time. You'll focus on the tasks and skills that increase productivity while working at your own pace and convenience.

We invite you to visit the Perspection Web site at:

www.perspection.com

Acknowledgements

The task of creating any book requires the talents of many hard-working people pulling together to meet impossible deadlines and untold stresses. We'd like to thank the outstanding team responsible for making this book possible: the writer, Steve Johnson; the technical editor, Alex Williams; the production team, Emily Atwood, Alex Williams, and Dori Hernandez; the editors and proofreaders, Emily Atwood and Holly Johnson; and the indexer, Katherine Stimson.

At Que publishing, we'd like to thank Greg Wiegand and Stephanie McComb for the opportunity to undertake this project, Michelle Newcomb for administrative support, and Sandra Schroeder for your production expertise and support.

Perspection

About The Author

Steve Johnson has written more than thirty-five books on a variety of computer software, including Microsoft Office 2003 and XP, Microsoft Windows XP, Apple Mac OS X Panther, Macromedia Flash MX 2004 and 8, Macromedia Director MX 2004, Macromedia Fireworks, and Adobe Photoshop CS and CS2. In 1991, after working for Apple Computer and Microsoft, Steve founded Perspection, Inc., which writes and produces software training. When he is not staying up late writing, he enjoys playing golf, gardening, and spending time with his wife, Holly, and three children, JP, Brett, and Hannah. When time permits, he likes to travel to such places as New Hampshire in October, and Hawaii. Steve and his family live in Pleasanton, California, but can also be found visiting family all over the western United States.

Contents

C

3 Working with Formulas and Functions 71

Introduction

Welcome to *Brilliant Microsoft Excel 2007*, a visual quick reference book that shows you how to work efficiently with Microsoft Office Excel. This book provides complete coverage of basic to advanced Excel skills.

How This Book Works

You don't have to read this book in any particular order. We've designed the book so that you can jump in, get the information you need, and jump out. However, the book does follow a logical progression from simple tasks to more complex ones. Each task is presented on no more than two facing pages, which lets you focus on a single task without having to turn the page. To find the information that you need, just look up the task in the table of contents or index, and turn to the page listed. Read the task introduction, follow the step-by-step instructions in the left column along with screen illustrations in the right column, and you're done.

What's New

If you're searching for what's new in Excel 2007, just look for the icon: **New!**. The new icon appears in the table of contents and through out this book so you can quickly and easily identify a new or improved feature in Excel 2007. A complete description of each new feature appears in the New Features guide in the back of this book.

Keyboard Shortcuts

Most menu commands have a keyboard equivalent, such as Ctrl+P, as a quicker alternative to using the mouse. A complete list of keyboard shortcuts is available on the Web at *www.perspection.com*.

How You'll Learn

How This Book Works

What's New

Keyboard Shortcuts

Step-by-Step Instructions

Real World Examples

Workshop

Microsoft Office Specialist

Get More on the Web

Introduction

Welcome to *Microsoft Office Excel 2007 On Demand*, a visual quick reference book that shows you how to work efficiently with Microsoft Office Excel. This book provides complete coverage of basic to advanced Excel skills.

How This Book Works

You don't have to read this book in any particular order. We've designed the book so that you can jump in, get the information you need, and jump out. However, the book does follow a logical progression from simple tasks to more complex ones. Each task is presented on no more than two facing pages, which lets you focus on a single task without having to turn the page. To find the information that you need, just look up the task in the table of contents or index, and turn to the page listed. Read the task introduction, follow the step-by-step instructions in the left column along with screen illustrations in the right column, and you're done.

What's New

If you're searching for what's new in Excel 2007, just look for the icon: **New!**. The new icon appears in the table of contents and through out this book so you can quickly and easily identify a new or improved feature in Excel 2007. A complete description of each new feature appears in the New Features guide in the back of this book.

Keyboard Shortcuts

Most menu commands have a keyboard equivalent, such as Ctrl+P, as a quicker alternative to using the mouse. A complete list of keyboard shortcuts is available on the Web at *www.perspection.com*.

iⁱ

Step-by-Step Instructions

This book provides concise step-by-step instructions that show you "how" to accomplish a task. Each set of instructions include illustrations that directly correspond to the easy-to-read steps. Also included in the text are time-savers, tables, and sidebars to help you work more efficiently or to teach you more in-depth information. A "Did You Know?" provides tips and techniques to help you work smarter, while a "See Also" leads you to other parts of the book containing related information about the task.

Real World Examples

This book uses real world examples files to give you a context in which to use the task. By using the example files, you won't waste time looking for or creating sample files. You get a start file and a result file, so you can compare your work. Not every topic needs an example file, such as changing options, so we provide a complete list of the example files used through out the book. The example files that you need for project tasks along with a complete file list are available on the Web at *www.perspection.com*.

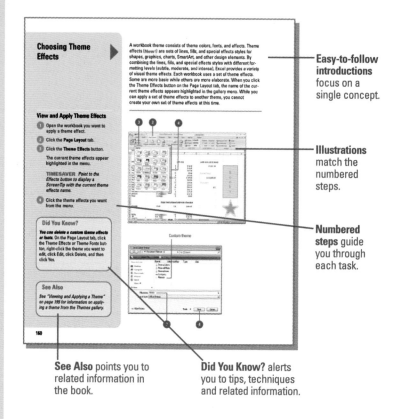

Easy-to-follow introductions focus on a single concept.

Illustrations match the numbered steps.

Numbered steps guide you through each task.

See Also points you to related information in the book.

Did You Know? alerts you to tips, techniques and related information.

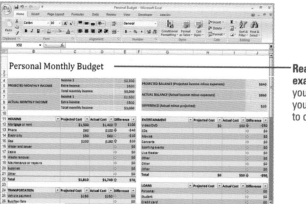

Real world examples help you apply what you've learned to other tasks.

Workshop

This book shows you how to put together the individual step-by-step tasks into indepth projects with the Workshop. You start each project with a sample file, work through the steps, and then compare your results with project results file at the end. The project files are available on the Web at *www.perspection.com*.

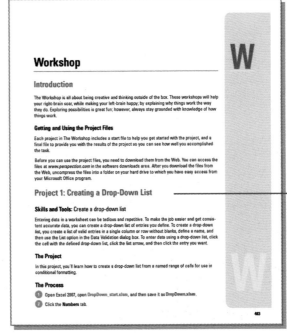

The **Workshop** walks you through indepth projects to help you put Microsoft Office to work.

Microsoft Certified Applications Specialist

This book prepares you for the Microsoft Certified Applications Specialist (MCAS) exam for Microsoft Office Excel 2007. Each MCAS certification exam has a set of objectives, which are organized into broader skill sets. To prepare for the certification exam, you should review and perform each task identified with a MCAS objective to confirm that you can meet the requirements for the exam. Throughout this book, content that pertains to an objective is identified with the following MCAS logo and objective number next to it.

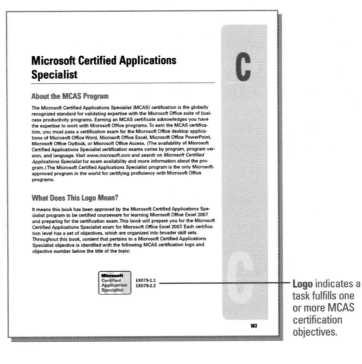

Logo indicates a task fulfills one or more MCAS certification objectives.

Get More on the Web

In addition to the information in this book, you can also get more information on the Web to help you get up to speed faster with Excel 2007. Some of the information includes:

Transition Helpers

◆ **Only New Features.** Download and print the new feature tasks as a quick and easy guide.

Productivity Tools

◆ **Keyboard Shortcuts.** Download a list of keyboard shortcuts to learn faster ways to get the job done.

More Content

◆ **Photographs.** Download photographs and other graphics to use in your Office documents.

◆ **More Content.** Download new content developed after publication. For example, you can download a complete chapter on Office SharePoint Server 2007.

You can access these additional resources on the Web at *www.perspection.com*.

Working Together on Office SharePoint Documents

S

Introduction

Microsoft Windows SharePoint Services is a collection of products and services which provide the ability for people to engage in communication, document and file sharing, calendar events, sending alerts, tasks planning, and collaborative discussions in a single community solution.

Office SharePoint Server 2007 is a product that uses Windows SharePoint Services 3.0 or later technology to work effectively with Microsoft Office 2007 programs. You can create a slide library on a Office SharePoint site in PowerPoint 2007 (New!), use Office SharePoint list data to create reports in Access 2007, create a meeting workspace and synchronize calendar and contacts in Outlook 2007, design browser form templates in InfoPath 2007 (New!), and save worksheets on an Office SharePoint site in Excel 2007. In many of the Office 2007 programs, you can update properties for a server document in a Document Information Panel (New!), and participate in workflows (New!), which is the automated movement of documents or items through a sequence of actions or tasks, such as document approval.

Office 2007 programs use the Document Management task pane to access many Office SharePoint Server 2007 features. The Document Management task pane allows you to see the list of team members collaborating on the current project, find out who is online, send an e-mail message, and review tasks and other resources. You can also use the Document Management task pane to create document workspaces where you can collect, organize, modify, share, and discuss Office documents.

Before you can use Office SharePoint Server 2007 the software needs to be set up and configured on a Windows 2003 Server or later by your network administrator. You can view Office SharePoint Server sites using a Web browser or a mobile device (New!) while you're on the road.

What You'll Do

View and Navigate Office SharePoint Sites

Create a Document Workspace Site

Create a Document Library Site

Add and Upload Documents to a Site

Add Pages to a Site

Publish Slides to a Library

Saving a File to a Document Management Server

View Versions of Documents

Check Documents In and Out to Edit

Work with Shared Workspace

View Team Members

Create Lists

Create Events

Hold Web Discussions

Set Up Alerts

Customize Quick Launch or Top Link Bar

1

Additional content is available on the Web. You can download a chapter on SharePoint.

Getting Started with Excel

Introduction

Microsoft Office Excel 2007 is a spreadsheet program that you can use to track and analyze sales, create budgets, and organize finances—both business and personal. You can also use Excel to manage inventory, set up investment reports or create loan amortizations. Microsoft Excel is a financial tool for performing calculations and other tasks automatically, which allows you to accomplish a variety of business or personal tasks in a fraction of the time it would take using pen and paper.

This chapter introduces you to the terminology and the basic Excel skills you can use in the program. In Excel, files are called **workbooks**. Each new workbook contains a default setting (which you can change) of three **worksheets**, which are similar to the pages in an accountant's ledger. You can format the worksheets for your specific project at hand, or you can download pre-made templates from Microsoft's Office Online Web site.

With the results-oriented visual interface, you navigate through various tasks with a click of the mouse, or by using shortcut keys on your keyboard. Microsoft Excel is set up with a tab-based Ribbon (New!) and dialog boxes that provide you with the tools you need when you need them to get tasks done. The customizable Quick Access Toolbar (New!) gives you easy access to commonly-used commands, such as Save and Print.

When you finish the design of your worksheet you can save it in a more efficient XML format (New!) or as a PDF or XPS document (New!), send it through e-mail for review, or even collaborate and share it with co-workers using a SharePoint library (New!). Should something happen to your workbook or worksheets, Excel has a recovery feature designed to help recover your worksheet.

Starting Excel

The two quickest ways to start Excel are to select it on the Start menu or double-click a shortcut icon on the desktop. By providing different ways to start a program, Office lets you work the way you like and start programs with a click of a button. When you start Excel, a program window opens, displaying a blank workbook, where you can begin working immediately.

Start Excel from the Start Menu

1. Click the **Start** button on the taskbar.

2. Point to **All Programs**.

3. Click **Microsoft Office**.

4. Click **Microsoft Office Excel 2007**.

   If Microsoft Office asks you to activate the program, follow the instructions to complete the process.

   TIMESAVER *To activate Microsoft Office later, click the Office button, click Excel Options, click Resources, and then click Activate.*

   If a Privacy dialog box appears, select the options you want, and then click OK.

Did You Know?

You can create a program shortcut from the Start menu to the desktop. Click the Start menu, point to All Programs, click Microsoft Office, right-click Microsoft Office Excel 2007, point to Send To, and then click Desktop (Create Shortcut).

You can start Excel and open a workbook from Windows Explorer. Double-clicking any Excel workbook icon in Windows Explorer opens that file and Excel.

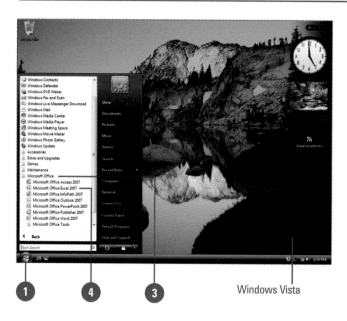

Windows Vista

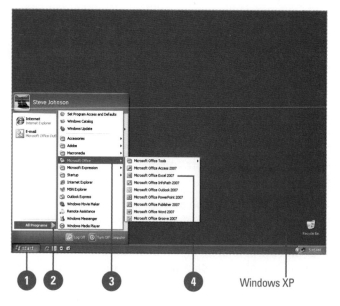

Windows XP

Viewing the Excel Window

Office button
Click to access Office file commands.

Quick Access Toolbar
Click to access command comments on this customizable toolbar.

Tabs
Click to access tools and commands.

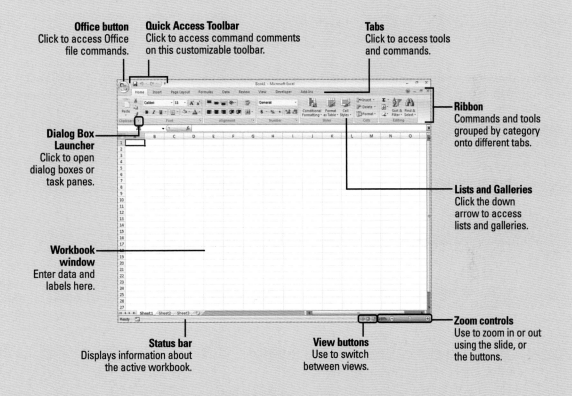

Dialog Box Launcher
Click to open dialog boxes or task panes.

Workbook window
Enter data and labels here.

Ribbon
Commands and tools grouped by category onto different tabs.

Lists and Galleries
Click the down arrow to access lists and galleries.

Status bar
Displays information about the active workbook.

View buttons
Use to switch between views.

Zoom controls
Use to zoom in or out using the slide, or the buttons.

Using the Ribbon

The **Ribbon** (New!) is a new look for Excel 2007. It replaces menus, toolbars, and most of the task panes found in Excel 2003. The Ribbon is located at the top of the workbook window and is comprised of **tabs** (New!) that are organized by task or objects. The controls on each tab are organized into **groups**, or sub-tasks. The controls, or **command buttons**, in each group execute a command, or display a menu of commands or a drop-down gallery. Controls in each group provide a visual way to quickly make workbook changes.

> **TIMESAVER** *To minimize the Ribbon, double-click the name of the tab that is displayed, or click the Customize Quick Access Toolbar list arrow, and then click Minimize the Ribbon. Click a tab to auto display it (Ribbon remains minimized). Double-click a tab to maximize it.*

If you prefer using the keyboard instead of the mouse to access commands on the Ribbon, Microsoft Office provides easy to use shortcuts. Simply press and release the [Alt] or [F10] key to display **KeyTips** (New!) over each feature in the current view, and then continue to press the letter shown in the KeyTip until you press the one that you want to use. To cancel an action and hide the KeyTips, press and release the [Alt] or [F10] key again. If you prefer using the keyboard shortcuts found in previous versions of Microsoft Office, such as Ctrl+P (for Print), all the keyboard shortcuts

and keyboard accelerators work exactly the same in Microsoft Office 2007. Office 2007 includes a legacy mode that you can turn on to use familiar Office 2003 keyboard accelerators.

Tabs

Excel provides three types of tabs on the Ribbon. The first type is called a **standard** tab—such as Home, Insert, Page Layout, Formulas, Data, Review, View, and Add-Ins—that you see whenever you start Excel. The second type is called a **contextual** tab—such as Picture Tools, Drawing, or Table—that appear only when they are needed based on the type of task you are doing. Excel recognizes what you're doing and provides the right set of tabs and tools to use when you need them. The third type is called a **program** tab—such as Print Preview—that replace the standard set of tabs when you switch to certain views or modes.

Live Preview

When you point to a gallery option, such as WordArt, on the Ribbon, Excel displays a **live preview** (New!) of the option change so that you can see exactly what your change will look like before committing to it.

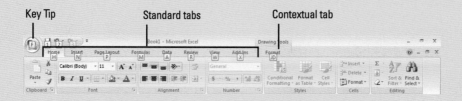

Key Tip   Standard tabs   Contextual tab

Choosing Commands

The Excel commands are organized in groups on the Ribbon, Office menu (**New!**), Quick Access Toolbar, and Mini-Toolbar. The Office button opens to display file related menu commands, while the Quick Access Toolbar and Mini-Toolbar display frequently used buttons that you may be already familiar with from Excel 2003. In addition to the Office menu, you can also open a **shortcut menu** with a group of related commands by right-clicking a Excel element.

Choose a Command from the Office Menu

1. Click the **Office** button on the Ribbon.

2. Click the command you want.

    If the command is followed by an arrow, point to the arrow to see a list of related options, and then click the option you want.

    TIMESAVER *You can use a shortcut key to choose a command. Press and hold down the first key and then press the second key. For example, press and hold the Ctrl key and then press S (or Ctrl+S) to select the Save command.*

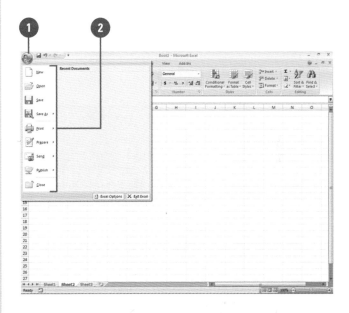

Choose a Command from a Shortcut Menu

1. Right-click an object (a cell or graphic element).

    TIMESAVER *Press Shift+F10 to display the shortcut menu for a selected command.*

2. Click a command on the shortcut menu. If the command is followed by an arrow, point to the command to see a list of related options, and then click the option you want.

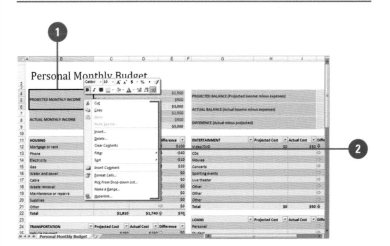

Working with Toolbars

Microsoft Certified Application Specialist EX07S-1.4.1

Excel includes its most common commands, such as Save and Undo, on the **Quick Access Toolbar** (New!). Click a toolbar button to choose a command. If you are not sure what a toolbar button does, point to it to display a ScreenTip. When Excel starts, the Quick Access Toolbar appears at the top of the Excel window, unless you've changed your settings. You can customize the toolbar by adding command buttons or groups to it. You can also move the toolbar below or above the Ribbon so it's right where you need it. In addition to the Quick Access Toolbar, Excel also displays the Mini-Toolbar when you point to selected text. The **Mini-Toolbar** (New!) appears above the selected text and provides quick access to formatting tools.

Choose a Command Using a Toolbar or Ribbon

◆ **Get command help**. If you're not sure what a button does, point to it to display a ScreenTip. If the ScreenTip includes *Press F1 for more help*, continue to point to the item, and then press F1.

◆ **Choose a command**. Click the button, or button arrow, and then click a command or option.

ScreenTip

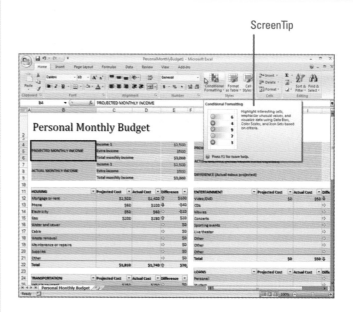

Did You Know?

You can move the Quick Access Toolbar to another location. Click the Customize Quick Access Toolbar list arrow, and then click Show Below the Ribbon or Show Above the Ribbon.

You can turn off ScreenTips or change the display. Click the Office button, click Excel Options, click Popular, click the ScreenTip Scheme list arrow, click Don't Show Enhanced ScreenTips or Don't Show ScreenTips, and then OK.

You can rest the Quick Access Toolbar to its original state. In the Excel Options dialog box, click Customize, click Reset, and then click OK.

You can minimize the Ribbon. Click the Customize Quick Access Toolbar list arrow, and then click Minimize the Ribbon. Click a tab to maximize it.

Add or Remove Items from the Quick Access Toolbar

◆ **Add or remove a common button**. Click the Customize Quick Access Toolbar list arrow, and then click a button name (checked item appears on the toolbar).

◆ **Add a Ribbon button or group**. Right-click the button or group name on the Ribbon, and then click Add to Quick Access Toolbar.

◆ **Remove a button or group**. Right-click the button or group name on the Quick Access Toolbar, and then click Remove from Quick Access Toolbar.

Customize Quick Access Toolbar list arrow   Click to add or remove frequently used buttons

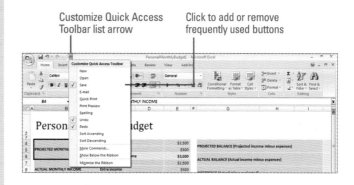

Click to add a button or group

Customize the Quick Access Toolbar

① Click the **Customize Quick Access Toolbar** list arrow, and then click **More Commands**.

② Click the **Choose commands from** list arrow, and then click **All Commands** or a specific Ribbon.

③ Click the **Customize Quick Access Toolbar** list arrow, and then click **For all documents (default)**.

Select the current workbook if you only want the commands available in the workbook.

④ Click the command you want to add (left column) or remove (right column), and then click **Add** or **Remove**.

TIMESAVER *Click <Separator>, and then click Add to insert a separator line between buttons.*

⑤ Click the **Move Up** and **Move Down** arrow buttons to arrange the order.

⑥ Click **OK**.

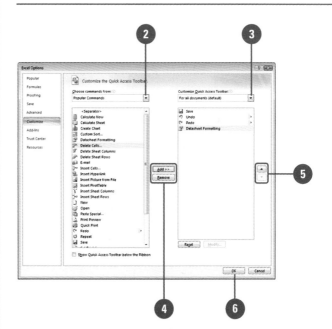

Choosing Dialog Box Options

A **dialog box** is a window that opens when you click a Dialog Box Launcher. **Dialog Box Launchers (New!)** are small icons that appear at the bottom corner of some groups. When you point to a Dialog Box Launcher, a ScreenTip with a thumbnail of the dialog box appears to show you which dialog box opens (**New!**). A dialog box allows you to supply more information before the program carries out the command you selected. After you enter information or make selections in a dialog box, click the OK button to complete the command. Click the Cancel button to close the dialog box without issuing the command. In many dialog boxes, you can also click an Apply button to apply your changes without closing the dialog box.

Choose Dialog Box Options

All dialog boxes contain the same types of options, including the following:

- ◆ **Tabs**. Click a tab to display its options. Each tab groups a related set of options.

- ◆ **Option buttons**. Click an option button to select it. You can usually select only one.

- ◆ **Up and down arrows**. Click the up or down arrow to increase or decrease the number, or type a number in the box.

- ◆ **Check box**. Click the box to turn on or off the option. A checked box means the option is selected; a cleared box means it's not.

- ◆ **List box**. Click the list arrow to display a list of options, and then click the option you want.

- ◆ **Text box**. Click in the box and type the requested information.

- ◆ **Button**. Click a button to perform a specific action or command. A button name followed by an ellipsis (...) opens another dialog box.

- ◆ **Preview box**. Many dialog boxes show an image that reflects the options you select.

Tabs

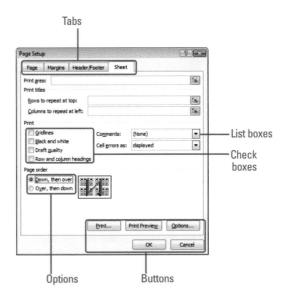

List boxes

Check boxes

Options   Buttons

For Your Information

Navigating a Dialog Box

Rather than clicking to move around a dialog box, you can press the Tab key to move from one box or button to the next. You can also use Shift+Tab to move backward, or Ctrl+Tab and Ctrl+Shift+Tab to move between dialog box tabs.

Using the Status Bar

The **Status bar** appears across the bottom of your screen and displays workbook information—such as cell mode, Office theme name, and current display zoom percentage—and some Excel controls, such as view shortcut buttons, zoom slider, and Fit To Window button. With the click of the mouse, you can quickly customize exactly what you see on the Status bar (**New!**). In addition to displaying information, the Status bar also allows you to check the on/off status of certain features (**New!**), such as Signatures, Permissions, Selection Mode, Page Number, Caps Lock, Num Lock, Macro Recording and Playback, and much more.

Add or Remove Items from the Status Bar

◆ **Add Item**. Right-click the Status bar, and then click an unchecked item.

◆ **Remove Item**. Right-click the Status bar, and then click a checked item.

> ### See Also
>
> See "Adding a Digital Signature" on page 344 or "Recording a Macro" on page 439 for information on changing the status of items on the Status bar.

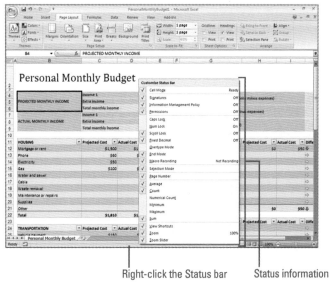

Right-click the Status bar   Status information

Creating a Blank Workbook

When you start Excel, the program window opens with a new workbook so that you can begin working in it. You can also start a new workbook whenever Excel is running, and you can start as many new workbooks as you want. Each new workbook displays a default name ("Book1," "Book2," and so on), numbered according to how many new workbooks you have started during the work session until you save it with a more meaningful name. The workbook name appears on the title bar, and taskbar buttons.

Start a Blank Workbook Within Excel

1. Click the **Office** button, and then click **New**.

   TIMESAVER *To create a blank workbook without a dialog box, press Ctrl+N.*

   The New Workbook dialog box appears.

2. In the left pane, click **Blank and recent**.

3. Click **Blank Workbook**.

4. Click **Create**.

   A new blank workbook appears in the Excel window.

> ## See Also
>
> *See "Setting New Workbook Options" on page 413 for information on personalizing options for new workbooks.*

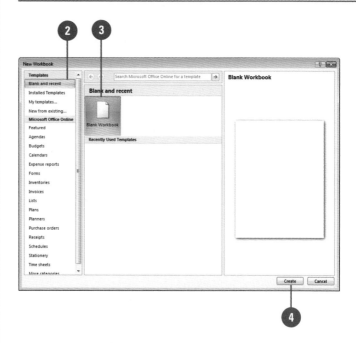

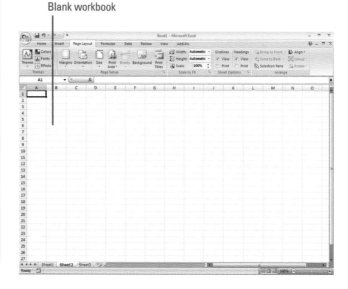

Blank workbook

10

Creating a Workbook Using a Template

Excel provides a collection of professionally designed templates that you can use to help you create workbooks. Start with a template when you have a good idea of your content but want to take advantage of a template's professional look. A **template** is an Excel workbook file (.xlsx) that provides you with a unified workbook design, which includes worksheets and themes, so you only need to add text and graphics. In the New Workbook dialog box, you can choose a template from those already installed with Excel or from Microsoft Office Online Web site, an online content library. You can choose a Microsoft Office Online template from one of the listed categories or from the Spotlight (**New!**) section in the Featured category. The Spotlight section highlights new Excel content, which you can set to automatically update.

Create a Workbook with a Template

1. Click the **Office** button, and then click **New**.

2. Choose one of the following:

   ◆ Click the **Blank and recent** category to open recently used templates.

   ◆ Click the **Installed Templates** category, and then click a template.

   ◆ Click the **My Templates** category to open a dialog box.

   ◆ Click the **Featured** category, and then click a template from the Spotlight section.

   ◆ Click a Microsoft Office Online template category, and then click a template.

3. Click **Create** or **Download**.

4. If necessary, click the template you want, and then click **OK**.

> **Did You Know?**
>
> *You can download template packs on the Web.* Go to *www.microsoft.com*, click the Office link, and then search for Excel Templates.

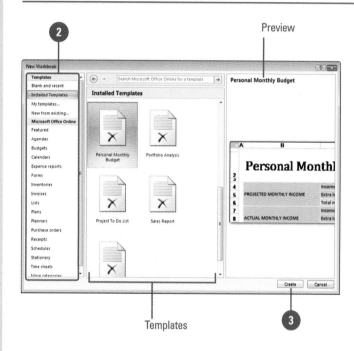

Preview

Templates

Opening an Existing Workbook

You can open an Excel workbook and start Excel simultaneously, or you can open an Excel workbook file or file created in another spreadsheet program after you start Excel. You can open an existing workbook from within Excel by using the Office button. On the Office menu, you can choose the Open command to locate and select the workbook you want or choose a recently used workbook from the Recent Documents list. Similar to the Windows Start menu, the Recent Documents list allows you to pin documents (**New!**) to the list that you want to remain accessible regardless of recent use. The Pin icon to the right of the file name on the Office menu makes it easy to pin or unpin as needed.

Open a Workbook from the Excel Window

1. Click the **Office** button, and then click **Open**, or click a recently used workbook.

2. If you want to open a specific file type, click the **Files of type** list arrow, and then click a file type.

3. If the file is located in another folder, click the **Look In** list arrow, and then navigate to the file.

4. Click the Excel file you want, and then click **Open**, or click the **Open** button arrow, and then click one of the following options:

   ◆ **Open Read-Only** to open the selected file with protection.

   ◆ **Open as Copy** to open a copy of the selected file.

   ◆ **Open in Browser** to open the selected Web file in a browser.

   ◆ **Open and Repair** to open the damaged file.

   ◆ **Show previous versions** to show previous versions of Excel documents.

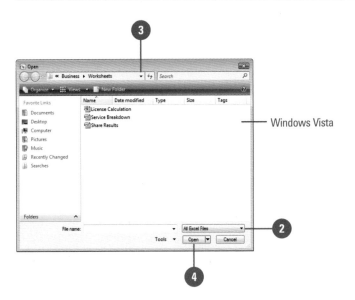

Windows Vista

For Your Information

Using the Excel Viewer

The Excel Viewer is a program used to open and view workbooks on computers that don't have Microsoft Excel installed. The Excel Viewer is available for download from the Microsoft Office Online Web site in the downloads section. Check the Microsoft Web site for software requirements.

Open a Recently Opened Workbook

1 Click the **Office** button.

2 Click the Excel workbook you want to open.

◆ **Pin a workbook**. Click the Pin icon (right-side) to display a green pin (document is pinned) on the Recent Documents list.

◆ **Unpin a workbook**. Click the Pin icon (right-side) to display a grey pin on the Recent Documents list.

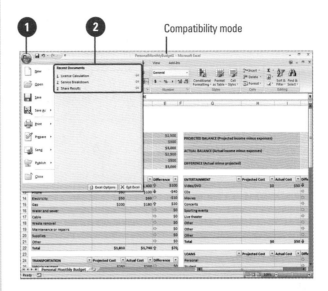

Compatibility mode

Did You Know?

You can change the number of recently opened files that appear on the Office menu. Click the Office button, click Excel Options, click Advanced, and then change the Number of documents in the Recent Documents list, and then click OK.

You can change the default file location of the Open dialog box. Click the Office button, click Excel Options, click Save, and then enter a new location in the Default File Location box, and then click OK.

You can delete or rename a file in a dialog box. In the Open or Save As dialog box, click the file, click the Tools list arrow, and then click Delete or Rename.

You can move or copy a file quickly in a dialog box. In the Open or Save As dialog box, right-click the file you want to move or copy, click Cut or Copy, open the folder where you want to paste the file, right-click a blank area, and then click Paste.

Excel 2007 Open File Formats

Opening Files with Different File Formats

Microsoft Excel can open a variety of different file formats using the Open dialog box. These include All Web Pages, XML Files, Text Files, All Data Sources, Access Databases, Query Files, dBASE Files, Microsoft Excel 4.0 Macros, Microsoft Excel 4.0 Workbooks, Worksheets, Workspaces, Templates, Add-Ins, Toolbars, SYLK Files, Data Interchange Format (DIF), and Backup Files. See "Saving a Workbook with Different Formats" on page 24 for a list and description of many of these formats.

Converting an Existing Workbook

When you open a workbook from Excel 97-2003, Excel 2007 goes into compatibility mode (**New!**)—indicated on the title bar—where it disables new features that cannot be displayed or converted well by previous versions. When you save a workbook, Excel 2007 saves Excel 97-2003 files in their older format using compatibility mode (**New!**). The workbook stays in compatibility mode until you convert it to the Excel 2007 file format.

Convert a Excel 97-2003 Workbook to Excel 2007

1. Open the Excel 97-2003 workbook you want to convert to the Excel 2007 file format

   The Excel 97-2003 workbook opens in compatibility mode.

2. Click the **Office** button, and then click **Convert**.

3. Click **OK** to convert the file to new Excel 2007 format.

   Excel exits compatibility mode, which is only turned on when a previous version is in use.

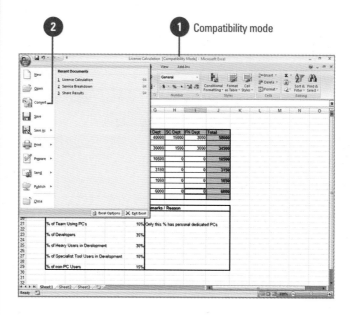

Compatibility mode

> ### Did You Know?
>
> *You can display extensions in the Save and Open dialog boxes and Recent Documents list.* Changing the Windows option also changes Excel. In the Folder Options dialog box on the View tab, clear the Hide extensions for known file types check box.

Using Task and Window Panes

Task panes are separate windows that appear when you need them, such as Document Recovery, or when you click a Dialog Box Launcher icon (**New!**), such as Office Clipboard and Clip Art. A task pane displays various options that relate to the current task. **Window panes** are sections of a window, such as a split window. If you need a larger work area, you can use the Close button in the upper-right corner of the pane to close a task or window pane, or move a border edge (for task panes) or **splitter** (for window panes) (**New!**) to resize it.

Work with Task and Window Panes

◆ **Open a Task Pane**. It appears when you need it or when you click a Dialog Box Launcher icon.

◆ **Close a Task or Window Pane**. Click the Close button in upper-right corner of the pane.

◆ **Resize a Task Pane**. Point to the Task Pane border edge until the pointer changes to double arrows, then drag the edge to resize it.

◆ **Resize a Window Pane**. Point to the window pane border bar until the pointer changes to a double bar with arrows, then drag the edge to resize it.

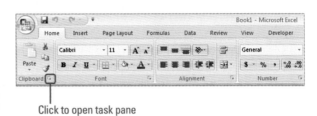

Click to open task pane

Task pane options

Close

> ### Did You Know?
>
> ***You can insert window panes.*** Click the View tab, click the Split button in the Window group.

> ### See Also
>
> *See "Splitting a Worksheet into Panes" on page 123 for more information on using the Split button.*

Moving Around the Workbook

You can move around a worksheet using your mouse or the keyboard. You might find that using your mouse to move from cell to cell is most convenient, while using various keyboard combinations is easier for quickly covering large areas of a worksheet. Or, you might find that entering numbers on the keypad and pressing Enter is a better method. Certain keys on the keyboard—Home, End, and Delete to name a few—are best used as shortcuts to navigate in the worksheet. However, there is no right way; whichever method feels the most comfortable is the one you should use.

Use the Mouse to Navigate

Using the mouse, you can navigate to:

◆ Another cell

◆ Another part of the worksheet

◆ Another worksheet

To move from one cell to another, point to the cell you what to move to, and then click.

When you click the wheel button on the IntelliMouse, the pointer changes shape. Drag the pointer in any direction to move to a new location quickly.

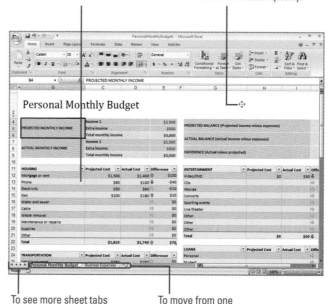

To see more sheet tabs without changing the location of the active cell, click a sheet scroll button

To move from one worksheet to another, click the tab of the sheet you want to move to.

For Your Information

Storing More Data in Excel 2007

Office Excel 2007 takes advantage of new technology to help you store more data and increase performance. Excel now supports over 1 million rows and 16 thousand columns in each worksheet, dual-processors and multi-threaded chips, memory management up to 2 GB, and up to 16 million colors (**New!**).

Use the Keyboard to Navigate

Using the keyboard, you can navigate in a worksheet to:

- ◆ Another cell
- ◆ Another part of the worksheet

  Refer to the table for keyboard shortcuts for navigating around a worksheet.

Did You Know?

You can change or move cell selections after pressing Enter. When you press Enter, the active cell moves down one cell. To change the direction, click the Office button, click Excel Options, click Advanced, click the Direction list arrow, select a direction, and then click OK.

Keys For Navigating in a Worksheet

Press This Key	To Move
Left arrow	One cell to the left
Right arrow	One cell to the right
Up arrow	One cell up
Down arrow	One cell down
Enter	One cell down
Tab	One cell to the right
Shift+Tab	One cell to the left
Page Up	One screen up
Page Down	One screen down
End+arrow key	In the direction of the arrow key to the next cell containing data or to the last empty cell in current row or column
Home	To column A in the current row
Ctrl+Home	To cell A1
Ctrl+End	To the last cell in the worksheet containing data

Go To a Specific Location

1 Click the **Home** tab.

2 Click the **Find & Select** button, and then click **Go To**.

3 Type the cell address to the cell location where you want to go.

4 To go to other locations (such as comments, blanks, last cell, objects, formulas, etc.), click **Special**, select an option, and then click **OK**.

   TIMESAVER *To open the Special dialog box directly, click the Find & Select button, and then click Go To Special.*

5 Click **OK**.

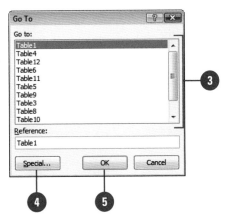

Arranging Windows

Microsoft Certified Application Specialist

EX07S-1.4.3

Every Office program and workbook opens inside a **window**, which contains a title bar, Ribbon, and work area, which is where you create and edit your data. Most often, you'll probably fill the entire screen with one window. But when you want to move or copy information between programs or documents, it's easier to display several windows at once. You can arrange two or more windows from one program or from different programs on the screen at the same time. However, you must make the window active to work in it. You can also click the document buttons on the taskbar to switch between open documents.

Resize and Move a Window

- **Maximize button**. Click to make a window fill the entire screen.

- **Restore Down button**. Click to reduce a maximized window to a reduced size.

- **Minimize button**. Click to shrink a window to a taskbar button. To restore the window to its previous size, click the taskbar button.

- **Close button**. Click to shut a window.

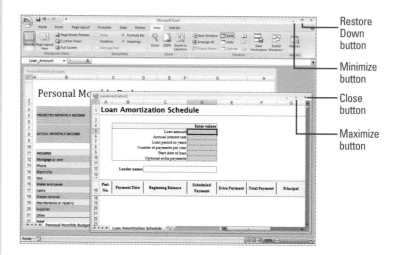

Restore Down button

Minimize button

Close button

Maximize button

Resize and Move a Window Using a Mouse

1. If the window is maximized, click the **Restore Down** button.

2. Use the following methods:

   - **Move**. Move the mouse over the title bar.

   - **Resize**. Move the mouse over one of the borders of the window until the mouse pointer changes into a two-headed arrow. The directions of the arrowheads show you the directions in which you can resize the window.

3. Drag to move or resize the window.

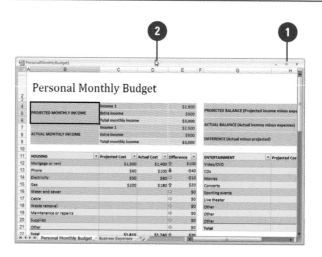

Arrange or Switch Between Windows

1 Open the workbooks you want to arrange or switch between.

2 Click the **View** tab.

3 In the Window group, perform any of the following:

◆ Click **Switch Windows**, and then click the workbook name you want.

◆ Click **Arrange**, click an arrange window option (Tiled, Horizontal, Vertical, or Cascade), and then click OK.

◆ Click **New Window** to open a new window containing a view of the current workbook.

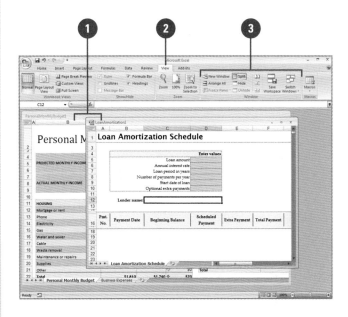

Compare Windows Side By Side

1 Open the workbooks you want to arrange or switch between.

2 Click the **View** tab.

3 In the Window group, perform any of the following:

◆ Click **View Side By Side** to compare two worksheets vertically.

◆ Click **Synchronous Scrolling** to synchronize the scrolling of two documents so that they scroll together. To enable this feature turn on View Side By Side.

◆ Click **Reset Window** to reset the window position of the documents being compared side-by-side so that they share the screen equally. To enable this feature turn on View Side By Side.

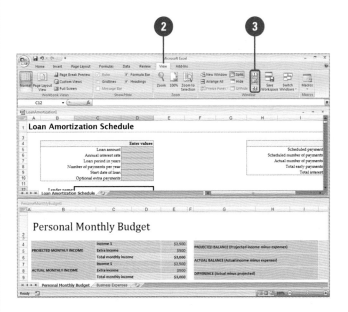

Getting Help While You Work

At some time, everyone has a question or two about the program they are using. The Excel Help Viewer provides the answers and resources you need, including feature help, articles, tips, templates, training, and downloads. By connecting to Microsoft Office Online, you not only have access to standard product help information, but you also have access to updated information over the Web without leaving the Help Viewer. The Web browser-like Help Viewer allows you to browse an extensive catalog of topics using a table of contents to locate information, or ask a question or enter phrases to search for specific information. When you use any of these help options, a list of possible answers is shown to you with the most likely answer or most frequently-used at the top of the list.

Using the Help Viewer to Get Answers

1. Click the **Help** button on the Ribbon.

   TIMESAVER *Press F1.*

2. Locate the Help topic you want.

   ◆ Click a Help category on the home page, and then click a topic (? icon).

   ◆ Click the **Table of Contents** button on the toolbar, click a help category (book icon) and then click a topic (? icon).

3. Read the topic, and then click any links to get Help information.

4. Click the **Back**, **Forward**, **Stop**, **Refresh**, and **Home** buttons on the toolbar to move around in the Help Viewer.

5. If you want to print the topic, click the **Print** button on the toolbar.

6. To keep the Help Viewer window (not maximized) on top or behind, click to toggle the **Keep On Top** button (pin pushed in) and **Not On Top** button (pin not pushed in) on the toolbar.

7. When you're done, click the **Close** button.

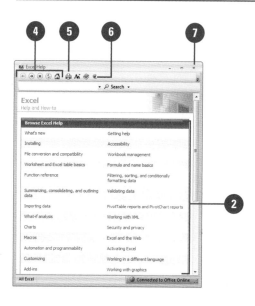

Topic

Search for Help

1. Click the **Help** button on the Ribbon.

2. Click the **Search button** list arrow below the toolbar, and then select the location and type of information you want.

3. Type one or more keywords in the Search For box, and then click the **Search** button.

4. Click a topic.

5. Read the topic, and then click any links to get information on related topics or definitions.

6. When you're done, click the **Close** button.

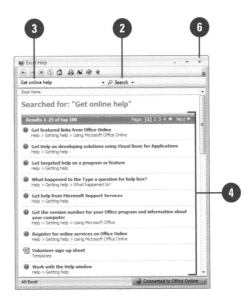

Check Help Connection Status

1. Click the **Help** button on the Ribbon.

2. Click the Connection Status at the bottom of the Help Viewer.

3. Click the connection option where you want to get help information:

   ◆ **Show content from Office Online** to get help from this computer and the internet (online).

   ◆ **Show content only from this computer** to get help from this computer only (offline).

   This setting is maintained for all Office 2007 program Help Viewers.

4. When you're done, click the **Close** button.

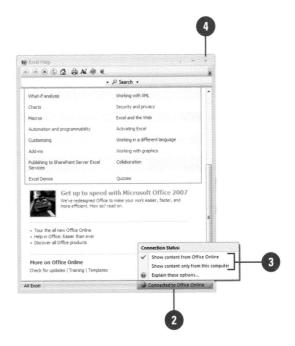

Saving a Workbook

Microsoft Certified Application Specialist

EX07S-5.4.1, EX07S-5.4.2

When you create an Excel workbook, save it as a file on your computer so you can work with it later. When you save a workbook for the first time or if you want to save a copy of a file, use the Save As command. When you want to save an open workbook, use the Save button on the Quick Access Toolbar. When you save a workbook, Excel 2007 saves Excel 97-2003 files in their older format using compatibility mode (**New!**) and new Excel 2007 files in an XML (Extensible Markup Language) based file format .xlsx (**New!**). The XML format significantly reduces file sizes, provides enhanced file recovery, and allows for increased compatibility, sharing, reuse, and transportability. An Excel 97-2003 workbook stays in compatibility mode—indicated on the title bar—until you convert it to the new Excel 2007 file format. Compatibility mode disables new features that cannot be displayed or converted well by previous versions.

Save a Workbook for Excel 2007

1. Click the **Office** button, point to **Save As**, and then click **Excel Workbook**.

   TIMESAVER *Press Ctrl+S, or click the Office button, and then click Save As.*

2. Click the **Save in** list arrow, and then click the drive or folder where you want to save the file.

   TIMESAVER *Click the New Folder button in the Save As dialog box to save the file to a new folder.*

3. Type a workbook file name.

4. Click the **File as type** list arrow, and then click **Excel Workbook**.

5. Click the Authors or Tags box to enter Document Properties.

6. Click **Save**.

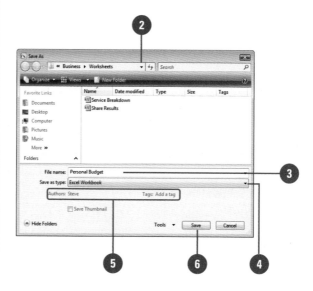

Did You Know?

You can access options from the Save dialog box. In the Save dialog box, click Tools, and then click the command option you want, either General, Web, or Compress Pictures.

Save an Excel 97-2003 Workbook

① Open the Excel 97-2003 workbook you want to continue to save in the Excel 97-2003 format.

The Excel 97-2003 workbook opens in compatibility mode.

② Click the **Save** button on the Quick Access Toolbar, or click **Office** button, and then click **Save**.

Excel stays in compatibility mode.

Set Save Options

① Click the **Office** button, and then click **Excel Options**.

② In the left pane, click **Save**.

③ Set the save options you want:

◆ **Default Save Format.** Click Save files in this format list arrow, and then click the default format you want.

◆ **Default File Location.** Specify the complete path to the folder location where you want to save your workbook.

④ Click **OK**.

Saving a Workbook with Different Formats

Microsoft
Certified
Application
Specialist

EX07S-5.4.2

Excel 2007 is a versatile spreadsheet program that allows you to save your workbook in a variety of different formats—see the table on the following page for a complete list and description. For example, you might want to save your workbook as a Web page that you can view in a Web browser. Or you can save a workbook in an earlier version of Excel (97-2003) in case the people you work with have not upgraded to Excel 2007. If you save a workbook to Excel 97-2003, some new features and formatting are converted to uneditable pictures or not retained. The new format is compatible with Office 2003, Office XP, and Office 2000 with a software patch. However, for best results, if you're creating a workbook for someone with Excel 97 to Excel 2003, it's better to save it with the .xls file format. In addition to the new XML-based file format, Excel also allows you to save a workbook in a binary file format (or BIFF12), which is based on the segmented compressed file format (**New!**). This file format is most useful for large or complex workbooks, and optimized for performance and backward compatibility.

Save a Workbook with Another Format

1. Click the **Office** button, point to **Save As**, and then click the format you want:

   ◆ **Excel 97-2003 Workbook.**

   ◆ **Excel Binary Workbook.**

   ◆ **Other Formats.**

2. Click the **Save in** list arrow, and then click the drive or folder where you want to save the file.

3. Type a workbook file name.

4. If necessary, click the **File as type** list arrow, and then click the file format you want.

5. Click **Save**.

See Also

See "Creating a PDF Document" on page 183 or "Creating an XPS Document" on page 184 for information on using and saving a workbook with different formats.

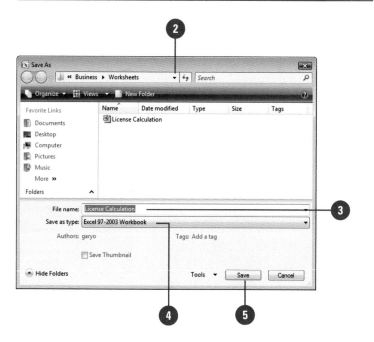

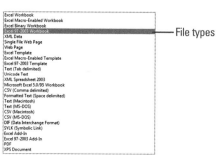

File types

Excel 2007 Save File Formats

Save As file type	Extension	Used to save
Excel Workbook (**New!**)	.xlsx	Excel 2007 workbook
Excel Macro-Enabled Workbook (**New!**)	.xlsm	Excel 2007 workbook that contains Visual Basic for Applications (VBA) code
Excel Binary Workbook (**New!**)	.xlsb	Excel 2007 workbook with a binary format of the segmented compressed file format for large or complex workbooks
Excel 97-2003 Workbook	.xls	Excel 97 to Excel 2003 workbook
XML Data	.xml	XML document
Single File Web Page	.mht; .mhtml	Web page as a single file with an .htm file
Web Page	.htm; .html	Web page as a folder with an .htm file
Excel Template (**New!**)	.xltx	Excel 2007 template
Excel Macro-Enabled Template (**New!**)	.xltm	Excel 2007 template that includes preapproved macros
Excel 97-2003 Template (**New!**)	.xlt	Excel 97-2003 template
Text (Tab delimited)	.txt	Text file with tabs between the data
Unicode Text	.txt	Character format; useful for complex languages, such as Greek, Chinese and Japanese.
XML Spreadsheet 2003	.xml	Excel workbook 2003 with the XML format
Microsoft Excel 5.0/95	.xls	Excel workbook in the Excel 5.0/95 version
CSV (Comma delimited)	.csv	Text file with commas separating data
Formatted Text (Space delimited)	.prn	Text file with spaces separating data
Text (Macintosh) or Text (MS-DOS)	.txt	Text file with the Macintosh or MS-DOS
CSV (Macintosh) or CSV (MS-DOS)	.csv	Text file with commas separating data
DIF (Data Interchange Format)	.dif	Text file with a header and body
SYLK (Symbolic Link)	.slk	File divided into records by a return or Enter key
Excel Add-in (**New!**)	.xlam	Excel 2007 add-in that stores specialized functionality, such as VBA code
Excel 97-2003 Add-in	.xla	Excel 97-2003 add-in that stores specialized functionality, such as VBA code
PDF Workbook (**New!**)	.pdf	Fixed-layout electronic file format that preserves document formatting developed by Adobe
XPS Document Format (**New!**)	.xps	Fixed-layout electronic file format that preserves document formatting developed by Microsoft

Checking Compatibility

EX07S-5.4.1

The Compatibility Checker (**New!**) identifies the potential loss of functionality when you save an Excel 2007 workbook in the Excel 97-2003 Workbook file format. The Compatibility Checker generates a report that provides a summary of the potential losses and the number of occurrences in the workbook. Use the report information to determine what caused each message and for suggestions on how to change it. If the loss is due to a new feature in Excel 2007—such as custom layouts or Quick Styles applied to shapes, pictures, and WordArt—you might be able to simply remove the effect or feature. In other cases, you might not be able to do anything about it. To maintain a visual appearance, SmartArt graphics and other objects with new effects are converted to bitmaps to preserve their overall look and cannot be edited.

Check Workbook Compatibility

1. Click the **Office** button, point to **Prepare**, and then click **Run Compatibility Checker**.

   Office checks compatibility of the workbook for non supported features in earlier versions of Excel.

2. View the compatibility summary information, so you can make changes, as necessary.

3. To have the compatibility checker check the workbook when Excel saves the file, select the **Check compatibility when saving this workbook** check box.

4. Click **OK**.

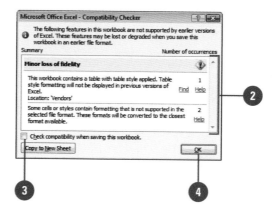

Documenting Workbook Properties

EX07S-5.3.3

Excel automatically documents workbook properties while you work, such as file size, save dates, and various statistics, and allows you to document other properties, such as title, author, subject, keywords, category, and status. You can view or edit standard document properties or create advanced custom properties by using the **Document Information Panel** (New!), which is actually an XML-based Microsoft InfoPath 2007 form hosted in Excel. You can use document properties—also known as metadata—to help you manage and track files; search tools can use the metadata to find a workbook based-on your search criteria. If you associate a document property to an item in the document, the document property updates when you change the item.

View and Edit Standard Workbook Properties

1 Click the **Office** button, point to **Prepare**, and then click **Properties**.

2 Enter the standard properties, such as author, title, subject, keywords, category, status, and comments, in the Document Information Panel.

3 Click the **Close** button on the Document Information Panel.

Document Properties

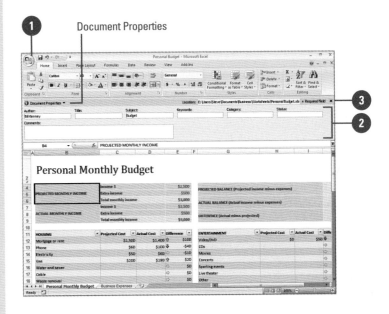

Did You Know?

Your Document Information Panel might look different. If you save your document to a SharePoint library or a document management server, your Document Information Panel might have additional properties.

You can view or change document properties when you open or save a file. In the Open or Save As dialog box, select the document you want, click the arrow next to the Views, and then click Details to view file size and last changed date, or click Properties to view all information. If you want to insert or change author names or keywords, click the Authors box or Tags box, and then type what you want.

Switching Views

Microsoft
Certified
Application
Specialist

EX07S-1.4.1

Excel includes a view selector (**New!**) in the lower-right of the workbook window, where you can use buttons to quickly switch between Excel views: Normal, Page Layout, and Page Break Preview. **Normal view** is the main view in Excel. It lets you focus on entering, modifying, and managing your data. **Page Layout view** (**New!**) is the printout related view. It lets you focus on how your worksheet is going to look when you print it. You can work with page setup, headers, footers, margins, and shapes in this view to make sure pages look the way you want. You use Page Break Preview view along with Page Layout view. **Page Break Preview view** lets you see how your worksheet data appears on pages. In addition to the view selector, you can also use the View tab to switch between views. On the View tab, you can also switch to Full Screen view, which allows you to see the maximum amount of worksheet data your screen can display without the Ribbon, tabs, or Status bar.

Switch Between Views

◆ **Use the View Selector.** On the right-side of the Status bar, click any of the following view buttons: **Normal View, Page Layout View,** or **Page Break Preview View**.

◆ **Use the View tab.** Click the View tab, and then click any of the following view buttons: **Normal View, Page Layout View, Page Break Preview View,** or **Full Screen**.

To exit Full Screen View, press Esc.

View tab buttons

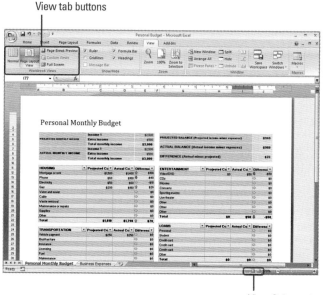

View Selector buttons

Getting Excel Updates on the Web

Excel offers a quick and easy way to update Excel with any new software downloads that improve the stability and security of the program. From the Resources area in the Excel Options dialog box, simply click the Check for Updates button to connect to the Microsoft Update Web site to have your computer scanned for necessary updates, and then choose which Office updates you want to download and install.

Get Excel Updates on the Web

1. Click the **Office** button, and then click **Excel Options**.

2. In the left pane, click **Resources**.

3. Click **Check for Updates** to open the Microsoft Update Web site.

4. Click one of the update buttons to find out if you need Excel updates, and then choose the updates you want to download and install.

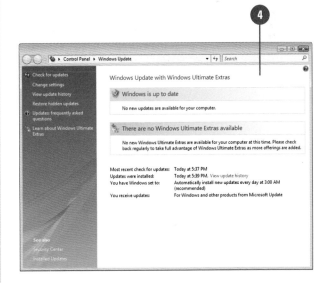

Did You Know?

You can contact Microsoft for help. You can get support over the phone, chat, or e-mail messages. To get online help, click the Office button, click Excel Options, click Resources, and then click Contact Us. To get offline help, click the Office button, click Excel Options, click Resources, click About, and then click Tech Support for contact information.

You can get better help information. At the bottom of a help topic, click Yes, No, or I don't know to give Microsoft feedback on the usefulness of a topic.

Recovering a Workbook

If Excel encounters a problem and stops responding, the program tries to recover the file the next time you open Excel. The recovered files appear in the Document Recovery task pane, which allows you to open the files, view what repairs were made, and compare the recovered versions. Each file appears in the task pane with a status indicator, either Original or Recovered, which shows what type of data recovery was performed. You can save one or all of the file versions. You can also use the AutoRecover feature to periodically save a temporary copy of your current file, which ensures proper recovery of the file.

Recover a Workbook

① When the Document Recovery task pane appears, click the list arrow next to the name of each recovered file, and then perform one of the following:

◆ Click **Open** to view the file for review.

◆ Click **Save As** to save the file.

◆ Click **Delete** to close the file without saving.

◆ Click **Show Repairs** to find out how Excel fixed the file.

② When you're done, click the **Close** button.

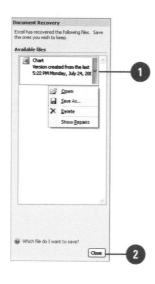

Use AutoRecover

① Click the **Office** button, and then click **Excel Options**.

② In the left pane, click **Save**.

③ Select the **Save AutoRecover information every _x_ minutes** check box.

④ Enter the number of minutes, or click the **Up** and **Down** arrows to adjust the minutes.

⑤ Specify the complete path to the folder location where you want to save your AutoRecover workbook file.

⑥ To disable AutoRecover for a specific workbook, perform the following:

  ◆ Click the **File** list arrow, select the workbook you want to disable.

  ◆ Select the **Disable AutoRecover for this workbook only** check box.

⑦ Click **OK**.

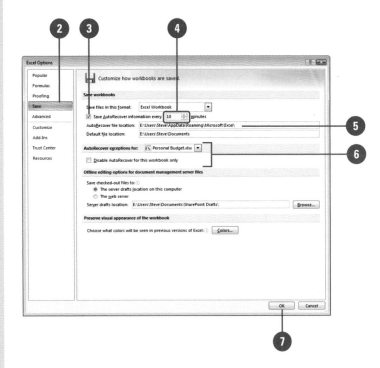

Diagnosing and Repairing Problems

At times you may determine that Excel is not working as efficiently as it once did. This sometimes happens when you install new software or move files into new folders. Use the Diagnose command to improve performance by repairing problems, such as missing files from setup, corrupted file by malicious viruses, and registry settings. Note that this feature does not repair personal files, such as your workbooks. If the Diagnose command does not fix the problem, you might have to reinstall Excel. If you need to add or remove features, reinstall Excel, or remove it entirely, you can use Office Setup's maintenance feature.

Diagnose and Repair Problems

① Click the **Office** button, and then click **Excel Options**.

② In the left pane, click **Resources**.

③ Click **Diagnose**.

> **TIMESAVER** *In Windows, click Start, point to All Programs, click Microsoft Office, click Microsoft Office Tools, and then click Microsoft Office Diagnostics.*

The Microsoft Office Diagnostics dialog box appears.

④ Click **Continue**, and then click **Run Diagnostics**.

Office runs several diagnostics to determine and fix any problems. This might take 15 minutes or more. A diagnostic report appears in your browser:

◆ **Setup.** Checks for corrupt files and registry settings.

◆ **Disk.** Checks error logs.

◆ **Memory.** Checks integrity of computer RAM.

◆ **Update.** Checks for Office updates on Web.

◆ **Compatibility.** Checks for conflicts with Outlook.

◆ **Check for known solutions.** Checks data on Office program crashes on your computer.

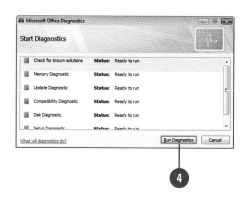

Perform Maintenance on Office Programs

1 Insert the Excel or Office CD in your drive.

2 In Windows Explorer, double-click the Setup icon on the Excel or Office CD.

3 Click one of the following maintenance buttons.

◆ **Add or Remove Features** to change which features are installed or remove specific features.

◆ **Repair** to reinstall or repair Microsoft Office 2007 to its original state.

◆ **Remove** to uninstall Microsoft Office 2007 from this computer.

4 Click **Continue**, and then follow the wizard instructions to complete the maintenance.

See Also

See "Working with Office Safe Modes" on page 360 for information on fixing problems with a Microsoft Office 2007 program.

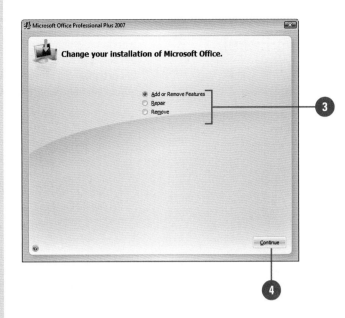

Add or Remove Features

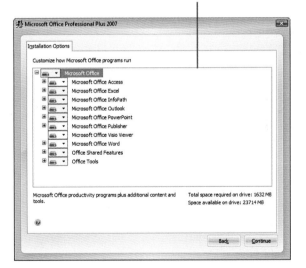

Closing a Workbook and Quitting Excel

After you finish working on a workbook, you can close it. Closing a file makes more computer memory available for other activities. Closing a workbook is different from quitting Excel; after you close a workbook, Excel is still running. When you're finished using Excel, you should quit the program. To protect your files, always save your workbooks and quit Excel before turning off the computer.

Close a Workbook

1. Click the **Close** button on the workbook window, or click the **Office** button, and then click **Close**.

   TIMESAVER *Press Ctrl+W.*

2. If you have made changes to any open files since last saving them, a dialog box opens, asking if you want to save changes. Click **Yes** to save any changes, or click **No** to ignore your changes.

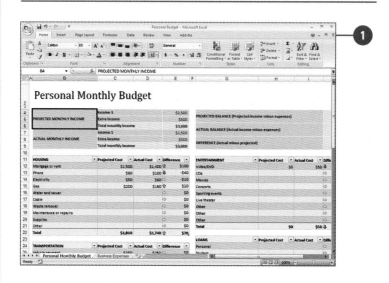

Exit Excel

1. Click the **Close** button on the Excel window, or click the **Office** button, and then click **Exit Excel**.

   TIMESAVER *Press Ctrl+Q.*

2. If you have made changes to any open files since last saving them, a dialog box opens asking if you want to save changes. Click **Yes** to save any changes, or click **No** to ignore your changes.

Excel window Close button

Basic Workbook Skills

2

Introduction

Creating a Microsoft Office Excel workbook is as easy as entering data in the cells of an Excel worksheet. Each cell has a **cell address** which is made up of its column and row intersection. Cells on a worksheet contain either labels or values, a formula or remain blank. Cell entries can be modified using the keyboard or mouse. You can select cells in ranges that are **contiguous** (selected cells are adjacent to each other) or **noncontiguous** (selected cells are in different parts of the worksheet). Selected cells are used in formulas, to copy and paste data, to AutoFill, to apply date and time and other formatting functions.

In addition, Excel offers a Find and Replace feature that allows you to look for labels and values and make changes as necessary. When you need to spell check your worksheet, Excel can check and suggest spelling corrections. You can even customize the spelling dictionary by adding company specific words into AutoCorrect so that the spell checker doesn't think it's a misspelled word. The Smart Tags feature works with other Microsoft Office programs to enhance your worksheets. Contact information can be pulled from your address book in Outlook, to your worksheet in Excel. Stock symbols can trigger a Smart Tag choice to import data on a publicly traded company. Additional research and language tools area available to build up the content of you workbooks.

If you accidentally make a change to a cell, you can use the Undo feature to remove, or "undo," your last change. Excel remembers your recent changes to the worksheet, and gives you the opportunity to undo them. If you decide to Redo the Undo, you can erase the previous change. This is useful when moving, copying, inserting and deleting cell contents.

What You'll Do

Make Label Entries

Select Cells, Row, Columns, and Special Ranges

Enter Labels and Values on a Worksheet

Enter Values Quickly with AutoFill

Edit and Clear Cell Contents

Understand How Excel Pastes Data

Store and Copy Cell Contents

Move Cell Contents

Insert and Delete Cell Contents

Find and Replace Cell Contents

Correct Cell Contents with AutoCorrect

Insert Information the Smart Way

Check Your Spelling

Change Proofing Options

Use Custom Dictionaries

Find the Right Words

Insert Research Material

Translate Text to Another Language

Use the English Assistant

Undo and Redo an Action

Making Label Entries

There are three basic types of cell entries: labels, values, and formulas. A **label** is text in a cell that identifies the data on the worksheet so readers can interpret the information. Excel does not use labels in its calculations. For example, the label *price* is used as a column header to identify the price of each item in the column. A **value** is a number you enter in a cell. Excel knows to include values in its calculations. To quickly and easily enter values, you can format a cell, a range of cells, or a column with a specific number-related format. Then, as you type, the cells are automatically formatted.

To perform a calculation in a worksheet, you enter a formula in a cell. A **formula** is a calculation that contains cell references, values, and arithmetic operators. The result of a formula appears in the worksheet cell where you entered the formula. The contents of the cell appears on the formula bar. Entering cell references rather than actual values in a formula has distinct advantages. When you change the data in the worksheet or copy the formula to other cells (copying this formula to the cell below), Excel automatically adjusts the cell references in the formula and returns the correct results.

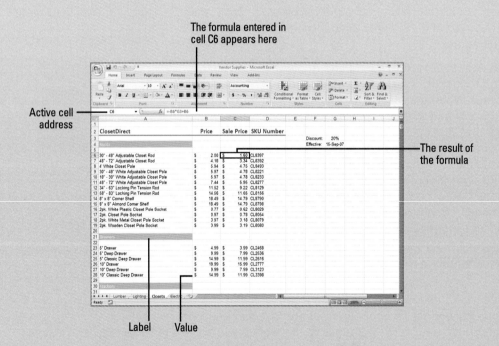

The formula entered in cell C6 appears here

Active cell address

The result of the formula

Label   Value

Selecting Cells

In order to work with a cell—to enter data in it, edit or move it, or perform an action—you **select** the cell so it becomes the active cell. When you want to work with more than one cell at a time—to move or copy them, use them in a **formula**, or perform any group action—you must first select the cells as a **range**. A range can be **contiguous** (where selected cells are adjacent to each other) or **non-contiguous** (where the cells may be in different parts of the worksheet and are not adjacent to each other). As you select a range, you can see the range reference in the Name box. A **range reference** contains the cell address of the top-left cell in the range, a colon (:), and the cell address of the bottom-right cell in the range.

Select a Contiguous Range

1. Click the first cell that you want to include in the range.

2. Drag the mouse to the last cell you want to include in the range.

   TIMESAVER *Instead of dragging, hold down the Shift key, and then click the lower-right cell in the range.*

   When a range is selected, the top-left cell is surrounded by the cell pointer, while the additional cells are selected.

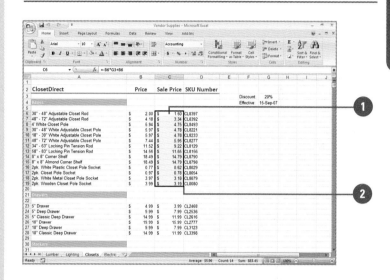

Select a Non-contiguous Range

1. Click the first cell you want to include in the range.

2. Drag the mouse to the last contiguous cell, and then release the mouse button.

3. Press and hold Ctrl, and then click the next cell or drag the pointer over the next group of cells you want in the range.

   To select more, repeat step 3 until all non-contiguous ranges are selected.

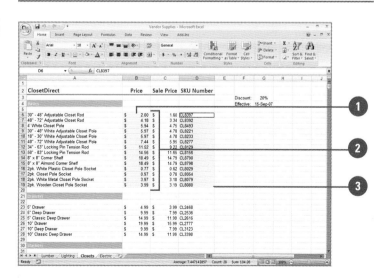

Selecting Rows, Columns, and Special Ranges

In addition to selecting a range of contiguous and non-contiguous cells in a single worksheet, you may need to select entire rows and columns, or even a range of cells across multiple worksheets. Cells can contain many different types of data, such as comments, constants, formulas, or conditional formats. Excel provides an easy way to locate these and many other special types of cells with the Go To Special dialog box. For example, you can select the Row Differences or Column Differences option to select cells that are different from other cells in a row or column, or select the Dependents option to select cells with formulas that refer to the active cell.

Select an Entire Rows or Columns

- To select a single row or column, click in the row or column heading, or select any cell in the row or column, and press Shift+spacebar.

- To select multiple adjacent rows or columns, drag in the row or column headings.

- To select multiple nonadjacent rows or columns, press Ctrl while you click the borders for the rows or columns you want to include.

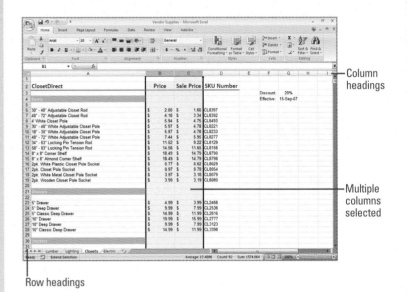

Column headings

Multiple columns selected

Row headings

Select Multisheet Ranges

① Select the range in one sheet.

② Select the worksheets to include in the range.

To select contiguous worksheets, press Shift and click the last sheet tab you want to include. To select non-contiguous worksheets, press Ctrl and click the sheets you want.

When you make a worksheet selection, Excel enters Group mode.

③ To exit Group mode, click any sheet tab.

Group selection

Make Special Range Selections

① If you want to make a selection from within a range, select the range you want.

② Click the **Home** tab.

③ Click the **Find & Select** button, and then click **Go To Special**.

TIMESAVER *Press F5 to open the Go To Special dialog box.*

④ Select the option in which you want to make a selection. When you click the Formulas option, select or clear the formula related check boxes.

⑤ Click **OK**.

If no cells are found, Excel displays a message.

Entering Labels on a Worksheet

Labels turn a worksheet full of numbers into a meaningful report by identifying the different types of information it contains. You use labels to describe the data in worksheet cells, columns, and rows. You can enter a number as a label (for example, the year 2007), so that Excel does not use the number in its calculations. To help keep your labels consistent, you can use Excel's **AutoComplete** feature, which automatically completes your entries (excluding numbers, dates, or times) based on previously entered labels.

Enter a Text Label

1. Click the cell where you want to enter a label.

2. Type a label. A label can include uppercase and lowercase letters, spaces, punctuation, and numbers.

3. Press Enter, or click the **Enter** button on the formula bar.

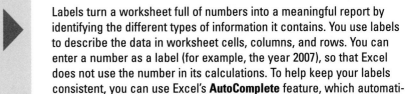

Enter a Number as a Label

1. Click the cell where you want to enter a number as a label.

2. Type ′ (an apostrophe). The apostrophe is a label prefix and does not appear on the worksheet.

3. Type a number value.

4. Press Enter, or click the **Enter** button on the formula bar.

   If a green triangle appears, it indicates a smart tag. Select the cell to display the Error Smart Tag button, where you can select options related to the label.

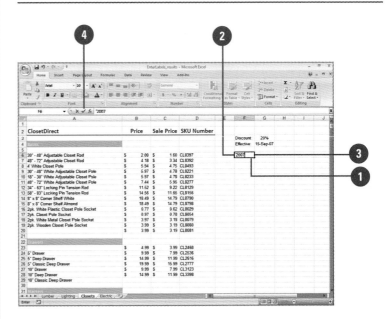

Enter a Label Using AutoComplete

① Type the first few characters of a label.

If Excel recognizes the entry, AutoComplete completes it.

② To accept the suggested entry, press Enter or click the **Enter** button on the formula bar.

③ To reject the suggested completion, simply continue typing.

Did You Know?

Excel doesn't recognize the entry.
The AutoComplete option may not be turned on. To turn on the feature, click the Office button, click Excel Options, click Advanced, select Enable AutoComplete for cell values check box, and then click OK.

Long labels might appear truncated.
When you enter a label that is wider than the cell it occupies, the excess text appears to spill into the next cell to the right—unless there is data in the adjacent cell. If that cell contains data, the label will appear truncated—you'll only see the portion of the label that fits in the cell's current width. Click the cell to see its entire contents displayed on the formula bar.

AutoComplete label

Entering Values on a Worksheet

You can enter values as whole numbers, decimals, percentages, or dates using the numbers on the top row of your keyboard, or by pressing your Num Lock key, the numeric keypad on the right. When you enter a date or the time of day, Excel automatically recognizes these entries (if entered in an acceptable format) as numeric values and changes the cell's format to a default date or time format. You can also change the way values, dates or times of day are shown.

Enter a Value

1. Click the cell where you want to enter a value.

2. Type a value.

3. Press Enter, or click the **Enter** button on the formula bar.

> ### Did You Know?
>
> *You can use the numeric keypad to enter numbers.* Make sure NUM appears in the lower-right corner of the status bar. before you begin using the numbers.

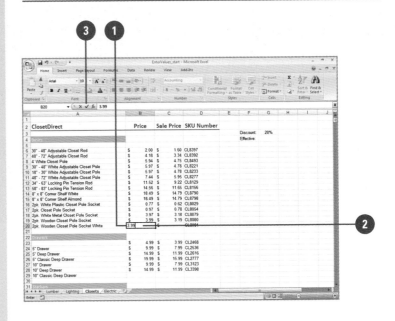

Enter a Date or Time

1. To enter a date, type the date using a slash (/) or a hyphen (-) between the month, day, and year in a cell or on the formula bar.

   To enter a time, type the hour based on a 12-hour clock, followed by a colon (:), followed by the minute, followed by a space, and ending with an "a" or a "p" to denote A.M. or P.M.

2. Press Enter, or click the **Enter** button on the formula bar.

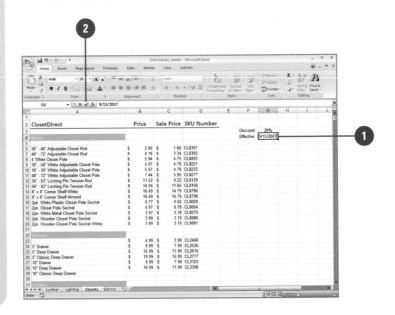

Format Values Quickly

① Click the cell that contains the date format you want to change.

② Click the **Home** tab.

③ Click the **Number Format** list arrow.

④ Click the number format you want, which includes:

◆ **General.** No specific format.

◆ **Number.** 38873.00

◆ **Currency.** $38,873.00

◆ **Accounting.** $ 38,873.00

◆ **Short Date.** 6/5/2006

◆ **Long Date.** Monday, June 5, 2006

◆ **Time.** 12:00:00 AM

◆ **Percentage.** 38873.00%

◆ **Fraction.** 38873

◆ **Scientific.** 3.89E+04

◆ **More Number Formats.** Opens the Format Cell dialog box, where you can format cells with multiple options at one time.

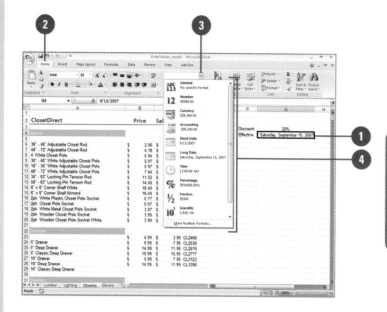

More Number Formats command

Entering Values Quickly with AutoFill

Microsoft Certified Application Specialist

EX07S-1.1.1,
EX07S-1.1.2

AutoFill is a feature that automatically fills in data based on the data in adjacent cells. Using the **fill handle**, you can enter data in a series, or you can copy values or formulas to adjacent cells. A single cell entry can result in a repeating value or label, or the results can be a more complex series. You can enter your value or label, and then complete entries such as days of the week, weeks of the year, months of the year, or consecutive numbering.

Enter Repeating Data Using AutoFill

1. Select the first cell in the range you want to fill.

2. Enter the starting value to be repeated.

3. Position the pointer on the lower-right corner of the selected cell. The pointer changes to the fill handle (a black plus sign).

4. Drag the fill handle over the range you want the value repeated.

5. To choose how to fill the selection, click the **AutoFill Options** button, and then click the option you want.

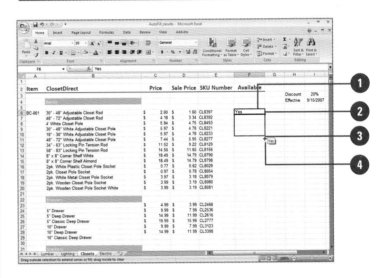

Create a Complex Series Using AutoFill

1. Enter the starting value for the series, and then press Enter.

2. Select the first cell in the range you want to fill.

3. Position the pointer on the lower-right corner of the selected cell. The pointer changes to the fill handle (a black plus sign).

4. Drag the fill handle over the range you want the value repeated.

5. To choose how to fill the selection, click the **AutoFill Options** button, and then click the option you want.

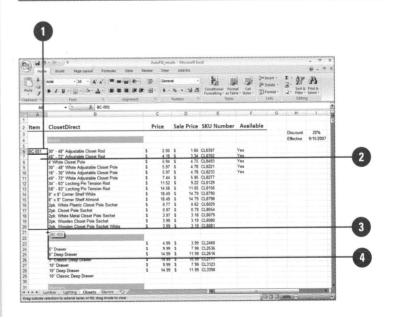

Fill with Contents of Adjacent Cells

1. Select the cell below, to the right, above, or to the left of the cell that contains the data you want to fill.

2. Click the **Home** tab.

3. Click the **Fill** button, and then click **Down**, **Right**, **Up** or **Left**.

   TIMESAVER *To quickly fill a cell with the contents of the cell above or to the left of it, press Ctrl+D or Ctrl+R.*

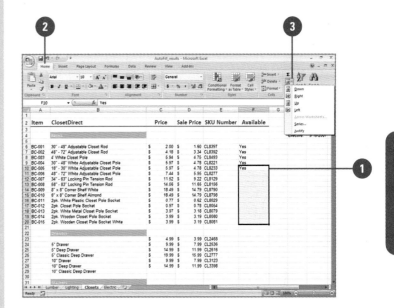

Did You Know?

You can suppress AutoFill. Hold down Ctrl while you drag the fill handle of a selection of two or more cells. The values are copied to the adjacent cells, and Excel does not extend a series.

Create a Custom Fill

1. If you want to use an existing list, select the list of items.

2. Click the **Office** button, and then click **Excel Options**.

3. In the left pane, click **Popular**.

4. Click **Edit Custom Lists**.

5. Click the option you want.

   ◆ **New list.** Click **NEW LIST**, type the entries you want, press Enter after each. Click **Add**.

   ◆ **Existing list.** Verify the cell reference of the selected list appears in the Import list, and then click **Import**.

6. Click **OK**, and then click **OK** again.

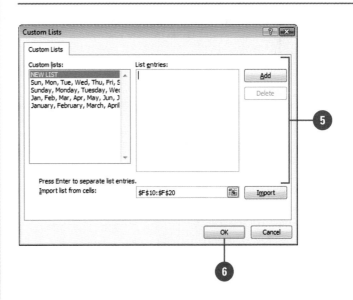

Editing Cell Contents

Even if you plan ahead, you can count on having to make changes on a worksheet. Sometimes it's because you want to correct an error. Other times it's because you want to see how your worksheet results would be affected by different conditions, such as higher sales, fewer units produced, or other variables. You can edit data just as easily as you enter it, using the formula bar or directly editing the active cell.

Edit Cell Contents

1 Double-click the cell you want to edit. The insertion point appears in the cell.

The Status bar now displays Edit instead of Ready.

2 If necessary, use the Home, End, and arrow keys to position the insertion point within the cell contents.

3 Use any combination of the Backspace and Delete keys to erase unwanted characters, and then type new characters as needed.

4 Click the **Enter** button on the formula bar to accept the edit, or click the Esc button to cancel the edit.

The Status bar now displays Ready instead of Edit.

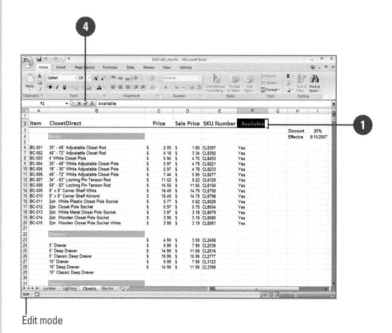

Edit mode

Did You Know?

You can change editing options. Click the Office button, click Excel Options, click Advanced, change the editing options you want, and then click OK.

You can edit cell contents using the formula bar. Click the cell you want to edit, click to place the insertion point on the formula bar, and then edit the cell contents.

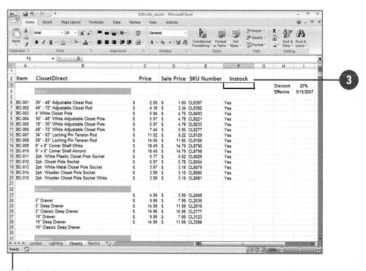

Ready mode

Clearing Cell Contents

You can clear a cell to remove its contents. Clearing a cell does not remove the cell from the worksheet; it just removes from the cell whatever elements you specify: data, comments (also called **cell notes**), or formatting instructions. When clearing a cell, you must specify whether to remove one, two, or all three of these elements from the selected cell or range.

Clear Cell Contents, Formatting, and Comments

1. Select the cell or range you want to clear.

2. Click the **Home** tab.

3. Click the **Clear** button, and then click any of the following options:

    ◆ **Clear All.** Clears contents and formatting.

    ◆ **Clear Formats.** Clears formatting and leaves contents.

    ◆ **Clear Contents.** Clears contents and leaves formatting.

    ◆ **Clear Comments.** Clears comments; removes purple triangle indicator.

    TIMESAVER *To quickly clear contents, select the cell or range you want to clear, right-click the cell or range, and then click Clear Contents, or press Delete.*

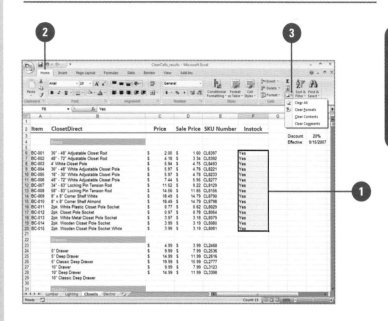

Did You Know?

You can find or replace cell contents. Click the cell or cells containing content you want to replace. Click Home tab, click the Find & Select button, click Find. You can click the Replace tab for additional options.

Understanding How Excel Pastes Data

Microsoft Certified Application Specialist

EX07S-1.3.1

If you want to use data that has already been entered on your worksheet, you can cut or copy it, and then paste it in another location. When you cut or copy data, the data is stored in an area of memory called the Clipboard. When pasting a range of cells from the Clipboard, you only need to specify the first cell in the new location. After you select the first cell in the new location and then click the Paste button, Excel automatically places all the selected cells in the correct order. Depending on the number of cells you select before you cut or copy, Excel pastes data in one of the following ways:

- ◆ **One to one**. A single cell in the Clipboard is pasted to one cell location.

- ◆ **One to many**. A single cell in the Clipboard is pasted into a selected range of cells.

- ◆ **Many to one**. Many cells are pasted into a range of cells, but only the first cell is identified. The entire contents of the Clipboard will be pasted starting with the selected cell. Make sure there is enough room for the selection; if not, the selection will copy over any previously occupied cells.

- ◆ **Many to many**. Many cells are pasted into a range of cells. The entire contents of the Clipboard will be pasted into the selected cells. If the selected range is larger than the selection, the data will be repeated in the extra cells. To turn off the selection marquee and cancel your action, press the Esc key.

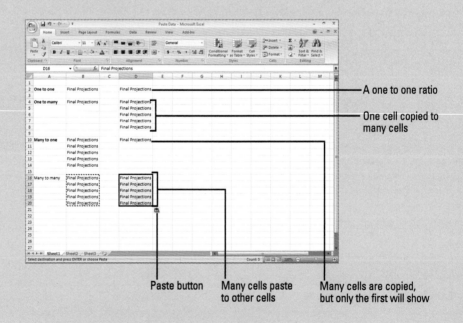

A one to one ratio

One cell copied to many cells

Paste button

Many cells paste to other cells

Many cells are copied, but only the first will show

Storing Cell Contents

Microsoft Certified Application Specialist

EX07S-1.3.1

With Microsoft Office, you can use the Office Clipboard to store multiple pieces of information from several different sources in one storage area shared by all Office programs. Unlike the Clipboard, which only stores a single piece of information at a time, the Office Clipboard allows you to copy text or pictures from one or more files. When you copy multiple items, you see the Office Clipboard, showing all the items you stored there. You can paste these pieces of information into any Office program, either individually or all at once.

Copy and Paste Data to the Office Clipboard

1. Click the **Home** tab.

2. Click the **Clipboard Dialog Box Launcher**.

3. Select the data you want to copy.

4. Click the **Copy** button.

   The data is copied into the first empty position on the Clipboard task pane.

5. Click the first cell or range where you want to paste data.

6. Click the Office Clipboard item you want to paste, or point to the item, click the list arrow, and then click **Paste**.

7. Click the **Close** button in the task pane.

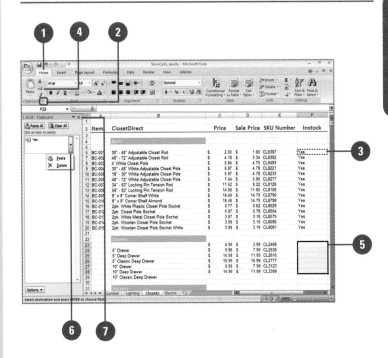

Did You Know?

You can change Office Clipboard options. At the bottom of the Office Clipboard, you can click the Options button to turn on and off any of the following options: Show Office Clipboard Automatically, Show Office Clipboard When Ctrl+C Pressed Twice, Collect Without Showing Office Clipboard, Show Office Clipboard Icon on Taskbar, or Show Status Near Taskbar When Copying.

Copying Cell Contents

Microsoft Certified Application Specialist

EX07S-1.3.1

You can **copy** and move data on a worksheet from one cell or range to another location on any worksheet in your workbook. When you copy data, a duplicate of the selected cells is placed on the Clipboard. To complete the copy or move, you must **paste** the data stored on the Clipboard in another location. With the Paste Special command, you can control what you want to paste and even perform mathematical operations. To copy or move data without using the Clipboard, you can use a technique called **drag-and-drop**. Drag-and-drop makes it easy to copy or move data short distances on your worksheet.

Copy Data Using the Clipboard

1. Select the cell or range that contains the data you want to copy.

2. Click the **Home** tab.

3. Click the **Copy** button.

   The data in the cells remains in its original location and an outline of the selected cells, called a **marquee**, shows the size of the selection. If you don't want to paste this selection, press Esc to remove the marquee.

4. Click the first cell or range where you want to paste the data.

5. Click the **Paste** button.

   The data remains on the Clipboard, available for further pasting, until you replace it with another selection.

   If you don't want to paste this selection anywhere else, press Esc to remove the marquee.

6. If you want to change the way the data pastes into the worksheet, click the **Paste Options** button, and then select the option you want.

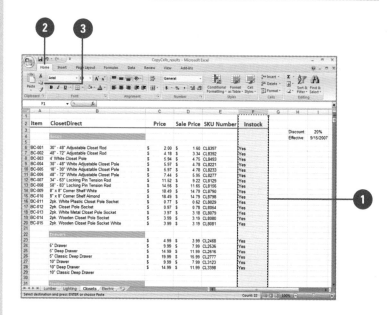

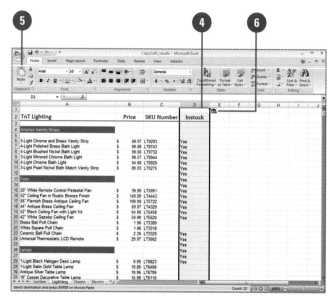

Copy Data Using Drag-and-Drop

1. Select the cell or range that contains the data you want to copy.

2. Move the mouse pointer to an edge of the selected cell or range until the pointer changes to an arrowhead.

3. Press and hold the mouse button and Ctrl.

4. Drag the selection to the new location, and then release the mouse button and Ctrl.

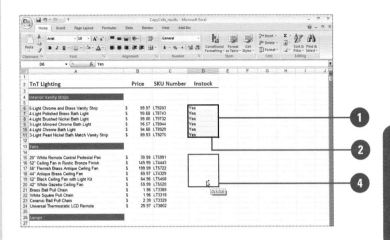

Paste Data with Special Results

1. Select the cell or range that contains the data you want to copy.

2. Click the **Home** tab.

3. Click the **Copy** button.

4. Click the first cell or range where you want to paste the data.

5. Click the **Paste** button, and then click **Paste Special**.

6. Click the option buttons with the paste results and mathematical operations you want.

7. Click **OK**.

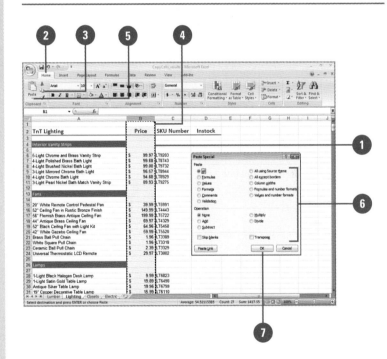

Did You Know?

You can use the Alt key to drag and drop to a different worksheet. Once cells are selected, press and hold Alt, and then drag the selection to the appropriate sheet tab. Release Alt, and then drag the selection to the desired location on the new worksheet.

Moving Cell Contents

Microsoft
Certified
Application
Specialist

EX07S-1.3.1

Unlike copied data, moved data no longer remains in its original location. Perhaps you typed data in a range of cells near the top of a worksheet, but later realized it should appear near the bottom of the sheet. **Moving** data lets you change its location without having to retype it. When you move data, you are cutting the data from its current location and pasting it elsewhere. **Cutting** removes the selected cell or range content from the worksheet and places it on the Clipboard.

Move Data Using the Clipboard

1. Select the cell or range that contains the data you want to move.

2. Click the **Home** tab.

3. Click the **Cut** button.

   An outline of the selected cells, called a marquee, shows the size of the selection. If you don't want to paste this selection, press Esc to remove the marquee.

4. Click the top-left cell of the range where you want to paste the data.

5. Click the **Paste** button.

   The marquee disappears. The data is still on the Clipboard and still available for further pasting until you replace it with another selection.

Did You Know?

You can use the Office Clipboard to cut multiple items. When the Office Clipboard task pane is displayed, selections you cut can be placed on this clipboard. You can move data to the Clipboard, and then paste it at a later time.

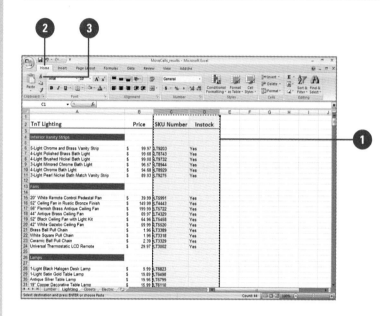

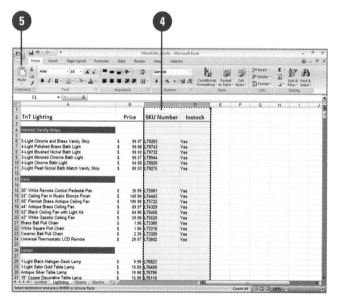

Move Data Using Drag-and-Drop

1. Select the cell or range that contains the data you want to move.

2. Move the mouse pointer to an edge of the cell until the pointer changes to an arrowhead.

3. Press and hold the mouse button while dragging the selection to its new location, and then release the mouse button.

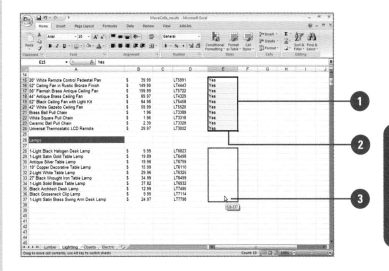

Paste Cells from Rows to Columns or Columns to Rows

1. Select the cells that you want to switch.

2. Click the **Home** tab.

3. Click the **Copy** button.

4. Click the top-left cell of where you want to paste the data.

5. Click the **Paste** button arrow, and then click **Transpose**.

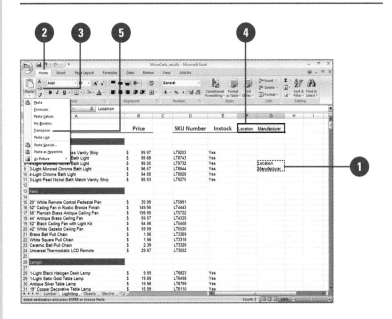

Inserting and Deleting Cell Contents

You can **insert** new, blank cells anywhere on the worksheet in order to enter new data or data you forgot to enter earlier. Inserting cells moves the remaining cells in the column or row in the direction of your choice, and Excel adjusts any formulas so they refer to the correct cells. You can also **delete** cells if you find you don't need them; deleting cells shifts the remaining cells to the left or up—just the opposite of inserting cells. When you delete a cell, Excel removes the actual cell from the worksheet.

Insert a Cell

1. Select the cell or cells where you want to insert the new cell(s).

2. Click the **Home** tab.

3. Click the **Insert Cells** button arrow, and then click **Insert Cells**.

    TIMESAVER *Click the Insert Cells button to quickly insert cells to the right.*

4. Click the option you want.

    ◆ **Shift Cells Right** to move cells to the right one column.

    ◆ **Shift Cells Down** to move cells down one row.

    ◆ **Entire Row** to move the entire row down one row.

    ◆ **Entire Column** to move entire column over one column.

5. Click **OK**.

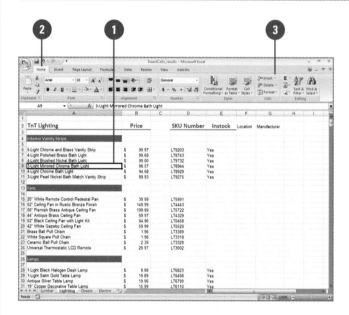

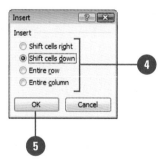

See Also

See "Finding and Replacing Cell Contents" on page 56 for information on substituting replacement text in a cell.

Delete a Cell

① Select the cell or range you want to delete.

② Click the **Home** tab.

③ Click the **Delete Cells** button arrow, and then click **Delete Cells**.

TIMESAVER *Click the Delete Cells button to quickly delete cells to the left.*

④ Click the option you want.

♦ **Shift Cells Left** to move the remaining cells to the left.

♦ **Shift Cells Up** to move the remaining cells up.

♦ **Entire Row** to delete the entire row.

♦ **Entire Column** to delete the entire column.

⑤ Click **OK**.

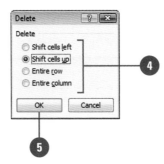

Did You Know?

There is a difference between deleting a cell and clearing a cell. Deleting a cell is different from clearing a cell: deleting removes the cells from the worksheet; clearing removes only the cell contents, or format, or both.

Finding and Replacing Cell Contents

The Find and Replace commands make it easy to locate or replace specific text or formulas in a document. For example, you might want to find each figure reference in a long report to verify that the proper graphic appears. Or you might want to replace all references to cell A3 in your Excel formulas with cell G3. The Find and Replace dialog boxes vary slightly from one Office program to the next, but the commands work essentially in the same way.

Find Cell Contents

1. Click at the beginning of the worksheet.

2. Click the **Home** tab.

3. Click the **Find & Select** button, and then click **Find**.

4. Type the text you want to find.

5. Click **Find Next** until the text you want to locate is highlighted.

   You can click **Find Next** repeatedly to locate each instance of the cell content.

6. To find all cells with the contents you want, click **Find All**.

7. If a message box opens when you reach the end of the worksheet, click **OK**.

8. Click **Close**.

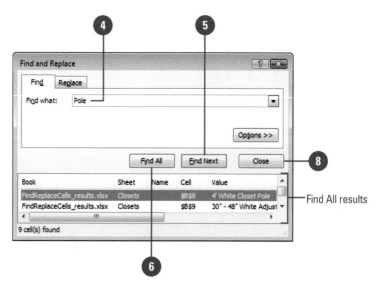

Find All results

Replace Cell Contents

① Click at the beginning of the worksheet.

② Click the **Home** tab.

③ Click the **Find & Select** button, and then click **Replace**.

④ Type the text you want to search for.

⑤ Type the text you want to substitute.

⑥ Click **Find Next** to begin the search, and then select the next instance of the search text.

⑦ Click **Replace** to substitute the replacement text, or click Replace All to substitute text throughout the entire worksheet.

You can click **Find Next** to locate the next instance of the cell content without making a replacement.

⑧ If a message box appears when you reach the end of the worksheet, click **OK**.

⑨ Click **Close**.

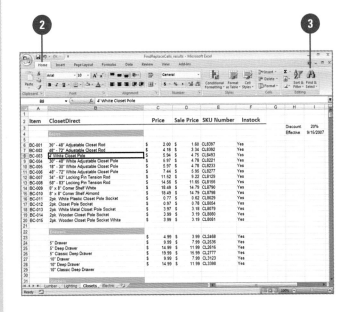

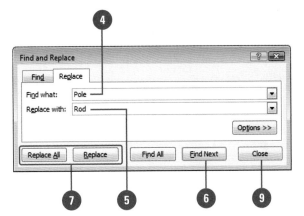

Correcting Cell Contents with AutoCorrect

Excel's **AutoCorrect** feature automatically corrects common capitalization and spelling errors as you type. AutoCorrect comes with hundreds of text and symbol entries you can edit or remove. You can add words and phrases to the AutoCorrect dictionary that you misspell, or add often-typed words and save time by just typing their initials. You could use AutoCorrect to automatically change the initials EPA to Environmental Protection Agency, for example. You can also use AutoCorrect to quickly insert symbols. For example, you can type (c) to insert ©. Use the AutoCorrect Exceptions dialog box to control how Excel handles capital letters. When you point to a word that AutoCorrect changed, a small blue box appears under the first letter. When you point to the small blue box, the AutoCorrect Options button appears, which gives you control over whether you want the text to be corrected. You can also display the AutoCorrect dialog box and change AutoCorrect settings.

Turn On AutoCorrect

1. Click the **Office** button, and then click **Excel Options**.

2. Click **Proofing**, and then click **AutoCorrect Options**.

3. Click the **AutoCorrect** tab.

4. Select the **Show AutoCorrect Options buttons** check box to display the button to change AutoCorrect option when corrections arise.

5. Select the **Replace Text As You Type** check box.

6. Select the capitalization related check boxes you want AutoCorrect to change for you.

7. To change AutoCorrect exceptions, click **Exceptions**, click the **First Letter** or **INitial CAps** tab, make the changes you want, and then click **OK**.

8. Click **OK**.

9. Click **OK** again.

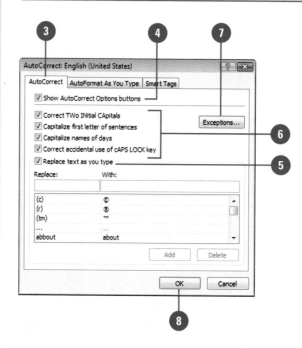

Add or Edit an AutoCorrect Entry

1. Click the **Office** button, and then click **Excel Options**.

2. Click **Proofing**, and then click **AutoCorrect Options**.

3. Click the **AutoCorrect** tab.

4. Do one of the following:

   ◆ **Add.** Type a misspelled word or an abbreviation.

   ◆ **Edit.** Select the one you want to change. You can either type the first few letters of the entry to be changed in the Replace box, or scroll to the entry, and then click to select it.

5. Type the replacement entry.

6. Click **Add** or **Replace**. If necessary, click Yes to redefine entry.

7. Click **OK**, and then click **OK** again.

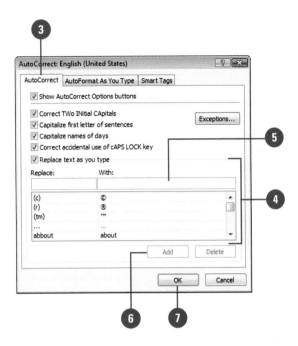

Did You Know?

You can correct text as you text. If Excel recognizes text to correct, it will correct the text and display the AutoCorrect button. Point to the small blue box under the corrected text, and then click the AutoCorrect Options button list arrow to view your options. Click an option, or click a blank area of the worksheet to deselect the AutoCorrect Options menu.

For Your Information

Inserting Symbols

Excel comes with a host of symbols for every need. Insert just the right one to keep from compromising a workbook's professional appearance with a missing mathematical symbol (å). To insert a symbol or special character, click the Insert tab, click the Symbol button, click a symbol, and then click Insert. In the Symbol dialog box, you can use the Recently used symbols list to quickly insert a symbol that you want to insert again. If you don't see the symbol you want, use the Font list to look at the available symbols for other fonts installed on your computer.

Inserting Information the Smart Way

Smart Tags help you integrate actions typically performed in other programs directly in Excel. For example, you can insert a financial symbol to get a stock quote, add a person's name and address in a worksheet to the contacts list in Microsoft Outlook, or copy and paste information with added control. Excel analyzes the data you type in a cell and recognizes certain types that it marks with smart tags. The types of actions you can take depend on the type of data in the cell with the smart tag.

Change Smart Tag Options

1. Click the **Office** button, and then click **Excel Options**.

2. In the left pane, click **Proofing**, and then click **AutoCorrect Options**.

3. Click the **Smart Tags** tab.

4. Select the **Label data with smart tags** check box.

5. Select the check boxes with the smart tags you want.

6. Click the **Show smart tags as** list arrow, and then select a display option.

7. To check the workbook for new smart tags, click **Check Workbook**.

8. To add more smart tags, click **More Smart Tags**, and then follow the online instructions.

9. To embed smart tags for future use, select the **Embed smart tags in this workbook** check box.

10. Click **OK**.

11. Click **OK** again.

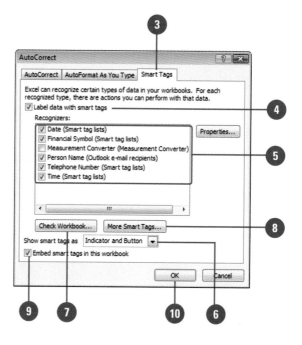

Online resource for Smart Tags

Insert Information Using a Smart Tag

1 Click a cell where you want to insert a smart tag.

2 Type the information needed for the smart tag, such as the date, a recognized financial symbol in capital letters, or a person's name from you contacts list, and then press Spacebar.

3 Click outside the cell, and then point to the purple triangle in the lower-right corner of the cell to display the Smart Tag button. The purple triangle in the corner of a cell indicates a smart tag is available for the cell contents.

4 Click the **Smart Tag** button, and then click the list arrow next to the button.

5 Click the smart tag option you want; options vary depending on the smart tag. For example, click Insert Refreshable Stock Price to insert a stock quote.

6 Click the **On a new sheet** option or the **Starting at cell** option, and then click **OK**.

A new worksheet is inserted in the workbook containing stock information.

Did You Know?

You can remove a smart tag from text. Point to the text with the smart tag, click the Smart Tag button, and then click Remove this Smart Tag.

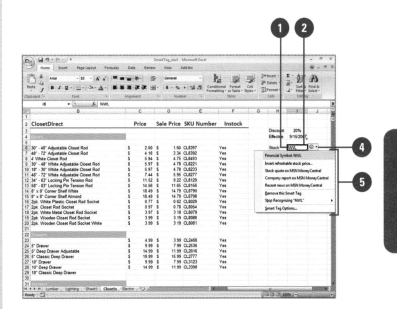

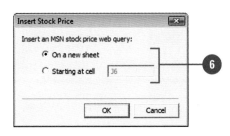

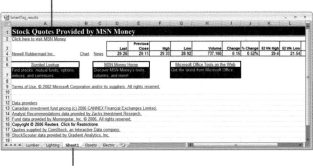

Stock information page

New worksheet

Checking Spelling

A worksheet's textual inaccuracies can distract the reader, so it's important that your text be error-free. Excel provides a spelling checker —common for all Office 2007 programs (New!)—so that you can check the spelling in an entire worksheet for words not listed in Excel's dictionary (such as misspellings, names, technical terms, or acronyms) or duplicate words (such as *the the*). You can correct these errors as they arise or after you finish the entire workbook. You can use the Spelling button on the Review tab to check the entire workbook using the Spelling dialog box, or you can avoid spelling errors on a worksheet by enabling the AutoCorrect feature to automatically correct words as you type.

Check Spelling All at Once

1. Click the **Review** tab.

2. Click the **Spelling** button.

3. If the Spelling dialog box opens, choose an option:

   ◆ Click **Ignore Once** to skip the word, or click **Ignore All** to skip every instance of the word.

   ◆ Click **Add to Dictionary** to add a word to your dictionary, so it doesn't show up as a misspelled word in the future.

   ◆ Click a suggestion, and then click **Change** or **Change All**.

   ◆ Select the correct word, and then click **AutoCorrect** to add it to the AutoCorrect list.

   ◆ If no suggestion is appropriate, click in the workbook and edit the text yourself. Click **Resume** to continue.

4. Excel will prompt you when the spelling check is complete, or you can click **Close** to end the spelling check.

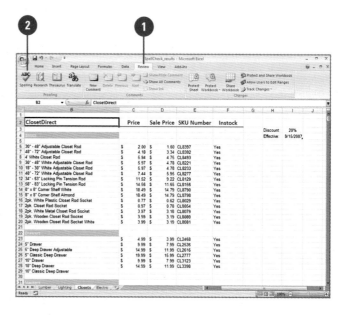

Word not recognized   Suggested corrections

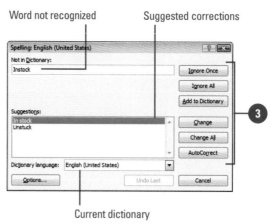

Current dictionary

Changing Proofing Options

You can customize the way Excel and Microsoft Office spell checks a workbook by selecting proofing settings in Excel Options. Some spelling options apply to Excel, such as Check spelling as you type, while other options apply to all Microsoft Office programs (New!), such as Ignore Internet and file addresses, and Flag repeated words. If you have ever mistakenly used their instead of *there*, you can use contextual spelling to fix it (New!). While you work in a workbook, you can can set options to have the spelling checker search for mistakes in the background.

Change Spelling Options for All Microsoft Programs

1. Click the **Office** button, and then click **Excel Options**.

2. In the left pane, click **Proofing**.

3. Select or clear the Microsoft Office spelling options you want.

   ◆ **Ignore words in UPPERCASE**.

   ◆ **Ignore words that contain numbers**.

   ◆ **Ignore Internet and file addresses (New!)**.

   ◆ **Flag repeated words (New!)**.

   ◆ **Enforce accented uppercase in French (New!)**.

   ◆ **Suggest from main dictionary only (New!)**. Select to exclude your custom dictionary.

4. Click **OK**.

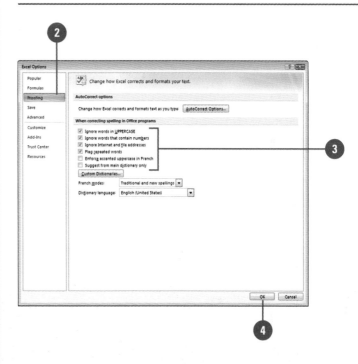

Using Custom Dictionaries

Before you can use a custom dictionary, you need to enable it first. You can enable and manage custom dictionaries by using the Custom Dictionaries dialog box (**New!**). In the dialog box, you can change the language associated with a custom dictionary, create a new custom dictionary, or add or remove existing custom dictionary. If you need to manage dictionary content, you can also change the default custom dictionary to which the spelling checker adds words, as well as add, delete, or edit words. All the modifications you make to your custom dictionaries are shared with all your Microsoft Office programs, so you only need to make changes once (**New!**). If you mistakenly type an obscene or embarrassing word, such as *ass* instead of *ask*, the spelling checker will not catch it because both words are spelled correctly. You can avoid this problem by using an exclusion dictionary (**New!**). When you use a language for the first time, Office automatically creates an exclusion dictionary. This dictionary forces the spelling checker to flag words you don't want to use.

Use a Custom Dictionary

1. Click the **Office** button, and then click **Excel Options**.

2. In the left pane, click **Proofing**.

3. Click **Custom Dictionaries**.

4. Select the check box next to **CUSTOM.DIC (Default)**.

5. Click the **Dictionary language** list arrow, and then select a language for a dictionary.

6. Click the options you want:

   ◆ Click **Edit Word List** to add, delete, or edit words.

   ◆ Click **Change Default** to select a new default dictionary.

   ◆ Click **New** to create a new dictionary.

   ◆ Click **Add** to insert an existing dictionary.

   ◆ Click **Remove** to delete a dictionary.

7. Click **OK** to close the Custom Dictionaries dialog box.

8. Click **OK**.

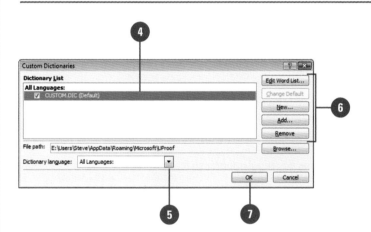

Find and Modify the Exclusion Dictionary

① In Windows Explorer, go to the folder location where the custom dictionaries are stored.

◆ **Windows Vista.** C:\Users*user name*\AppData\Roaming \Microsoft\UProof

◆ **Windows XP**. C:\Documents and Settings*user name* \Application Data\Microsoft \UProof

TROUBLE? *If you can find the folder, change folder settings to show hidden files and folders.*

② Locate the exclusion dictionary for the language you want to change.

◆ The file name you want is ExcludeDictionary *Language CodeLanguage LCID*.lex.

For example, ExcludeDictionary EN0409.lex, where EN is for English.

Check Excel Help for an updated list of LCID (Local Identification Number) number for each language.

③ Open the file using Microsoft Notepad or WordPad.

④ Add each word you want the spelling check to flag as misspelled. Type the words in all lowercase and then press Enter after each word.

⑤ Save and close the file.

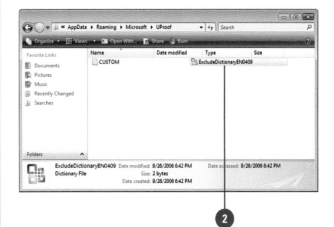

Finding the Right Words

Repeating the same word in a workbook can reduce a message's effectiveness. Instead, replace some words with synonyms or find antonyms. If you need help finding exactly the right words, use the shortcut menu to look up synonyms quickly or search a Thesaurus for more options. This feature can save you time and improve the quality and readability of your workbook. You can also install a Thesaurus for another language. Foreign language thesauruses can be accessed under Research Options on the Research task pane.

Use the Thesaurus

1. Select the text you want to translate.

2. Click the **Review** tab.

3. Click the **Thesaurus** button.

4. Click the list arrow, and then select a **Thesaurus**, if necessary.

5. Point to the word in the Research task pane.

6. Click the list arrow, and then click one of the following:

    ◆ **Insert** to replace the word you looked up with the new word.

    ◆ **Copy** to copy the new word and then paste it within the workbook.

    ◆ **Look Up** to look up the word for other options.

7. When you're done, click the **Close** button on the task pane.

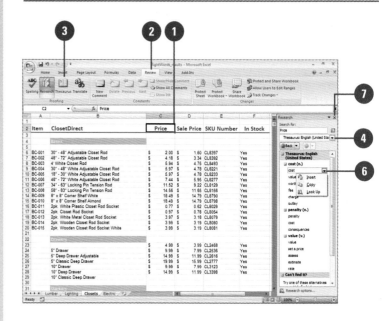

Inserting Research Material

With the Research task pane, you can access data sources and insert research material right into your text without leaving your Excel workbook. The Research task pane can help you access electronic dictionaries, thesauruses, research sites, and proprietary company information. You can select one reference source or search in all reference books. This research pane allows you to find information and quickly and easily incorporate it into your work.

Research a topic

1. Click the **Review** tab.

2. Click the **Research** button.

3. Type the topic you would like to research.

4. Click the list arrow, and then select a reference source, or click **All Reference Books**.

5. To customize which resources are used for translation, click **Research options**, select the reference books and research sites you want, and then click **OK**.

6. Click the **Start Searching** button (green arrow).

7. Select the information in the Research task pane that you want to copy.

   To search for more information, click one of the words in the list or click a link to an online site, such as MSN Encarta.

8. Select the information you want, and then copy it.

   In the Research task pane, you can point to the item you want, click the list arrow, and then click **Copy**.

9. Paste the information into your workbook.

10. When you're done, click the **Close** button on the task pane.

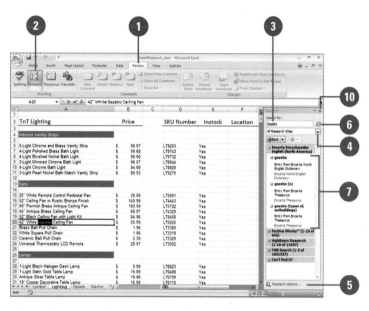

Translating Text to Another Language

With the Research task pane, you can translate single words or short phrases into different languages by using bilingual dictionaries. The Research task pane provides you with different translations and allows you to incorporate it into your work. If you need to translate an entire document for basic subject matter understanding, Web-based machine translations services are available. A machine translation is helpful for general meaning, but may not preserve the full meaning of the content.

Research a Topic

1. Select the text you want to translate.

2. Click the **Review** tab.

3. Click the **Translate** button.

   If this is the first you have used translation services, click **OK** to install the bilingual dictionaries and enable the service.

4. If necessary, click the list arrow, and then click **Translation**.

5. Click the **From** list arrow, and then select the language of the selected text.

6. Click the **To** list arrow, and then select the language you want to translate into.

7. To customize which resources are used for translation, click **Translation options**, select the look-up options you want, and then click **OK**.

8. Right-click the translated text in the Research task pane that you want to copy, and then click **Copy**.

9. Paste the information into your workbook.

10. When you're done, click the **Close** button on the task pane.

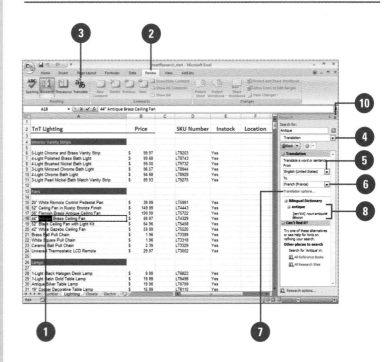

Using the English Assistant

The English Assistant (**New!**) is a Microsoft Office Online service that helps people for whom English is a second language write professional English text. The English Assistant provides tools for spelling, explanation, and usage. It also provides suggestions for synonyms and collocations (the association between two words that are typically or frequently used together), and related example sentences.

Use the English Assistant

1. Click the **Review** tab.

2. Click the **Research** button.

3. Click the list arrow, and then **English Assistant (PRC)** or **English Assistant (Japan)**.

4. If the English assistances are not available, click **Research options**, select the assistances you want, and then click **OK**.

5. Select the text in which you need help:

   ◆ **Single word.** Press Alt, and then click the word.

   ◆ **Phrase.** Type the phrase in the Search for box.

6. Click the **Start Searching** button (green arrow).

7. Point to the information in the Research task pane that you want to copy.

8. Click the list arrow, and then click **Copy**.

9. Paste the information into your workbook.

10. When you're done, click the **Close** button on the task pane.

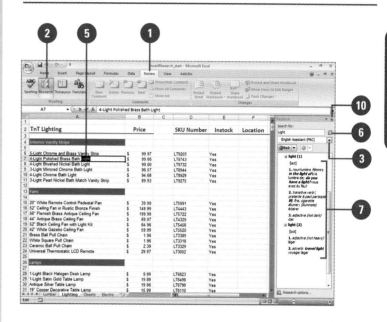

Undoing and Redoing an Action

You may realize you've made a mistake shortly after completing an action or a task. The Undo feature lets you "take back" one or more previous actions, including data you entered, edits you made, or commands you selected. For example, if you were to enter a number in a cell, and then decide the number was incorrect, you could undo the entry instead of selecting the data and deleting it. A few moments later, if you decide the number you deleted was correct after all, you could use the Redo feature to restore it to the cell.

Undo an Action

1. Click the **Undo** button on the Quick Access Toolbar to undo the last action you completed.

2. Click the **Undo** button arrow on the Quick Access Toolbar to see recent actions that can be undone.

3. Click an action. Excel reverses the selected action and all actions above it.

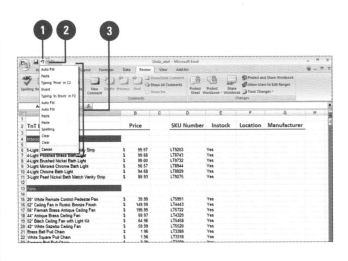

Redo an Action

1. Click the **Redo** button on the Quick Access Toolbar to restore your last undone action.

   TROUBLE? *If the Redo button is not available on the Quick Access Toolbar, click the Customize Quick Access Toolbar list arrow, and then click Redo.*

2. Click the **Redo** button arrow on the Quick Access Toolbar to see actions that can be restored.

3. Click the action you want to restore. All actions above it will be restored as well.

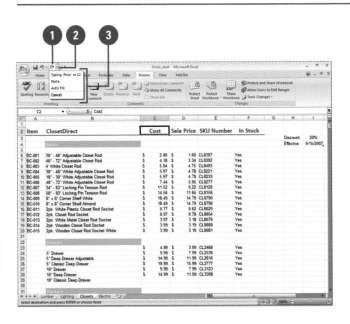

Working with Formulas and Functions

3

Introduction

Once you enter data in a worksheet, you'll want to add formulas to perform calculations. Microsoft Office Excel can help you get the results you need. Formulas can be very basic entries to more complex ones. The difficulty of the formula depends on the complexity of the result you want from your data. For instance, if you are simply looking to total this months sales, then the formula would add your sales number and provide the result. However, if you were looking to show this months sales, greater than $100.00 with repeat customers, you would take a bit more time to design the formula.

Because Microsoft Excel automatically recalculates formulas, your worksheets remain accurate and up-to-date no matter how often you change the data. Using absolute cell references anchors formulas to a specific cell. Excel provides numerous built-in functions to add to your worksheet calculations. Functions, such as AVERAGE or SUM, allow you to perform a quick formula calculation.

Another way to make your formulas easier to understand is by using name ranges in them. Name ranges—a group of selected cells named as a range—can help you understand your more complicated formulas. It is a lot easier to read a formula that uses name ranges, then to look at the formula and try to decipher it. Excel offers a tool to audit your worksheet. Looking at the "flow" of your formula greatly reduces errors in the calculation. You can see how your formula is built, one level at a time through a series of arrows that point out where the formula is pulling data from. As you develop your formula, you can make corrections to it.

Understanding Formulas

Introduction

A formula calculates values to return a result. On an Excel worksheet, you can create a formula using constant values (such as 147 or $10.00), operators (shown in the table), references, and functions. An Excel formula always begins with the equal sign (=).

A **constant** is a number or text value that is not calculated, such as the number 147, the text "Total Profits", and the date 7/22/2008. On the other hand, an **expression** is a value that is not a constant. Constants remain the same until you or the system change them. An **operator** performs a calculation, such as + (plus sign) or - (minus sign). A cell **reference** is a cell address that returns the value in a cell. For example, A1 (column A and row 1) returns the value in cell A1 (see table below).

Cell Reference Examples

Reference	Meaning
A1	Cell in column A and row 1
A1:A10	Range of cells in column A and rows 1 through 10
A1:F1	Range of cells in row 1 and columns A through F
1:1	All cells in row 1
1:5	All cells in rows 5 through 10
A:A	All cells in column A
A:F	All cells in columns A through F
Profits!A1:A10	Range of cells in column A and rows 1 through 10 in worksheet named Profits

A **function** performs predefined calculations using specific values, called arguments. For example, the function SUM(B1:B10) returns the sum of cells B1 through B10. An argument can be numbers, text, logical values such as TRUE or FALSE, arrays, error values such as #NA, or cell references. Arguments can also be constants, formulas, or other functions, known as **nested functions**. A function starts with the equal sign (=), followed by the function name, an opening parenthesis, the arguments for the function separated by commas, and a closing parenthesis. For example, the function, AVERAGE(A1:A10, B1:B10), returns a number with the average for the contents of cells A1 through A10 and B1 through B10. As you type a function, a ToolTip appears with the structure and arguments needed to complete the function. You can also use the Insert Function dialog box to help you add a function to a formula.

Perform Calculations

By default, every time you make a change to a value, formula, or name, Excel performs a calculation. To change the way Excel performs calculations, click the Formulas tab, click the Calculation Options button, and then click the option you want: Automatic, Automatic Except Data Tables, or Manual. To manually recalculate all open workbooks, click the Calculate Now button (or press F9). To recalculate the active worksheet, click the Calculate Sheet button (or press Shift+F9).

Precedence Order

Formulas perform calculations from left to right, according to a specific order for each operator. Formulas containing more than one operator follow precedence order: exponentiation, multiplication and division, and then addition and subtraction. So, in the formula 2 + 5 * 7, Excel performs multiplication first and addition next for a result of 37. Excel calculates operations within parentheses first. The result of the formula (2 + 5) * 7 is 49.

Types of Operators		
Operator	**Meaning**	**Example**
Arithmetic		
= (plus sign)	Addition	2+7
- (minus sign)	Subtraction	7-2
	Negative	-2
* (asterisk)	Multiplication	2*7
/ (forward slash)	Division	7/2
% (percent)	Percent	70%
^ (caret)	Exponentiation	2^7
Comparison		
= (equal sign)	Equal to	A2=B7
> (greater than sign)	Greater than	A2>B7
< (less than sign)	Less than	A2<B7
>= (greater than or equal to sign)	Greater than or equal to	A2>=B7
<= (less than or equal to sign)	Less than or equal to	A2<=B7
<> (not equal to sign)	Not equal to	A2<>B7
Text concatenation		
& (ampersand)	Connects, or concatenates, two values to produce one continuous text value	"Total"&"Profit"
Reference		
: (colon)	Range operator, which produces one reference to all the cells between two references	A1:A10
, (comma)	Union operator, which combines multiple references into one reference	SUM(A1:A10,B1:B10)
(space)	Intersection operator, which produces on reference to cells common to the two references	A1:A10 B1:B10

Creating a Simple Formula

EX07S-3.8

A **formula** calculates values to return a result. On an Excel worksheet, you can create a formula using values (such as 147 or $10.00), arithmetic operators (shown in the table), and cell references. An Excel formula always begins with the equal sign (=). The equal sign, when entered, automatically formats the cell as a formula entry. The best way to start a formula is to have an argument. An **argument** is the cell references or values in a formula that contribute to the result. Each function uses function-specific arguments, which may include numeric values, text values, cell references, ranges of cells, and so on. To accommodate long, complex formulas, you can resize the formula bar (**New!**) to prevent formulas from covering other data in your worksheet. By default, only formula results are displayed in a cell, but you can change the view of the worksheet to display formulas instead of results.

Enter a Formula

1. Click the cell where you want to enter a formula.

2. Type = (an equal sign). If you do not begin with an equal sign, Excel will display, not calculate, the information you type.

3. Enter the first argument. An argument can be a number or a cell reference.

   TIMESAVER *To avoid typing mistakes, click a cell to insert its cell reference in a formula rather than typing its address.*

4. Enter an arithmetic operator.

5. Enter the next argument.

6. Repeat steps 4 and 5 as needed to complete the formula.

7. Click the **Enter** button on the formula bar, or press Enter.

   Notice that the result of the formula appears in the cell (if you select the cell, the formula itself appears on the formula bar).

   TIMESAVER *To wrap text in a cell, press Alt+Enter, which manually inserts a line break.*

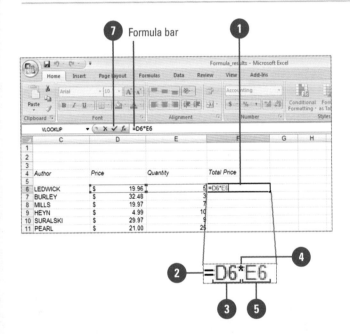

For Your Information

Understanding Order of Precedence

Formulas containing more than one operator follow the order of precedence: exponentiation, multiplication and division, and then addition and subtraction. So, in the formula 5 + 2 * 3, Excel performs multiplication first and addition next for a result of 11. Excel calculates operations within parentheses first. The result of the formula (5 + 2) * 3 is 21.

Resize the Formula Bar

◆ To switch between expanding the formula box to three or more lines or collapsing it to one line, click the double-down arrow at the end of the formula bar (**New!**). You can also press Ctrl+Shift+U.

◆ To precisely adjust the height of the formula box, point to the bottom of the formula box until the pointer changes to a vertical double arrow, and then drag up or down, and then click the vertical double arrow or press Enter.

◆ To automatically fit the formula box to the number of lines of text in the active cell, point to the formula box until the pointer changes to a vertical double arrow, and then double-click the vertical arrow.

Double-down arrow

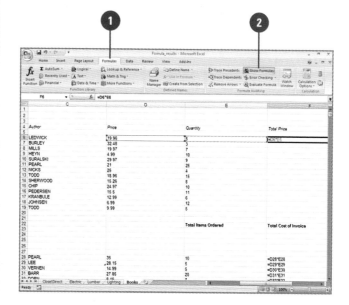

Display Formulas in Cells

① Click the **Formulas** tab.

② Click the **Show Formulas** button.

TIMESAVER *Press Ctrl+'* (**New!**).

③ To turn off formula display, click the **Show Formulas** button again.

Did You Know?

Pointing to cells reduces errors. When building formulas, pointing to a cell rather than typing its address ensures that the correct cell is referenced.

You can print formulas. Click the Formulas tab, click the Show Formulas button to show formulas, click the Office button, click Print, and then click OK.

Creating a Formula Using Formula AutoComplete

To minimize typing and syntax errors, you can create and edit formulas with Formula AutoComplete (**New!**). After you type an = (equal sign) and begin typing to start a formula, Excel displays a dynamic drop-down list of valid functions, arguments, defined names, table names, special item specifiers—including [(open bracket), , (comma), : (colon)—and text string that match the letters you type. An argument is the cell references or values in a formula that contribute to the result. Each function uses function-specific arguments, which may include numeric values, text values, cell references, ranges of cells, and so on.

Enter Items in a Formula Using Formula AutoComplete

1. Click the cell where you want to enter a formula.

2. Type = (an equal sign), and beginning letters or a display trigger to start Formula AutoComplete.

   For example, type *su* to display all value items, such as SUBTOTAL and SUM.

   The text before the insertion point is used to display the values in the drop-down list.

3. As you type, a drop-down scrollable list of valid items is displayed.

   Icons represent the type of entry, such as a function or table reference, and a ScreenTip appears next to a selected item.

4. To insert the selected item in the drop-down list into the formula, press Tab or double-click the item.

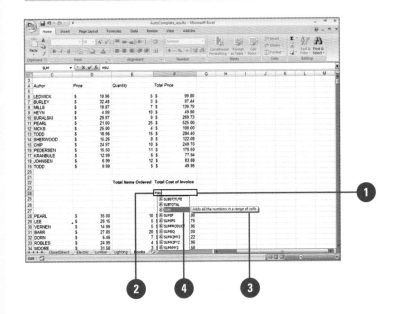

Use the Keyboard to Navigate

Using the keyboard, you can navigate the Formula AutoComplete drop-down list to quickly find the entry you want.

◆ Refer to the table for keyboard shortcuts for navigating the Formula AutoComplete drop-down list.

Keys For Navigating AutoComplete List

Press This Key	To Move
Left arrow	Move insertion point to the left
Right arrow	Move the insertion point to the right
Up arrow	Move the selection up one item
Down arrow	Move the selection down one item
End	Select the last item
Home	Select the first item
Page Down	Move down one page and select a new item
Page Up	Move up one page and select a new item
Esc	Close the drop-down list
Alt+Down arrow	Turn on or off Formula AutoComplete

Turn on Formula AutoComplete

1. Click the **Office** button, and then click **Excel Options**.

2. In the left pane, click **Formulas**.

3. Select the **Formula AutoComplete** check box.

4. Click **OK**.

Did You Know?

Some items don't appear on the Formula AutoComplete drop-down list. Defined names that you create for enumerated constants, such as the ones used in the SUBTOTAL function, and Cube function connections do not appear in the Formula AutoComplete drop-down list, but you can still type them.

Editing a Formula

You can edit formulas just as you do other cell contents, using the formula bar or working in the cell. You can select, cut, copy, paste, delete, and format cells containing formulas just as you do cells containing labels or values. Using **AutoFill**, you can quickly copy formulas to adjacent cells. If you need to copy formulas to different parts of a worksheet, use the Office Clipboard.

Edit a Formula Using the Formula Bar

1. Select the cell that contains the formula you want to edit.

2. Press F2 to change to Edit mode.

3. If necessary, use the Home, End, and arrow keys to position the insertion point within the cell contents.

4. Use any combination of Backspace and Delete to erase unwanted characters, and then type new characters as needed.

5. Click the **Enter** button on the formula bar, or press Enter.

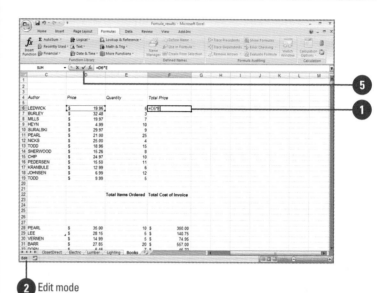

2 Edit mode

Copy a Formula Using AutoFill

1. Select the cell that contains the formula you want to copy.

2. Position the pointer (fill handle) on the lower-right corner of the selected cell.

3. Drag the mouse down until the adjacent cells where you want the formula pasted are selected, and then release the mouse button.

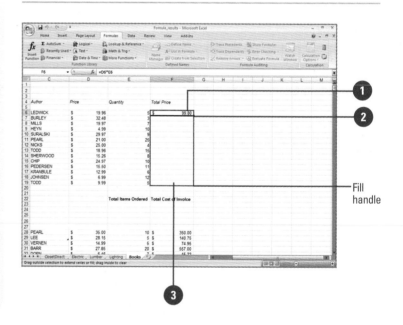

Fill handle

Copy a Formula Using the Clipboard

① Select the cell that contains the formula you want to copy.

② Click the **Home** tab.

③ Click the **Copy** button.

④ Select one or more cells where you want to paste the formula.

⑤ Click the **Paste** button.

⑥ Click the **Paste Options** button, and then select what type of formatting option you want.

If you don't want to paste this selection anywhere else, press Esc to remove the marquee.

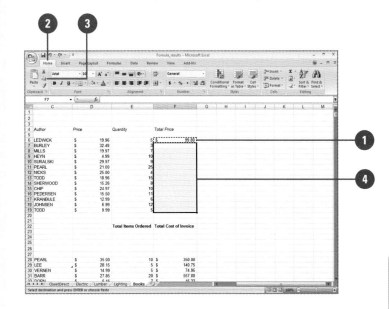

Did You Know?

You can use Paste Special to copy only formulas. Select the cells containing the formulas you want to copy, click the Copy button on the Home tab, click where you want to paste the data, click the Paste button arrow, click Paste Special, click the Formulas button, and then click OK.

You can use keyboard commands to recalculate formulas. Press F9 to recalculate formulas that have changed since the last calculation in all open workbooks. Press Shift+F9 to recalculate formulas that have changed since the last calculation in the active worksheet. Press Ctrl+Alt+F9 to recalculate all formulas in all open workbooks, regardless of whether formulas have changed. Press Ctrl+Shift+Alt+F9 to recheck dependent formulas in all open workbooks, regardless of whether formulas have changed.

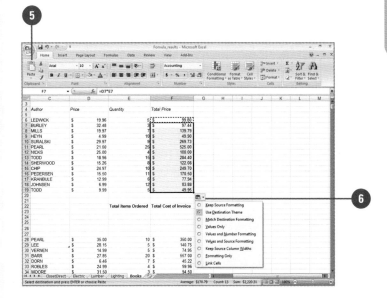

Understanding Cell Referencing

Microsoft Certified Application Specialist   EX07S-3.1.1, EX07S-3.1.2

Each cell, the intersection of a column and row on a worksheet, has a unique address, or **cell reference**, based on its column letter and row number. For example, the cell reference for the intersection of column D and row 4 is D4.

Cell References in Formulas

The simplest formula refers to a cell. If you want one cell to contain the same value as another cell, type an equal sign followed by the cell reference, such as =D4. The cell that contains the formula is known as a **dependent cell** because its value depends on the value in another cell. Whenever the cell that the formula refers to changes, the cell that contains the formula also changes.

Depending on your task, you can use **relative cell references**, which are references to cells relative to the position of the formula, **absolute cell references**, which are cell references that always refer to cells in a specific location, or **mixed cell references**, which use a combination of relative and absolute column and row references. If you use macros, the R1C1 cell references make it easy to compute row and column positions.

Relative Cell References

When you copy and paste or move a formula that uses relative references, the references in the formula change to reflect cells that are in the same relative position to the formula. The formula is the same, but it uses the new cells in its calculation. Relative addressing eliminates the tedium of creating new formulas for each row or column in a worksheet filled with repetitive information.

Absolute Cell References

If you don't want a cell reference to change when you copy a formula, make it an absolute reference by typing a dollar sign ($) before each part of the reference that you don't want to change. For example, A1 always refers to cell A1. If you copy or fill the formula down columns or across rows, the absolute reference doesn't change. You can add a $ before the column letter and the row number. To ensure accuracy and simplify updates, enter constant values (such as tax rates, hourly rates, and so on) in a cell, and then use absolute references to them in formulas.

Mixed Cell References

A mixed reference is either an absolute row and relative column or absolute column and relative row. You add the $ before the column letter to create an absolute column or before the row number to create an absolute row. For example, $A1 is absolute for column A and relative for row 1, and A$1 is absolute for row 1 and relative for column A. If you copy or fill the formula across rows or down columns, the relative references adjust, and the absolute ones don't adjust.

3-D References

3-D references allow you to analyze data in the same cell or range of cells on multiple worksheets within a workbook. A 3-D reference includes the cell or range reference, preceded by a range of worksheet names. For example, =AVERAGE(Sheet1:Sheet4!A1) returns the average for all the values contained in cell A1 on all the worksheets between and including Sheet 1 and Sheet 4.

Using Absolute Cell References

When you want a formula to consistently refer to a particular cell, even if you copy or move the formula elsewhere on the worksheet, you need to use an absolute cell reference. An absolute cell reference is a cell address that contains a dollar sign ($) in the row or column coordinate, or both. When you enter a cell reference in a formula, Excel assumes it is a relative reference unless you change it to an absolute reference. If you want part of a formula to remain a relative reference, remove the dollar sign that appears before the column letter or row number.

Create an Absolute Reference

1. Click a cell where you want to enter a formula.

2. Type = (an equal sign) to begin the formula.

3. Select a cell, and then type an arithmetic operator (+, -, *, or /).

4. Select another cell, and then press the F4 key to make that cell reference absolute.

   You can continue to press F4 to have Excel cycle through the different reference types.

5. If necessary, continue entering the formula.

6. Click the **Enter** button on the formula bar, or press Enter.

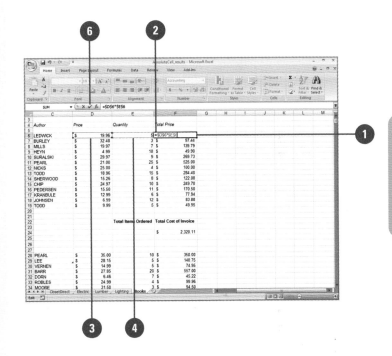

Did You Know?

You can change an absolute reference back to a relative reference. In the cell with the absolute formula, repeatedly press F4 until all the dollar signs are removed from the reference. You press F4 to cycle through all the reference types. For example, if you enter A1 to start a formula, press F4 to display A1. Press again to display A$1. Press again to display $A1. Press it again to display A1.

Using Mixed Cell References

Microsoft Certified Application Specialist

EX07S-3.1.1, EX07S-3.1.2

Create a Mixed Reference

1. Click a cell where you want to enter a formula.

2. Type = (an equal sign) to begin the formula.

3. Select the cells you want to use and then complete the formula.

4. Click the insertion point in the formula bar, and then type $ before the column or row you want to make absolute.

5. Click the **Enter** button on the formula bar, or press Enter.

A mixed cell reference is either an absolute column and relative row or absolute row and relative column. When you add the $ before the column letter you create an absolute column or before the row number you create an absolute row. For example, $A1 is absolute for column A and relative for row 1, and A$1 is absolute for row 1 and relative for column A. If you copy or fill the formula across rows or down columns, the relative references adjust, and the absolute ones don't adjust.

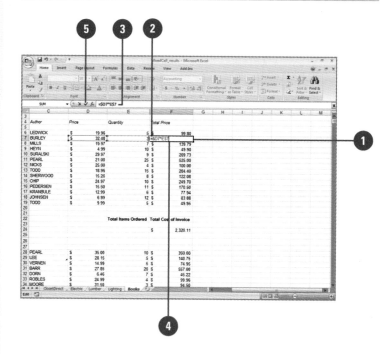

Using 3-D Cell References

Microsoft
Certified
Application
Specialist

EX07S-3.1.1,
EX07S-1.1.2

If you want to analyze data in the same cell or range of cells on multiple worksheets within a workbook, use a mixed 3-D reference. For example, =SUM(Sheet3:Sheet6!A1:A10) returns the sum for all the values contained in the range of cells A1 through A10 on all the worksheets between and including Sheet 3 and Sheet 6. 3-D references work with the following functions: AVERAGE, AVERAGEA, COUNT, COUNTA, MAX, MAXA, MIN, MINA, PRODUCT, STDEV, STDEVA, STDEVPA, VAR, VARA, VARP, and VARPA. However, 3-D references cannot be used with array formulas, the intersection operator (a single space), or the implicit intersection. If you move, insert, or copy sheets between the ones included in the range, Excel adds the values from the sheets in the calculations. If you move or remove sheets between the ones included in the range, Excel removes the values from the calculation.

Create a 3-D Cell Reference

1. Click a cell where you want to enter a formula.

2. Type = (an equal sign) to begin the formula.

3. Type the function you want to use followed by a ((left bracket).

4. Type the first worksheet name, followed by a : (colon), and then the last worksheet name in the range.

5. Type ! (exclamation).

6. Type or select the cell or cell range you want to use in the function.

7. Type) (right bracket).

8. Click the **Enter** button on the formula bar, or press Enter.

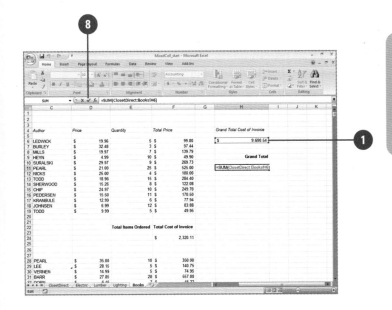

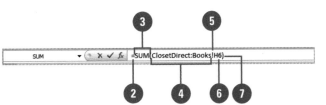

See Also

See "Performing Calculations Using Functions" on page 101 and "Creating Functions" on page 102 for information on creating and using functions.

Naming Cells and Ranges

To make working with ranges easier, Excel allows you to name them. The name BookTitle, for example, is easier to remember than the range reference B6:B21. Named ranges can be used to navigate large worksheets. Named ranges can also be used in formulas instead of typing or pointing to specific cells. When you name a cell or range, Excel uses an absolute reference for the name by default, which is almost always what you want. You can see the absolute reference in the Refers to box in the New Name dialog box. There are two types of names you can create and use: defined name and table name. A **defined name** represents a cell, a range of cells, formula or constant, while a **table name** represents an Excel table, which is a collection of data stored in records (rows) and fields (columns). You can define a name for use in a worksheet or an entire workbook, also known as **scope**. To accommodate long names, you can resize the name box in the formula bar (**New!**). The worksheet and formula bar work together to avoid overlapping content.

Name a Cell or Range Using the Name Box

1. Select the cell or range, or nonadjacent selections you want to name.

2. Click the Name box on the formula bar.

3. Type a name for the range.

   A range name can include up to 255 characters, uppercase or lowercase letters (not case sensitive), numbers, and punctuation, but no spaces or cell references.

   By default, names use absolute cell references.

4. To adjust the width of the Name box, point between the Name box and the Formula box until the pointer changes to a horizontal double arrow, and then drag left or right (**New!**).

5. Press Enter. The range name will appear in the Name box whenever you select the range in the workbook.

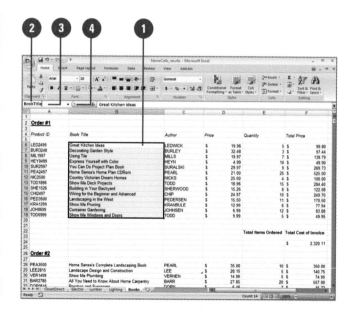

Let Excel Name a Cell or Range

1. Select the cells, including the column or row header, you want to name.

2. Click the **Formulas** tab.

3. Click the **Create from Selection** button.

4. Select the check box with the position of the labels in relation to the cells.

   Excel automatically tries to determine the position of the labels, so you might not have to change any options.

5. Click **OK**.

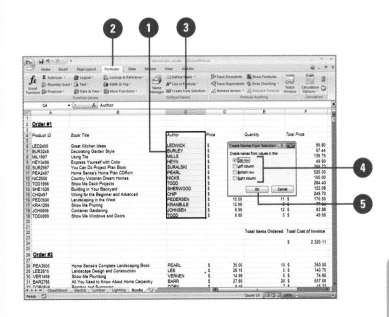

Name a Cell or Range Using the New Name Dialog Box

1. Select the cell or range, or nonadjacent selections you want to name.

2. Click the **Formulas** tab.

3. Click the **Define Name** button.

4. Type a name for the reference.

5. Click the **Scope** list arrow, and then click **Workbook** or a specific worksheet.

6. If you want, type a description of the name.

   The current selection appears in the Refer to box.

7. Click the **Collapse Dialog** button, select different cells and click the **Expand Dialog** button, or type = (equal sign) followed by a constant value or a formula.

8. Click **OK**.

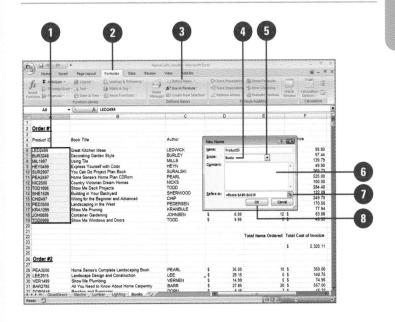

Entering Named Cells and Ranges

Microsoft
Certified
Application
Specialist

EX07S-3.1.4

After you define a named cell or range, you can enter a name by typing, using the Name box, using Formula AutoComplete (New!), or selecting from the Use in Formula command. As you begin to type a name in a formula, Formula AutoComplete displays valid matches in a drop-down list, which you can select and insert into a formula. You can also select a name from a list of available from the Use in Formula command. If you have already entered a cell or range address in a formula or function, you can apply a name to the address instead of re-creating it.

Enter a Named Cell or Range Using the Name Box

1. Click the **Name box** list arrow on the formula bar.

2. Click the name of the cell or range you want to use.

The range name appears in the Name box, and all cells included in the range are highlighted on the worksheet.

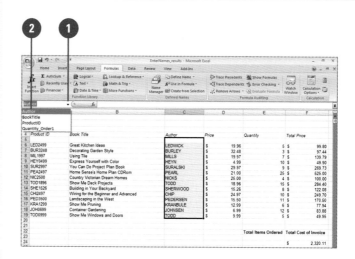

Enter a Named Cell or Range Using Formula AutoComplete

1. Type = (equal sign) to start a formula, and then type the first letter of the name.

2. To insert a name, type the first letter of the name to display it in the Formula AutoComplete drop-down list.

3. Scroll down the list, if necessary, to select the name you want, and then press Tab or double-click the name to insert it.

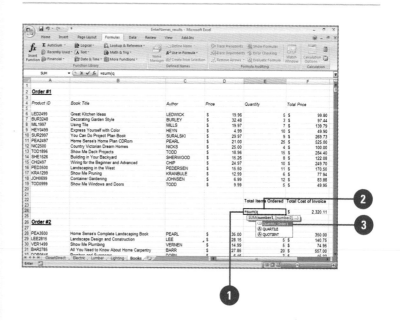

Enter a Named Cell or Range from the Use in Formula Command

1. Type = (equal sign) to start a formula.

2. Click the **Formulas** tab.

3. When you want to insert a name, click the **Use in Formula** button.

4. Use one of the following menu options:

   ◆ Click the name you want to use.

   ◆ Click **Paste Names**, select a name, and then click **OK**.

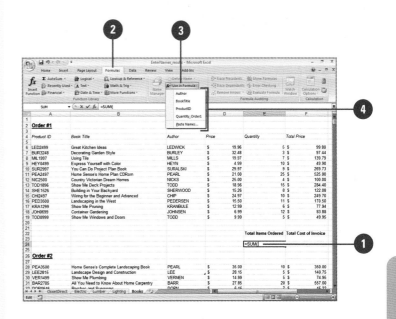

Apply a Name to a Cell or Range Address

1. Select the cells in which you want to apply a name.

2. Click the **Formulas** tab.

3. Click the **Define Name** button arrow, and then click **Apply Names**.

4. Click the name you want to apply.

5. Click **OK**.

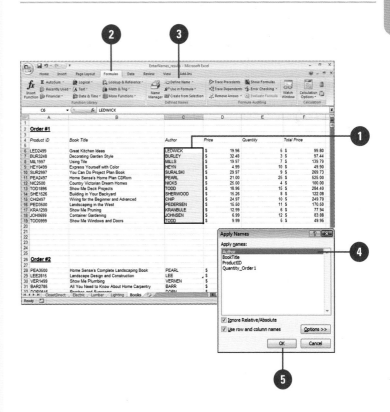

Did You Know?

Should I select the Use row and column names option? When you select this option, Excel uses the range row and column headings to refer to the range you've selected (if a cell does not have its own name, but it part of a named range).

Managing Names

Microsoft
Certified
Application
Specialist

EX07S-3.1.3

The Name Manager (**New!**) makes it easy to work with all the defined names and table names in a workbook from one location. You can display the value and reference of a name, specify the scope—either worksheet or workbook level—of a name, find names with errors, and view or edit name descriptions. In addition, you can add, change, or delete names, and sort and filter the names list. You can also use table column header names in formulas instead of cell references (**New!**).

Organize and View Names

1. Click the **Formulas** tab.

2. Click the **Name Manager** button.

   TROUBLE? *You cannot use the Name Manager dialog box while you're editing a cell. The Name Manager doesn't display names defined in VBA or hidden names.*

3. Use one of the following menu options:

   - **Resize columns.** Double-click the right side of the column header to automatically size the column to fit the largest value in that column.

   - **Sort names.** Click the column header to sort the list of names in ascending or descending order.

   - **Filter names.** Click the Filter button, and then select the filter command you want. See table for filter option details.

4. Click **Close**.

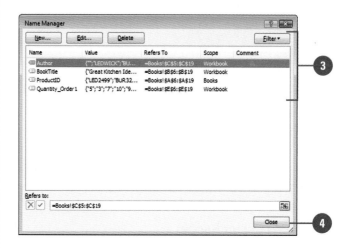

Did You Know?

What happens when you zoom in on a name range? When you zoom the view of the worksheet to 39 percent or less, Excel adds a blue border around the labels you have created. The blue border does not print.

Name Manager Filter Options

Option	Result
Names Scoped to Worksheet	Displays names local to a worksheet
Names Scoped to Workbook	Displays names global to a workbook
Names with Errors	Displays names with values that contain errors (such as #NAME, #VALUE, etc.)
Names without Errors	Displays names without errors
Defined Names	Displays names defined by you or by Excel
Table Names	Displays table names

Change a Name

① Click the **Formulas** tab.

② Click the **Names Manager** button.

③ Click the name you want to change.

④ Click **Edit**.

⑤ Type a new name for the reference in the Name box.

⑥ Change the reference.

⑦ Click **OK**.

⑧ In the Refers to area, make any changes you want to the cell, formula, or constant represented by the name.

To cancel unwanted changes, click the Cancel button or press Esc, or to save changes, click the Commit button or press Enter.

⑨ Click **Close**.

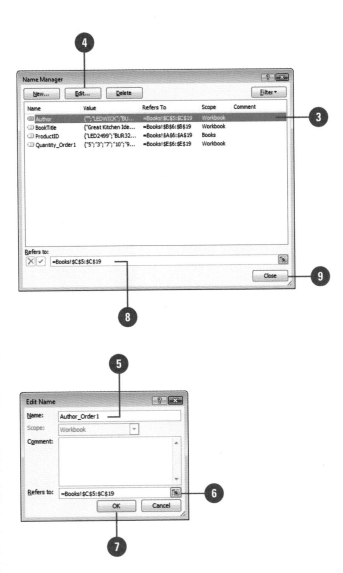

Did You Know?

You can delete a name range. Click the Formulas tab, click the Name Manager button, select the names you want to delete, click Delete or press Delete, click OK to confirm, and then click Close.

What happens when you change a label reference? If you change the name of a reference label, Excel automatically makes the same change to every formula in which the name is used.

You can label names that are relative. When you use a label name in a formula or function, Excel sees it as a relative reference. You can copy the formula to other cells, or use AutoFill to copy it and the reference changes.

Simplifying a Formula with Ranges

Microsoft Certified Application Specialist

EX07S-3.1.4

You can simplify formulas by using ranges and range names. For example, if 12 cells on your worksheet contain monthly budget amounts, and you want to multiply each amount by 10%, you can insert one range address in a formula instead of inserting 12 different cell addresses, or you can insert a range name. Using a range name in a formula helps to identify what the formula does; the formula =TotalOrder*0.10, for example, is more meaningful than =SUM(F6:F19)*0.10.

Use a Range in a Formula

1. Put your cursor where you would like the formula. Type an equal sign =SUM(.

2. Click the first cell of the range, and then drag to select the last cell in the range. Excel enters the range address for you.

3. Complete the formula by entering a close parentheses, or another function, and then click the **Enter** button.

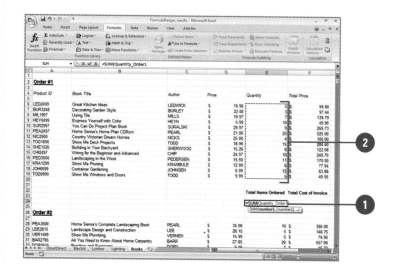

Use a Range Name in a Formula

1. Put your cursor where you would like the formula. Type an equal sign =SUM(.

2. Press F3 to display a list of named ranges.

   You can also click the Use in Formula button on the Formulas tab, and then click Paste.

3. Click the name of the range you want to insert.

4. Click **OK**.

5. Complete the formula by entering a close parentheses, or another function, and then click the **Enter** button.

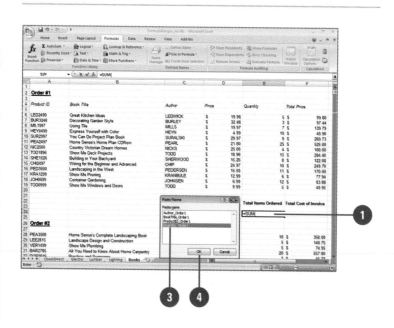

Displaying Calculations with the Status Bar

You can simplify your work using the Status bar calculations when you don't want to insert a formula, but you want to quickly see the results of a simple calculation. The Status bar automatically displays the sum, average, maximum, minimum, or count of the selected values. The Status bar results do not appear on the worksheet when printed but are useful for giving you quick answers while you work. If a cell contains text, it's ignored, except when you select the Count option.

Calculate a Range Automatically

① Select the range of cells you want to calculate.

The sum, average, and count of the selected cells appears on the status bar by default.

② If you want to change the type of calculations that appear on the Status bar, right-click anywhere on the Status bar to display a shortcut menu.

The shortcut menu displays all the available status information you can track. The right side of the menu displays the current values for the different calculations.

③ Click to toggle (on or off) the available types of calculations.

- ◆ Average
- ◆ Count
- ◆ Numerical Count
- ◆ Minimum
- ◆ Maximum
- ◆ Sum

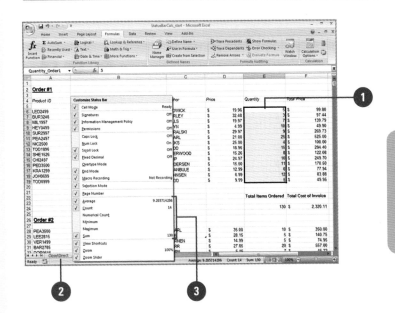

Calculating Totals with AutoSum

Microsoft Certified Application Specialist

EX07S-4.5.2

A range of cells can easily be added using the **AutoSum** button on the Standard toolbar. AutoSum suggests the range to sum, although this range can be changed if it's incorrect. AutoSum looks at all of the data that is consecutively entered, and when it sees an empty cell, that is where the AutoSum stops. You can also use AutoSum to perform other calculations, such as AVERAGE, COUNT, MAX, and MIN. Subtotals can be calculated for data ranges using the Subtotals dialog box. This dialog box lets you select where the subtotals occur, as well as the function type.

Calculate Totals with AutoSum

1. Click the cell where you want to display the calculation.

   - To sum with a range of numbers, select the range of cells you want.

   - To sum with only some of the numbers in a range, select the cells or range you want using the Ctrl key. Excel inserts the sum in the first empty cell below the selected range.

   - To sum both across and down a table of number, select the range of cells with an additional column to the right and a row at the bottom.

2. Click the **Formulas** tab.

3. Click the **AutoSum** button.

   TIMESAVER *Press Alt+= to access the AutoSum command.*

4. Click the **Enter** button on the formula bar, or press Enter.

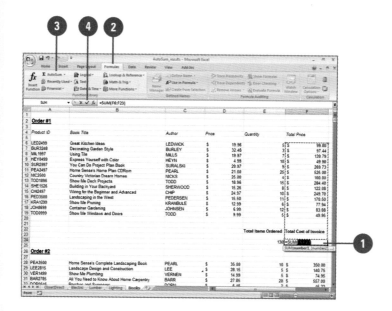

Did You Know?

You can select additional AutoFill commands. Click the Edit menu, and then click Fill to select additional commands such as Up, Down, Left, Right, Series, or Justify.

Calculate with Extended AutoSum

1. Click the cell where you want to display the calculation.

2. Click the **Formulas** tab.

3. Click the **AutoSum** button arrow.

4. Click the function you want to use, such as AVERAGE, COUNT, MAX, and MIN.

5. Press Enter to accept the range selected.

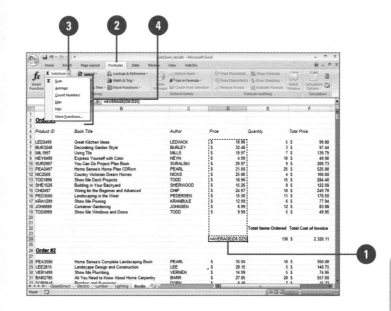

Calculate Subtotals and Totals

1. Click anywhere within the data to be subtotaled.

2. Click the **Data** tab.

3. Click the **Subtotals** button.

   If a message box appears, read the message, and then click the appropriate button.

4. Select the appropriate check boxes to specify how the data is subtotaled.

5. Click **OK**.

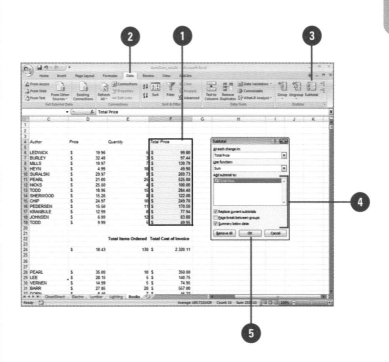

Did You Know?

You can use AutoSum to calculate a subtotal. If you're working with a table, you can use the AutoSum button to insert the Subtotal function rather than the SUM function. The function only sums the visible cells in a filtered list.

Performing One Time Calculations

Sometimes you may want to perform simple calculations, such as dividing each value in a range by 4, without having to take the time to use a formula. You can use the Paste Special command to perform simple mathematical operations, such as Add, Subtract, Multiply, and Divide. If you want to perform a more complex function, you can create a temporary formula to accomplish a one-time task. For example, if you want to display a list of names in proper case with only the first letter of each name in uppercase, you can use the Proper function.

Perform One Time Simple Calculations without Using a Formula

1. Select an empty cell, and then enter the number you want to use in a calculation.

2. Click the **Home** tab.

3. Click the **Copy** button.

4. Select the range you want to use in the calculation.

5. Click the **Paste** button arrow, and then click **Paste Special**.

6. Click the operation option you want to use: **Add**, **Subtract**, **Multiply**, or **Divide**.

7. Click **OK**.

8. Press Esc to cancel Copy mode.

   The operation is applied to the contents of each cell in the range. The formula in each cell is changed to include the new operation.

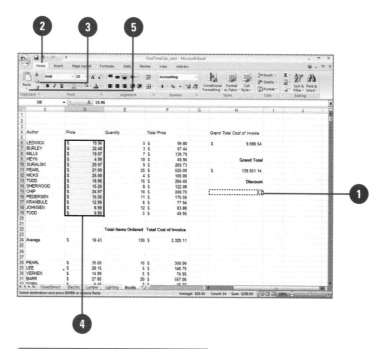

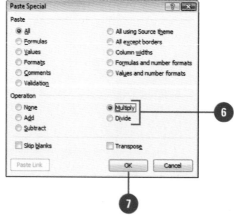

Perform One Time Calculations Using a Formula

① Create a temporary formula in an unused cell, typically a column out of the way. Select an empty cell at the top, type = (equal sign), and then type a function, such as Proper().

② Click the **Home** tab.

③ If you want to change a range of data, use the fill down handle to copy the formula to unused cells.

④ Select the cell or range with the formula.

⑤ Click the **Copy** button.

⑥ Select the cell you want to change the contents with the formula.

⑦ Click the **Paste** button arrow, and then click **Paste Special**.

⑧ Click the **Values** option.

⑨ Click **OK**.

The original data is replaced with the changed data.

⑩ When you're done with the temporary formulas, select the cells, and delete them.

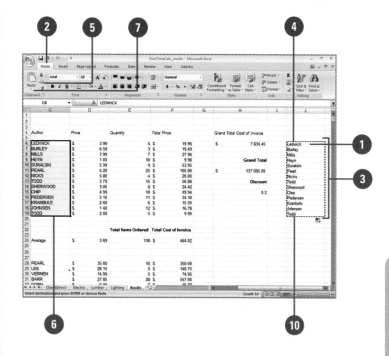

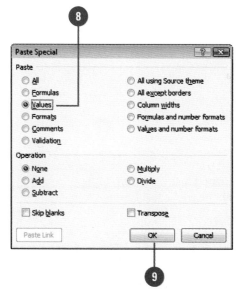

Converting Formulas and Values

If you have a range of cells that contain formulas, you can convert the cells to values only. This is useful when you have a range of cells that you don't want to change anymore. You use the Paste Special command to paste the contents of the selected range back into place as a value instead of a formula. If you're working with an input form in Excel, you probably need to delete values, but keep the formulas. You can do it with the help of the Go To Special dialog box.

Convert a Formula to a Value

1. Select the range of cells with formulas you want to convert to values.

2. Click the **Home** tab.

3. Click the **Copy** button.

4. Click the **Paste** button arrow, and then click **Paste Special**.

5. Click the **Values** option.

6. Click **OK**.

7. Press Esc to cancel Copy mode.

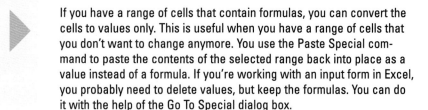

Delete Values and Keep Formulas

1. Click the **Home** tab.

2. Click the **Find & Select** button, and then click **Go To Special.**

3. Click the **Constants** option.

4. Select the **Numbers** check box, and then clear the other check boxes under Formula.

5. Click **OK**.

6. Press Delete to remove the selected values.

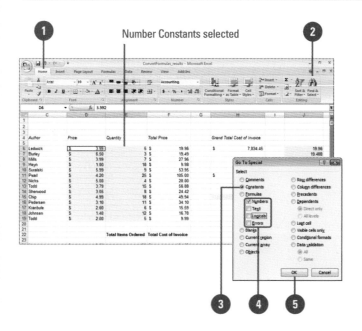

Number Constants selected

Correcting Calculation Errors

When Excel finds a possible error in a calculation, it displays a green triangle in the upper left corner of the cell. If Excel can't complete a calculation it displays an error message, such as "#DIV/0!". You can use the Error smart tag to help you fix the problem. In a complex worksheet, it can be difficult to understand the relationships between cells and formulas. Auditing tools enable you to clearly determine these relationships. When the Auditing feature is turned on, it uses a series of arrows to show you which cells are part of which formulas. When you use the auditing tools, tracer arrows point out cells that provide data to formulas and the cells that contain formulas that refer to the cells. A box is drawn around the range of cells that provide data to formulas.

Review and Correct Errors

1. Select a cell that contains a green triangle in the upper left corner.

2. Click the **Error Smart Tag** button.

3. Click one of the troubleshooting options (menu options vary depending on the error).

   ◆ To have Excel fix the error, click one of the available options specific to the error.

   ◆ To find out more about an error, click **Help on this Error**.

   ◆ To remove the error alert, click **Ignore Error**.

   ◆ To fix the error manually, click **Edit in Formula Bar**.

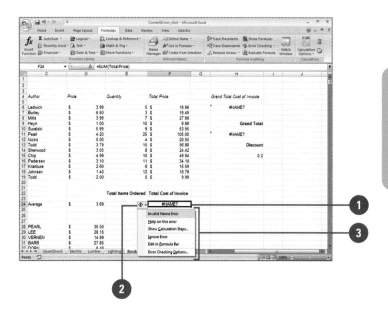

For Your Information

Avoiding Error Displays in Formulas

If you include empty cells in a formula, an error message, such as #DIV/0! might appear in the formula cell. You can avoid this message by adding a function to check for errors. If the formula generating an error message for empty cells is =*Formula*, then change it to =IF(ISERROR(*Formula*),"",*Formula*). If the ISERROR function is true, the IF function returns an empty string, instead of an error message.

Correcting Formulas

Excel has several tools to help you find and correct problems with formulas. One tool is the **Watch window** and another is the **Error checker**. The Watch window keeps track of cells and their formulas as you make changes to a worksheet. Excel uses an error checker in the same way Microsoft Word uses a grammar checker. The Error checker uses certain rules, such as using the wrong argument type, a number stored as text or an empty cell reference, to check for problems in formulas.

Watch Cells and Formulas

1. Select the cells you want to watch.

2. Click the **Formulas** tab.

3. Click the **Watch Window** button.

4. Click the **Add Watch** button on the Watch Window dialog box.

5. Click **Add**.

6. Click **Close**.

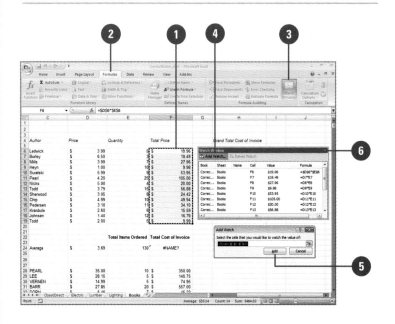

Remove Cells from the Watch Window

1. Click the **Formulas** tab.

2. Click the **Watch Window** button.

3. Select the cells you want to delete. Use the Ctrl key to select multiple cells.

4. Click **Delete Watch**.

5. Click **Close**.

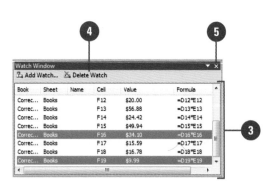

Set Error Checking Options

1. Click the **Office** button, and then click **Excel Options**.

2. In the left pane, click **Formulas**.

3. Select the **Enable background error checking** check box.

4. Point to the help icons at the end of the error checking rule options to display a ScreenTip describing the rule.

5. Select the error checking rules check boxes you want to use.

6. Click **OK**.

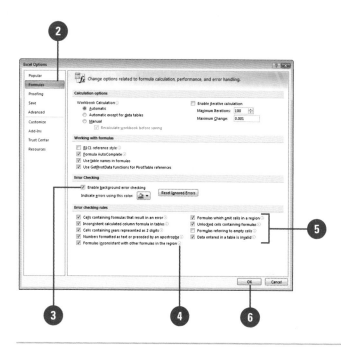

Correct Errors

1. Open the worksheet where you want to check for errors.

2. Click the **Formulas** tab.

3. Click the **Error Checking** button.

   The error checker scans the worksheet for errors, generating the Error Checker dialog box every time it encounters an error.

4. If necessary, click **Resume**.

5. Choose a button to correct or ignore the problem.

   ◆ **Help on this error.**

   ◆ **Show Calculation Steps.** Click Evaluate to see results.

   ◆ **Ignore Error.**

   ◆ **Edit in Formula Bar.**

   ◆ **Previous** or **Next.**

6. If necessary, click **Close**.

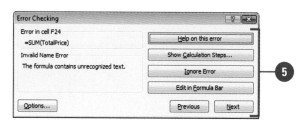

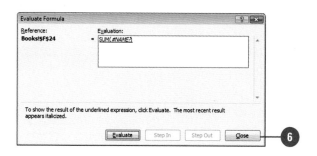

Auditing a Worksheet

In a complex worksheet, it can be difficult to understand the relationships between cells and formulas. Auditing tools enable you to clearly determine these relationships. When the **Auditing** feature is turned on, it uses a series of arrows to show you which cells are part of which formulas. When you use the auditing tools, **tracer arrows** point out cells that provide data to formulas and the cells that contain formulas that refer to the cells. A box is drawn around the range of cells that provide data to formulas.

Trace Worksheet Relationships

1. Click the **Formulas** tab.

2. Use any of the following options:

   ◆ Click the **Trace Precedents** button to find cells that provide data to a formula.

   ◆ Click the **Trace Dependents** button to find out which formulas refer to a cell.

   ◆ Click the **Error Checking** button arrow, and then click **Trace Error** to locate the problem if a formula displays an error value, such as #DIV/0!.

   ◆ Click **Remove Arrows** button arrow, and then click **Remove Precedent Arrows**, **Remove Dependent Arrows**, or **Remove All Arrows** to remove precedent and dependent arrows.

3. If necessary, click **OK** to locate the problem.

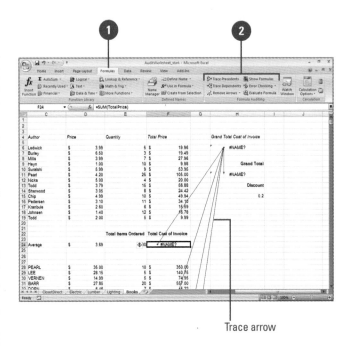

Trace arrow

Locating Circular References

A **circular reference** occurs when a formula directly or indirectly refers to its own cell. This causes the formula to use its result in the calculation, which can create errors. When a workbook contains a circular reference, Excel cannot automatically perform calculations. You can use error checking in Excel to locate circular references in a formula, and then remove them. If you leave them in, Excel calculates each cell involved in the circular reference by using the results of the previous iteration. An iteration is a repeated recalculation until a specific numeric condition is met. By default, Excel stops calculating after 100 iterations or after all values in the circular reference change by less than 0.001 between iterations, unless you change the Excel option.

Locate a Circular Reference

① Click the **Formulas** tab.

② Click the **Error Checking** button arrow, point to **Circular References**, and then click the first cell listed in the submenu.

③ Review the formula cell.

④ If you cannot figure out if the cell is the cause of the circular reference, click the next cell in the Circular References submenu, if available.

⑤ Continue to review and correct the circular reference until the status bar no longer displays the word "Circular."

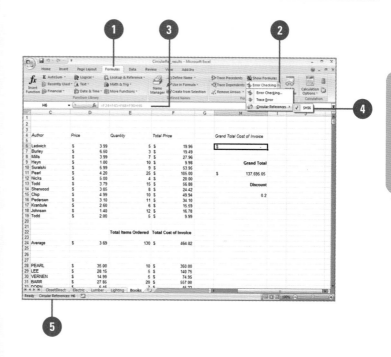

Did You Know?

You can enable and increase formula iterations to make a circular reference work. Click the Office button, click Excel Options, click Formulas, select the Enable iterative calculation check box, enter the maximum number of iterations you want (higher the number, the more time Excel needs to calculate a worksheet), and set the maximum amount of change you want to accept between calculation results (smaller the number, the more accurate the results).

Performing Calculations Using Functions

Microsoft Certified Application Specialist   EX07S-3.2.1

Functions are predesigned formulas that save you the time and trouble of creating commonly used or complex equations. Excel includes hundreds of functions that you can use alone or in combination with other formulas or functions. Functions perform a variety of calculations, from adding, averaging, and counting to more complicated tasks, such as calculating the monthly payment amount of a loan. You can enter a function manually if you know its name and all the required arguments, or you can easily insert a function using AutoComplete, which helps you select a function and enter arguments with the correct format.

Enter a Function

1. Click the cell where you want to enter the function.

2. Type = (an equal sign), type the name of the function, and then type ((an opening parenthesis).

   As you type, you can scroll down the Formula AutoComplete list, select the function you want, and then press Tab.

3. Type the argument or select the cell or range you want to insert in the function, and then type) (a closed parenthesis) to complete the function.

4. Click the **Enter** button on the formula bar, or press Enter.

   Excel will automatically add the closing parenthesis to complete the function.

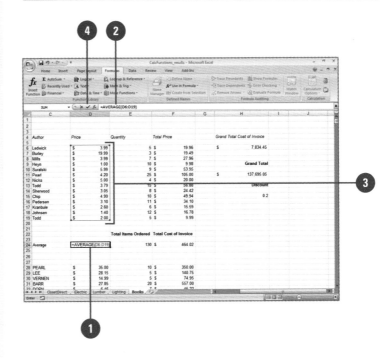

See Also

See "Creating a Formula Using Formula AutoComplete" on page 76 for information on using Formula AutoComplete.

Commonly Used Excel Functions

Function	Description	Sample
SUM	Displays the sum of the argument	=SUM(argument)
AVERAGE	Displays the average value in the argument	=AVERAGE(argument)
COUNT	Calculates the number of values in the argument	=COUNT(argument)
PMT	Determines the monthly payment of a loan	=PMT(argument)

Creating Functions

Microsoft
Certified
Application
Specialist

EX07S-3.2.1

Trying to write a formula that calculates various pieces of data, such as calculating payments for an investment over a period of time at a certain rate, can be difficult and time-consuming. The **Insert Function** feature simplifies the process by organizing Excel's built-in formulas, called functions, into categories so they are easy to find and use. A function defines all the necessary components (also called arguments) you need to produce a specific result; all you have to do is supply the values, cell references, and other variables. You can even combine one or more functions if necessary.

Enter a Function Using Insert Function

1. Click the cell where you want to enter the function.

2. Click the **Insert Function** button on the Formula bar or click the **Function Wizard** button on the Formulas tab.

3. Type a brief description that describes what you want to do in the Search for a function box, and then click **Go**.

4. If necessary, click a function category you want to use.

5. Click the function you want to use.

6. Click **OK**.

7. Enter the cell addresses in the text boxes. Type them or click the Collapse Dialog button to the right of the text box, select the cell or range using your mouse, and then click the Expand Dialog button.

8. Click **OK**.

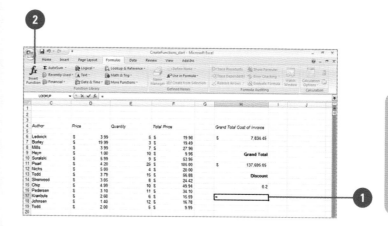

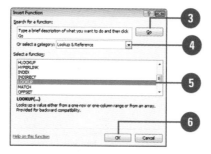

For Your Information

Inserting Placeholder Arguments

If you don't know the cell references you want to use for a function, you can insert argument names as placeholders, and then fill in the actual argument later. Press Ctrl+Shift+A after you type the functions name. Excel uses the arguments names as arguments. For example,

=VLOOKUP(lookup_value, table_array, col_index_num, range_lookup).

Creating Functions Using the Library

EX07S-3.2.1

To make it easier to find the function you need for a specific use, Excel has organized functions into categories—such as Financial, Logical, Text, Date & Time, Lookup & Reference, Math & Trig, and other functions—on the Formulas tab. After you use a function, Excel places it on the recently used list. When you insert a function from the Function Library, Excel inserts the function in the formula bar and opens a Function Argument dialog box, where you can enter or select the cells you want to use in the function.

Enter a Function Using the Function Library

1. Click the cell where you want to enter the function.

2. Click the **Formulas** tab.

3. Type = (an equal sign).

4. Click the button (**Financial, Logical, Text, Date & Time, Lookup & Reference, Math & Trig, More Functions**, or **Recently Used**) from the Function Library with the type of function you want to use, click a submenu if necessary, and then click the function you want to insert into a formula.

   Excel inserts the function you selected into the formula bar with a set of parenthesis, and opens the Function Arguments dialog box.

5. Type the argument or select the cell or range you want to insert in the function.

   You can click the Collapse Dialog button to the right of the text box, select the cell or range using your mouse, and then click the Expand Dialog button.

6. Click **OK**.

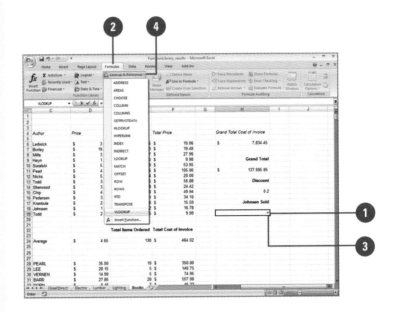

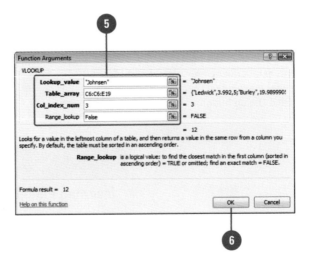

Calculating Multiple Results

Microsoft
Certified
Application
Specialist

EX07S-3.2.1

An array formula can perform multiple calculations and then return either a single or multiple result. For example, when you want to count the number of distinct entries in a range, you can use an array formula, such as {=SUM(1/COUNTIF(range,range))}. You can also use an array formula to perform a two column lookup using the LOOKUP function. An array formula works on two or more sets of values, known as **array arguments**. Each argument must have the same number of rows and columns. You can create array formulas in the same way that you create other formulas, except you press Ctrl+Shift+Enter to enter the formula. When you enter an array formula, Excel inserts the formula between {} (brackets).

Create an Array Formula

1. Click the cell where you want to enter the array formula.

2. Click the **Formulas** tab.

3. Type = (an equal sign).

4. Use any of the following methods to enter the formula you want.

   ◆ Type the function.

   ◆ Type and use Formula AutoComplete.

   ◆ Use the Function Wizard.

   ◆ Use button in the Function Library.

5. Press Ctrl+Shift+Enter.

   {} (brackets) appear around the function to indicate it's an array formula.

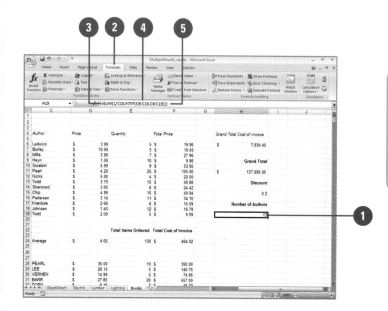

Using Nested Functions

Microsoft Certified Application Specialist

EX07S-3.6.1

A nested function (**New!**) uses a function as one of the arguments. Excel allows you to nest up to 64 levels of functions. Users typically create nested functions as part of a conditional formula. For example, IF(AVERAGE(B2:B10)>100,SUM(C2:G10),0). The AVERAGE and SUM functions are nested within the IF function. The structure of the IF function is IF(condition_test, if_true, if_false). You can use the AND, OR, NOT, and IF functions to create conditional formulas. When you create a nested formula, it can be difficult to understand how Excel performs the calculations. You can use the Evaluate Formula dialog box to help you evaluate parts of a nested formula one step at a time.

Create a Conditional Formula Using a Nested Function

1. Click the cell where you want to enter the function.

2. Click the **Formulas** tab.

3. Type = (an equal sign).

4. Click a button from the Function Library with the type of function you want to use, click a submenu if necessary, and then click the function you want to insert into a formula.

   For example, click the Logical & Reference button, and then click COUNTIF.

   Excel inserts the function you selected into the formula bar with a set of parenthesis, and opens the Function Arguments dialog box.

5. Type a function as an argument to create a nested function, or a regular argument.

   For example, =COUNTIF(E6:E19), ">"&AVERAGE(E6:E19)).

6. Click **OK**.

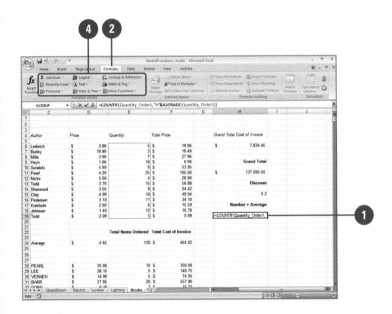

Conditional Formula Examples	
Formula	**Result**
=AND(A2>A3, A2<A4)	If A2 is greater than A3 and less than A4, then return TRUE, otherwise return FALSE
=OR(A2>A3, A2<A4)	If A2 is greater than A3 or A2 is less than A4, then return TRUE, otherwise return FALSE
=NOT(A2+A3=24)	If A2 plus A3 is not equal to 24, then return TRUE, otherwise return FALSE
IF(A2<>15, "OK", "Not OK")	If the value in cell A2 is not equal to 15, then return "OK", otherwise return "Not OK"

Evaluate a Nested Formula One Step at a Time

1. Select the cell with the nested formula you want to evaluate. You can only evaluate one cell at a time.

2. Click the **Formulas** tab.

3. Click the **Evaluate Formula** button.

4. Click **Evaluate** to examine the value of the underlined reference.

   The result of the evaluation appears in italics.

5. If the underlined part of the formula is a reference to another formula, click **Step In** to display the other formula in the Evaluation box.

   The Step In button is not available for a reference the second time the reference appears in the formula, or if the formula refers to a cell in a separate workbook.

6. Continue until each part of the formula has been evaluated, and then click **Close**.

7. To see the evaluation again, click **Restart**.

   Some parts of formulas that use IF and CHOOSE functions are not evaluated, and #NA is displayed. If a reference is blank, a zero value (0) is displayed.

   IMPORTANT *Some functions recalculate each time the worksheet changes, and can cause the Evaluate Formula to display different results. These functions include RAND, AREAS, INDEX, OFFSET, CELL, INDIRECT, ROWS, COLUMNS, NOW, TODAY, AND RANDBETWEEN.*

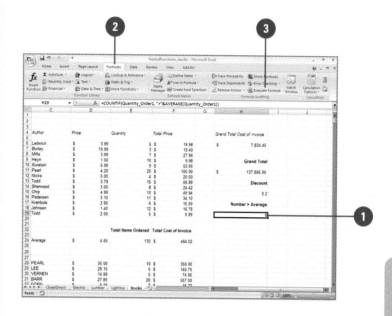

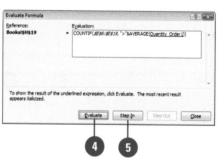

Using Constants and Functions in Names

Instead of using a cell to store a constant value or function for use in a formula, you can create a name to store it and then use the name in a formula. If you wanted to calculate sales tax, for example, you could create a name called Sales Tax and assign it a constant value. You can also store text in a name. Instead of typing a long name, such as Environmental Protection Agency, you could create a name called EPA and then use the easy-to-type three letter abbreviation in a formula. When you use EPA in a formula as a text string, Excel replaces it with Environmental Protection Agency. It also works for functions and nested functions.

Use a Constant or Function in a Name

1. Click the **Formulas** tab.

2. Click the **Define Name** button.

3. Type a name for the reference.

4. Click the **Scope** list arrow, and then click **Workbook** or a specific worksheet.

5. If you want, type a description of the name.

   The current selection appears in the Refer to box.

6. In the Refer to box, type = (equal sign) followed by the constant, text, or function you want to use.

   =.0875, or ="Environmental Protection Agency"

7. Click **OK**.

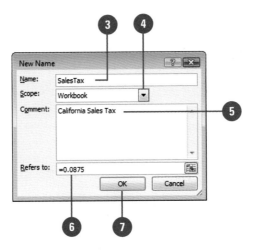

> **Did You Know?**
>
> **You can edit the contents of the Refers to box in the New Names dialog box.**
> Since the contents of the Refer to box is in point mode, you can not use the insertion point and arrow keys to edit it. Press F2 to switch to edit mode, where you can use the insertion point and arrow keys to edit it.

Constant name used in formula

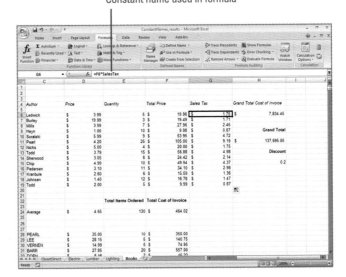

108

Modifying Worksheets and Workbooks

4

Introduction

At times, you'll need to reorganize a workbook by adding additional worksheets, moving their appearance order within the workbook, or even deleting an unused or outdated worksheet. You can rename worksheets to better show the theme of your workbook. When using your workbook, there may be times when you'll want to hide certain worksheets due to sensitive or confidential information. You can also freeze the column and row headings to ease viewing a long list of data.

On any worksheet, you can insert and delete cells, rows, and columns. You can adjust column width and row height so that you can structure the worksheet exactly the way you want. It's easy to make changes because Microsoft Office Excel updates cell references in existing formulas as necessary whenever you modify a worksheet and automatically recalculates formulas to ensure that the results are always up-to-date.

Perhaps each month you create an inventory worksheet in which you enter repetitive information; all that changes is the actual data. By creating your own template, you can have a custom form that is ready for completion each time you take inventory. Formatting, formulas and other settings are already set up, so that you can begin working on the task at hand. A template file saves all the customization you made to reuse in other workbooks. Microsoft Excel comes with a variety of pre-made templates that you can use for your own business and personal needs.

Selecting and Naming a Worksheet

Microsoft
Certified
Application
Specialist

EX07S-1.5.3

Each new workbook opens with three worksheets (or sheets), in which you store and analyze values. You can work in the active, or selected, worksheet. The default worksheet names are Sheet1, Sheet2, and Sheet3, which appear on the sheet tab, like file folder labels. As you create a worksheet, give it a meaningful name to help you remember its contents. The sheet tab size adjusts to fit the name's length, so using short names means more sheet tabs will be visible. If you work on a project that requires more than three worksheets, add additional sheets to the workbook so all related information is stored in one file.

Select a Worksheet

1. If necessary, click a sheet tab scroll button to display other tabs.

2. Click a sheet tab to make it the active worksheet.

3. To select multiple worksheets, press and hold Ctrl as you click other sheet tabs. When multiple worksheets are selected, [Group] appears in the title bar.

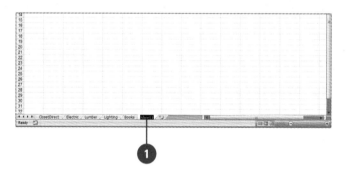

Name or Rename a Worksheet

1. Double-click the sheet tab you want to name.

   ◆ You can also click the **Home** tab, click the **Format** button, and then click **Rename**.

2. Type a new name.

3. Press Enter.

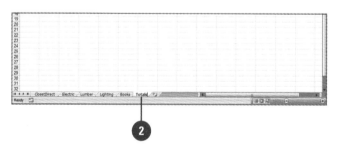

Did You Know?

You can select all worksheets. Right-click any sheet tab, and then click Select All Sheets.

Inserting and Deleting a Worksheet

Microsoft
Certified
Application
Specialist

EX07S-1.5.5

You can add or delete sheets in a workbook. If, for example, you are working on a project that requires more than three worksheets, you can insert additional sheets in one workbook rather than open multiple workbooks. You can insert as many sheets in a workbook as you want. If, on the other hand, you are using only one or two sheets in a workbook, you can delete the unused sheets to save disk space. Before you delete a sheet from a workbook, make sure you don't need the data. You cannot undo the deletion.

Insert a Worksheet

1. Click the sheet tab to the right of where you want to insert the new sheet.

2. Click the **Insert Worksheet** icon at the end of the sheet tabs (**New!**).

   TIMESAVER *Press Shift+F11.*

   ◆ You can also click the **Home** tab, click the **Insert Cells** button, and then click **Insert Sheet**.

   A new worksheet is inserted to the left of the selected worksheet.

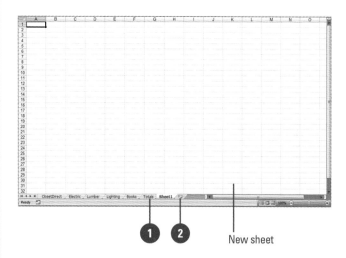

New sheet

Delete a Worksheet

1. Click the sheet tab of the worksheet you want to delete.

2. Click the **Home** tab.

3. Click the **Delete Cells** button arrow, and then click **Delete Sheet**.

4. Click **Delete** to confirm the deletion.

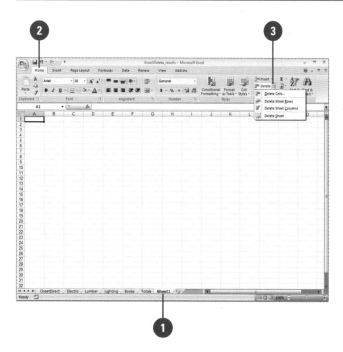

Moving and Copying a Worksheet

Microsoft
Certified
Application
Specialist

EX07S-1.5.1,
EX07S-1.5.2

After adding several sheets to a workbook, you might want to reorganize them. You can arrange sheets in chronological order or in order of importance. You can easily move or copy a sheet within a workbook or to a different open workbook. Copying a worksheet is easier and often more convenient then re-entering similar information on a new sheet. If you are moving or copying a worksheet a short distance, you should use the mouse. For longer distances, you should use the Move or Copy command.

Move a Worksheet Within a Workbook

1. Click the sheet tab of the worksheet you want to move, and then hold down the mouse button.

2. When the mouse pointer changes to a sheet of paper, drag it to the right of the sheet tab where you want to move the worksheet.

3. Release the mouse button.

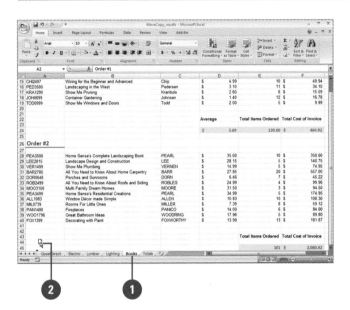

Did You Know?

You can use the Create a copy check box to move a worksheet. Clear the Create a copy check box in the Move or Copy dialog box to move a worksheet rather than copy it.

You can give your worksheet a different background. Click the tab of the sheet on which you want to insert a background, click the Format menu, point to Sheet, and then click Background. Select the picture you want to use as a background, and then click Insert.

You can use groups to affect multiple worksheets. Click a sheet tab, press and hold Shift, and click another sheet tab to group worksheets. Right-click a grouped sheet tab, and then click Ungroup Sheet on the shortcut menu.

Copy a Worksheet

1. Click the sheet tab of the worksheet you want to copy.

   TIMESAVER *Press and hold the Ctrl key while you drag a sheet name to copy a worksheet.*

2. Click the **Home** tab.

3. Click the **Format** button arrow, and then click **Move or Copy Sheet**.

4. If you want to copy the sheet to another open workbook, click the **To book** list arrow, and then select the name of that workbook. The sheets of the selected workbook appear in the Before Sheet list.

   TROUBLE? *If the workbook you want to copy to does not show up in the To Book drop-down list, you must first open the workbook.*

5. Click a sheet name in the Before Sheet list. Excel inserts the copy to the left of this sheet.

6. Select the **Create a copy** check box.

7. Click **OK**.

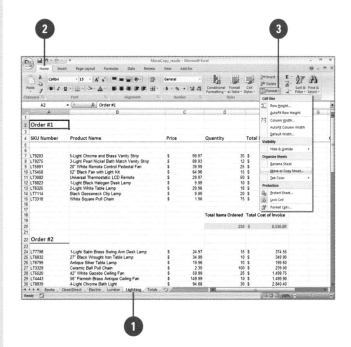

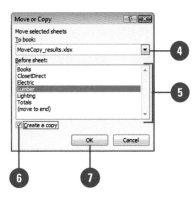

Did You Know?

You can copy or move a sheet to a different workbook. You must first open the other workbook, and then switch back to the workbook of the sheet you want to copy or move.

Hiding and Unhiding Worksheets and Workbooks

Microsoft
Certified
Application
Specialist

EX07S-1.5.4

Not all worksheets and workbooks should be available to everyone. You can hide sensitive information without deleting it by hiding selected worksheets or workbooks. For example, if you want to share a workbook with others, but it includes confidential employee salaries, you can simply hide a worksheet. Hiding worksheets does not affect calculations in the other worksheets; all data in hidden worksheets is still referenced by formulas as necessary. Hidden worksheets do not appear in a printout either. When you need the data, you can unhide the sensitive information.

Hide a Worksheet

1. Click the sheet tab you want to hide.

2. Click the **Home** tab.

3. Click the **Format** button, point to **Hide & Unhide**, and then click **Hide Sheet**.

   TIMESAVER *Right-click the sheet you want to hide, and then click Hide.*

Unhide a Worksheet

1. Click the **Home** tab.

2. Click the **Format** button, point to **Hide & Unhide**, and then click **Unhide Sheet**.

3. Select the worksheet you want to unhide.

4. Click **OK**.

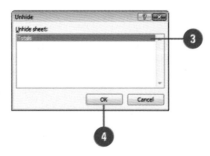

Hide a Workbook

1. Open the workbook you want to hide.

2. Click the **View** tab.

3. Click the **Hide** button.

Did You Know?

You can change the color of the sheet tab names. By right-clicking the sheet tab of the worksheet you want, and point to Tab Color, and then select a color. Click No Color to remove a color.

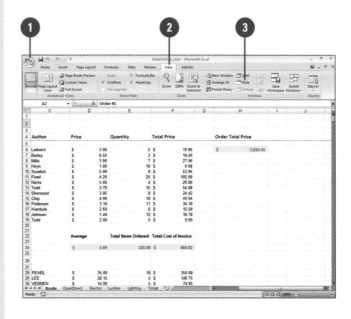

Unhide a Workbook

1. Click the **View** tab.

2. Click the **Unhide** button.

3. Select the workbook you want to unhide.

4. Click **OK**.

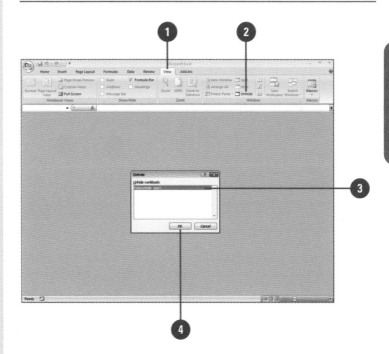

Selecting a Column or Row

You can select one or more columns or rows in a worksheet in order to apply formatting attributes, insert or delete columns or rows, or perform other group actions. The header buttons above each column and to the left of each row indicate the letter or number of the column or row. You can select multiple columns or rows even if they are non-contiguous—that is, not next to one another in the worksheet.

Select a Column or Row

1. Click the column or row header button of the column or row you want to select.

   An arrow appears when you point to a header button.

> **Did You Know?**
>
> *You can select the entire worksheet quickly.* Click the Select All button located above the row number 1 and the left of column A.

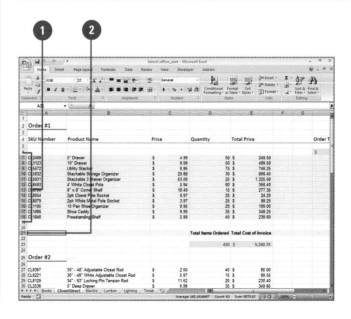

Select Multiple Columns or Rows

1. Drag the mouse over the header buttons of any contiguous columns or rows you want to select.

2. To select non-contiguous columns or rows, press and hold Ctrl while clicking each additional column or row header button.

   An arrow appears when you point to a header button.

Hiding and Unhiding a Column or Row

Microsoft Certified Application Specialist EX07S-2.2.3

Not all the data on a worksheet should be available to everyone. You can hide sensitive information without deleting it by hiding selected columns or rows. For example, if you want to share a worksheet with others, but it includes confidential employee salaries, you can simply hide the salary column. Hiding columns and rows does not affect calculations in a worksheet; all data in hidden columns and rows is still referenced by formulas as necessary. Hidden columns and rows do not appear in a printout either. When you need the data, you can unhide the sensitive information.

Hide a Column or Row

1. Click the column or row header button of the column or row you want to hide. (Drag to select multiple header buttons to hide more than one column or row.)

2. Click the **Home** tab.

3. Click the **Format** button, point to **Hide & Unhide**, and then click **Hide Columns** or **Hide Rows**.

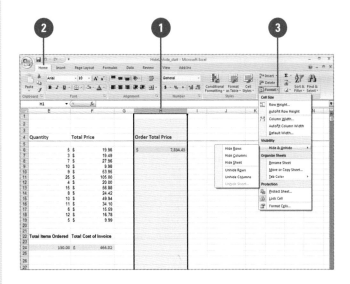

Unhide a Column or Row

1. Drag to select the column or row header buttons on either side of the hidden column or row.

2. Click the **Home** tab.

3. Click the **Format** button, point to **Hide & Unhide**, and then click **Unhide Columns** or **Unhide Rows**.

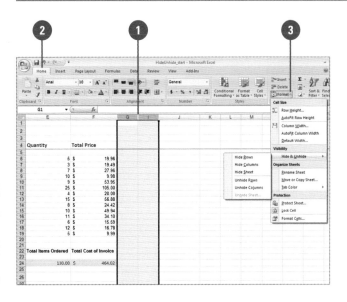

Inserting a Column or Row

Microsoft
Certified
Application
Specialist

EX07S-2.2.1

Insert a Column or Row

1. Click to the right of the location of the new column you want to insert.

   To insert a row, click the row immediately below the location of the row you want to insert.

2. Click the **Home** tab.

3. Click the **Insert Cells** button, and then click **Insert Sheet Columns** or **Insert Sheet Rows**.

4. To adjust formatting, click the **Insert Options** button, and then click a formatting option.

Insert Multiple Columns or Rows

1. Drag to select the column header buttons for the number of columns you want to insert.

   To insert multiple rows, drag to select the row header buttons for the number of rows you want to insert.

2. Click the **Home** tab.

3. Click the **Insert Cells** button, and then click **Insert Sheet Columns** or **Insert Sheet Rows**.

4. To adjust formatting, click the **Insert Options** button, and then click a formatting option.

You can insert blank columns and rows between existing data, without disturbing your worksheet. Excel repositions existing cells to accommodate the new columns and rows and adjusts any existing formulas so that they refer to the correct cells. Formulas containing absolute cell references will need to be adjusted to the new columns or rows. When you insert one or more columns, they insert to the left. When you add one or more rows, they are inserted above the selected row.

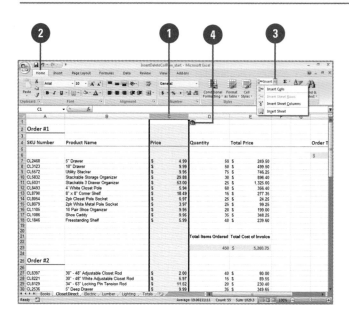

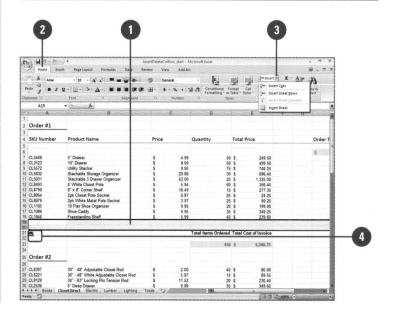

Deleting a Column or Row

Microsoft Certified Application Specialist

EX07S-2.2.1

At some point in time, you may want to remove an entire column or row of data from a worksheet rather than deleting or editing individual cells. You can delete columns and rows just as easily as you insert them. Formulas will need to be checked in your worksheet prior to deleting a row or column, especially when referencing absolute cell addresses. Remaining columns and rows move to the left or up to join the other remaining data.

Delete a Column or Row

1. Select the column header button or row header button that you want to delete.

2. Click the **Home** tab.

3. Click the **Delete Cells** button, and then click **Delete Sheet Columns** or **Delete Sheet Rows**.

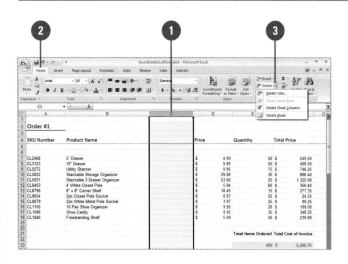

Delete Multiple Columns or Rows

1. Select the columns header buttons or rows header buttons that you want to delete.

2. Click the **Home** tab.

3. Click the **Delete Cells** button, and then click **Delete Sheet Columns** or **Delete Sheet Rows**.

Did You Know?

You can re-check your formulas. When deleting columns or rows that are referenced in a formula, it is important to adjust your formula for recalculations.

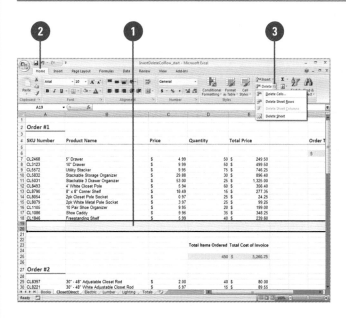

Adjusting Column Width and Row Height

Microsoft Certified Application Specialist

EX07S-2.2.4

You've entered labels and values, constructed formulas, and even formatted the cells, but now some of your data isn't visible; the value displays as #### in the cell. Also, some larger-sized labels are cut off. You can narrow or widen each column width to fit its contents and adjust your row heights as needed. As you build your worksheet, you can change the default width of some columns or the default height of some rows to accommodate long strings of data or larger font sizes. You can manually adjust column or row size to fit data you have entered, or you can use AutoFit to resize a column or row to the width or height of its largest entry.

Adjust Column Width or Row Height

1. Click the column or row header button for the first column or row you want to adjust.

2. If you want, drag to select more columns or rows.

3. Click the **Home** tab.

4. Click the **Format** button, and then click click **Column Width** or **Row Height**.

   TIMESAVER *Right-click the selected column(s) or row(s), and then click Column Width or Row Height.*

5. Type a new column width or row height in points.

6. Click **OK**.

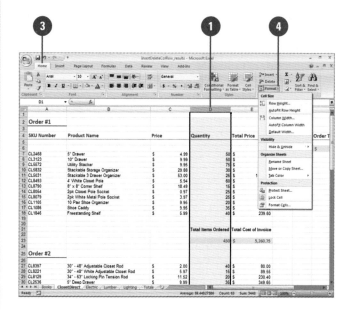

Did You Know?

What is a point? A point is a measurement unit used to size text and space on a worksheet. One inch equals 72 points.

You can change the default column width. Click the Home tab, click the Format button, click Default Width, type a column width in points, and then click OK.

Adjust Column Width or Row Height Using the Mouse

1. Position the mouse pointer on the right edge of the column header button or the bottom edge of the row header button for the column or row you want to change.

2. When the mouse pointer changes to a double-headed arrow, click and drag the pointer to a new width or height.

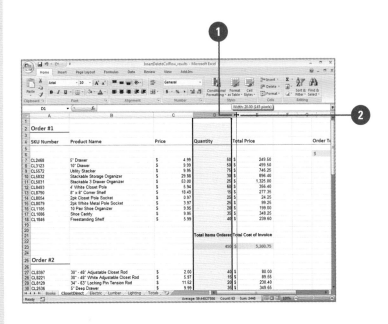

Change Column Width or Row Height Using AutoFit

1. Position the mouse pointer on the right edge of the column header button or the bottom edge of the row header button for the column or row you want to change.

2. When the mouse pointer changes to a double-headed arrow, double-click the mouse.

   ◆ You can also click the **Home** tab, click the **Format** button, and then click click **AutoFit Column Width** or **AutoFit Row Height**.

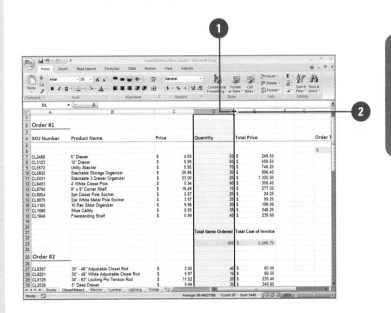

Freezing and Unfreezing a Column or Row

Large worksheets can be difficult to work with, especially on low-resolution or small screens. If you scroll down to see the bottom of the list, you can no longer see the column names at the top of the list. Instead of repeatedly scrolling up and down, you can temporarily set, or **freeze**, those column or row headings so that you can see them no matter where you scroll in the list. When you freeze a row or column, you are actually splitting the screen into one or more panes (window sections) and freezing one of the panes. You can split the screen into up to four panes and can freeze up to two of these panes. You can edit the data in a frozen pane just as you do any Excel data, but the cells remain stationary even when you use the scroll bars; only the unfrozen part of the screen scrolls. When you freeze a pane, it has no effect on how a worksheet looks when printed.

Freeze and Unfreeze a Column or Row

1. Select the column to the right of the columns you want to freeze, or select the row below the rows you want to freeze.

   To freeze both, click the cell to the right and below of the column and row you want to freeze.

2. Click the **View** tab.

3. Click the **Freeze Panes** button, and then click the option you want.

   ◆ **Freeze Panes.** Keeps rows and columns visible based on the current selection.

   ◆ **Freeze Top Row.** Keeps top row visible.

   ◆ **Freeze First Column.** Keeps first column visible.

   When you freeze a pane horizontally, all the rows **above** the active cell freeze. When you freeze a pane vertically, all the columns to the **left** of the active cell freeze.

4. To unfreeze a column or row, click the **Freeze Panes** button, and then click **Unfreeze Panes**.

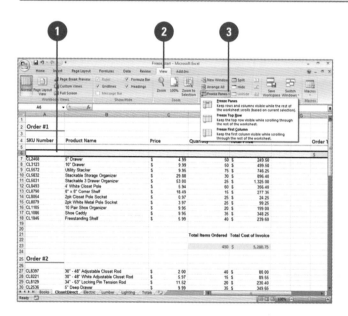

Splitting a Worksheet into Panes

Microsoft
Certified
Application
Specialist

EX07S-1.4.2

If you are working on a large worksheet, it can be time consuming and tiring to scroll back and forth between two parts of the worksheet. You can split the worksheet into four panes and two scrollable windows that you can view simultaneously but edit and scroll independently using the Split button (New!). As you work in two parts of the same worksheet, you can resize the window panes to fit your task. Drag the split bar between the panes to resize the windows. No matter how you display worksheets, Excel's commands and buttons work the same as usual.

Split a Worksheet into Panes

1. Select the row, column, or cell location where you want to split a worksheet into panes.

   A column or row selection creates two panes, while a cell selection creates four panes.

2. Click the **View** tab.

3. Click the **Split** button.

   The button appears highlighted.

4. To remove the split, click the **Split** button again.

   The button doesn't appear highlighted.

Did You Know?

You can search for a value or data in a cell, and then replace it with different content. Click the cell or cells containing content you want to replace. Click the Home tab, click Find & Select button, click Replace, specify the values or data you want to find and replace, and then click the appropriate Find or Replace buttons.

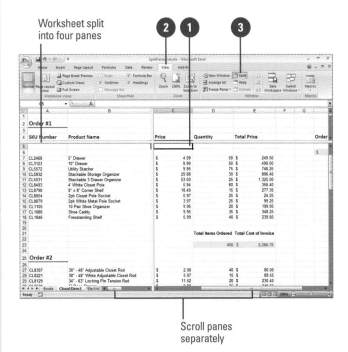

Worksheet split into four panes

Scroll panes separately

Showing and Hiding Workbook Elements

When you open a new or existing workbook, Excel displays a standard set of elements, such as the Formula Bar, Headings (columns and rows), Gridlines, Message Bar for security purposes, and Ruler, which is available in Page Layout view. If you need a little more display room to see your data or you want to see how your data looks without the gridlines, you can quickly select or clear view settings on the Data tab in Excel to show or hide these elements.

Show or Hide Workbook Elements

1. Click the **View** tab.

2. Select or clear the check box for the element you want to show or hide.

    ◆ **Ruler** (New!). In Page Layout view, the horizontal and vertical rulers.

    ◆ **Gridlines**. The gray outline around cells.

    ◆ **Message Bar** (New!). The bar below the Ribbon when a security alert appears.

    ◆ **Formula Bar**. The bar below the Ribbon.

    ◆ **Headings**. The column (letters) and row (numbers) headings.

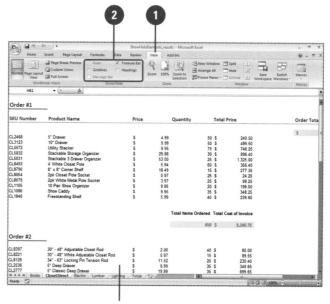

No gridlines or headings

Did You Know?

You can view a workbook in full screen without the Ribbon, tabs, and toolbars. Click the View tab, click the Full Screen button. To exit Full Screen view, right-click anywhere on the worksheet, and then click Close Full Screen.

Zooming the View In and Out

 EX07S-1.4.1

Change the View

1. Use any of the following zoom options available on the Status bar (New!):

   ◆ **Zoom Out**. Click to zoom out (percentage gets smaller).

   ◆ **Zoom In**. Click to zoom in (percentage gets larger).

   ◆ **Slider**. Drag to zoom out or in to the percentage you want.

   ◆ **Zoom Level**. Click to display the Zoom dialog box, where you can select the magnification you want.

2. For additional zoom options, click the **View** tab, and then use any of the following options:

   ◆ **Zoom**. Click to display the Zoom dialog box, where you can select the magnification you want.

   This is the same as Zoom Level above.

   ◆ **100%**. Click to display the view at 100%.

   ◆ **Zoom to Selection**. Click to zoom the current selection in view.

Working with the Zoom tools gives you one more way to control exactly what you see in an Excel worksheet. The Zoom tools are located in the bottom-right corner of the window. Large worksheet are difficult to work with and difficult to view. Many worksheets, when viewed at 100%, are larger than the maximized size of the window. When this happens, viewing the entire worksheet requires reducing the zoom.

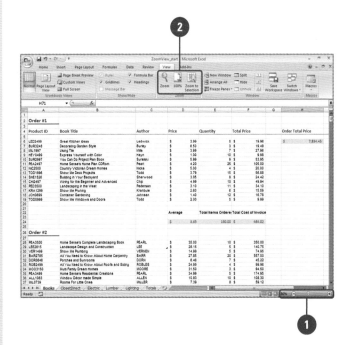

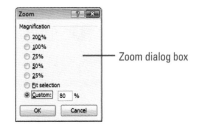

Zoom dialog box

Creating Custom Views

A **view** is a set of display and print settings that you can name and apply to a workbook. In Excel, you can create multiple custom views—such as one for developing a worksheet and another for entering data—in the same workbook without having to save separate copies. If you include print settings in a view, the view includes the defined print area. If the sheet has no defined print area, the view displays the entire worksheet. If one or more worksheets contain an Excel list, the Custom Views command is disabled for the entire workbook.

Create a Custom View

① Set up the workbook to appear the way you want to view and print it.

② Click the **View** tab.

③ Click the **Custom Views** button.

④ Click **Add**.

⑤ Type a name for the custom view.

To make it easier to identify, use the sheet name in the view name.

⑥ Select or clear the **Print settings** check box and the **Hidden rows, columns and filter settings** check box.

⑦ Click **OK**.

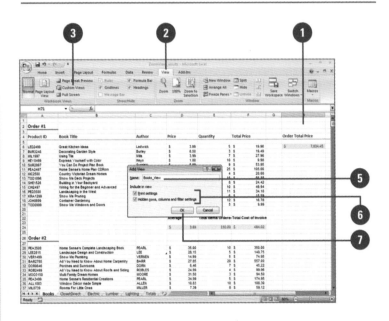

Show or Delete a Custom View

① Click the **View** tab.

② Click the **Custom Views** button.

③ Click the view you want to display.

④ Click **Show**.

Excel switches to the sheet that was active when you created the view and displays the custom view.

⑤ To delete a view, click **Delete**, and then click **Yes** to confirm.

⑥ If you deleted a view, click **Close**.

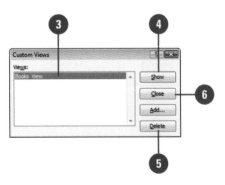

Saving a Workspace Layout

If you continually need to set up your working environment in Excel every time you want to work on a specific workbook, you can use the Save Workspace command to save your current window display settings. The Save Workspace command saves your current window display as a file in the Workspace file format so that you can open and view it again later with the same window sizes, print areas, screen magnification, and display settings. The workspace file doesn't contain the workbooks themselves; Excel opens each workbook saved in the workspace. To open a workspace file, you can use the Open dialog box.

Save a Workspace Layout of Windows

1. Size and arrange the workbook windows as you want them to appear when you open the workspace.

2. Click the **View** tab.

3. Click the **Save Workspace** button.

   The Save as type appears with the Workspaces file format.

4. Click the **Save in** list arrow, and then click the drive or folder where you want to save the file.

5. Type a workspace file name.

6. Click **Save**.

7. If necessary, click **Yes** to save changes, and then save the workspace.

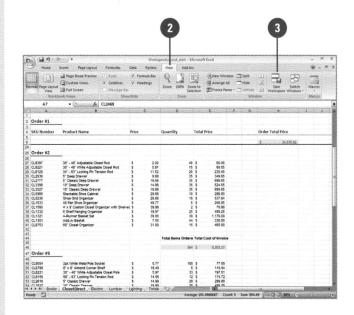

> ### Did You Know?
>
> **You can open a workspace file.** Click the Office button, click Open, click the Files of type list arrow, click Workspace, navigate to and select the workspace file, and then click Open.

Creating a Template

You can create your own template as easily as you create a worksheet. Like those that come with Excel, custom templates can save you time. Perhaps each month you create an inventory worksheet in which you enter repetitive information; all that changes is the actual data. By creating your own template, you can have a custom form that is ready for completion each time you take inventory. A template file (.xltx) saves all the customization you made to reuse in other workbooks. Although you can store your template anywhere you want, you may find it handy to store it in the Templates folder that Excel and Microsoft Office uses to store its templates. If you store your design templates in the Templates folder, those templates appear as options when you choose the New command on the Office menu, and then click My Templates.

Create a Template

1 Enter all the necessary information in a new workbook—including formulas, labels, graphics, and formatting.

2 Click the **Office** button, point to **Save As**, and then click **Other Formats**.

3 Click the **Save as type** list arrow, and then select a template format.

◆ **Excel Template**. Creates a template for Excel 2007.

◆ **Excel Macro-Enabled Template**. Creates a template for Excel 2007 with macros.

◆ **Excel 97-2003 Template**. Creates a template for Excel 97-2003.

Microsoft Office templates are typically stored in the following location:

Windows Vista. C:/Users /*your name*/AppData/Roaming /Microsoft/Templates

Windows XP. C:/Documents and Settings/*your name*/Application Data/Microsoft/Templates

4 Type a name for your template.

5 Click **Save**.

Templates folder

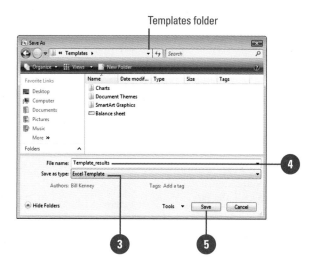

Opening a Template

You may not realize it, but every workbook you create is based on a template. When you start a new workbook without specifying a template, Excel creates a new workbook based on the **default template**, which includes three worksheets and no special formulas, labels, or formatting. When you specify a particular template in the New dialog box, whether it's one supplied by Excel or one you created yourself, Excel starts a new workbook that contains the formulas, labels, graphics, and formatting contained in that template. The template itself does not change when you enter data in the new workbook, because you are working on a new file, not with the template file.

Open a Template

1. Click the **Office** button, and then click **Open**.

2. Click the **Files of type** list arrow, and then click **Templates**.

3. Click the **Look in** list arrow, and then select the drive and folder that contain the template you want to open.

   Microsoft Office templates are typically stored in the following location:

   Windows Vista. C:/Users /*your name*/AppData/Roaming /Microsoft/Templates

   Windows XP. C:/Documents and Settings/*your name*/Application Data/Microsoft/Templates

4. Click the file name of the template you want to open.

5. Click **Open**.

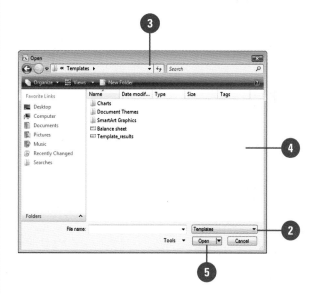

Changing a Template

Microsoft Excel has a selection of premade templates designed for you to use. These templates are available in the New Workbook dialog box under the Installed Templates. If you like one of these templates, you can use it as the basis to create your own template. To customize one of the Microsoft Installed Templates, open the actual template, make the changes you want, and then save it. If you save the original template back in the same location with the same name as the original, you create a new default template. The original one is replaced by the newly saved template. If you don't want to change the original, save the template with a new name. You can also use the same procedure to change one of your own templates.

Change an Excel Template

1. Click the **Office** button, and then click **New**.

2. Open the template you want to change using the following:

   ◆ **Microsoft Templates.** Click **Installed Templates**, click the template you want, and then click **Create**.

   ◆ **My Templates.** Click **My Templates**, click the template you want, and then click **OK**.

3. Make the changes you want to the template.

4. Click the **Office** button, and then click **Save As**.

5. Click the **Save as type** list arrow, and then click **Excel Template**.

   The location defaults to the folder for My Templates.

   If you want to save your template with Installed Templates, then navigate to the following:

   C:/Program Files/Microsoft Office/Templates/1033/

6. Type a new file name or the same as the existing name to replace it.

7. Click **Save**, and then click **Yes**, if necessary, to replace the file.

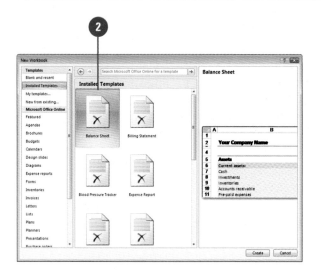

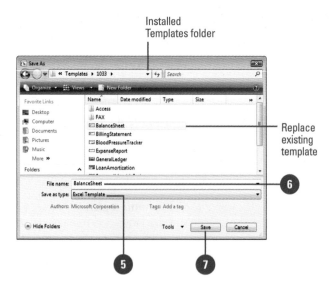

Installed Templates folder

Replace existing template

Formatting a Worksheet

5

Introduction

Microsoft Office Excel offers several tools for making your worksheets look more attractive and professional. Without formatting, a worksheet can look like a sea of meaningless data. To highlight important information, you can change the appearance of selected numbers and text by adding dollar signs, commas, and other numerical formats, or by applying attributes, such as boldface, italics, and underline.

Once you've set up your worksheet, additional changes are available to customize your worksheet's look. You can change the default font and font size, or maybe you'd like to adjust the alignment of data in cells. In addition to column, row, or font changes, you can add colors to cells or fonts, and include patterns to cells. You can also add borders around columns of data to help visually group them, or even add some clip art, a company logo, or some pictures.

Not everyone has an eye for color, and pulling it all together can be daunting, so Excel provides you with professionally designed themes, which you can apply to any workbook. A **theme** is a set of unified design elements that provides a consistent look for a workbook by using color themes, fonts, and effects, such as shadows, shading, and animations. However, if you simply want to format a range of cells in a worksheet you can quickly apply a cell style. A **cell style** is a defined collection of formats—font, font size, attributes, numeric formats, and so on—that you can store as a set and later apply to other cells. You can use one of Excel's built-in cell styles, or create one of your own.

If you need to find the various formatting attributes and change them, you can use the Find and Replace Formatting feature to change them all at once instead of making individual changes.

Formatting Numbers

Microsoft Certified Application Specialist

EX07S-2.2.2,
EX07S-2.3.1

You can change the appearance of the data in the cells of a worksheet without changing the actual value in the cell. You can apply **numeric formats** to numbers to better reflect the type of information they represent—dollar amounts, dates, decimals, and so on. For example, you can format a number to display up to 15 decimal places or none at all. If you don't see the number format you need, you can create a custom one.

Format Numbers Quickly

1. Select a cell or range that contains the number(s) you want to format.

2. Click the **Home** tab.

3. Click the **Number Format** list arrow (**New!**), and then click any of the following formats:

   - **General.** No specific format.

   - **Number.** 0.75

   - **Currency.** $0.75

   - **Accounting.** $ 0.75

   - **Short Date.** 3/17/2008

   - **Long Date.** Wednesday, March 17, 2008

   - **Time.** 6:00:00 PM

   - **Percentage.** 75.00%

   - **Fraction.** 3/4

   - **Scientific.** 7.50E-01

4. To fine-tune the format, click any of the following format buttons:

   - **Currency Style.** Click the button arrow to select a currency symbol.

   - **Percent Style.**

   - **Comma Style.**

   - **Increase Decimal.**

   - **Decrease Decimal.**

   You can apply multiple attributes to the range.

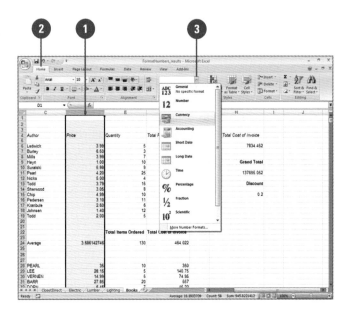

Format a Number Using the Format Cells Dialog Box

1. Select a cell or range that contains the number(s) you want to format.

2. Click the **Home** tab.

3. Click the **Number Dialog Box Launcher**.

   The dialog box opens, displaying the Number tab.

4. Click to select a category.

5. Select the options you want to apply.

   To create a custom format, click Custom, type the number format code, and then use one of the existing codes as a starting point.

6. Preview your selections in the Sample box.

7. Click **OK**.

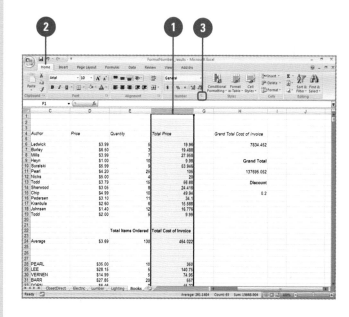

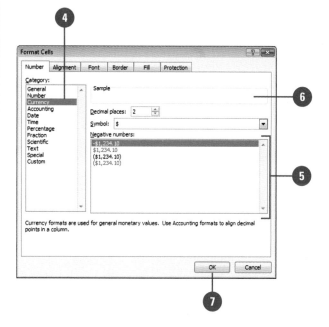

Did You Know?

You can format numbers in international currencies. In the Format Cells dialog box, click the Number tab, click Currency in the Category list, click the Symbol list arrow, and then click an international currency symbol.

You can quickly remove a numeric format or font attribute. The buttons on the Home tab Ribbon and the Mini-Toolbar are toggle buttons, which means you simply click to turn them on and off. To add or remove a numeric format or a font attribute, select the cell, range, or text, and then click the appropriate button on the the Home tab or the Mini-Toolbar to turn the format or attribute off.

Formatting Text

Microsoft
Certified
Application
Specialist

EX07S-2.2.2,
EX07S-2.3.4

A **font** is a collection of alphanumeric characters that share the same typeface, or design, and have similar characteristics. Most fonts are available in a number of styles (such as bold and italic) and sizes. You can format text and numbers with font attributes, such as bolding, italics, or underlining, to enhance data to catch the reader's attention. The basic formats you apply to text are available on the Home tab in the Font group or in the Font dialog box. Some of the formats available in the Font dialog box include strikethrough, and single or double normal and accounting underline. When you point to selected text, Excel displays the Mini-Toolbar above it. The **Mini-Toolbar (New!)** provides easy access to common formatting toolbar buttons, such as font, font size, increase and decrease font size, bold, italic, font color, and increase and decrease list level. If you don't want to display the Mini-Toolbar, you can use Excel Options to turn it off.

Format Text Quickly

1 Select the text you want to format.

2 Click the **Home** tab.

3 To change fonts, click the **Font** list arrow on the Ribbon or Mini-Toolbar, and then point for a live preview (New!), or click the font you want, either a theme font (New!) or any available fonts.

The font name appears in the font style.

To change the font size, click one or more of the font size buttons on the Ribbon or Mini-Toolbar:

◆ Click the **Font Size** list arrow, and then click the font size you want.

◆ Click the **Increase Font Size** button (New!) or **Decrease Font Size** button (New!).

To apply other formatting, click one or more of the formatting buttons on the Ribbon or Mini-Toolbar: **Bold**, **Italic**, **Underline**, **Shadow**, **Strikethrough** (New!), or **Font Color**.

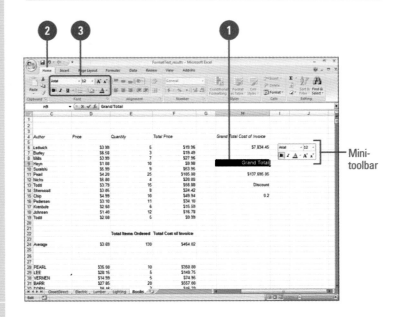

Mini-toolbar

Format Text Using the Format Cells Dialog Box

1. Select the text you want to format.

2. Click the **Home** tab.

3. Click the **Font Dialog Box Launcher**.

   The dialog box opens, displaying the Font tab.

4. Select the font, font style, and font size you want.

5. Select or clear the effects you want or don't want: **Strikethrough**, **Superscript**, and **Subscript**.

6. If you want, click **Font Color**, and then click a color.

7. If you want, click **Underline** list arrow, and then click a style.

8. Click **OK**.

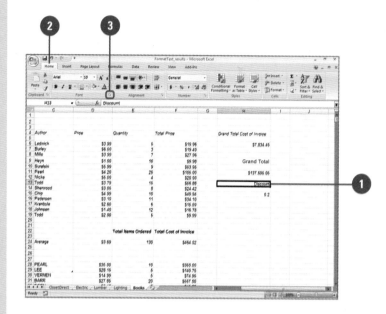

Did You Know?

You can tell the difference between a TrueType and printer font. A TrueType (outline) font is a font that uses special software capabilities to print exactly what is seen on the screen. A printer (screen) font is a font that comes only in specified sizes. If you are creating a worksheet for publication, you need to use printer fonts.

What is a point? The size of each font character is measured in points (a point is approximately 1/72 of an inch). You can use any font that is installed on your computer on a worksheet, but the default is 10-point Arial.

Each computer has different fonts installed. Users with whom you share files may not have all the fonts you've used in a workbook installed on their computers.

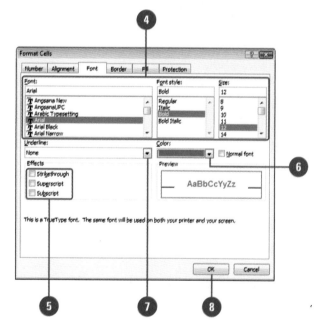

Applying Conditional Formatting

Microsoft
Certified
Application
Specialist

EX07S-4.3.2,
EX07S-4.3.3

You can make your worksheets more powerful by setting up **conditional formatting**, which lets the value of a cell determine its formatting. For example, you might want this year's sales total to be displayed in red and italics if it's less than last year's total, but in green and bold if it's more. The formatting is applied to the cell values only if the values meet the a condition that you specify. Otherwise, no conditional formatting is applied to the cell values. With Excel 2007, you can apply conditional formatting only to cells that contain text, number, or date or time values (**New!**). You can quickly format only top or bottom ranked values, values above or below average, unique or duplicate values, or use a formula to determine which cells to format (**New!**).

Format Cell Contents Based on Comparison

1. Select a cell or range you want to conditionally format.

2. Click the **Home** tab.

3. Click the **Conditional Formatting** button, and then point to **Highlight Cell Rules**.

4. Click the comparison rule you want to apply to conditionally format the selected data.

   ◆ **Greater Than.**

   ◆ **Less Than.**

   ◆ **Between.**

   ◆ **Equal To.**

   ◆ **Text that Contains.**

   ◆ **A Date Occurring.**

   ◆ **Duplicate Values.**

5. Specify the criteria you want. Each rule supplies different criteria.

6. Click **OK**.

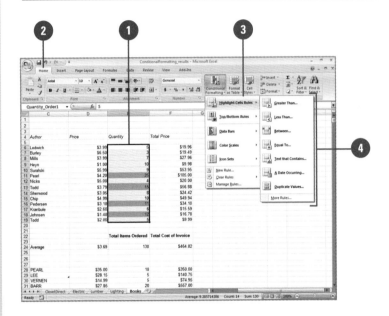

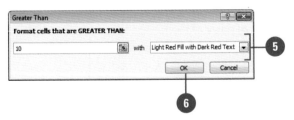

Format Cell Contents Based on Ranking and Average

1. Select a cell or range you want to conditionally format.

2. Click the **Home** tab.

3. Click the **Conditional Formatting** button, and then point to **Top/Bottom Rules**.

4. Click the comparison rule you want to apply to conditionally format the selected data.

   ◆ **Top 10 Items.**

   ◆ **Top 10 %.**

   ◆ **Bottom 10 Items.**

   ◆ **Bottom 10 %.**

   ◆ **Above Average.**

   ◆ **Below Average.**

5. Specify the criteria you want. Each rule supplies different criteria.

6. Click **OK**.

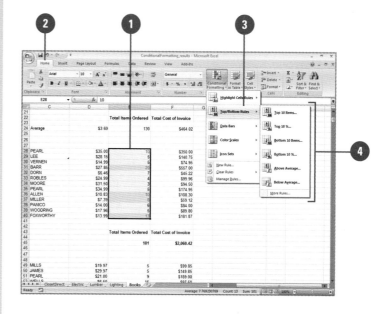

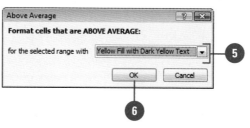

Applying Specialized Conditional Formatting

Microsoft Certified Application Specialist

EX07S-4.3.2,
EX07S-4.3.3

With Excel 2007, you can apply specialized conditional formatting by using data bars, color scales, and icon sets. A colored **data bar** (New!) helps you see the value of a cell relative to other cells. The length of the data bar represents the value in the cell. A longer bar represents a higher value. A **color scale** (New!) is a visual guide that helps you understand data distribution and variation using a two or three color gradient. The shade of the color represents the value in the cell. A two-color scale represents higher and lower values, while a three-color scale represents higher, middle, and lower values. An **icon set** (New!) helps you annotate and classify data into three to five categories separated by a threshold value. Each icon represents a value in the cell.

Format Using Data Bars

1. Select a cell or range you want to conditionally format.

2. Click the **Home** tab.

3. Click the **Conditional Formatting** button, and then point to **Data Bars**.

4. Click the colored data bar you want: Blue, Green, Red, Orange, Light Blue, or Purple.

5. To create a custom data bar, click **More Rules**, specify the description you want, and then click **OK**.

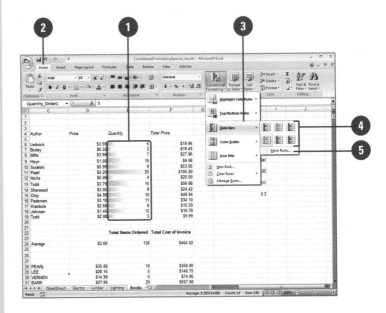

Format Using Color Scales

1. Select a cell or range you want to conditionally format.

2. Click the **Home** tab.

3. Click the **Conditional Formatting** button, and then point to **Color Scales**.

4. Click the two or three colored scale you want.

   The top color represents higher values, the center color represents middle values (for three-color), and the bottom color represents lower values.

5. To create a custom color scale, click **More Rules**, specify the description you want, and then click **OK**.

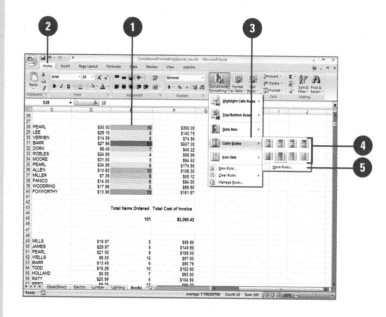

Format Using Icon Sets

1. Select a cell or range you want to conditionally format.

2. Click the **Home** tab.

3. Click the **Conditional Formatting** button, and then point to **Icon Sets**.

4. Click the colored icon sets you want.

5. To create a custom icon sets, click **More Rules**, specify the description you want, and then click **OK**.

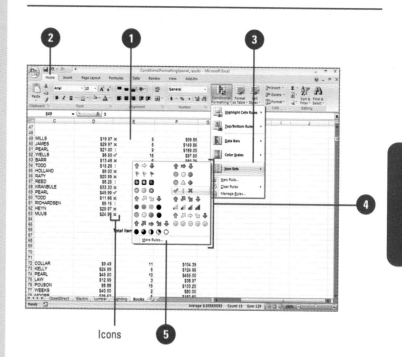

Icons

Creating Conditional Formatting

Microsoft Certified Application Specialist

EX07S-4.3.1

Instead of using one of the built-in conditional formatting rules, you can create your own rules. The New Formatting Rule dialog box (**New!**) allows you to create rules based on different rule types, such as format all cells based on their values, or use a formula to determine which cells to format. After you select a rule type, you specify the rule criteria to trigger conditional formatting. Many of the rule types include the Format button, which opens the familiar Format Cells dialog box. You can specify number, font, border, and fill formatting options.

Create Conditional Formatting Rules

1. Click the **Home** tab.

2. Click the **Conditional Formatting** button, and then click **New Rules**.

3. Click the rule type you want.

   ◆ Format all cells based on their values.

   ◆ Format only cells that contain.

   ◆ Format only top or bottom ranked values.

   ◆ Format only values that are above or below average.

   ◆ Format only unique or duplicate values.

   ◆ Use a formula to determine which cells to format.

4. Specify the rule criteria you want to create a conditional format. Each rule type provides a different set of options you can set.

   If available, click **Format** to specify number, font, border, and fill formatting options in the Format Cells dialog box.

5. Click **OK**.

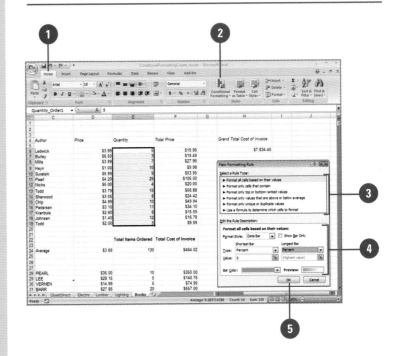

Clearing Conditional Formatting

EX07S-4.3.1

If you no longer need the conditional formatting applied to a cell, range, table, or PivotTable, you can quickly clear the formatting using any of the Clear Rules commands on the Conditional Formatting menu. You can clear rules from selected cells, entire sheet, table, or PivotTable (New!). When you clear conditional formatting rules, the contents of the cell, range, table or PivotTable remain intact. Only the cell formatting is removed.

Clear Conditional Formatting Rules

1 Select the cell or range with the conditional formatting rules you want to clear.

2 Click the **Home** tab.

3 Click the **Conditional Formatting** button, and then point to **Clear Rules**.

4 Click the clear rule option you want:

- ◆ **Clear Rules from Selected Cells.**

- ◆ **Clear Rules form Entire Sheet.**

- ◆ **Clear Rules from This Table.**

- ◆ **Clear Rules from This PivotTable.**

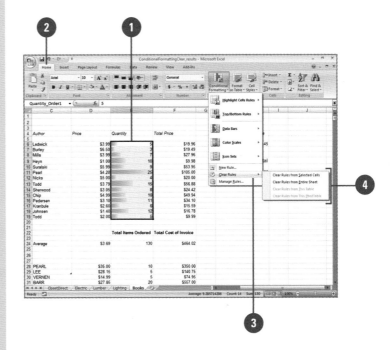

Managing Conditional Formatting

Microsoft
Certified
Application
Specialist

EX07S-4.3.1

When you apply conditional formatting to a cell or range of cells, Excel stores the rules associated with the conditional formatting in the Conditional Formatting Rules Manager (**New!**). You can use the Conditional Formatting Rules Manager to create, edit, delete, and view all conditional formatting rules in a workbook. When two or more conditional formatting rules apply to the same cells (that conflict or not), the rules are evaluated in order of precedence as they appear in the dialog box. You can move a rule up or down in the precedence list. Conditional formatting takes precedence over a manual format, which doesn't appear in the Conditional Formatting Rules Manager.

Edit Conditional Formatting Rule Precedence

1. If you want, select the cell or range with the conditional formatting rules you want to edit.

2. Click the **Home** tab.

3. Click the **Conditional Formatting** button, and then click **Manage Rules**.

4. Click the **Show formatting rulers for** list arrow, and then select an option to show the rules you want.

5. Select the rule you want to change.

6. To move the selected rule up or down in precedence, click **Move Up** or **Move Down**.

7. To stop rule evaluation at a specific rule, select the **Stop If True** check box.

   Select this option for backwards compatibility with previous versions of Excel that don't support multiple conditional formatting rules.

8. To delete a rule, click **Delete Rule**.

9. To edit a rule, click **Edit Rule**, make the changes you want, and then click **OK**.

10. Click **OK**.

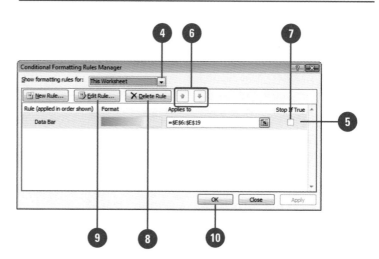

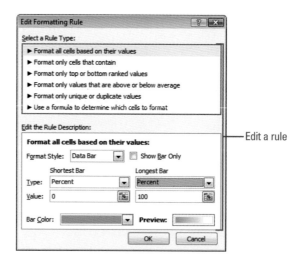

Edit a rule

Finding Conditional Formatting

If you have cells in your workbook that contain conditional formatting, you can quickly find them using the Find & Select button in order to change, copy or delete the formatting. You can use the Conditional Formatting command (**New!**) to find all cells that have a conditional format, or use the Go To Special command to find only cells that have the same conditional format.

Find Cells with Conditional Formatting

1. Select any cell without a conditional format.

2. Click the **Home** tab.

3. Click the **Find & Select** button arrow, and then click **Conditional Formatting**.

Find Cells with the Same Conditional Format

1. Select a cell with the conditional format you want to find.

2. Click the **Home** tab.

3. Click the **Find & Select** button arrow, and then click **Go To Special**.

4. Click the **Conditional formats** option.

5. Click the **Same** option.

6. Click **OK**.

Changing Data Alignment

EX07S-2.3.4

When you enter data in a cell, Excel aligns labels on the left edge of the cell and aligns values and formulas on the right edge of the cell. **Horizontal alignment** is the way in which Excel aligns the contents of a cell relative to the left or right edge of the cell; **vertical alignment** is the way in which Excel aligns cell contents relative to the top and bottom of the cell. Excel also provides an option for changing the flow and angle of characters within a cell. The **orientation** of the contents of a cell is expressed in degrees. The default orientation is 0 degrees, in which characters are horizontally aligned within a cell.

Change Alignment Using the Ribbon

1. Select a cell or range containing the data to be realigned.

2. Click the **Home** tab.

3. Click any of the alignment buttons on the Ribbon:

   ◆ Click **Align Left**, **Center**, or **Align Right** to align cell contents left to right.

   ◆ Click **Top Align**, **Middle Align**, or **Bottom Align** to align cell contents from top to bottom.

   ◆ Click **Decrease Indent** or **Increase Indent** to shift cell contents to the left or right.

   ◆ Click **Orientation**, and then click **Angle Counterclockwise**, **Angle Clockwise**, **Vertical Text**, **Rotate Text Up**, or **Rotate Text Down** to rotate cell contents.

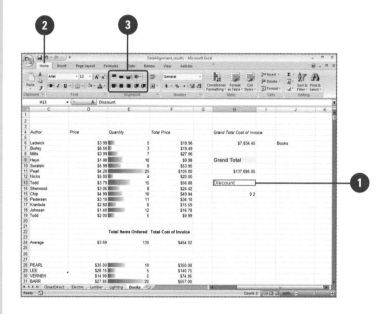

Change Alignment Using the Format Dialog Box

1. Select a cell or range containing the data to be realigned.

2. Click the **Home** tab.

3. Click the **Alignment Dialog Box Launcher**.

   The Format Cells dialog box opens, displaying the Alignment tab.

4. Click the **Horizontal** list arrow or the **Vertical** list arrow, and then select an alignment.

5. Select an orientation. Click a point on the map, or click the **Degrees** up or down arrow.

6. If you want, select one or more of the Text Control check boxes.

7. Click the **Text Direction** list arrow, and then select a direction: **Context, Left-to-Right,** or Right-to-Left.

8. Click **OK**.

Did You Know?

You can use the Format Cells dialog box to select other alignment options. Many more alignment options are available from the Format Cells dialog box, but for centering across columns and simple left, right, and center alignment, it's easier to use the Formatting toolbar buttons.

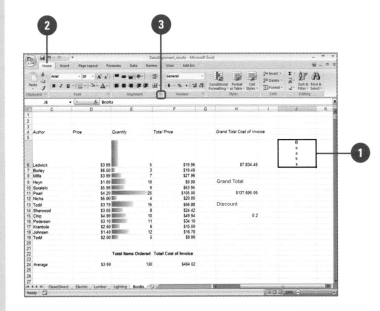

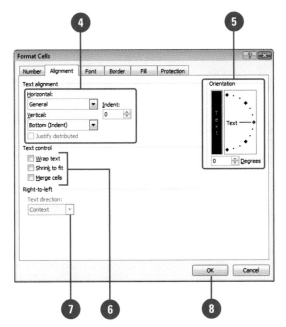

Controlling Text Flow ▶

Microsoft
Certified
Application
Specialist   EX07S-2.3.6

The length of a label might not always fit within the width you've chosen for a column. If the cell to the right is empty, text spills over into it, but if that cell contains data, the text will be truncated (that is, cut off). A cell can be formatted so its text automatically wraps to multiple lines or cell contents can also be shrunk to fit within the available space; that way, you don't have to widen the column to achieve an attractive effect. If the cell to the right is empty, cell contents can be combined, or merged, with the contents of other cells.

Control the Flow of Text in a Cell

1. Select a cell or range whose text flow you want to change.

2. Click the **Home** tab.

3. To center cell contents across selected columns, click the **Merge & Center** button arrow, and then click one of the options:

   ◆ **Merge & Center.**

   ◆ **Merge Across.**

   ◆ **Merge Cells.**

   ◆ **Unmerge Cells.**

4. To wrap text in a cell, click the **Wrap text** button.

5. To set multiple alignment options at the same time or shrink text to fit in a cell, click the **Alignment Dialog Box Launcher**.

   The Format Cells dialog box opens, displaying the Alignment tab.

6. Select one or more Text Control check boxes.

   ◆ **Wrap text** moves the text to multiple lines within a cell.

   ◆ **Shrink to fit** reduces character size to fit within a cell.

   ◆ **Merge cells** combines selected cells into a single cell.

7. Click **OK**.

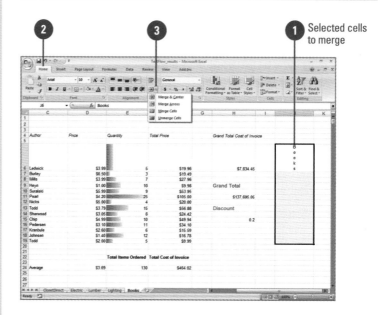

Selected cells to merge

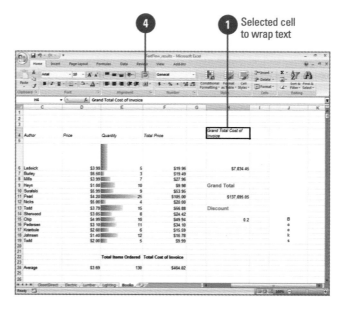

Selected cell to wrap text

Changing Data Color

Change Font Color

 Select a cell or range that contains the text you want to change.

2 Click the **Home** tab.

3 Click the **Font Color** button arrow.

4 Click a color.

Did You Know?

The Font Color button on the Ribbon displays the last font color you used. To apply this color to another selection, simply click the button, not the list arrow.

You can change the color of the numbers and text on a worksheet. Strategic use of **font color** can be an effective way of tying similar values together. For instance, on a sales worksheet you might want to display sales in green and returns in red. Or, you may want to highlight column or row headers with colored labels. Either way, using color to highlight numbers and texts makes deciphering your worksheet data easier.

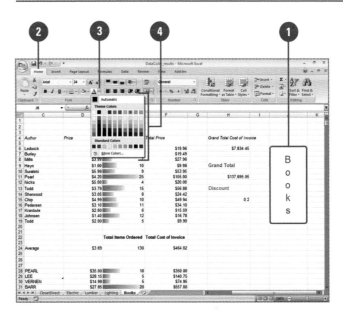

Adding Color and Patterns to Cells

You can **fill** the background of a cell with a color and a pattern to make its data stand out. Fill colors and patterns can also lend consistency to related information on a worksheet. On a sales worksheet, for example, formatting all fourth-quarter sales figures with a blue background and all second-quarter sales with a yellow background would make each group of figures easy to identify. You can use fill colors and patterns in conjunction with text attributes, fonts, and font colors to further enhance the appearance of your worksheet. If you no longer need cell shading, you can remove it.

Apply Solid Colors to Cells

1. Select a cell or range you want to apply cell color.

2. Click the **Home** tab.

3. Click the **Fill Color** button arrow, and then click the color on the palette you want.

   TIMESAVER *To apply the most recently selected color, click the Fill Color button.*

4. To remove the cell shading, click the **Fill Color** button arrow, and then click **No Fill**.

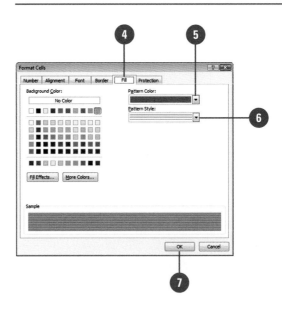

Apply Color and Pattern to Cells

1. Select a cell or range you want to apply cell shading.

2. Click the **Home** tab.

3. Click the **Font Dialog Box Launcher**.

4. Click the **Fill** tab.

5. Click the **Pattern Color** list arrow, and then click a pattern color.

6. Click the **Pattern Style** list arrow, and then click a pattern.

7. Click **OK**.

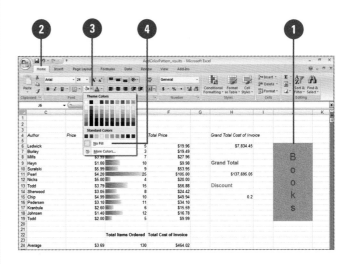

Adding Custom Colors

In addition to the standard and theme colors (**New!**), Excel allows you to add more colors to your workbook. These additional colors are available on each color button palette on the Ribbon or in a dialog box, such as the Fill Color or Font Color button. These colors are useful when you want to use a specific color, but the workbook color theme does not have that color. Colors that you add to a workbook appear in all color palettes and remain in the palette even if the color theme changes.

Add a Color to the Menus

1 Click the **Font Color** button on the Home tab, and then click **More Colors**.

This is one method. You can also use other color menus to access the Colors dialog box.

2 Click the **Custom** tab.

3 Click the **Color Mode** list arrow, and then click **RGB** or **HSL**.

4 Select a custom color using one of the following methods:

- ◆ If you know the color values, enter them, either Hue, Sat, Lum, or Red, Green, and Blue.

- ◆ Drag across the palette until the pointer is over the color you want. Drag the black arrow to adjust the amount of black and white in the color.

  The new color appears above the current color at the bottom right.

5 Click **OK**.

The current selection is changed to the new color, plus the new color is added to the Recent Colors section of all workbook color menus.

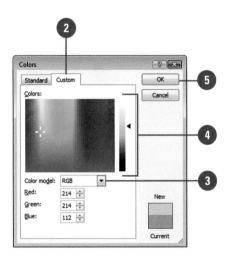

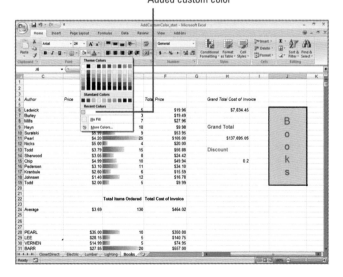

Added custom color

> ### See Also
>
> See "Creating Theme Colors" on page 156 for information on using color.

Adding Borders to Cells

Microsoft Certified Application Specialist

EX07S-2.3.7

Apply or Remove a Border Using the Ribbon

1 Select a cell or range to which you want to apply a border.

2 Click the **Home** tab.

3 Click the **Borders** button arrow.

TIMESAVER *To apply the most recently selected border, click the Borders button.*

4 Select a border from the submenu.

5 To remove cell borders, click **No Border**.

Draw a Border

1 Click the **Home** tab.

2 Click the **Borders** button arrow.

3 Select a draw borders option from the submenu.

♦ Point to **Line Color**, and then click the color you want.

♦ Point to **Line Style**, and then click the style you want.

♦ Click **Draw Border**, and then drag a border.

♦ Click **Draw Border Grid**, and then drag a border.

♦ Click **Erase Border**, and then drag a border.

4 Press Esc to exit.

The light gray grid that appears on the worksheet helps your eyes move from cell to cell. Although you can print these gridlines, sometimes a different grid pattern better emphasizes your data. For example, you might put a decorative line border around the title or a double-line bottom border below cells with totals. You can add borders of varying colors and widths to any or all sides of a single cell or range. If you prefer, you can draw (**New!**) a border outline or grid directly on a worksheet.

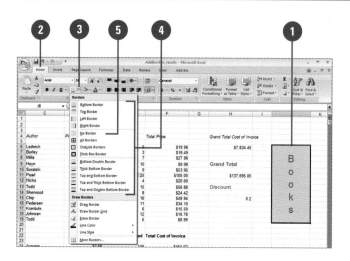

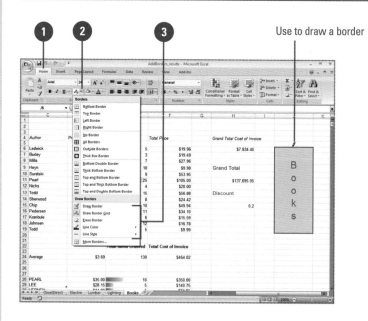

Use to draw a border

Apply a Border Using the Format Cells Dialog Box

1 Select a cell or range to which you want to apply borders.

2 Click the **Home** tab.

3 Click the **Borders** button arrow, and then click **More Borders**.

The Format Cells dialog box opens, displaying the Border tab.

4 Select a line style.

5 Click the **Color** list arrow, and then click a color for the border.

6 If you want a border on the outside of a cell or range, click **Outline**. If you want a border between cells, click **Inside**. If you want to remove a border, click **None**.

7 To set a custom border, click a Border button, or click the Preview Border box where you want to add a border.

Use these buttons to create a diagonal border.

8 Click **OK**.

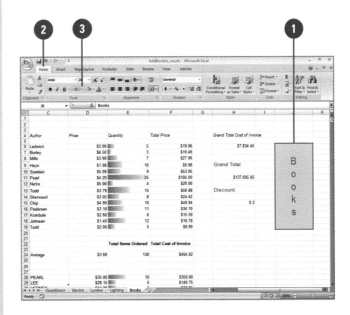

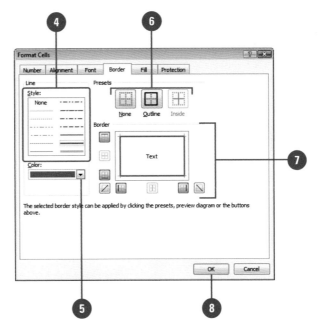

Did You Know?

You can quickly switch between Draw Border and Draw Border Grid. Click the Borders button arrow on the Home tab, click Draw Border or Draw Border Grid. Hold down the Ctrl key to switch to the other border drawing cursor.

You can use the Select All button. To place a border around the entire worksheet, click the Select All button, and then apply the border.

Formatting Tabs and Background

Microsoft Certified Application Specialist EX07S-2.1.3, EX07S-2.1.4

Depending on your screen size, the sheet tabs at the bottom of your workbook can be hard to view. You can add color to the sheet tabs to make them more distinguishable. If you want to add artistic style to your workbook or you are creating a Web page from your workbook, you can add a background picture. When you add a background to a worksheet, the background does not print, and it's not included when you save an individual worksheet as a Web page. You need to publish the entire workbook as a Web page to include the background.

Add or Remove Color to Worksheet Tabs

1. Click the sheet tab you want to color.

2. Click the **Home** tab.

3. Click the **Format** button, point to **Tab Color**, and then do any of the following:

   ◆ **Add.** Click a color.

   ◆ **Remove.** Click **No Color**.

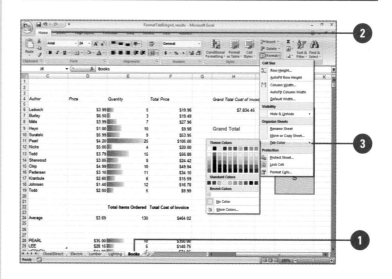

Add or Remove a Background

1. Click the sheet tab to which you want to add a background.

2. Click the **Page Layout** tab.

3. Click the **Background** button.

4. Select the folder with the graphic file you want to use.

5. Select the graphic you want.

6. Click **Insert**.

   The Background button changes to the Delete Background button.

7. To remove the background, click **Delete Background** on the Page Layout tab.

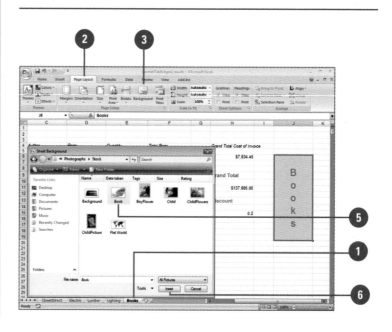

Copying Cell Formats ▶

After formatting a cell on a worksheet, you might want to apply those same formatting changes to other cells on the worksheet. For example, you might want each subtotal on your worksheet to be formatted in italic, bold, 12-point Times New Roman, with a dollar sign, commas, and two decimal places. Rather than selecting each subtotal and applying the individual formatting to each cell, you can **paint** (that is, copy) the formatting from one cell to others. The Format Painter lets you "pick up" the style of one section and apply, or "paint," it to another. To apply a format style to more than one item, double-click the Format Painter button on the Home tab instead of a single-click. The double-click keeps the Format Painter active until you want to press Esc to disable it, so you can apply formatting styles to any text or object you want in your workbook.

Apply a Format Style Using the Format Painter

1. Select a cell or range containing the formatting you want to copy.

2. Click the **Home** tab.

3. Click the **Format Painter** button.

   If you want to apply the format to more than one item, double-click the Format Painter button.

4. Drag to select the text or click the object to which you want to apply the format.

5. If you double-clicked the Format Painter button, drag to select the text or click the object to which you want to apply the format, and then press Esc when you're done.

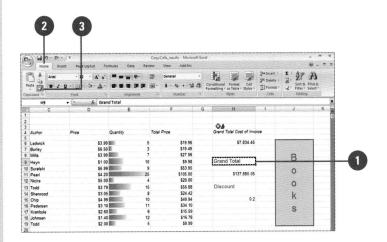

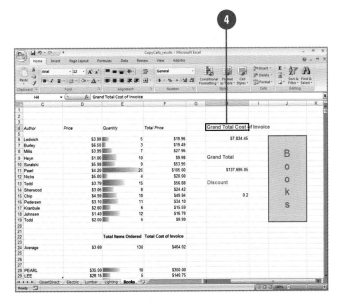

Did You Know?

You can use the Esc key to cancel format painting. If you change your mind about painting a format, cancel the marquee by pressing Esc.

Understanding Color Themes

A theme helps you create professional-looking workbooks that use an appropriate balance of color for your workbook content. You can use a default color theme (New!) or create a custom one.

Themes in Excel are made up of a palette of twelve colors (New!). These colors appear on color palettes when you click a color-related button, such as Fill Color or Font Color button on the Home tab or in a dialog box. These twelve colors correspond to the following elements in a workbook:

Four Text and Background. The two background colors (light and dark combinations) are the canvas, or drawing area, color of the worksheet. The two text colors (light and dark combinations) are for typing text and drawing lines, and contrast with the background colors.

Six Accent. These colors are designed to work as a complementary color palette for

objects, such as shadows and fills. These colors contrast with both the background and text colors.

One hyperlink. This color is designed to work as a complementary color for objects and hyperlinks.

One followed hyperlink. This color is designed to work as a complementary color for objects and visited hyperlinks.

The first four colors in the Theme Colors list represent the workbook text and background colors (light and dark for each). The remaining colors represent the six accent and two hyperlink colors for the theme. When you apply another theme or change any of these colors to create a new theme, the colors shown in the Theme Colors dialog box and color palettes change to match the current colors.

Accent 5   Accent 4   Accent 6   Accent 1   Accent 3

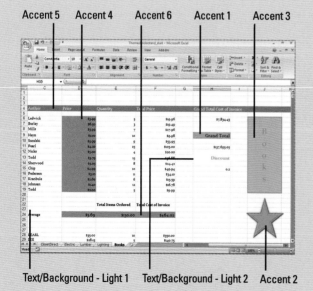

Text/Background - Light 1   Text/Background - Light 2   Accent 2

Twelve theme colors   **Sample color themes:** Dark and Light

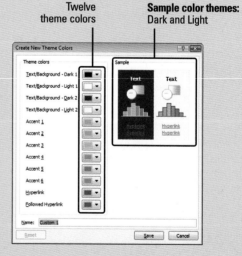

Viewing and Applying a Theme

A workbook theme (**New!**) consists of theme colors, fonts, and effects. You can quickly format an entire worksheet with a professional look by applying a theme. To quickly see if you like a theme, point to one on the themes gallery to display a ScreenTip with name and information about it, and a live preview (**New!**) of it on the current worksheet. If you like the theme, you can apply it. When you apply a theme, the background, text, graphics, charts, and tables all change to reflect the theme. You can choose from one or more standard themes. When you add new content, the worksheet elements change to match the theme ensuring all of your material will look consistent. You can even use the same theme in other Microsoft Office 2007 programs, such as Word and PowerPoint, so all your work matches. Can't find a theme you like? Search Microsoft Office Online.

View and Apply a Theme

1. Open the workbook you want to apply a theme.

2. Click the **Page Layout** tab.

3. Click the **Themes** button to display the themes gallery.

   The current theme appears highlighted in the gallery.

4. Point to a theme.

   A live preview (**New!**) of the theme appears in the worksheet, along with a ScreenTip.

5. Click the theme you want to apply to the active worksheet.

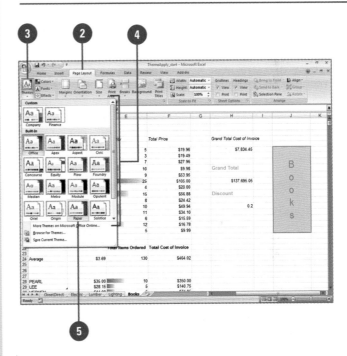

Did You Know?

You can search for themes at Microsoft Office Online. Click the Page Layout tab, click the Themes button, and then click Search Office Online. Follow Microsoft Office Online Web site instructions to download and use online themes.

You can create a new workbook based on a theme. Click the Office button, click New, click Installed Themes in the left pane, click the theme you want, and then click Create.

Creating Theme Colors

Microsoft
Certified
Application
Specialist
EX07S-2.1.1

You may like a certain color theme except for one or two colors. You can change an existing color theme (**New!**) and apply your changes to the entire workbook. You can add other custom colors to your theme by using RGB (Red, Green, and Blue) or HSL (Hues, Saturation, and Luminosity) color modes. The RGB color mode is probably the most widely used of all the color modes. You can accomplish this by using sliders, dragging on a color-space, or entering a numeric value that corresponds to a specific color. Once you create this new color theme, you can add it to your collection of color themes so that you can make it available to any workbook.

Apply or Create Theme Colors

1 Open the workbook you want to apply a color theme.

2 Click the **Page Layout** tab.

3 To apply theme colors to a workbook, click the **Theme Colors** button, and then click a color theme.

4 To create theme colors, click the **Theme Colors** button, and then click **Create New Theme Colors**.

5 Click the Theme Colors buttons (Text/Background, Accent, or Hyperlink, etc.) for the colors you want to change.

6 Click a new color, or click **More Colors** to select a color from the **Standard** or **Custom** tab, and then click **OK**.

7 If you don't like your color choices, click the **Reset** button to return all color changes to their original colors.

8 Type a new name for the color theme.

9 Click **Save**.

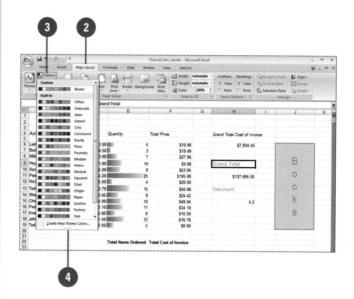

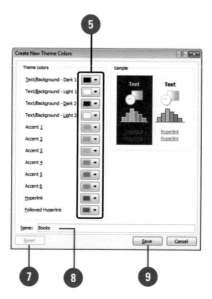

Select Custom Colors

1. Select a cell or range you want to apply a custom color.

2. Click the **Font Color** button on the Home tab, and then click **More Colors**.

   This is one method. You can also use other color menus to access the Colors dialog box.

3. Click the **Custom** tab.

4. Click the **Color Mode** list arrow, and then click **RGB** or **HSL**.

5. Select a custom color using one of the following methods:

   ◆ If you know the color values, enter them, either Hue, Sat, Lum, or Red, Green, and Blue.

   ◆ Drag across the palette until the pointer is over the color you want. Drag the black arrow to adjust the amount of black and white in the color.

   The new color appears above the current color at the bottom right.

6. Click **OK**.

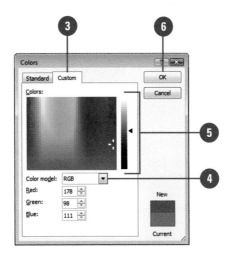

Did You Know?

You can edit a custom color theme. On the Page Layout tab, click the Theme Colors button, right-click the theme color you want to edit, click Edit, make changes, and then click Save.

You can delete a custom color theme. On the Page Layout tab, click the Theme Colors button, right-click the theme color you want to edit, click Edit, click Delete, and then click Yes.

The Properties of Color

Characteristic	Description
Hue	The color itself; every color is identified by a number, determined by the number of colors available on your monitor.
Saturation	The intensity of the color. The higher the number, the more vivid the color.
Luminosity	The brightness of the color, or how close the color is to black or white. The larger the number, the lighter the color.
Red, Green, Blue	Primary colors of the visible light spectrum. RGB generates color using three 8-bit channels: 1 red, 1 green, and 1 blue. RGB is an additive color system, which means that color is added to a black background. The additive process mixes various amounts of red, green and blue light to produce other colors.

Choosing Theme Fonts

Microsoft Certified Application Specialist

EX07S-2.1.1

A workbook theme consists of theme colors, fonts, and effects. Theme fonts (**New!**) include heading and body text fonts. Each workbook uses a set of theme fonts. When you click the Theme Fonts button on the Page Layout tab, the name of the current heading and body text font appear highlighted in the gallery menu. To quickly see if you like a theme font, point to one on the menu, and a live preview (**New!**) of it appears on the current worksheet. If you want to apply the theme, click it on the menu. You can apply a set of theme fonts to another theme or create your own set of theme fonts.

Apply and Choose Theme Fonts

1. Open the workbook you want to apply theme fonts.

2. Click the **Home** tab.

3. Select the cell or range you want to change, click the **Font** list arrow, and then click the theme font you want.

   TIMESAVER *To select the entire worksheet, press Ctrl+A .*

4. Click the **Page Layout** tab.

5. Click the **Theme Fonts** button.

   The current theme fonts appear highlighted in the menu.

   TIMESAVER *Point to the Fonts button to display a ScreenTip with the current theme fonts.*

6. Click the theme fonts you want from the gallery menu.

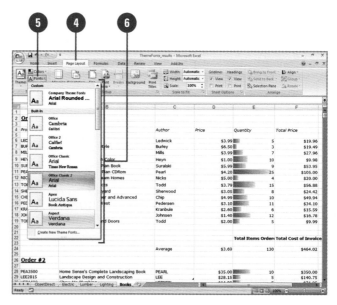

Create Theme Fonts

1. Click the **Page Layout** tab.

2. Click the **Theme Fonts** button, and then click **Create New Theme Fonts**.

3. Click the **Heading font** list arrow, and then select a font.

4. Click the **Body font** list arrow, and then select a font.

5. Type a name for the custom theme fonts.

6. Click **Save**.

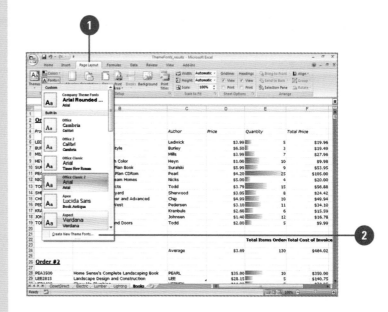

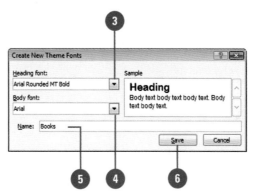

Choosing Theme Effects

Microsoft
Certified
Application
Specialist

EX07S-2.1.1

A workbook theme consists of theme colors, fonts, and effects. Theme effects (**New!**) are sets of lines, fills, and special effects styles for shapes, graphics, charts, SmartArt, and other design elements. By combining the lines, fills, and special effects styles with different formatting levels (subtle, moderate, and intense), Excel provides a variety of visual theme effects. Each workbook uses a set of theme effects. Some are more basic while others are more elaborate. When you click the Theme Effects button on the Page Layout tab, the name of the current theme effects appears highlighted in the gallery menu. While you can apply a set of theme effects to another theme, you cannot create your own set of theme effects at this time.

View and Apply Theme Effects

1. Open the workbook you want to apply a theme effect.

2. Click the **Page Layout** tab.

3. Click the **Theme Effects** button.

   The current theme effects appear highlighted in the menu.

   TIMESAVER *Point to the Effects button to display a ScreenTip with the current theme effects name.*

4. Click the theme effects you want from the menu.

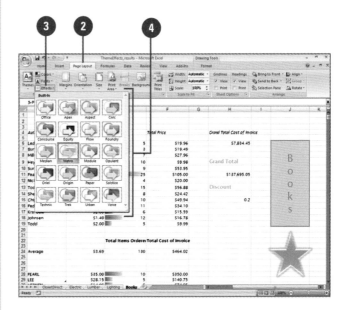

Did You Know?

You can delete a custom theme effects or fonts. On the Page Layout tab, click the Theme Effects or Theme Fonts button, right-click the theme you want to edit, click Edit, click Delete, and then click Yes.

See Also

See "Viewing and Applying a Theme" on page 155 for information on applying a theme from the Themes gallery.

Creating a Custom Theme

Microsoft Certified Application Specialist EX07S-2.1.1

If you have special needs for specific colors, fonts, and effects, such as a company sales or marketing workbook, you can create your own theme by customizing theme colors, theme fonts, and theme effects, and saving them as a theme file (.thmx) (**New!**), which you can reuse. You can apply the saved theme to other workbooks. When you save a custom theme, the file is automatically saved in the Document Themes folder and added to the list of custom themes used by Excel 2007 and other Office 2007 programs. When you no longer need a custom theme, you can delete it.

Create a Custom Theme

1. Click the **Page Layout** tab, and then create a theme by customizing theme colors, theme fonts, and theme effects.

2. Click the **Themes** button, and then click **Save Current Theme**.

3. Type a name for the theme file.

4. Click **Save**.

Did You Know?

You can remove a custom theme from the gallery menu. Simply move or delete the theme file from the Document Themes folder into another folder.

Custom theme

Choosing a Custom Theme

Microsoft
Certified
Application
Specialist

EX07S-2.1.1

When you can create your own theme by customizing theme colors, theme fonts, and theme effects, and saving them as a theme file (.thmx) (**New!**), you can apply the saved theme to other workbooks. When you save a custom theme file in the Document Themes folder, you can choose the custom theme from the Themes gallery, available on the Page Layout tab. If you save a custom theme file in another folder location, you can use the Browse for Themes command to locate and select the custom theme file you want to reuse. When you no longer need a custom theme, you can delete it from the Browse dialog box.

Choose and Apply a Custom Theme

1. Click the **Page Layout** tab.

2. Click the **Themes** button to see additional themes.

3. Point to gallery to want to display the theme name, and then click the one you want.

See Also

See "Viewing and Applying a Theme" on page 155 for information on applying a theme from the Themes gallery.

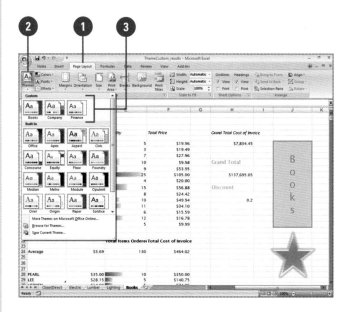

Select and Apply a Custom Theme From a File

1. Open the workbook you want to apply a theme.

2. Click the **Page Layout** tab.

3. Click the **Themes** button, and then click **Browse for Themes**.

4. If you want to open a specific file type, click the **Files of type** list arrow, and then click a file type.

   ◆ **Office Themes and Themed Documents.**

   ◆ **Office Themes.**

   ◆ **Office Themes and Excel Templates.**

5. If the file is located in another folder, click the **Look in** list arrow, and then navigate to the file.

6. Click the theme file you want.

7. Click **Open**.

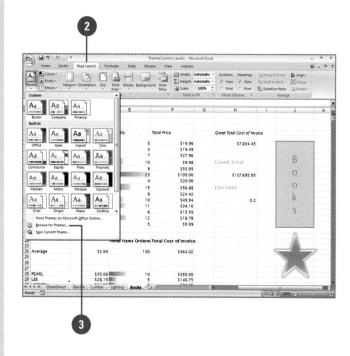

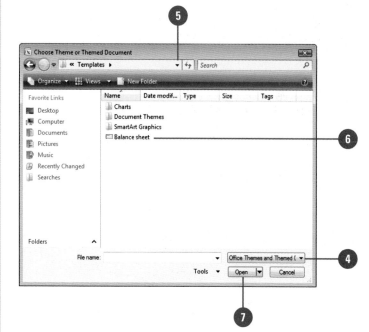

Applying and Creating Cell Styles

Microsoft
Certified
Application
Specialist

EX07S-2.3.2,
EX07S-2.3.3

A **cell style** is a defined collection of formats—font, font size, attributes, numeric formats, and so on—that you can store as a set and later apply to other cells. For example if you always want subtotals to display in blue 14-point Times New Roman, bold, italic, with two decimal places and commas, you can create a style that includes all these formats. A cell style can help you quickly create a consistent look for your workbook. If you plan to enter repetitive information, such as a list of dollar amounts in a row or column, it's often easier to apply the desired style to the range before you enter the data. That way you can simply enter each number, and Excel formats it as soon as you press Enter. You can use one of Excel's built-in cell styles (**New!**), or create one of your own. Once you create a style, it is available to you in every workbook. If you need to prevent users from making changes to specific cells, you can use a cell style that locks cells.

Apply a Cell Style

1. Select a cell or range you want to apply cell shading.

2. Click the **Home** tab.

3. Click the **Cell Styles** button, and then click the cell style you want to apply.

See Also

See "Modifying a Cell Style" on page 166 for information on merging a style from another workbook.

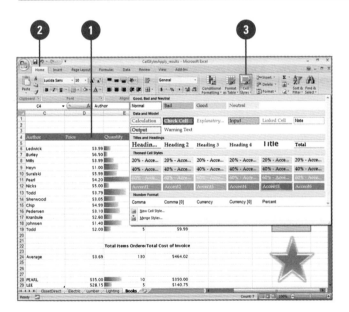

Create a Custom Cell Style

① Select a cell or range you want to apply cell shading.

② Click the **Home** tab.

③ Click the **Cell Styles** button, and then click **New Cell Style**.

④ Type a name for the cell style.

⑤ Click **Format**.

The Format Cells dialog box opens.

⑥ Select the formatting you want on the Number, Alignment, Font, border, Fill, and Protection tabs, and then click **OK**.

⑦ Clear the check boxes for any formatting you don't want to use.

◆ **Number.**

◆ **Alignment.**

◆ **Font.**

◆ **Border.**

◆ **Fill.**

◆ **Protection.**

⑧ Click **OK**.

The new cell style is available on the Cell Styles gallery.

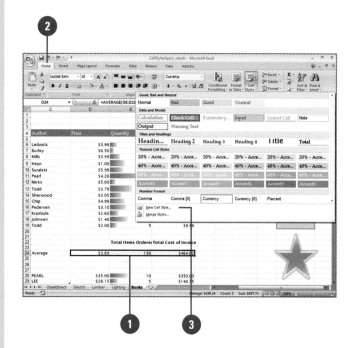

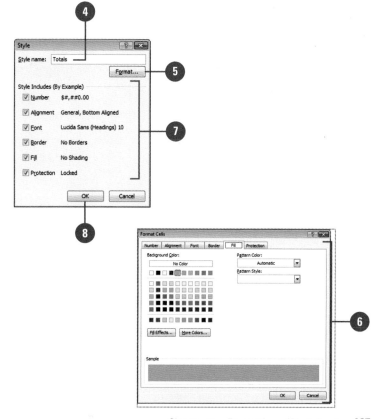

Modifying a Cell Style

Microsoft Certified Application Specialist

EX07S-2.3.2,
EX07S-2.3.3

Any style—whether it was supplied by Excel or created by you or someone else—can be modified (New!). Suppose you created a style containing fonts and colors your company uses. If those specifications changed, you could modify the style to include the new attributes. If you want to use styles created or modified in another workbook, you can merge the styles into the open workbook. If you no longer use a style, you can delete it from the workbook.

Modify a Custom Cell Style

1. Click the **Home** tab.

2. Click the **Cell Styles** button.

3. Right-click the custom cell style you want to change, and then click **Modify**.

4. To create a new style based on an existing style, type a name for the cell style.

5. Click **Format**.

   The Format Cells dialog box opens.

6. Select the formatting you want on the Number, Alignment, Font, border, Fill, and Protection tabs, and then click **OK**.

7. Clear the check boxes for any formatting you don't want to use.

   ◆ **Number.**

   ◆ **Alignment.**

   ◆ **Font.**

   ◆ **Border.**

   ◆ **Fill.**

   ◆ **Protection.**

8. Click **OK**.

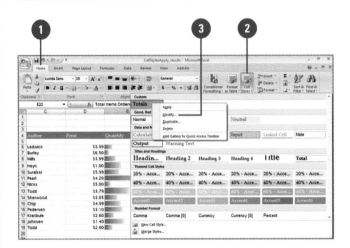

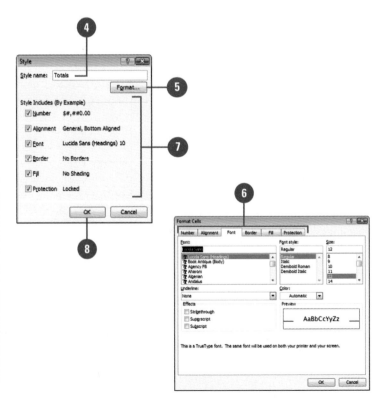

Merge Cell Styles

1. Open the workbook that contains the styles you want to merge first, and then open the workbook to which you want to merge styles.

2. Click the **Home** tab.

3. Click the **Cell Styles** button, and then click **Merge Styles**.

4. Click the workbook that contains the styles you want to merge with the current workbook.

5. Click **OK**.

6. Click **Yes or No** to merge or not merge styles with the same name.

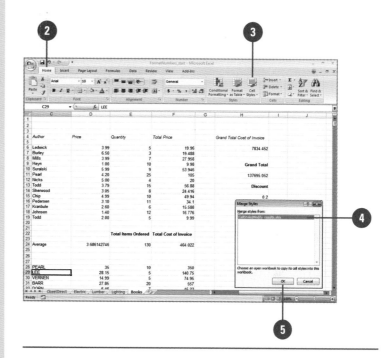

Delete a Cell Style

1. Click the **Home** tab.

2. Click the **Cell Styles** button.

3. To delete the cell style and remove it from all cells using it, right-click the cell style, and then click **Delete**.

Did You Know?

You can remove a custom cell style from a cell. Select the cell or range with the custom style you want to remove, click the Home tab, click the Cell Styles button, and then click Normal.

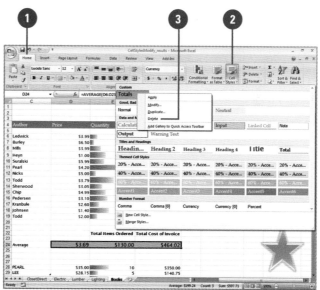

Finding and Replacing Cell Formatting

The Find and Replace commands make it easy to locate or replace specific text, numbers, and formatting in a workbook. For example, you might want to replace all the references to cell A6 in your formulas with data contained in cell H2, or you might want to replace bold text with italic text. Or, you may want to change a client name or contact on all of your financial reports. You can be specific in your replacing, by replacing one at a time, or all matches found.

Find or Replace Cell Formatting

1. Click the **Home** tab.

2. Click the **Find & Select** button, and then click **Find** or **Replace**.

3. If you want, enter the word or words you want to find.

4. Click **Options** to display formatting options. If necessary, click **Format**, and then click **Clear Formatting From Cell** to clear previous criteria.

5. Click **Format**.

6. Specify the formatting you want to locate, and then click **OK**.

   TIMESAVER *To quickly specify formatting, click Choose Format From Cell, and then click the cell with the format you want to find..*

7. To replace text and formatting, click the **Replace** tab, and then enter the word or words you want to replace in the Replace With text box.

8. Click the **Format** button next to Replace with, specify the formatting you want to replace, and then click **OK**.

9. Click **Find Next** or **Find All** to select the next instance of the formatted text or click **Replace** or **Replace All** to substitute formatting.

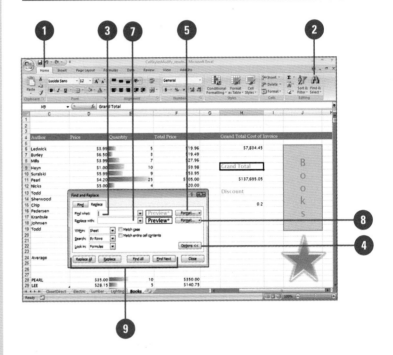

Click to select a cell with the format you want to find.

Viewing and Printing Worksheets and Workbooks

6

Introduction

When your Microsoft Office Excel worksheet is completed, you can preview and print its contents. While previewing the worksheet, you might find that rows of data might flow better on one page or the other. You can add page breaks to segment what you want to appear on a page. You can insert page breaks to control what you print on each page. You can change the orientation of the page from the default of portrait (vertical) to landscape (horizontal). This is helpful when you have wide or multiple columns that would look better on one page. You can also adjust your margins to better fit the worksheet on the page. Previewing a worksheet before printing saves you time and money by not printing unnecessary copies.

After you make layout adjustments you can add headers and footers on the page in Page Layout view (**New!**), which lets you focus on how your worksheet is going to look when you print it. Headers are typically a descriptive title about your worksheet or workbook. Footers can include date printed, page numbers, or other company related information. You can add additional elements to your printout by showing gridlines or column letters and row numbers.

When you're ready to print your work, you can quickly print the entire worksheet, or print only part of the worksheet. Excel provides options to set the print area and customize what you want to print. For example, you might want to print a different range in a worksheet for different people. After you set the print area, you can choose to print your worksheet. The Print dialog box allows you to customize all the options and more, and then you can send your worksheet or entire workbook to the printer.

If you need to send a workbook to others, which cannot be changed, Excel provides the option to save a workbook as an XPS or PDF file (**New!**), which are secure fixed-layout formats.

Setting Up the Page

Microsoft
Certified
Application
Specialist   EX07S-5.5.5

You can set up the worksheet page to print just the way you want. In Page Layout view, you can choose **page orientation**, which determines whether Excel prints the worksheet data portrait (vertically) or landscape (horizontally), and paper size (to match the size of paper in your printer). With the Page Setup dialog box, you can also adjust the **print scaling** (to reduce or enlarge the size of printed characters). Changes made in the Page Setup dialog box are not reflected in the worksheet window. You can see them only when you preview or print the worksheet.

Change Page Orientation

1. Click the **Page Layout** tab.

2. Click the **Orientation** button.

   The current orientation is highlighted on the submenu.

3. Click **Portrait** or **Landscape** from the submenu.

Did You Know?

You can print comments. Display the comments you want to print. Click the Page Layout tab, click the Page Setup Dialog Box Launcher, click the Sheet tab, click the Comments list arrow, click As displayed on sheet or At end of sheet option, and then click Print.

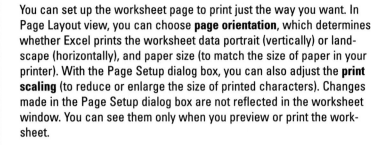

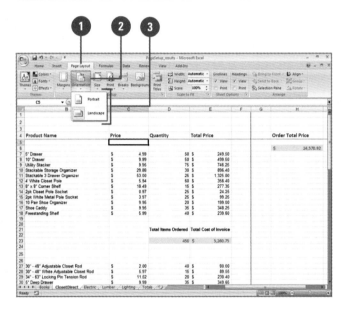

Change the Page Size

1 Click the **Page Layout** tab.

2 Click the **Size** button from the submenu.

The current margin setting is highlighted on the submenu.

3 Click **Letter** (8.5 x 11), **Letter Small** (8.5 x 11), **Tabloid** (11 x 17), **Ledger** (17 x 11, **Legal** (8.5 x 14), **Statement** (5.5 x 8.5), **Executive** (7.25 x 10.5), **A3** (11.69 x 16.54), **A4** (8.27 x 11.69), **A4 Small** (8.27 x 11.69) from the submenu.

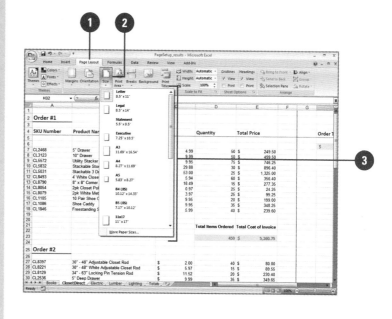

Customize the Page Size

1 Click the **Page Layout** tab.

2 Click the **Size** button, and then click **More Paper Sizes**.

The Page Setup dialog box opens, displaying the Page tab.

3 To scale the page, click the **Adjust to** or **Fit to** option, and then specify the adjust to percentage, or fit to the option you want.

4 Click the **Paper size** list arrow, and then select a paper size.

5 Click the **Print quality** list arrow, and then select a quality option; higher the number, the better the quality.

6 To start the first page on a specific number, enter the number you want.

7 Click **OK**.

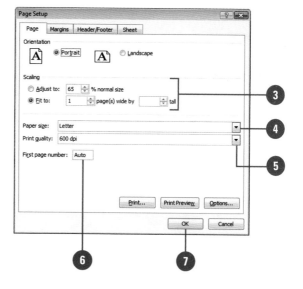

Adjusting Page Margins

Microsoft Certified Application Specialist

EX07S-5.5.3

A page margin is the blank areas along each edge of the paper. You can set up page margins to print your worksheets just the way you want. If you need to quickly set margins, you can use the Margins button on the Page Layout tab (**New!**). Otherwise, you can use the mouse pointer to adjust margins visually for the entire document in Page Layout view, or you can use the Page Setup dialog box to set precise measurements for an entire document or a specific section. You can resize or realign the left, right, top, and bottom margins (the blank areas along each edge of the paper). Changes made in the Page Setup dialog box are not reflected in the worksheet window. You can see them only when you preview or print the worksheet.

Change the Margin Settings

1. Click the **Page Layout** tab.

2. Click the **Margins** button.

   The current margin setting is highlighted on the submenu.

3. Click the option you want from the submenu.

   ◆ **Last Custom Setting.** Only available if you previously changed margin settings.

   ◆ **Normal.**

   ◆ **Wide.**

   ◆ **Narrow.**

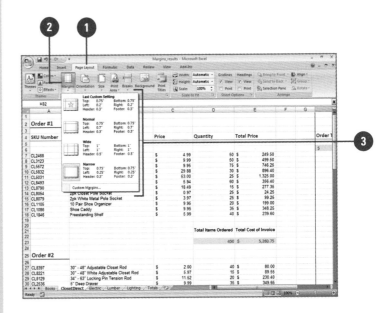

Change the Margin Using the Mouse in Page Layout View

1. Click the **View** tab.

2. Click the **Page Layout View** button.

3. Select the **Ruler** check box.

4. Position the cursor over the left, right, top, or bottom edge of the ruler until the cursor changes to a double arrow.

   A ScreenTip appears indicating the margin name and current position.

5. Drag to change the margin.

6. To exit Page Layout view, click the **Normal** button.

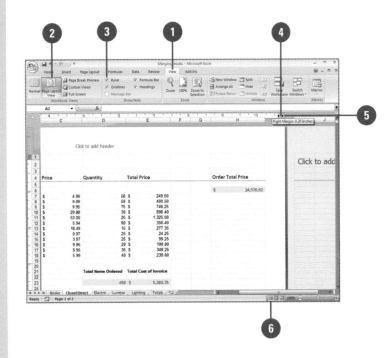

Customize Margin Settings

1. Click the **Page Layout** tab.

2. Click the **Margins** button, and then click **Custom Margins**.

   The Page Setup dialog box opens, displaying the Margins tab.

3. Click the **Top**, **Bottom**, **Left**, and **Right** up or down arrows to adjust the margins.

4. To automatically center your data, select the **Horizontally and Vertically** check boxes under Center on page.

5. Click **OK**.

   ◆ Or click **Print Preview** to see how the margin changes look.

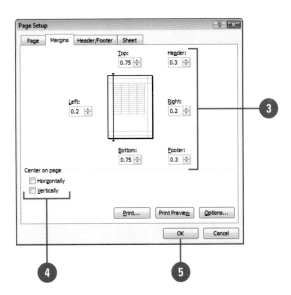

Adding Headers and Footers

Microsoft Certified Application Specialist

EX07S-2.1.2, EX07S-2.1.4, EX07S-5.5.4

Adding a header or footer to a workbook is a convenient way to make your printout easier for readers to follow. Using the Design tab under Header & Footer Tools, you can add predefined header or footer information (**New!**)—such as a page number and worksheet title—at the top and bottom of each page or section of a worksheet or workbook. If a predefined header or footer doesn't work, you can insert individual elements such as your computer system's date and time, the name of the workbook and sheet, a picture, or other custom information. When you insert elements in a header or footer, Excel inserts an ampersand followed by brackets with the name of the element, such as &[Page] for Page Number. Excel change the code to the actual element when you exit headers or footers. Instead of having the same header or footer on every page, you can select options on the Design tab to create a different first page, or different odd and even pages.

Add a Predefined Header or Footer in Page Layout View

1. Click the **Insert** tab.

2. Click the **Header & Footer** button.

   The worksheet appears in Page Layout view.

3. To insert predefined header and footer information, click the **Header** or **Footer** button, and then click the information you want.

   A sample of the information appears on the menu. After you make a selection, Excel exits the Design tab.

4. To add more header or footer text, click the left, center, or right header or footer boxes at the top or at the bottom of the worksheet page where you want to add text to place the insertion point.

   To change a header or footer, select the current text.

5. Type the text you want.

   To start a new line in a header or footer text box, press Enter.

6. To close the headers or footers, click anywhere in the worksheet, or press Esc.

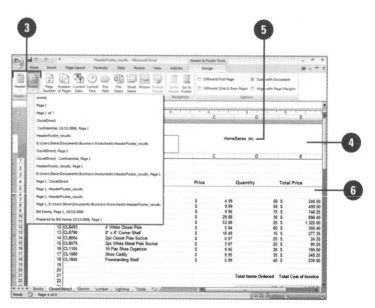

Insert Elements in a Header or Footer in Page Layout View

1. Click the **Insert** tab.

2. Click the **Header & Footer** button.

   The worksheet appears in Page Layout view.

3. Click the left, center, or right header or footer text at the top or at the bottom of the worksheet page where you want to insert an element.

4. Click the **Design** tab under Header & Footer Tools.

5. To insert individual elements, click the button in the Header & Footer Elements group you want.

6. Select or clear the options you want:

   ◆ **Different First Page.** Removes headers and footer from the first page.

   ◆ **Different Odd & Even Pages.** Different header or footer for odd and even pages.

   ◆ **Scale with Document.** Use the same font size and scaling as the worksheet.

   ◆ **Align with Page Margins.** Align header or footer margin with page margins.

7. To close the headers or footers, click anywhere in the worksheet, or press Esc.

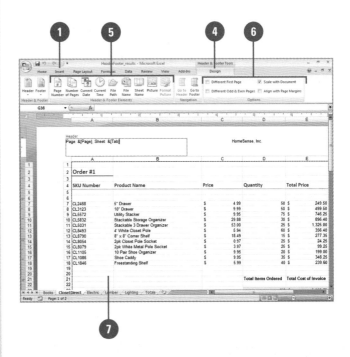

Did You Know?

You can enter an & in a header or footer. To include a single ampersand (&) within the text of a header or footer, use two ampersands (&&).

For Your Information

Inserting a Watermark

The watermark feature is not available in Excel. However, you can still perform the same function by inserting a picture in a header or footer. The picture appears behind the text and on every printed page. Click the Insert tab, click the Header & Footer button, click in the header or footer box where you want to insert a picture, click the Picture button, and then double-click the picture you want. To resize or scale the picture, click Format Picture, select the options you want on the Size tab, and then click OK. To add space above or below the picture, use the Enter key. To replace a picture, select &[Picture], click the Picture button, and then click Replace. You might need to adjust the margins so the picture and any text fit on the page the way you want.

Inserting Page Breaks

Microsoft
Certified
Application
Specialist

EX07S-5.5.2

If you want to print a worksheet that is larger than one page, Excel divides it into pages by inserting **automatic page breaks**. These page breaks are based on paper size, margin settings, and scaling options you set. You can change which rows or columns are printed on the page by inserting **horizontal** or **vertical page breaks**. In page break preview, you can view the page breaks and move them by dragging them to a different location on the worksheet.

Insert a Page Break

1. Select the location where you want to insert a page break:

   ◆ **Horizontal.** To insert a horizontal page break, click the row where you want to insert a page break.

   ◆ **Vertical.** To insert a vertical page break, click the column where you want to insert a page break.

   ◆ **Cell.** To insert a horizontal and vertical page break, click the cell below and to the right from where you want to insert a page break.

2. Click the **Page Layout** tab.

3. Click the **Breaks** button, and then click **Insert Page Break**.

   A dotted line appears on the worksheet indicating the location of the page break.

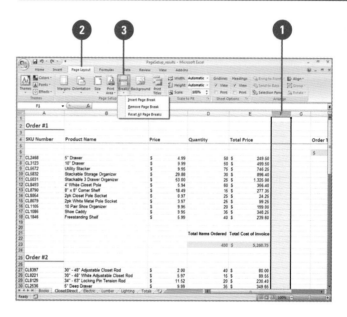

Preview and Move a Page Break

1. Click the **View** tab.

2. Click the **Page Break Preview** button.

   If the Welcome to Page Break Preview dialog box appears, select the **Do not show this dialog box again** check box, and then click **OK**.

3. Drag a page break (a thick solid or dashed blue line) to a new location.

4. When you're done, click the **Normal View** button on the Status bar.

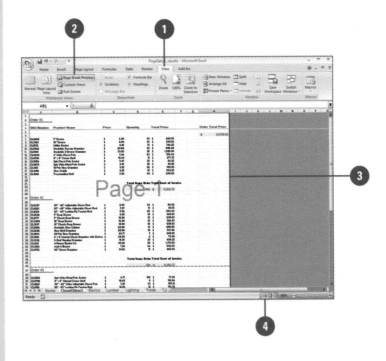

Remove a Page Break

1. Select the column or row next to the page break you want to remove.

2. Click the **Page Layout** tab.

3. Click the **Breaks** button, and then click **Remove Page Break**.

Did You Know?

You can reset page breaks back to the default. Click the Page Layout tab, click the Breaks button, and then click Reset All Page Breaks.

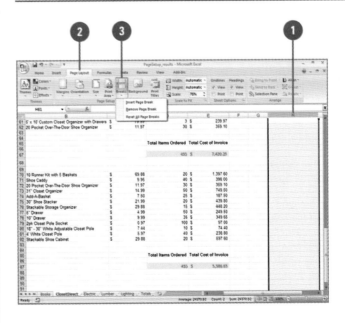

Customizing Worksheet Printing

At some point you'll want to print your worksheet so you can distribute it to others or use it for other purposes. You can print all or part of any worksheet, and you can control the appearance of many features, such as whether gridlines are displayed, whether column letters and row numbers are displayed, or whether to include print titles, columns and rows that are repeated on each page. If you have already set a print area, it will appear in the Print Area box on the Sheet tab of the Page Setup dialog box. You don't need to re-select it.

Print Part of a Worksheet

1. Click the **Page Layout** tab.

2. Click the **Page Setup Dialog Box Launcher.**

3. Click the **Sheet** tab.

4. Type the range you want to print. Or click the **Collapse Dialog** button, select the cells you want to print, and then click the **Expand Dialog** button to restore the dialog box.

5. Click **OK**.

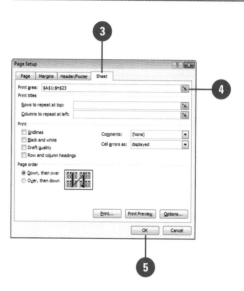

Print Row and Column Titles on Each Page

1. Click the **Page Layout** tab.

2. Click the **Print Titles** button.

   The Page Setup dialog box opens, display the Sheet tab.

3. Enter the number of the row or the letter of the column that contains the titles. Or click the **Collapse Dialog** button, select the row or column with the mouse, and then click the **Expand Dialog** button to restore the dialog box.

4. Click **OK**.

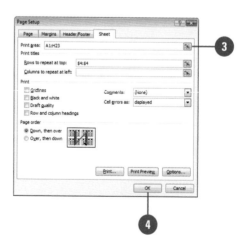

Print Gridlines, Column Letters, and Row Numbers

① Click the **Page Layout** tab.

② Select the **Print** check box under Gridlines.

③ Select the **Print** check box under Headings.

◆ You can also click the **Sheet Options Dialog Box Launcher** to select these print options.

Fit a Worksheet on a Specific Number of Pages

① Click the **Page Layout** tab.

② Select a scaling option.

◆ Click the **Height** list arrow and the **Width** list arrow, then select the number of pages you want to force a worksheet to print.

◆ Click the **Scale** up and down arrows to scale the worksheet using a percentage.

◆ You can also click the **Scale to Fit Dialog Box Launcher** to select these options.

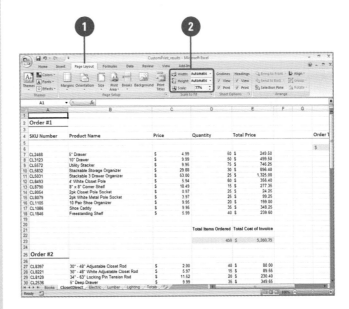

Setting the Print Area

Microsoft
Certified
Application
Specialist   EX07S-5.5.1

When you're ready to print your worksheet, you can choose several printing options. The **print area** is the section of your worksheet that Excel prints. You can set the print area when you customize worksheet printing or any time when you are working on a worksheet. For example, you might want to print a different range in a worksheet for different people. In order to use headers and footers, you must first establish, or set, the print area. You can set a single cell or a contiguous or non-contiguous range.

Set the Print Area

1. Select the range of cells you want to print.

2. Click the **Page Layout** tab.

3. Click the **Print Area** button, and then click **Set Print Area**.

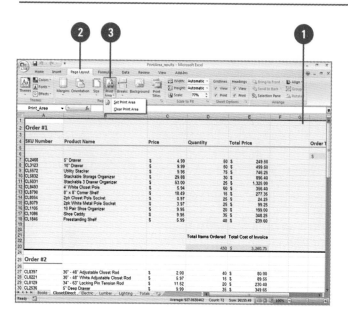

> ### Did You Know?
>
> **You can add to a print area.** Click the cell where you want to extend the print area, click the Page Layout tab, click the Print Area button, and then click Add to Print Area.

Clear the Print Area

1. Click the **Page Layout** tab.

2. Click the **Print Area** button, and then click **Clear Print Area**.

> ### Did You Know?
>
> **You can avoid repeating rows and columns.** For best results when printing a multipage worksheet, you'll want to coordinate the print area with specified print titles so that columns or rows are not repeated on a single page.

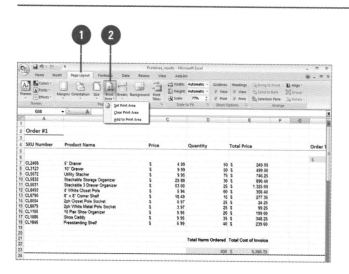

Previewing a Worksheet

Before printing, you should verify that the page looks the way you want. You save time, money, and paper by avoiding duplicate printing. **Print Preview** shows you the exact placement of your data on each printed page. You can view all or part of your worksheet as it will appear when you print it. The Print Preview tab makes it easy to zoom in and out to view data more comfortably, set margins and other page options, preview page breaks, and print.

Preview a Worksheet

1 Click the **Office** button, point to **Print**, and then click **Print Preview**.

2 Click the **Zoom** button, or position the Zoom pointer anywhere on the worksheet, and then click it to enlarge a specific area of the page.

3 To adjust margins visually, select the **Show Margins** check box, and then drag the margin lines where you want.

4 If you do not want to print from Print Preview, click the **Close Print Preview** button to return to the worksheet.

5 If you want to print from Print Preview, click the **Print** button.

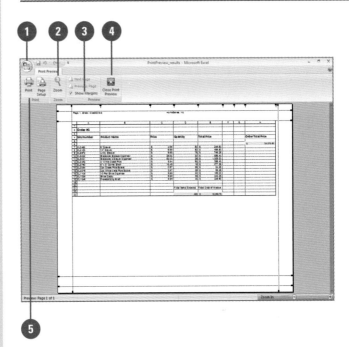

Did You Know?

You can preview your work from the Print dialog box. In the Print dialog box, click Preview. After previewing, you can click the Print button on the Print Preview tab to print the worksheet or click the Close Print Preview button to return to your worksheet.

Printing a Worksheet and Workbook

When you're ready to print your worksheet, you can choose several printing options. You can print all or part of any worksheet and control the appearance of many features, such as whether gridlines are displayed, whether column letters and row numbers are displayed, and whether to include print titles, which are the columns and rows that repeat on each page. You can quickly print a copy of your worksheet to review it by clicking the Quick Print button on the Quick Access Toolbar or on the Office menu Print submenu. You can also use the Print dialog box to specify several print options, such as choosing a new printer, selecting the number of pages in the worksheet you want printed, and specifying the number of copies.

Print All or Part of a Worksheet

1. Click the **Office** button, point to **Print**, and then click **Print**.

   TIMESAVER *To print without the Print dialog box, press Ctrl+P, click the Quick Print button on the Quick Access Toolbar, or click the Office button, point to Print, and then click Quick Print.*

2. If necessary, click the **Name** list arrow, and then click the printer you want to use.

3. To change printer properties, click **Properties**, select the options you want, and then click **OK**.

4. Select whether you want to print the entire document or only the pages you specify.

5. Select whether you want to print the selected text or objects, tables, the selected worksheets, or all the worksheets in the workbook with data.

6. Click the **Number of copies** up or down arrow to specify the number of copies you want.

7. Click **OK**.

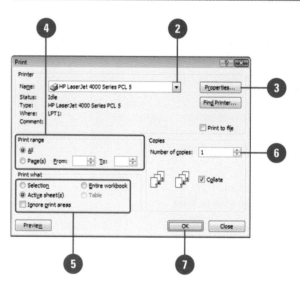

Creating a PDF Document

Microsoft Certified Application Specialist

EX07S-5.4.2

Portable Document Format (PDF) is a fixed-layout format developed by Adobe Systems that retains the form you intended on a computer monitor or printer. A PDF is useful when you want to create a document primarily intended to be read and printed, not modified. Excel allows you to save a workbook as a PDF file (**New!**), which you can send to others for review in an e-mail. To view a PDF file, you need to have Acrobat Reader—free downloadable software from Adobe Systems—installed on your computer. If the PDF or XPS command is not available on the Save As submenu, you'll need to download and install the Publish as PDF or XPS add-in for Microsoft Office 2007 from the Microsoft Web site.

Save a Workbook as a PDF Document

1. Click the **Office** button, point to **Save As**, and then click **PDF or XPS**.

2. Click the **Save as type** list arrow, and then click **PDF**.

3. Click the **Save in** list arrow, and then click the drive or folder where you want to save the file.

4. Type a PDF file name.

5. To open the file in Adobe Reader after saving, select the **Open file after publishing** check box.

6. Click the **Standard** or **Minimize size** option to specify how you want to optimize the file.

7. Click **Options**.

8. Select the publishing options you want, such as what to publish, range to publish, whether to include non-printing information, or PDF options.

   These options are similar to Print dialog box options.

9. Click **OK**.

10. Click **Publish**.

11. If necessary, install Adobe Acrobat Reader and related software as directed.

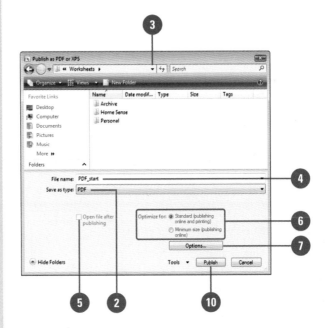

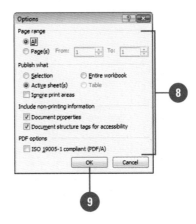

Creating an XPS Document

Microsoft
Certified
Application
Specialist
EX07S-5.4.2

XML Paper Specification (XPS) is a secure fixed-layout format developed by Microsoft that retains the form you intended on a monitor or printer. An XPS is useful when you want to create a document primarily intended to be read and printed, not modified. Excel allows you to save a workbook as an XPS file (**New!**), which you can send to others for review in an e-mail. XPS includes support for digital signatures and is compatible with Windows Rights Management for additional protection. The XPS format also preserves live links with documents, making files fully functional. To view an XPS file, you need to have a viewer—free downloadable software from Microsoft Office Online—installed on your computer. If the PDF or XPS command is not available on the Save As submenu, you'll need to download and install the Publish as PDF or XPS add-in for Microsoft Office 2007 from the Microsoft Web site.

Save a Workbook as an XPS Document

1. Click the **Office** button, point to **Save As**, and then click **PDF or XPS**.

2. Click the **Save as type** list arrow, and then click **XPS Document.**

3. Click the **Save in** list arrow, and then click the drive or folder where you want to save the file.

4. Type an XPS file name.

5. To open the file in viewer after saving, select the **Open file after publishing** check box.

6. Click the **Standard** or **Minimize size** option to specify how you want to optimize the file.

7. Click **Options**.

8. Select the publishing options you want, such as what to publish, range to publish, whether to include non-printing information, or XPS options.

9. Click **OK**.

10. Click **Publish**.

11. If necessary, click **Install** to download and install the Microsoft .NET Framework.

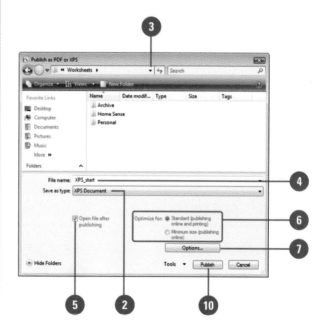

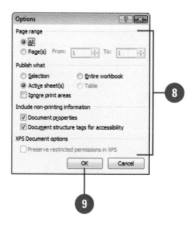

Inserting and Modifying Graphics

7

Introduction

Although well-illustrated worksheets can't make up for a lack of content, you can capture your audiences' attention if your worksheets are vibrant and visually interesting. You can easily enhance a worksheet by adding a picture—one of your own or one of the hundreds that come with Microsoft Office Excel. If you have the appropriate hardware, such as a sound card and speakers, you can also include sound files and video clips in your workbook.

Microsoft Office comes with a vast array of Clip Art, and there are endless amounts available through other software packages or on the Web. When going online to look at clips, you can categorize them so that it's easier to find the best choice for your workbook. You can use the Microsoft Online Web site to search for and download additional clip art.

If you need to modify your pictures, you can resize them, compress them for storage, change their brightness or contrast, recolor them, or change their shape by cropping them.

WordArt is another feature that adds detail to your workbook. Available in other Office applications, WordArt can bring together your worksheets—you can change its color, shape, shadow, or size. Because WordArt comes with so many style choices, time spent customizing your worksheets is minimal.

In Excel and other Microsoft Office programs, you can insert SmartArt graphics (**New!**) to create diagrams that convey processes or relationships. Excel offers a wide-variety of built-in SmartArt graphic types from which to choose, including graphical lists, process, cycle, hierarchy, relationship, matrix, and pyramid. Using built-in SmartArt graphics makes it easy to create and modify charts without having to create them from scratch.

Locate and Insert Clip Art

Insert Media Clips

Add and Remove Clips

Organize Clips into Categories

Access Clip Art on the Web

Insert a Picture

Add a Quick Style to a Picture

Apply a Shape and Border to a Picture

Apply Picture Effects

Modify Picture Size

Modify Picture Brightness and Contrast

Crop, Rotate and Recolor a Picture

Create and Format WordArt Text

Apply and Modify WordArt Text Effects

Create Smart Graphics

Use the Same Text Pane with SmartArt Graphics

Modify, Resize, and Format a SmartArt Graphic

Format a Shape in a SmartArt Graphic

Create and Modify an Organization Chart

Locating and Inserting Clip Art

To add a clip art image to a worksheet, you can click the Insert Clip Art button on the Insert tab to open the Clip Art task pane. The Clip Art task pane helps you search for clip art and access the clip art available in the Clip Organizer. You can limit search results to a specific collection of clip art or a specific type of media file. After you find the clip art you want, you can click it to insert it, or point to it to display a list arrow. Then click an available command, such as Insert, Find Similar Style, Edit Keywords, and Delete from Clip Organizer.

Locate and Insert Clip Art

1. Click the **Insert** tab.

2. Click the **Clip Art** button.

3. Type the keyword(s) associated with the clip you are looking for.

   To narrow your search, do one of the following:

   - To limit search results to a specific collection of clip art, click the **Search In** list arrow, and then select the collections you want to search.

   - To limit search results to a specific type of media file, click the **Results Should Be** list arrow, and then select the check box next to the types of clips you want to find.

4. Click **Go**.

   Clips matching the keywords appear in the Results list.

5. Click the clip you want, and then resize it, if necessary.

6. Click the **Close** button on the task pane.

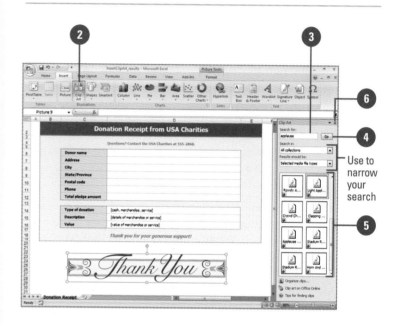

Use to narrow your search

For Your Information

Understanding Clip Art Objects

Clip art objects (pictures and animated pictures) are images made up of geometric shapes, such as lines, curves, circles, squares, and so on. These images, known as vector images, are mathematically defined, which makes them easy to resize and manipulate. A picture in the Microsoft Windows Metafile (.wmf) file format is an example of a vector image.

Inserting Media Clips

You can insert sounds or motion clips into a workbook by accessing them using the Clip Gallery. A **motion clip** is an animated picture—also known as an animated GIF—frequently used in Web pages. When you insert a sound, a small icon appears representing the sound file. To play sound and motion clips in Microsoft Clip Organizer or in your documents, you need to have Microsoft DirectShow or Microsoft Windows Media Player on your computer. For sounds other than your computer's internal sounds, you also need a sound card and speakers.

Insert a Clip Gallery Sound or Motion Clip

1. Click the **Insert** tab.

2. Click the **Clip Art** button.

3. Click the **Results Should Be** list arrow, and then make sure the **Movies** and/or **Sounds** check boxes are selected.

4. Type the keyword(s) associated with the clip you are looking for.

5. Click **Go**.

   Clips matching the keywords appear in the Results list.

6. To preview a media clip, point to the clip, click the list arrow, click **Preview/Properties**. When you're done, click **Close**.

7. Click the media you want to insert.

8. To play a sound using Windows Media Player, double-click the sound icon.

   To play a motion clip, preview your workbook as a Web page, or save your workbook or worksheet as a Web page, and then view it in a Web browser.

9. Click the **Close** button on the task pane.

Accessing Clip Art on the Web

If you can't find the image that you want in the Clip Organizer, you can search for additional images in Clip art on Office Online, a clip gallery that Microsoft maintains on its Web site. To access Clip Art on Office Online, you can click the link at the bottom of the Clip Art task pane or click the Clips Online button on the Clip Organizer toolbar. This launches your Web browser and navigates you directly to the Office Online Web site, where you can access thousands of free clip art images.

Open Clips Online

1. Click the **Insert** tab.

2. Click the **Clip Art** button.

3. Click **Clip art on Office Online**.

4. Establish a connection to the Internet.

   Your Web browser displays the Microsoft Office Online Clip Art and Media Home Web page.

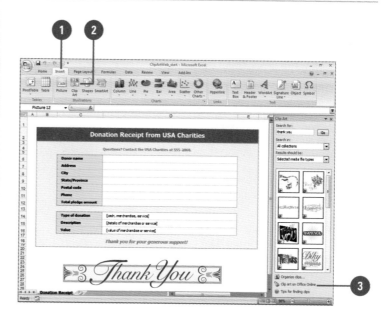

View Clips in a Category

1. If necessary, click the **Accept** button on the Clips Online Web page.

2. Scroll down to the Browse Clip Art And Media section, and then click the name of the category you want.

Search for a Clip

1. Click the **Search** list arrow on the Office Online Web page, and then select the media type you want: Clip Art, Photos, Animations, or Sounds.

2. Click the **Search** box.

3. Type a keyword.

4. Click the **Search** button.

Download a Clip

1. Once you have displayed a list of clips on the Office Online Web page, select the check box below a clip to add it to your selection basket.

   You can select as many as you want. Clear the check box to deselect a clip.

2. Click Download 1 Item (will vary depending on the number of items you are downloading), review the Terms of Use, and then click Accept.

3. If a security virus warning dialog box appears, click **Yes**, and then click **Continue**.

4. Click **Download Now**, and then click **Open**.

5. The clip is stored on your hard disk and shown in your Clip Organizer where you can categorize it.

Organizing Clips into Categories

The clips that come with Excel are already organized, but if you've added clips without organizing them, it's probably hard to find what you need in a hurry. The Microsoft Clip Organizer sorts clip art images, pictures, sounds, and motion clips into categories. The Clip Organizer allows you to organize and select clips from Microsoft Office, from the Web, and from your personal collection of clips. To help you quickly locate a clip, you can place it in one or more categories. You can also assign one or more keywords to a clip and modify the description of a clip. When you add media files, Clip Organizer automatically creates new sub-collections under My Collections. These files are named after the corresponding folders on your hard disk. The Clip Art task pane helps you search for clip art and access the clip art available in the Clip Organizer.

Categorize a Clip

1. Click the **Insert** tab.

2. Click the **Clip Art** button.

3. Click **Organize Clips** at the bottom of the Clip Art task pane.

4. In Clip Organizer, click the **File** menu, point to **Add Clips to Organizer**, and then click **On My Own**.

5. Locate the folder that contains the clip you want to add, and then select the clip.

6. Click the **Add To** button.

7. Click the collection to which you want to add the clip, or click **New** to create a new folder.

8. Click **OK**.

9. Click **Add**.

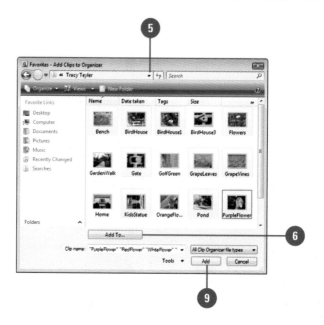

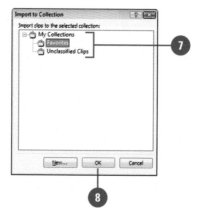

> **Did You Know?**
>
> **You can create a new collection.** In the Clip Organizer, click the File menu, click New Collection, type a new collection name, and then click OK.

190

Change Clip Properties

1 Click the **Insert** tab.

2 Click the **Clip Art** button.

3 Click **Organize Clips** at the bottom of the Clip Art task pane.

4 To create a new collection folder, click the **File** menu, click **New Collection**, type a name, select a location, and then click **OK.**

5 In the Clip Organizer, find and point to the clip you want to categorize or change the properties of, click the list arrow, and then click one of the following:

- ◆ Click **Copy to Collection** to place a copy of the clip in another category.

- ◆ Click **Move to Collection** to move the clip to another category.

- ◆ Click **Edit Keywords** to edit the caption of the clip and to edit keywords used to find the clip.

6 Click the **Close** button to close the Clip Organizer dialog box.

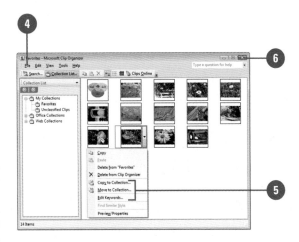

Create a new collection

Edit keywords

> **Did You Know?**
>
> **You can change clip properties in the Clip Art task pane.** In the Clip Art task pane, point to a clip, click the list arrow next to the clip, and then click Copy to Collection, Move to Collection, Edit Keywords, and Delete from Clip Organizer.

Adding and Removing Clips

You might want to add pictures and categories to the Clip Organizer for easy access in the future. You can import your own clips (pictures, photographs, sounds, and videos) into the Clip Organizer. For example, if you have a company logo that you plan to include in more than one workbook, add it to the Clip Organizer. You can also add groups of clips to the Clip Organizer. If you no longer need a picture in the Clip Organizer, you can remove it, which also saves space on your computer.

Add a Clip

1. Click the **Insert** tab.

2. Click the **Clip Art** button, and then click **Organize Clips** at the bottom of the Clip Art task pane.

3. Click the **File** menu, point to **Add Clips to Organizer**, and then click **On My Own**.

4. Click the **Look in** list arrow, and then select the drive and folder that contain the clip you want to import.

5. Click the **File as type** list arrow, and then select the file type.

6. Click the clips you want to import.

7. Click **Add**.

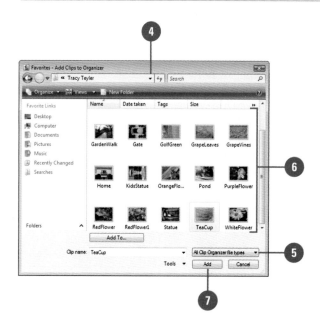

Remove a Clip

1. Click the **Insert** tab.

2. Click the **Clip Art** button, and then click **Organize Clips** at the bottom of the Clip Art task pane.

3. Point to the clip you want to remove, and then click the list arrow.

4. To delete the clip from all Clip Organizer categories, click **Delete from Clip Organizer**.

   To remove the clip from just one category, click **Delete** From the listed category.

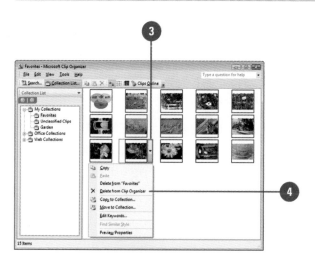

Inserting a Picture

Microsoft Certified Application Specialist

EX07S-4.4.1

Excel makes it possible for you to insert pictures, graphics, scanned photographs, art, photos, or artwork from a CD-ROM or other program into a worksheet. When you use the Picture button on the Insert tab, you specify the source of the picture. When you insert pictures from files on your hard disk drive, scanner, digital camera, or Web camera, Excel allows you to select multiple pictures, view thumbnails of them, and insert them all at once, which speeds up the process.

Insert a Picture from a File

1. Click the **Insert** tab.

2. Click the **Picture** button.

3. Click the **Look in** list arrow, and then select the drive and folder that contain the file you want to insert.

4. Click the file you want to insert.

5. Click **Insert**.

   ◆ To link a picture file, click the **Insert** button arrow, and then click **Link to File**.

   ◆ To insert and link a picture file, click the **Insert** button arrow, and then click **Insert and Link**.

   TROUBLE? *If you see a red "x" instead of a picture or motion clip in your workbook, then you don't have a graphics filter installed on your computer for that clip.*

Did You Know?

You can change a picture. Select the picture, click the Change Picture button on the Format tab, select a picture, and then click Insert.

You can add graphic formats. If the graphic format you want to insert is not in the list, you can use Office Setup's Add or Remove Features option to install additional graphic formats.

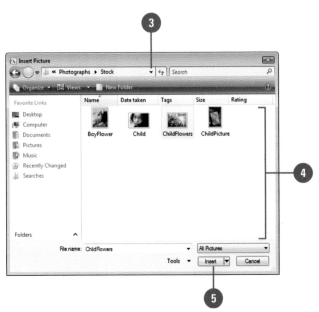

Adding a Quick Style to a Picture

Microsoft
Certified
Application
Specialist

EX07S-4.4.1

Instead of changing individual attributes of a picture—such as shape, border, and effects—you can quickly add them all at once with the Picture Quick Style gallery. The Picture Quick Style gallery (**New!**) provides a variety of different formatting combinations. To quickly see if you like a Picture Quick Style, point to a thumbnail in the gallery to display a live preview (**New!**) of it in the selected shape. If you like it, you can apply it.

Add a Quick Style to a Picture

1. Click the picture you want to change.

2. Click the **Format** tab under Picture Tools.

3. Click the scroll up or down arrow, or click the **More** list arrow in the Picture Styles group to see additional styles.

    The current style appears highlighted in the gallery.

4. Point to a style.

    A live preview (**New!**) of the style appears in the current shape.

5. Click the style you want from the gallery to apply it to the selected picture.

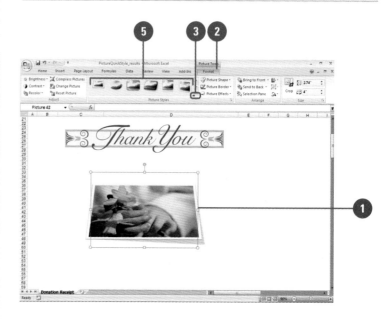

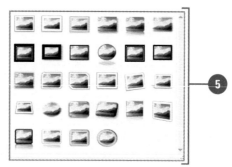

Did You Know?

You can save a shape as a picture in the PNG format. Right-click the shape, click Save as Picture, type a name, and then click Save.

You can copy the window or screen contents. To make a copy of the active window, press Alt+Print Scrn. To copy the entire screen as it appears on your monitor, press Print Scrn.

Applying a Shape to a Picture

After you insert a picture into your workbook, you can select it and apply one of Excel's shapes to it (**New!**). The picture appears in the shape just like its been cropped. The Picture Shape gallery makes it easy to choose the shape you want to use. Live preview is not available with the Picture Shape gallery. You can try different shapes to find the one you want. If you don't find the one you want, you can use the Reset Picture button to return the picture back to its original state.

Apply a Shape to a Picture

1. Click the picture you want to change.

2. Click the **Format** tab under Picture Tools.

3. Click the **Picture Shape** button.

4. Select the shape you want to apply to the selected picture.

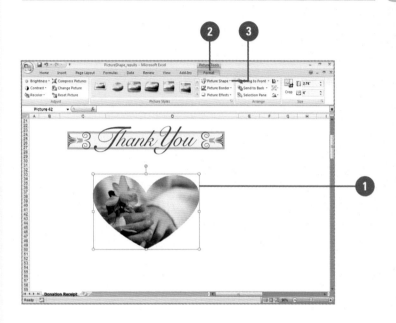

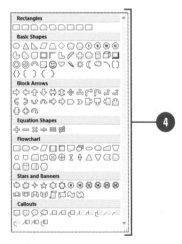

Did You Know?

You can quickly return a picture back to its original form. Select the picture, click the Format tab, and then click the Reset Picture button.

Applying a Border to a Picture

After you insert a picture, you can add and modify the picture border by changing individual outline formatting using the Picture Border button on the Format tab under Picture Tools. The Picture Border button works just like the Shape Outline button, and provides similar options to add a border, select a border color, and change border width and style. You can try different border combinations to find the one you want. If you don't find one that works for you, you can use the No Outline command on the Picture Border gallery to remove it.

Apply a Border to a Picture

1. Click the picture you want to change.

2. Click the **Format** tab under Picture Tools.

3. Click the **Picture Border** button.

4. Click a color, or point to **Weight**, or **Dashes**, and then select a style, or click **More Lines** to select multiple options.

5. Drag a sizing handle to change the size or angle of the line or arrow.

Did You Know?

You can remove a border. Select the picture, click the Format tab, click the Picture Border button, and then click No Outline.

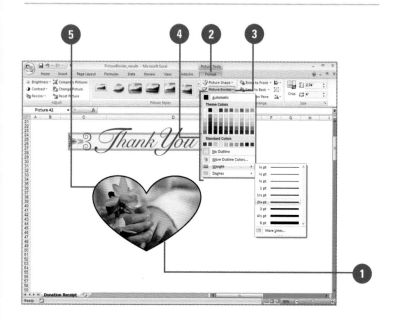

Applying Picture Effects

You can change the look of a picture by applying effects (**New!**), such as shadows, reflections, glow, soft edges, and 3-D rotations. You can also apply effects to a shape by using the Picture Effects gallery for quick results, or by using the Format Shape dialog box for custom results. From the Picture Effects gallery, you can apply a built-in combination of 3-D effects or individual effects to a picture. To quickly see if you like a picture effect, point to a thumbnail in the Picture Effects gallery to display a live preview (**New!**) of it. If you like it, you can apply it. If you no longer want to apply a picture effect to an object, you can remove it. Simply select the picture, point to the effect type on the Picture Effects gallery, and then select the No effect type option.

Add an Effect to a Picture

1. Click the picture you want to change.

2. Click the **Format** tab under Picture Tools.

3. Click the **Picture Effects** button, and then point to one of the following:

   ◆ **Preset** to select No 3-D, one of the preset types, or More 3-D Settings.

   ◆ **Shadow** to select No Shadow, one of the shadow types, or More Shadows.

   ◆ **Reflection** to select No Reflection or one of the Reflection Variations.

   ◆ **Glow** to select No Glow, one of the Glow Variations, or More Glow Colors.

   ◆ **Soft Edges** to select No Soft Edges or a point size to determine the soft edge amount.

   ◆ **3-D Rotation** to select No Rotation, one of the rotation types, or More 3-D Settings.

   When you point to an effect, a live preview (**New!**) of the style appears in the current shape.

4. Click the effect you want from the gallery to apply it to the selected shape.

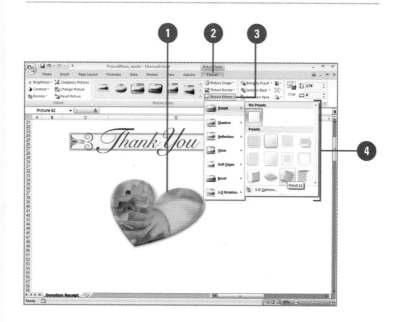

Modifying Picture Size

Microsoft Certified Application Specialist

EX07S-4.4.1

Once you have inserted a picture, clip art and other objects into your workbook, you can adapt them to meet your needs. Like any object, you can resize a picture. You can use the sizing handles to quickly resize a picture or use height and width options in the Size group on the Format tab to resize a picture more precisely. If you want to set unique or multiple options at the same time, you can use the Size and Position dialog box. These options allow you to make sure your pictures keep the same relative proportions as the original and lock size proportions.

Resize a Picture

1. Click the object you want to resize.

2. Drag one of the sizing handles to increase or decrease the object's size.

   ◆ Drag a middle handle to resize the object up, down, left, or right.

   ◆ Drag a corner handle to resize the object proportionally.

Resize a Picture Precisely

1. Click the object you want to resize.

2. Click the **Format** tab under Picture Tools.

3. Click the up and down arrows or enter a number (in inches) in the Height and Width boxes on the Ribbon and press Enter.

   If the **Lock aspect ratio** check box is selected in the Size and Position dialog box, height or width automatically changes when you change one of them. Click the **Size Dialog Box Launcher** to change the option.

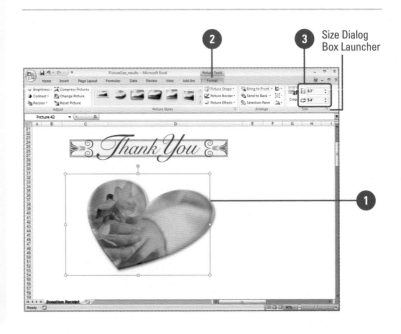

Size Dialog Box Launcher

Precisely Scale a Picture

1. Click the object you want to resize.

2. Click the **Format** tab under Picture Tools.

3. Click the **Size Dialog Box Launcher**.

4. To keep the picture proportional, select the **Lock aspect ratio** check box.

5. To keep the picture the same relative size, select the **Relative to original picture size** check box.

6. Click the up and down arrows or enter a number in the Height and Width boxes in one of the following:

   ◆ **Size.** Enter a size in inches.

   ◆ **Scale.** Enter a percentage size.

   If the Lock aspect ratio check box is selected, height or width automatically changes when you change one of them.

7. If you want to remove your changes, click **Reset**.

8. Click **Close**.

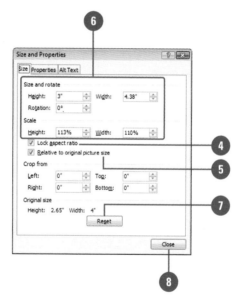

Compressing a Picture

Excel allows you to compress pictures in order to minimize the file size of the image. In doing so, however, you may lose some visual quality, depending on the compression setting. You can pick the resolution that you want for the pictures in a workbook based on where or how they'll be viewed (for example, on the Web or printed). You can also set other options, such as Delete Cropped Areas Of Picture, to get the best balance between picture quality and file size or automatically compress pictures when you save your workbook.

Compress a Picture

① Click to select the pictures you want to compress.

② Click the **Format** tab under Picture Tools.

③ Click the **Compress Pictures** button.

④ Select the **Apply to selected pictures only** check box to apply compression setting to only the selected picture. Otherwise, clear the check box to compress all pictures in your workbook.

⑤ Click **Options**.

⑥ Select or clear the **Automatically perform basic compression on save** check box.

⑦ Select or clear the **Delete cropped areas of pictures** check box to reduce file.

⑧ Click the **Print, Screen,** or **E-mail** option to specify a target output.

⑨ Click **OK** to close the Compression Settings dialog box.

⑩ Click **OK**.

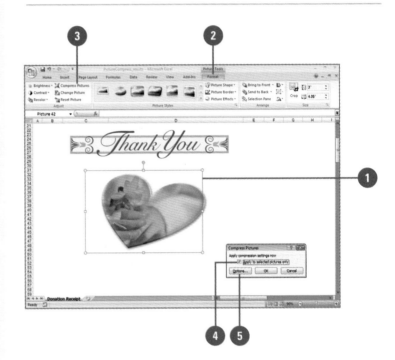

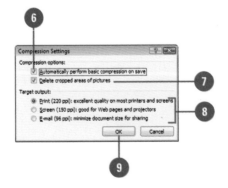

Modifying Picture Brightness and Contrast

Once you have inserted a picture, you can control the image's colors, brightness, and contrast using Picture tools. The brightness and contrast controls let you make simple adjustments to the tonal range of a picture. The brightness and contrast controls change a picture by an overall lightening or darkening of the image pixels. You can experiment with the settings to get the look you want. If you don't like the look, you can use the Reset Picture button to return the picture back to its original starting point.

Change Brightness

1. Click the picture whose brightness you want to increase or decrease.

2. Click the **Format** tab under Picture Tools.

3. Click the **Brightness** button, and then do one of the following:

   ◆ Click a positive brightness to lighten the object colors by adding more white, or click a negative brightness to darken the object colors by adding more black.

   ◆ Click **Picture Corrections Options** to set other specific brightness percentages.

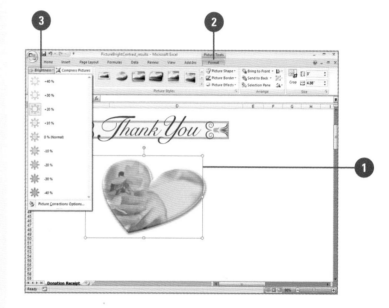

Change Contrast

1. Click the picture whose contrast you want to increase or decrease.

2. Click the **Format** tab under Picture Tools.

3. Click the **Contrast** button, and then do one of the following:

   ◆ Click a positive contrast to increase color intensity, resulting in less gray, or click a negative contrast to decrease color intensity, resulting in more gray.

   ◆ Click **Picture Corrections Options** to set other specific contrast percentages.

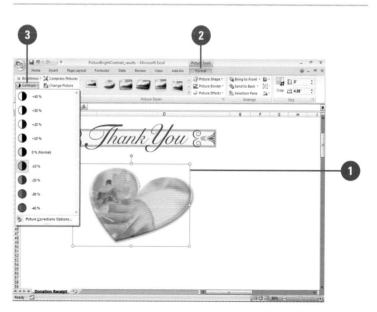

Recoloring a Picture

Microsoft
Certified
Application
Specialist

EX07S-4.4.1

You can recolor clip art and other objects to match the color scheme of your workbook. For example, if you use a flower clip art as your business logo, you can change shades of pink in the spring to shades of orange in the autumn. The Recolor Picture Quick Style gallery (**New!**) provides a variety of different formatting combinations. To quickly see if you like a Recolor Picture Quick Style, point to a thumbnail in the gallery to display a live preview (**New!**) of it in the selected shape. If you like it, you can apply it. You can also use a transparent background in your picture to avoid conflict between its background color and your worksheet's background. With a transparent background, the picture takes on the same background as your workbook.

Recolor a Picture

1. Click the picture whose color you want to change.

2. Click the **Format** tab under Picture Tools.

3. Click the **Recolor** button.

4. Click one of the Color options.

    ◆ **No Recolor.** Click this option to remove a previous recolor.

    ◆ **Color Modes.** Click an option to apply a color type:

    Grayscale. Converts colors into whites, blacks and shades of gray between black and white.

    Sepia. Converts colors into very light gold and yellow colors like a picture from the old west.

    Washout. Converts colors into whites and very light colors.

    Black and White. Converts colors into only white and black.

    ◆ **Light and Dark Variations.** Click an option to apply an accent color in light or dark variations.

    ◆ **More Dark Variations.** Point to this option to select a specific color.

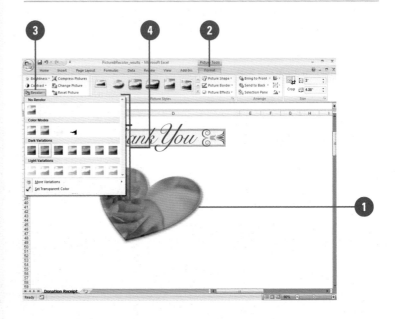

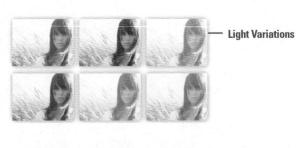

Light Variations

Dark Variations

Set a Transparent Background

1. Click the picture you want to change.

2. Click the **Format** tab under Picture Tools.

3. Click the **Recolor** button, and then click **Set Transparent Color**.

4. Move the pointer over the object until the pointer changes shape.

5. Click the color you want to set as transparent.

6. Move the pointer over the picture where you want to apply the transparent color, and then click to apply it.

7. When you're done, click outside the image.

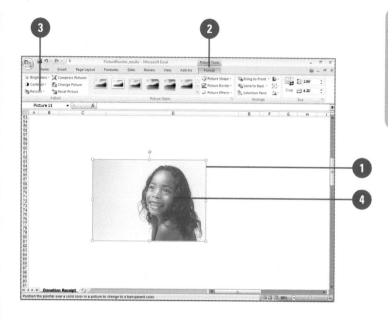

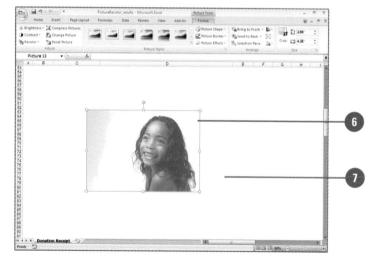

Cropping and Rotating a Picture

You can crop clip art to isolate just one portion of the picture. Because clip art uses vector image technology, you can crop even the smallest part of it and then enlarge it, and the clip art will still be recognizable. You can also crop bitmapped pictures, but if you enlarge the area you cropped, you lose picture detail. Use the crop button to crop an image by hand. You can also crop using the Size and Position dialog box, which gives you precise control over the dimensions of the area you want to crop. You can also rotate a picture by increments or freehand.

Crop a Picture Quickly

1. Click the picture you want to crop.

2. Click the **Format** tab under Picture Tools.

3. Click the **Crop** button.

4. Drag the sizing handles until the borders surround the area you want to crop.

5. Click outside the image when you are finished.

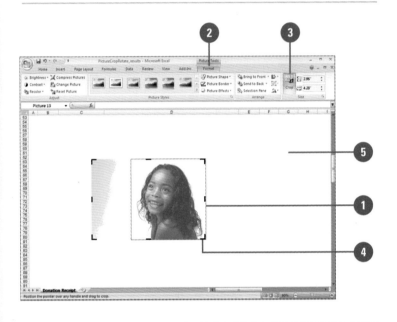

Redisplay a Cropped Picture

1. Click the picture you want to restore.

2. Click the **Format** tab under Picture Tools.

3. Click the **Crop** button.

4. Drag the sizing handles to reveal the areas that were originally cropped.

5. Click outside the image when you are finished.

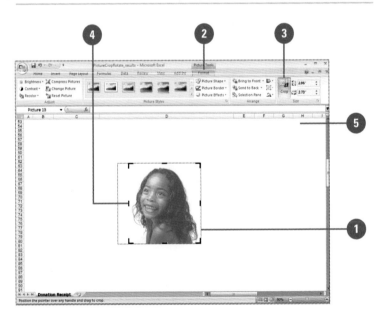

Crop a Picture Precisely

① Click the object you want to crop.

② Click the **Format** tab under Picture Tools.

③ Click the **Size Dialog Box Launcher**.

④ Adjust the values in the **Left**, **Right**, **Top**, and **Bottom** boxes to crop the image to the exact dimensions you want.

⑤ If you want to remove your changes, click **Reset**.

⑥ Click **Close**.

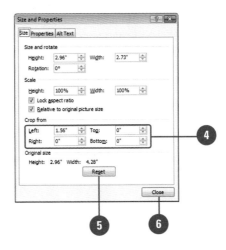

Rotate a Picture

① Click the object you want to rotate.

② Position the pointer (which changes to the Free Rotate pointer) over the green rotate lever at the top of the object, and then drag to rotate the object.

③ Click outside the object to set the rotation.

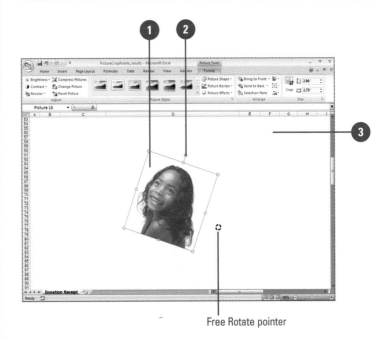

Free Rotate pointer

Creating WordArt Text

The WordArt feature lets you create stylized text to draw attention to your most important words. Most users apply WordArt to a word or a short phrase, such as *Make a Difference*. You should apply WordArt to a worksheet sparingly. Its visual appeal and unique look requires uncluttered space. When you use WordArt, you can choose from a variety of text styles that come with the WordArt Quick Style gallery (**New!**), or you can create your own using tools in the WordArt Styles group. To quickly see if you like a WordArt Quick Style, point to a thumbnail in the gallery to display a live preview (**New!**) of it in the selected text. If you like it, you can apply it. You can also use the free angle handle (pink diamond) inside the selected text box to adjust your WordArt text angle.

Insert WordArt Text

1 Click the **Insert** tab.

2 Click the **WordArt** button, and then click one of the WordArt styles.

A WordArt text box appears on the worksheet with selected placeholder text.

3 Type the text you want WordArt to use.

4 If applicable, use the Font and Paragraph options on the Home tab to modify the text you entered.

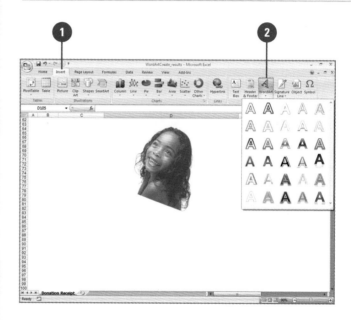

Did You Know?

You can convert text in a text box to WordArt. Select the text box, click the Format tab under Drawing Tools, and then click the WordArt text style you want from the Ribbon.

You can remove WordArt text. Select the WordArt text you want to remove, click the Format tab, click the Quick Styles button, and then click Clear WordArt.

Edit WordArt Text

1. Click the WordArt object you want to edit.

2. Click to place the insertion point where you want to edit, and then edit the text.

3. Click outside the object to deselect it.

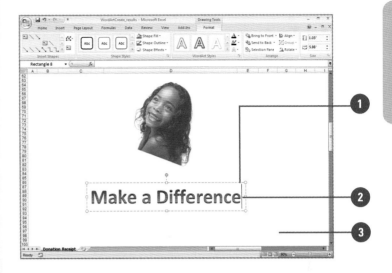

Formatting WordArt Text

In addition to applying one of the preformatted WordArt styles, you can also create your own style by shaping your text into a variety of shapes, curves, styles, and color patterns. The WordArt Styles group gives you tools for changing the fill and outline of your WordArt text. To quickly see if you like a WordArt Style, point to a thumbnail in the gallery to display a live preview (**New!**) of it in the selected text. If you like it, you can apply it.

Apply a Different WordArt Style to Existing WordArt Text

1. Click the WordArt object whose style you want to change.

2. Click the **Format** tab under Drawing Tools.

3. Click the scroll up or down arrow, or click the **More** list arrow in the WordArt Styles group to see additional styles.

   The current style appears highlighted in the gallery.

4. Point to a style.

   A live preview (**New!**) of the style appears in the current shape text.

5. Click the style you want from the gallery to apply it to the selected shape.

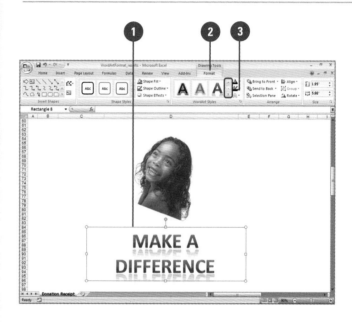

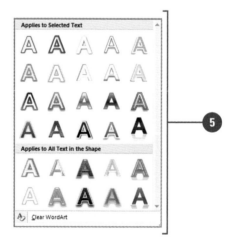

> **Did You Know?**
>
> **You can add more formatting to WordArt text.** Select the WordArt object, click the Home tab, and then use the formatting button in the Font and Paragraph groups.
>
> **You can change the WordArt fill color to match the background.** Click the WordArt object, right-click the object, click Format Shape, click the Background option, and then click Close.

Apply a Fill to WordArt Text

1. Click the WordArt object you want to change.

2. Click the **Format** tab under Drawing Tools.

3. Click the **Text Fill** button arrow, and then click or point to one of the following:

   ◆ **Color** to select a theme or standard color.

   ◆ **Picture** to select a picture file.

   ◆ **Gradient** to select No Gradient, one of the shadow types, or More Gradients.

   ◆ **Texture** to select one of the of the texture types, or More Textures.

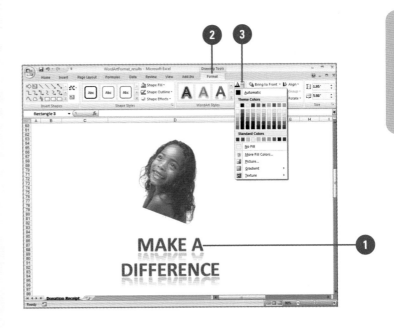

Apply an Outline to WordArt Text

1. Click the WordArt object you want to change.

2. Click the **Format** tab under Drawing Tools.

3. Click the **Text Outline** button arrow.

4. Click a color, or point to **Weight** or **Dashes**, and then select a style.

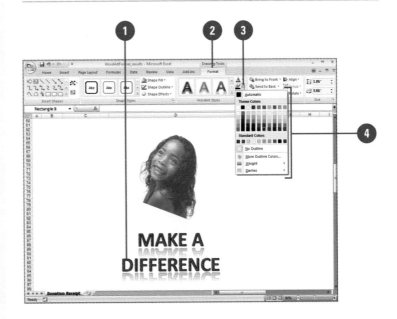

Applying WordArt Text Effects

You can change the look of WordArt text by applying effects (**New!**), such as shadows, reflections, glow, soft edges, 3-D rotations, and transformations. You can apply effects to a shape by using the Text Effects gallery for quick results. From the Text Effects gallery you can apply a built-in combination of 3-D effects or individual effects to WordArt text. To quickly see if you like the effect, point to a thumbnail in the Text Effects gallery to display a live preview (**New!**) of it. If you like it, you can apply it. If you no longer want to apply the effect, you can remove it. Simply, select the WordArt text, point to the effect type on the Text Effects gallery, and then select the No effect type option.

Apply an Effect to WordArt Text

1. Click the WordArt object you want to change.

2. Click the **Format** tab under Drawing Tools.

3. Click the **Text Effects** button, and then point to one of the following:

   ◆ **Shadow** to select No Shadow, one of the shadow types (Outer or Inner), or More Shadows.

   ◆ **Reflection** to select No Reflection or one of the Reflection Variations.

   ◆ **Glow** to select No Glow, one of the Glow Variations, or More Glow Colors.

   ◆ **Bevel** to select No Bevel, one of the bevel variations, or More 3-D Settings.

   ◆ **3-D Rotation** to select No Rotation, one of the rotation types (Parallel, Perspective, or Oblique), or More 3-D Settings.

   ◆ **Transform** to select No Transform, or one of the transform types (Follow Path or Warp).

   When you point to an effect, a live preview (**New!**) of the style appears in the current shape.

4. Click the effect you want from the gallery to apply it to the selected shape.

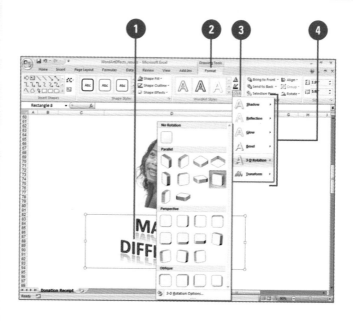

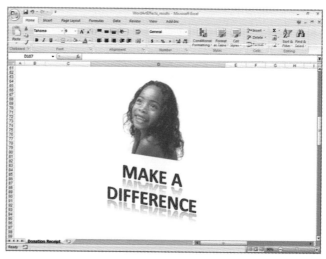

Modifying WordArt Text Position

You can apply a number of text effects to your WordArt objects that determine alignment and direction. The effects of some of the adjustments you make are more pronounced for certain WordArt styles than others. Some of these effects make the text unreadable for certain styles, so apply these effects carefully. You can apply effects to a shape by using the Format Shape dialog box for custom results. You can also use the free rotate handle (green circle) at the top of the selected text box to rotate your WordArt text.

Change WordArt Text Direction

1. Right-click the WordArt object you want to change, and then click **Format Shape**.

2. If necessary, click **Text Box** in the left pane.

3. Click the **Vertical alignment** or **Horizontal alignment** list arrow, and then select an option: Top, Middle, Bottom, Top Center, Middle Center, or Bottom Center.

4. Click the **Text Direction** list arrow, and then select an option: **Horizontal, Rotate all text 90°, Rotate all text 270°**, or **Stacked**.

5. Click **Close**.

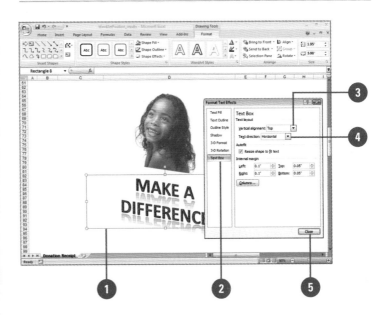

Rotate WordArt Text

1. Click the WordArt object you want to change.

2. Drag the free rotate handle (green circle) to rotate the object in any direction you want.

3. When you're done, release the mouse button.

4. Click outside the object to deselect it.

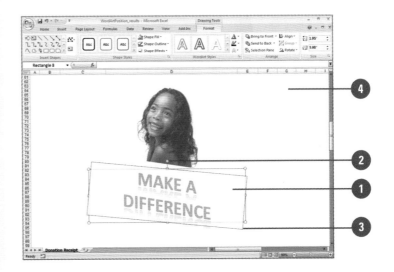

Creating SmartArt Graphics

Microsoft Certified Application Specialist

EX07S-4.4.2

SmartArt graphics (**New!**) allow you to create diagrams that convey processes or relationships. Excel offers a wide variety of built-in SmartArt graphic types, including graphical lists, process, cycle, hierarchy, relationship, matrix, and pyramid. Using built-in SmartArt graphics makes it easy to create and modify charts without having to create them from scratch. To quickly see if you like a SmartArt graphic layout, point to a thumbnail in the gallery to display a live preview (**New!**) of it in the selected shape. If you like it, you can apply it.

Create a SmartArt Graphic

1. Click the **Insert** tab.

2. Click the **SmartArt** button.

   TIMESAVER *In a content placeholder, you can click the SmartArt icon to start.*

3. In the left pane, click a category, such as All, List, Process, Cycle, Hierarchy, Relationship, Matrix, or Pyramid.

4. In the right pane, click a SmartArt graphic style type.

5. Click **OK**.

   The SmartArt graphic appears in the worksheet.

Did You Know?

Shorter amounts of text work best for SmartArt graphics. Most of the layouts for SmartArt graphics work the best with smaller amounts of text. However, if you have larger amounts, layouts in the List category work better than others.

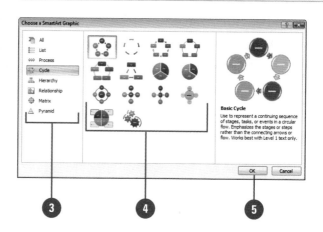

SmartArt Graphic Purposes

Type	Purpose
List	Show non-sequential information
Process	Show steps in a process or timeline
Cycle	Show a continual process
Hierarchy	Show a decision tree or create an organization chart
Relationship	Illustrate connections
Matrix	Show how parts relate to a whole
Pyramid	Show proportional relationships up and down

6 If necessary, click the **Text Pane** button, or click the control with two arrows along the left side of the SmartArt graphic selection to show the Text pane.

7 Label the shapes by doing one of the following:

- Type text in the [Text] box.

  You can use the arrow keys to move around the Text pane.

- Click a shape, and then type text directly into the shape.

8 When you're done, click outside of the SmartArt graphic.

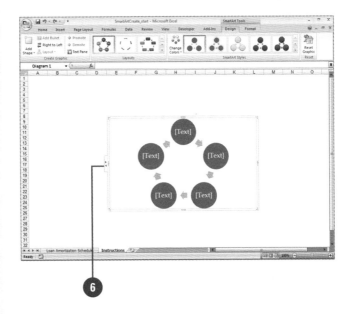

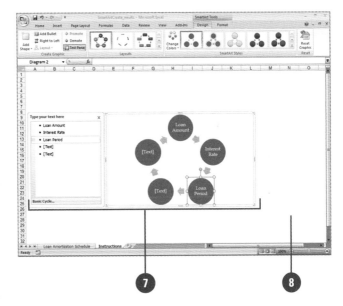

Using the Text Pane with SmartArt Graphics

After you create a layout for a SmartArt graphic, a Text pane (**New!**) appears next to your selected SmartArt graphic. The bottom of the Text pane displays a description of the SmartArt graphic. The Text pane and SmartArt graphic contain placeholder text. You can change the placeholder text in the Text pane or directly in the SmartArt graphic. The Text pane works like an outline or a bulleted list and the text corresponds directly with the shape text in the SmartArt graphic. As you add and edit content, the SmartArt graphic automatically updates, adding or removing shapes as needed while maintaining the design. If you see a red "x" in the Text pane, it means that the SmartArt graphic contains a fixed number of shapes, such as Counterbalance Arrows (only two).

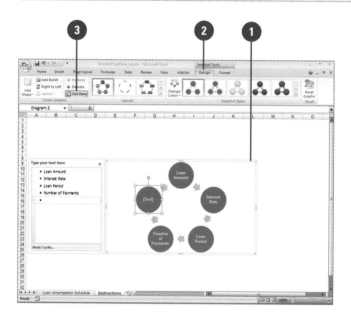

Show or Hide the Text Pane

1. Click the SmartArt graphic you want to modify.

2. Click the **Design** tab under SmartArt Tools.

3. Do any of the following:

   ◆ **Show**. Click the **Text Pane** button, or click the control with two arrows along the left side of the SmartArt graphic selection to show the Text pane.

   ◆ **Hide.** Click the **Text Pane** button, click the **Close** button on the Text pane, deselect the SmartArt graphic.

   The Text Pane button toggles to show or hide the Text pane.

Did You Know?

You can resize the Text pane. To resize the Text pane, point to any edge (pointer changes to double-headed arrow), and then drag to resize it.

You can move the Text pane. To move the Text pane, drag the top of the pane. The Text pane location resets when you exit Excel.

Work with Text in the Text Pane

1 Click the SmartArt graphic you want to modify.

2 Click the **Design** tab under SmartArt Tools.

3 If necessary, click the **Text Pane** button to show the Text pane.

4 Do any of the following tasks:

◆ **New line**. At the end of a line, press Enter.

◆ **Indent line right**. Press Tab, or click the **Promote** button.

◆ **Indent line left**. Press Shift+Tab, or click the **Demote** button.

◆ **Delete line**. Select the line text, and then press Delete.

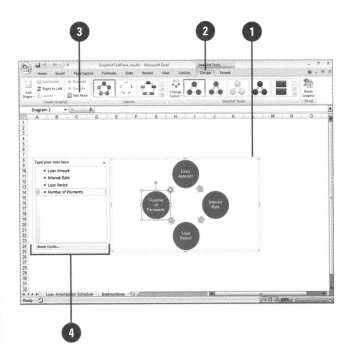

Modifying a SmartArt Graphic

After you create a SmartArt graphic, you can add, remove, change, or rearrange shapes to create a custom look. For shapes within a SmartArt graphic, you can change the shape from the Shape gallery or use familiar commands, such as Bring to Front, Send to Back, Align, Group, and Rotate, to create your own custom SmartArt graphic (**New!**). If you no longer want a shape you've added, simply select it, and then press Delete to remove it.

Add a Shape to a SmartArt Graphic

1. Select the shape in the SmartArt graphic you want to modify.

2. Click the **Design** tab under SmartArt Tools.

3. Click the **Add Shape** button to insert a shape at the end, or click the **Add Shape** button arrow, and then select the position where you want to insert a shape.

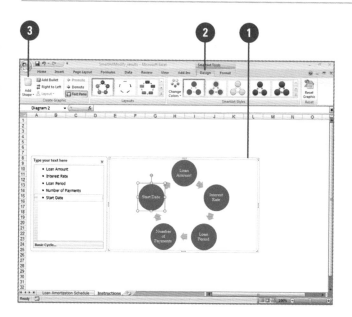

Change Shapes in a SmartArt Graphic

1. Select the shapes in the SmartArt graphic you want to modify.

2. Click the **Format** tab under SmartArt Tools.

3. Click the **Change Shape** button, and then click a shape.

> ### Did You Know?
>
> **You can reset a SmartArt graphic back to its original state.** Select the SmartArt graphic, click the Design tab for SmartArt Tools, and then click the Reset Graphic button.

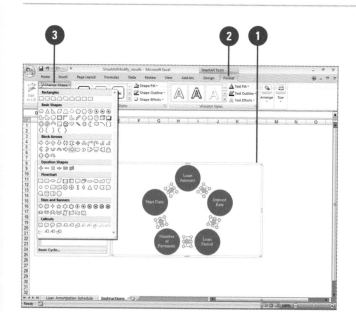

Resizing a SmartArt Graphic

You can change the size of individual shapes within a SmartArt graphic or of an entire SmartArt graphic. If the size of an individual shape within a SmartArt graphic changes, the other shapes in the graphic may also change based on the type of layout. When you resize a shape with text or increase or decrease text size, the text may automatically resize to fit the shape depending on the space available in the SmartArt graphic. When you resize an entire SmartArt graphic, shapes within it scale proportionally or adjust to create the best look.

Resize a SmartArt Graphic

1. Select the shapes in the SmartArt graphic or the entire SmartArt graphic you want to modify.

2. Click the **Format** tab under SmartArt Tools.

3. Use one of the following methods:

   ◆ Drag a middle handle to resize the object up, down, left, or right.

   ◆ Drag a corner handle to resize the object proportionally.

   ◆ Click the **Size** button, and then specify the size you want.

   ◆ Click the **Larger** or **Smaller** button to increase or decrease the object in standard increments.

Larger and Smaller buttons

Size button

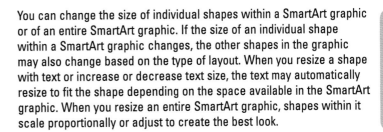

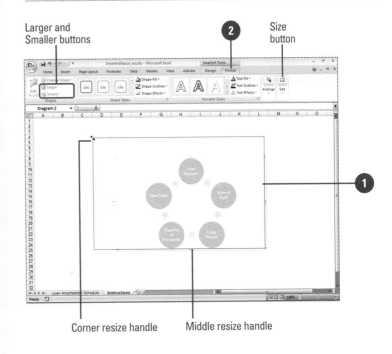

Corner resize handle   Middle resize handle

Did You Know?

You can arrange shapes in a SmartArt graphic. Select the shape in the SmartArt graphic, click the Format tab under SmartArt Tools, click the Arrange button, and then use any of the arrange button options: Bring to Front, Send to Back, Align, Group, or Rotate.

You can edit a SmartArt graphic shape in 2-D. Select the SmartArt graphic with the 3-D style, click the Format tab under SmartArt Tools, and then click the Edit in 2-D button.

Formatting a SmartArt Graphic

If your current SmartArt graphics don't quite convey the message or look you want, use live preview (**New!**) to quickly preview layouts in the Quick Styles (**New!**) and Layout Styles (**New!**) groups and select the one you want. If you only want to change the color, you can choose different color schemes using theme colors by using the Change Color button (**New!**). If the flow of a SmartArt graphic is not the direction you want, you can change the orientation.

Apply a Quick Style to a SmartArt Graphic

1. Click the SmartArt graphic you want to modify.

2. Click the **Design** tab under SmartArt Tools.

3. Click the scroll up or down arrow, or click the **More** list arrow in the Quick Styles group to see additional styles.

   The gallery displays the current layout with different theme colors.

4. Point to a style.

   A live preview (**New!**) of the style appears in the current shape.

5. Click the layout for the SmartArt graphic you want from the gallery.

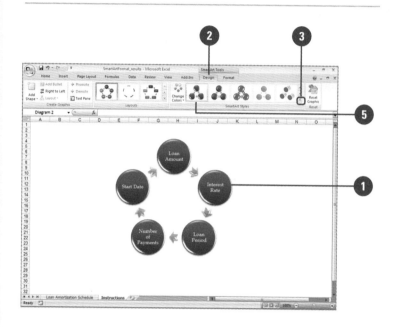

Change a Smart Graphic Orientation

1. Click the SmartArt graphic you want to modify.

2. Click the **Design** tab under SmartArt Tools.

3. Click the **Right to Left** button.

   The button toggles, so you can click it again to switch back.

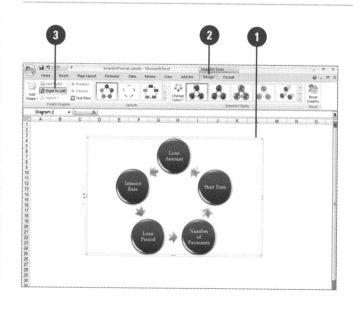

Change a SmartArt Graphic Layout

1. Click the SmartArt graphic you want to modify.

2. Click the **Design** tab under SmartArt Tools.

3. Click the scroll up or down arrow, or click the **More** list arrow in the Layout Styles group to see additional styles.

   The gallery displays layouts designed for bulleted lists.

4. To view the entire list of diagram layouts, click **More Layouts**.

5. Point to a layout.

   A live preview (**New!**) of the style appears in the current shape.

6. Click the layout for the SmartArt graphic you want from the gallery.

7. If you opened the entire list of layouts, click **OK**.

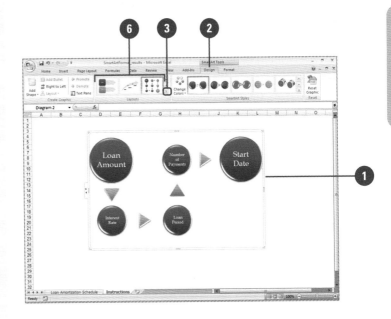

Change a SmartArt Graphic Colors

1. Click the SmartArt graphic you want to modify.

2. Click the **Design** tab under SmartArt Tools.

3. Click the **Change Colors** button.

   The gallery displays the current layout with different theme colors.

4. Point to a style.

   A live preview (**New!**) of the style appears in the current shape.

5. Click the layout for the SmartArt graphic you want from the gallery.

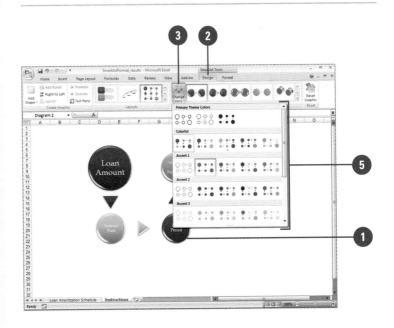

Formatting a Shape in a SmartArt Graphic

Microsoft
Certified
Application
Specialist

EX07S-4.4.2

In the same way you can apply shape fills, outlines, and effects to a shape, you can also apply them to shapes in a SmartArt graphic. You can modify all or part of the SmartArt graphic by using the Shape Fill, Shape Outline, and Shape Effects buttons (New!). Shape Fill can be set to be a solid, gradient, texture or picture, or set the Shape Outline to be a solid or gradient (New!). In addition, you can change the look of a SmartArt graphic by applying effects (New!), such as glow and soft edges. If a shape in a SmartArt graphic contains text, you can use WordArt style galleries to modify shape text.

Apply a Shape Fill to a SmartArt Graphic

1. Select the shapes in the SmartArt graphic you want to modify.

   TIMESAVER *You can hold Ctrl while you click to select multiple shapes, or press Ctrl+A to select all the shapes.*

2. Click the **Format** tab under SmartArt Tools.

3. Click the **Shape Fill** button.

4. Click a color, **No Fill**, or **Picture** to select an image, or point to **Gradient**, or **Texture**, and then select a style.

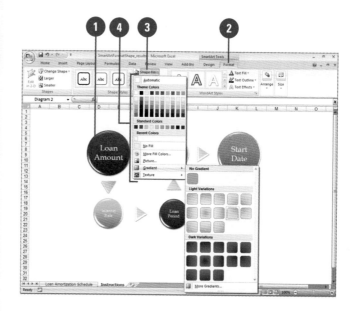

Apply a Shape Outline to a SmartArt Graphic

1. Select the shapes in the SmartArt graphic you want to modify.

2. Click the **Format** tab under SmartArt Tools.

3. Click the **Shape Outline** button.

4. Click a color or **No Outline**, or point to **Weight** or **Dashes**, and then select a style.

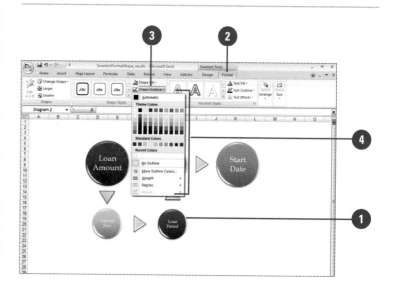

Apply a Shape Effect to a SmartArt Graphic

1. Select the shapes in the SmartArt graphic you want to modify.

2. Click the **Format** tab under SmartArt Tools.

3. Click the **Shape Effects** button, and then point to one of the following:

   ◆ **Preset** to select No 3-D, one of the preset types, or More 3-D Settings.

   ◆ **Shadow** to select No Shadow, one of the shadow types, or More Shadows.

   ◆ **Reflection** to select No Reflection or one of the Reflection Variations.

   ◆ **Glow** to select No Glow, one of the Glow Variations, or More Glow Colors.

   ◆ **Soft Edges** to select No Soft Edges or a point size to determine the soft edge amount.

   ◆ **Bevel** to select No Bevel, one of the bevel types, or More 3-D Settings.

   ◆ **3-D Rotation** to select No Rotation, one of the rotation types, or More 3-D Settings.

   When you point to an effect, a live preview (**New!**) of the style appears in the current shape.

4. Click the effect you want from the gallery to apply it to the selected shape.

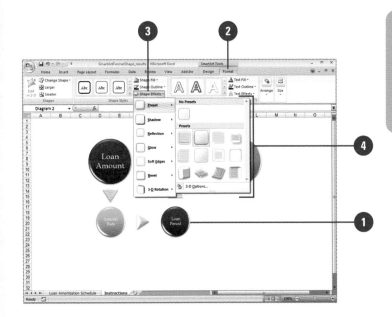

See Also

See "Formatting WordArt Text" on page 208 for information on applying WordArt styles to a SmartArt graphic.

Creating an Organization Chart

An organization chart shows the reporting relationships between individuals in an organization. For example, you can show the relationship between a manager and employees within a company. You can create an organization chart using a SmartArt graphic (**New!**) or using Microsoft Organization Chart. If you're creating a new organization chart, a SmartArt graphic is your best choice. If you need to match an existing organization chart from a previous version of Excel, Microsoft Organization Chart—an embedded application—is your best choice. A SmartArt graphic organization chart makes it easy to add shapes using the graphic portion or the Text pane.

Create an Organization Chart Using a SmartArt Graphic

1. Click the **Insert** tab.

2. Click the **SmartArt** button.

3. In the left pane, click **Hierarchy**.

4. In the right pane, click a SmartArt organization chart type.

5. Click **OK**.

   The SmartArt graphic appears with a Text pane to insert text.

6. Label the shapes by doing one of the following:

   - Type text in the [Text] box.

     You can use the arrow keys to move around the Text pane.

   - Click a shape, and then type text directly into the shape.

7. To add shapes from the Text pane, place the insertion point at the beginning of the text where you want to add a shape, type the text you want, press Enter, and then to indent the new shape, press Tab or to de-indent, press Shift+Tab.

8. When you're done, click outside of the SmartArt graphic.

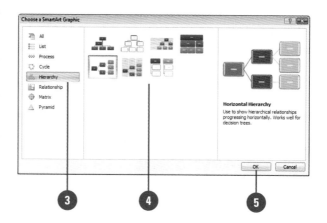

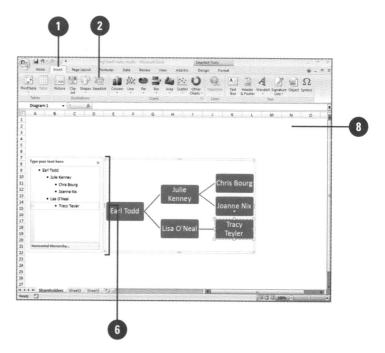

Add a Shape to an Organization Chart

1. Select the shapes in the SmartArt graphic you want to modify.

2. Click the **Design** tab under SmartArt Tools.

3. Click the shape with the layout you want to change.

4. Click the **Add Shape** button arrow, and then select the option you want:

   ◆ **Add Shape After or Add Shape Before.** Inserts a shape at the same level.

   ◆ **Add Shape Above or Add Shape Below.** Inserts a shape one level above or below.

   ◆ **Add Assistant.** Inserts a shape above, but it's displayed at the same level at the end in the Text pane.

5. When you're done, click outside of the SmartArt graphic.

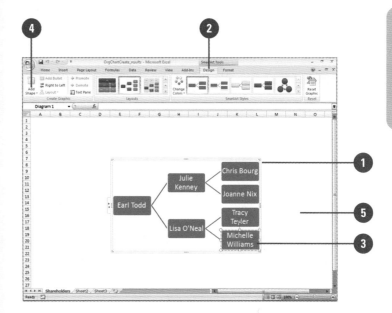

Modifying an Organization Chart

Like any SmartArt graphic, you can add special effects—such as soft edges, glows, or 3-D effects, and animation—to an organization chart. If your organization chart doesn't quite look the way you want, live preview (**New!**) can help you preview layouts in the Quick Styles (**New!**) and Layout Styles (**New!**) groups and select the one you want. If you only want to change the color, you can choose different color schemes using theme colors by using the Change Color button (**New!**).

Change the Layout or Apply a Quick Style to an Organization Chart

1. Click the SmartArt graphic you want to modify.

2. Click the **Design** tab under SmartArt Tools.

3. Click the scroll up or down arrow, or click the **More** list arrow in the Layouts group or Quick Styles group to see additional styles.

   The gallery displays different layouts or the current layout with different theme colors.

4. Point to a style.

   A live preview (**New!**) of the style appears in the current shape.

5. Click the layout or style for the SmartArt graphic you want from the gallery.

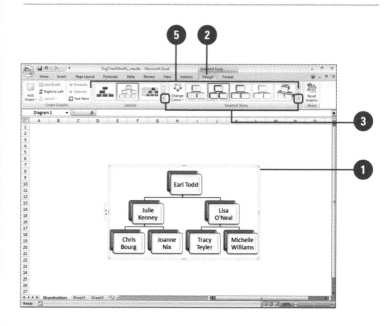

Did You Know?

You can change organization chart lines to dotted lines. Right-click the line you want to modify, click Format Object, click Line Style, click Dash type, click a style, and then click Close.

You can change the colors of an organization chart. Click the SmartArt graphic you want to modify, click the Design tab under SmartArt Tools, click the Change Colors button, and then click the color theme you want.

Drawing and Modifying Shapes

8

Introduction

When you want to add objects to a workbook, you can use Microsoft Office Excel as a drawing package. Excel offers a wide range of predesigned shapes, line options or freeform tools that allow you to draw, size, and format your own shapes and forms.

You can add several types of drawing objects to your Excel workbooks—shapes, text boxes, lines, and freeforms. **Shapes** are preset objects, such as stars, circles, or ovals. **Text boxes** are objects with text, a shape without a border. **Lines** are simply the straight or curved lines (arcs) that can connect two points or are used as arrows. **Freeforms** are irregular curves or polygons that you can create as a free-hand drawing.

Once you create a drawing object, you can move, resize, nudge, copy or delete it on your worksheets. You can also change its style, by adding color, creating a fill pattern, rotating it, and applying a shadow or 3-D effect. Take a simple shape and by the time you are done adding various effects, it could become an attractive piece of graphic art for your workbook. If you'd like to use it later, you can save it to the Clip Organizer.

Object placement on your worksheets is a key factor to all of your hard work. Multiple objects should be grouped if they are to be considered one larger object. Grouping helps you make changes later on, or copy your objects to another worksheet. Excel has the ability to line up your objects with precision—rulers and guides are part of the alignment process to help you. By grouping and aligning, you are assured that your drawing objects will be accurately placed.

Drawing and Resizing Shapes

Microsoft Certified Application Specialist EX07S-4.4.3

Excel supplies ready-made shapes, ranging from hearts to lightning bolts to stars. The ready-made shapes are available directly on the Shapes gallery on the Insert and Format tabs. Once you have placed a shape on a worksheet, you can resize it using the sizing handles. Many shapes have an **adjustment handle**, a small yellow or pink diamond located near a resize handle that you can drag to alter the shape. For precision when resizing, use the Size Dialog Box Launcher (**New!**) to specify the new size of the shape.

Draw a Shape

1. Click the **Insert** tab.

2. Click the **Shapes** button.

3. Click the shape you want to draw.

4. Drag the pointer on the worksheet where you want to place the shape until the drawing object is the shape and size that you want.

   The shape you draw uses the line and fill color defined by the workbook's theme.

   TIMESAVER *To draw a proportional shape, hold down Shift as you drag the pointer.*

Did You Know?

You can quickly delete a shape. Click the shape to select it, and then press Delete.

You can draw a perfect circle or square. To draw a perfect circle or square, click the Oval or Rectangle button on the Shapes gallery, and then press and hold Shift as you drag.

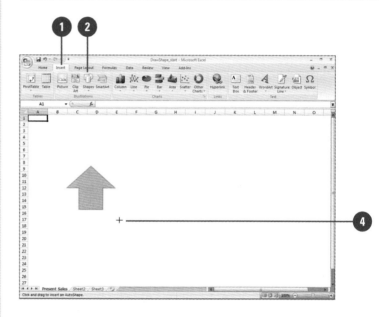

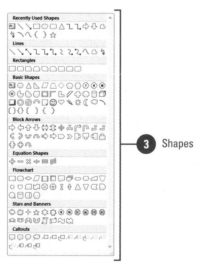

3 Shapes

Resize a Shape

1. Select the shape you want to resize.

2. Drag one of the sizing handles.

   - To resize the object in the vertical or horizontal direction, drag a sizing handle on the side of the selection box.

   - To resize the object in both the vertical and horizontal directions, drag a sizing handle on the corner of the selection box.

   - To resize the object with precise measurements, click the **Format** tab under Drawing Tools, and then specify exact height and width settings in the Size group.

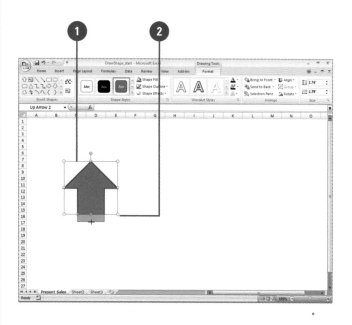

Adjust a Shape

1. Select the shape you want to adjust.

2. Click one of the adjustment handles (small yellow diamonds), and then drag the handle to alter the form of the shape.

Did You Know?

You can replace a shape. Replace one shape with another, while retaining the size, color, and orientation of the shape. Click the shape you want to replace, click the Format tab, click the Edit Shape button, point to Change Shape, and then click the new shape you want.

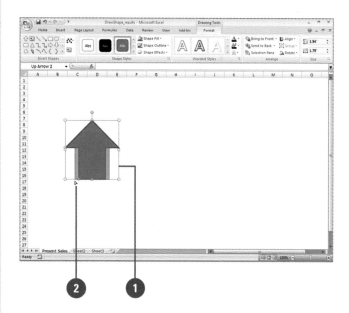

Inserting Multiple Shapes

Microsoft Certified Application Specialist

EX07S-5.4.2

If you need to draw the same shape several times on one or more worksheets in your workbook, you can use Excel's Lock Drawing Mode to draw as many of the same shapes as you want without having to reselect it from the Shapes gallery. This can be a timesaver and save you extra mouse clicks. Excel stays in Lock Drawing Mode until you press Esc. If a shape doesn't look the way you want, you can change the shape instead of redrawing it.

Insert Multiple Shapes

1. Click the **Insert** tab.

2. Click the **Shapes** button.

3. Right-click the shape you want to add, and then click **Lock Drawing Mode**.

4. Drag the pointer on the worksheet where you want to place the shape until the drawing object is the shape and size that you want. Continue to draw shapes as you want in your workbook.

5. When you're done, press Esc.

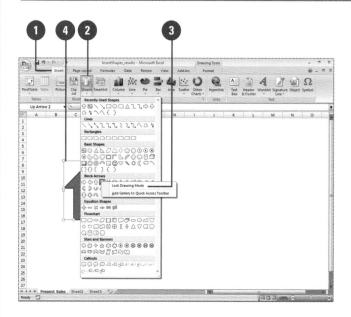

Change a Shape to Another Shape

1. Select the shape you want to modify.

2. Click the **Format tab** under Drawing Tools.

3. Click the **Edit Shape** button, point to **Change Shape**.

4. Click the shape you want to use from the Shapes gallery.

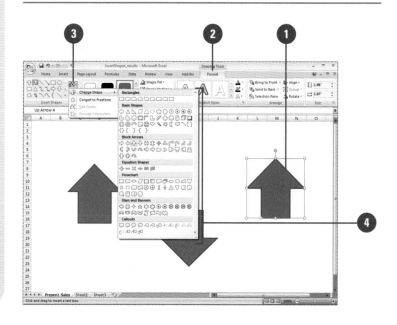

Adding Text to a Shape

You can add text to a shape in the same way you add text to a text box. Simply, select the shape object, and then start typing. Shapes range from rectangles and circles to arrows and stars. When you place text in a shape, the text becomes part of the object. If you rotate or flip the shape, the text rotates or flips too. You can use tools, such as an alignment button or Font Style, on the Mini-toolbar and Home tab to format the text in a shape like the text in a text box.

Add Text to a Shape

1. Select the shape in which you want to add text.

2. Type the text you want.

3. To edit the text in a shape, click the text to place the insertion point, and then edit the text.

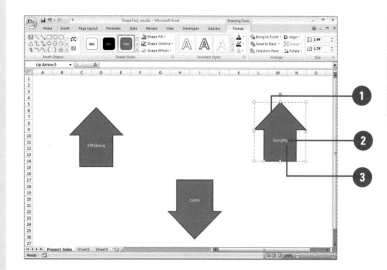

Create a Text Box

1. Click the **Insert** tab.

2. Click the **Text Box** button.

3. Perform one of the following:

   ◆ To add text that wraps, drag to create a box, and then start typing.

   ◆ To add text that doesn't wrap, click and then start typing.

4. To delete a text box, select it, and then press Delete.

5. Click outside the selection box to deselect the text box.

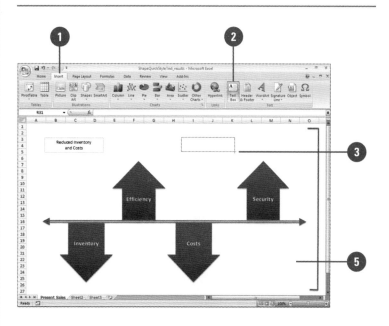

Drawing Lines and Arrows

The most basic drawing objects you can create on your worksheets are lines and arrows. Use the Line shape to create line segments or the Arrow shape to create arrows that emphasize key features of your workbook. You can quickly add multiple formatting to a line or arrow using Shape Quick Styles (**New!**) or change individual formatting—solid, dashed, or a combination—using the Shape Outline button. The Shape Outline button lets you change the type of line or arrow you want to create. You can add arrowheads to any lines on your worksheet.

Draw a Straight Line or Arrow

1. Click the **Insert** tab.

2. Click the **Shapes** button, and then click a Line or Arrow shape in the Shapes gallery.

3. Drag the pointer to draw a line. The endpoints of the line or arrow are where you start and finish dragging.

4. Release the mouse button when the line or arrow is the correct length. Sizing handles appear at both ends of the line. Use these handles to resize your line or move an endpoint.

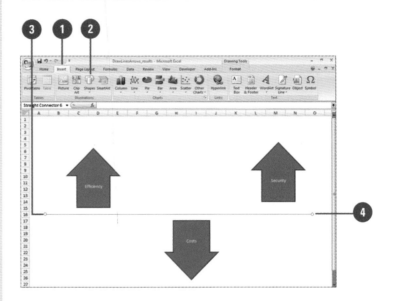

Add a Quick Style to a Line

1. Select the shape you want to modify.

2. Click the **Format** tab under Drawing Tools.

3. Click the scroll up or down arrow, or click the **More** list arrow in the Shapes Styles group to see additional styles.

4. Point to a style.

   A live preview (**New!**) of the style appears in the current shape.

5. Click the style you want from the gallery to apply it to the selected line.

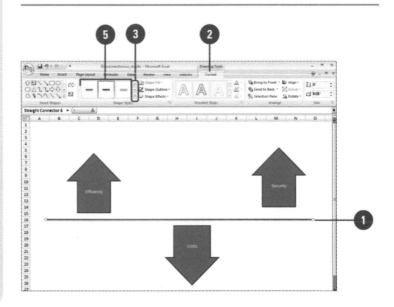

Change a Line or Arrow

1. Select the line or arrow you want to edit.

2. Click the **Format** tab under Drawing Tools.

3. Click the **Shape Outline** button to select a line or arrow style or thickness.

4. Click a color, or point to **Weight**, **Dashes**, or **Arrows**, and then select a style.

5. Drag a sizing handle to change the size or angle of the line or arrow.

Modify a Line or Arrow

1. Select the line or arrow you want to edit.

2. Click the **Format** tab under Drawing Tools.

3. Click the **Shape Outline** button, point to **Weight**, **Dashes**, or **Arrows**, and then click **More Lines** or **More Arrows**.

4. For a line and arrow, select a width, compound type (double or triple lines), dash type, cap type— end of line style (square, round, or flat end), or join type—style used to connect two lines together (round, bevel, or miter).

5. For an arrow, select a begin type, end type, begin size, and end size.

6. Click **Close**.

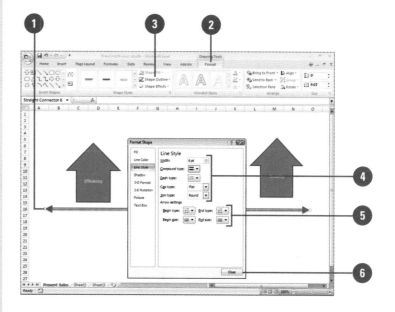

Creating and Editing Freeforms

When you need to create a customized shape, use the Excel freeform tools. Choose a freeform tool from the Lines category in the list of shapes. Freeforms are like the drawings you make with a pen and paper, except that you use a mouse for your pen and a worksheet for your paper. A freeform shape can either be an open curve or a closed curve. You can edit a freeform by using the Edit Points command to alter the vertices that create the shape.

Draw a Freeform Polygon

1 Click the **Insert** tab.

2 Click the **Shapes** button and then **Freeform** in the Shapes gallery under Lines.

3 Click the worksheet where you want to place the first vertex of the polygon.

4 Move the pointer, and then click to place the second point of the polygon. A line joins the two points.

◆ To draw a line with curves, drag a line instead of clicking in steps 3 and 4.

5 Continue moving the mouse pointer and clicking to create additional sides of your polygon.

6 Finish the polygon. For a closed polygon, click near the starting point. For an open polygon, double-click the last point in the polygon.

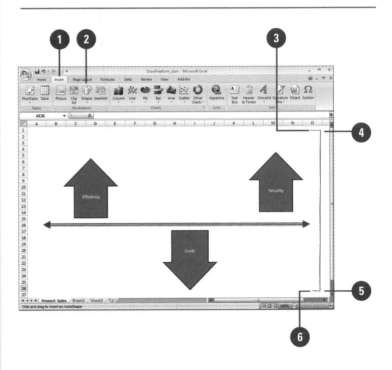

Did You Know?

You can convert a shape to a freeform. Select the shape, click the Edit Shape button, and then click Convert to Freeform.

You can switch between a closed curve and an open curve. Right-click the freeform drawing, and then click Close Path or Open Path.

For Your Information

Modifying a Freeform

Each vertex indicated by a black dot (a corner in an irregular polygon and a bend in a curve) has two attributes: its position, and the angle at which the curve enters and leaves it. You can move the position of each vertex and control the corner or bend angles. You can also add or delete vertices as you like. When you delete a vertex, Excel recalculates the freeform and smooths it among the remaining points. Similarly, if you add a new vertex, Excel adds a corner or bend in your freeform. To edit a freeform, click the freeform object, click the Format tab under Drawing Tools, click the Edit Shape button, click Edit Points, modify any of the points (move or delete), and then click outside to set the new shape.

Copying and Moving Objects

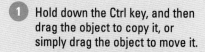

After you create a drawing object, you can copy or move it. Use the mouse to quickly move objects, or if you want precise control over the object's new position, use Excel's Size and Position dialog box to specify the location of the drawing object. You can copy a selected one or more objects to the Office Clipboard and then paste them in other parts of the current workbook or another existing workbook, or Office document. You can paste these items, either individually or all at once.

Copy or Move an Object in One Step

1. Hold down the Ctrl key, and then drag the object to copy it, or simply drag the object to move it.

   Make sure you aren't dragging a sizing handle or adjustment handle. If you are working with a freeform and you are in Edit Points mode, drag the interior of the object, not the border, or you will end up resizing or reshaping the object, not moving it.

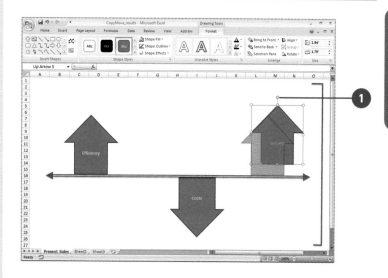

Copy or Move an Object

1. Select the objects you want to copy or move.

2. Click the **Home** tab.

3. Click the **Copy** button (to copy) or click the **Cut** button (to move).

4. Display the worksheet on which you want to paste the object.

5. Use one of the following methods:

   ◆ Click the **Paste** button.

   ◆ Click the **Clipboard Dialog Box Launcher**, and then click an item to paste it on the worksheet.

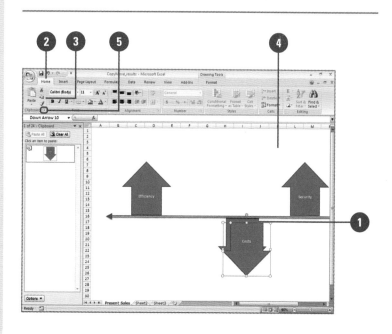

Adding a Quick Style to a Shape

Microsoft
Certified
Application
Specialist

EX07S-4.4.3

Instead of changing individual attributes of a shape—such as shape fill, shape outline, and shape effects—you can quickly add them all at once with the Shape Quick Style gallery. The Shape Quick Style gallery (**New!**) provides a variety of different formatting combinations. To quickly see if you like a Shape Quick Style, point to a thumbnail in the gallery to display a live preview (**New!**) of it in the selected shape. If you like it, you can apply it.

Add a Quick Style to a Shape

1. Select the shapes you want to modify.

2. Click the **Format** tab under Drawing Tools.

3. Click the scroll up or down arrow, or click the **More** list arrow in the Shapes Styles group to see additional styles.

   The current style appears highlighted in the gallery.

4. Point to a style.

   A live preview (**New!**) of the style appears in the current shape.

5. Click the style you want from the gallery to apply it to the selected shape.

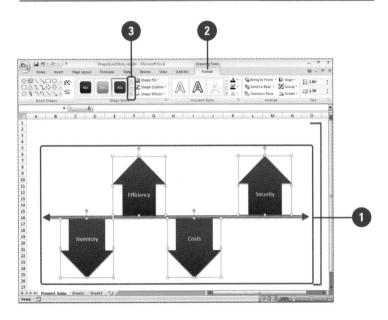

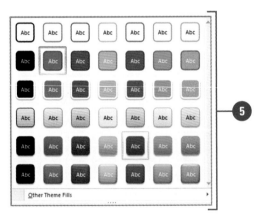

Adding a Quick Style to Shape Text

Add a Quick Style to Shape Text

1. Select the shapes with the text you want to modify.

2. Click the **Format** tab under Drawing Tools.

3. Click the scroll up or down arrow, or click the **More** list arrow in the WordArt Styles group to see additional styles.

   The current style appears highlighted in the gallery.

4. Point to a style.

   A live preview (**New!**) of the style appears in the current shape text.

5. Click the style you want from the gallery to apply it to the selected shape.

Instead of changing individual attributes of text in a shape, such as text fill, text outline, and text effects, you can quickly add them all at once with the WordArt Quick Style gallery. The WordArt Quick Style gallery (**New!**) provides a variety of different formatting combinations. To quickly see if you like a WordArt Quick Style, point to a thumbnail in the gallery to display a live preview (**New!**) of it in the selected shape. If you like it, you can apply it.

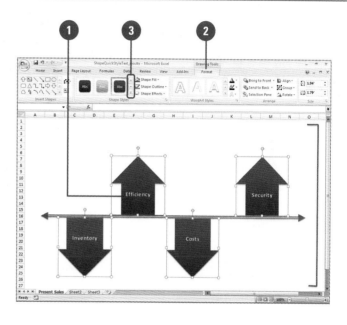

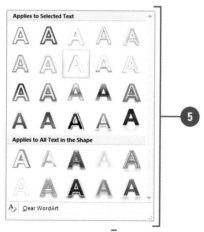

Applying Color Fills

When you create a closed drawing object such as a square, it applies the Shape Fill color to the inside of the shape, and the Shape Outline color to the edge of the shape. A line drawing object uses the Shape Outline color. You can set the Shape Fill to be a solid, gradient, texture or picture, and the Shape Outline can be a solid or gradient (**New!**). If you want to make multiple changes to a shape at the same time, the Format Shape dialog box allows you to do everything in one place. If the solid color appears too dark, you can make the color fill more transparent. If you no longer want to apply a shape fill to an object, you can remove it.

Apply a Color Fill to a Shape

1. Select the shape you want to modify.

2. Click the **Format** tab under Drawing Tools.

3. Click the **Shape Fill** button.

4. Select the fill color option you want.

5. To remove a color fill, click the **Shape Fill** button, and then click **No Fill**.

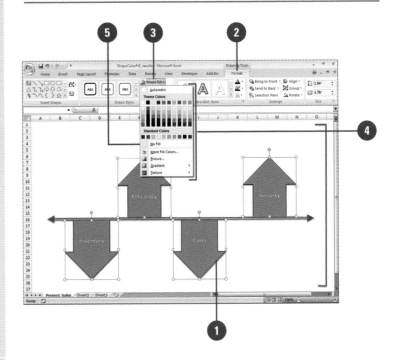

Did You Know?

You can set the color and line style for an object as the default. Right-click the object, and then click Set as Default Shape. Any new objects you create will use the same styles.

You can use the workbook background as the fill for a shape. Right-click the object, click Format Shape, click Fill in the left pane, click the Background option, and then click Close.

You can undo changes made in the Format Shape dialog box. Since changes made in the Shape Format dialog box are instantly applied, it's not possible to Cancel the dialog box. To remove changes, click the Undo button on the Quick Access Toolbar.

Apply a Shape Color Fill with a Transparency

1. Right-click the shape you want to modify, and then click **Format Shape**.

2. In the left pane, click **Fill**.

3. Click the **Solid Fill** option.

4. Click the **Color** button, and then select the fill color you want.

5. Drag the **Transparency** slider or enter a number from 0 (fully opaque) to 100 (fully transparent).

   All your changes are instantly applied to the shape.

6. Click **Close**.

   TROUBLE? *To cancel changes, click the Undo button on the Quick Access Toolbar.*

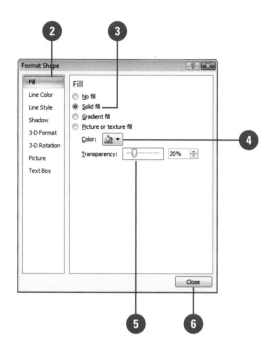

Apply a Color Outline to a Shape

1. Select the shape you want to modify.

2. Click the **Format** tab under Drawing Tools.

3. Click the **Shape Outline** button.

4. Select the outline color you want.

5. To remove an outline color, click the **Shape Outline** button, and then click **No Outline**.

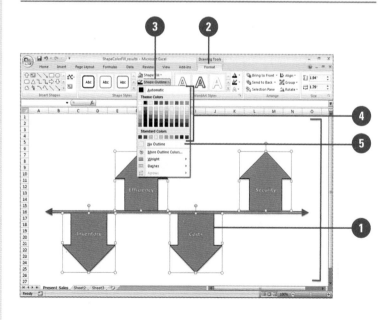

Applying Picture Fills

Applying a shape fill to a drawing object can add emphasis or create a point of interest in your workbook. You can insert a picture or clip art into a shape. You can insert a picture from a file or clip art from the Clip Art task pane, or paste one in from the Office Clipboard. Stretch a picture to fit across the selected shape or repeatedly tile the same picture horizontally and vertically to fill the shape. When you stretch a picture, you can also set offsets, which determine how much to scale a picture to fit a shape relative to the edges. A positive offset number moves the picture edge toward the center of the shape, while a negative offset number moves the picture edge away from the shape. If the picture appears too dark, you can make the picture more transparent.

Apply a Picture Fill to a Shape

1. Select the shape you want to modify.

2. Click the **Format** tab under Drawing Tools.

3. Click the **Shape Fill** button, and then click **Picture**.

4. Locate and select a picture file you want.

5. Click **Insert**.

Did You Know?

You can undo changes made in the Format Shape dialog box. Since changes made in the Shape dialog box are instantly applied to the shape, it is not possible to Cancel the dialog box. To remove changes, you can click the Undo button on the Quick Access Toolbar.

You can apply a custom picture fill. Right-click the object you want to modify, click Format Shape, click Fill, click the Picture or texture fill option, click File, Clipboard, or Clip Art to select a picture, select the tile, stretch, and transparency options you want, and then click Close.

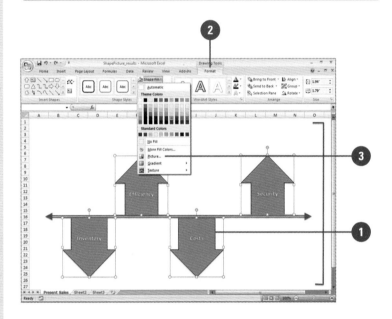

Applying Texture Fills

You can quickly apply a texture fill to a shape by using the Texture gallery or using the Format Shape dialog box to select custom options. Stretch a texture to fit across the selected shape or repeatedly tile the texture horizontally and vertically to fill the shape. If you tile a texture, you can also set offset, scale, alignment, and mirror options to determine the appearance of the texture in the selected shape. The offset x and y options determine how much to scale a texture to fit a shape relative to the edges, while scale x and y options determine horizontal and vertical scaling. If you want to play with the tile look, you can change the mirror type to determine whether the alternating tiles display a mirror or flip image with every other tile. If the texture doesn't provide enough contrast in the shape, you can make the texture more transparent.

Apply a Texture Fill to a Shape

1 Select the shape you want to modify.

2 Click the **Format** tab under Drawing Tools.

3 Click the **Shape Fill** button.

4 Point to **Texture**, and then select a texture from the gallery.

Did You Know?

You can apply a custom texture fill.
Right-click the object you want to modify, click Format Shape, click Fill, click the Picture or texture fill option, click the Texture button, select a texture, select the offset, scale, alignment, mirror and transparency options you want, and then click Close.

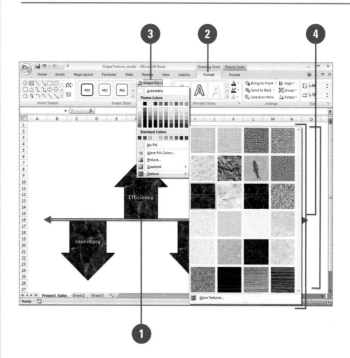

Applying Gradient Fills

Gradients are made up of two or more colors that gradually fade into each other. They can be used to give depth to a shape or create realistic shadows. Apply a gradient fill to a shape—now including lines (**New!**)—by using a gallery or presets for quick results, or by using the Format Shape dialog box for custom results. A gradient is made up of several gradient stops, which are used to create non-linear gradients. If you want to create a gradient that starts blue and goes to green, add two gradient stops, one for each color. Gradient stops consist of a position, a color, and a transparency percentage.

Apply a Gradient Fill to a Shape

1 Select the shape you want to modify.

2 Click the **Format** tab under Drawing Tools.

3 Click the **Shape Fill** button.

4 Point to **Gradient**, and then select a gradient from the gallery.

Four gradient modes are available: linear (parallel bands), radial (radiate from center), rectangle (radiate from corners), and path (radiate along path).

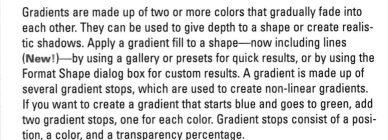
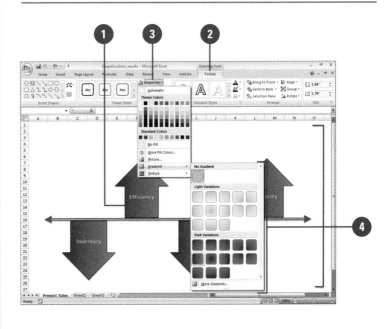

Apply a Gradient Fill with Presets

1 Right-click the shape you want to modify, and then click **Format Shape**.

2 In the left pane, click **Fill**.

3 Click the **Gradient fill** option.

4 Click the **Preset colors** button arrow, and then select the built-in gradient fill you want.

All your changes are instantly applied to the shape.

5 Click **Close**.

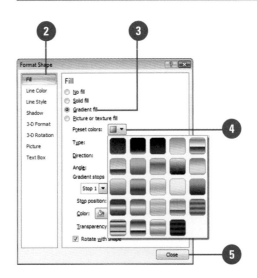

Apply a Custom Gradient Fill

1. Right-click the shape you want to modify, and then click **Format Shape**.

2. In the left pane, click **Fill**.

3. Click the **Gradient fill** option.

4. Click the **Preset colors** button arrow, and then select the built-in gradient fill you want.

5. Click the **Type** list arrow, and then select a gradient direction.

6. Click the **Direction** list arrow, and then select a shading progression. The options available depend on the gradient type.

7. If you selected the Linear type, specify the angle (in degrees) the gradient is rotated in the shape.

8. Specify the following tiling options:

   ◆ **Add.** Click Add, and then set the Stop position, Color, and Transparency you want.

   ◆ **Remove.** Click the Stop number list arrow, select a gradient stop, and then click Remove.

   ◆ **Stop position.** Specify a location for the color and transparency change in the gradient fill.

   ◆ **Color.** Click the Color button, and then select a color for the gradient stop.

   ◆ **Transparency.** Drag the Transparency slider or enter a number from 0 (fully opaque) to 100 (fully transparent) for the selected stop position.

9. Select the **Rotate with shape** check box to rotate the gradient with the shape's rotation.

   All your changes are instantly applied to the shape.

10. Click **Close**.

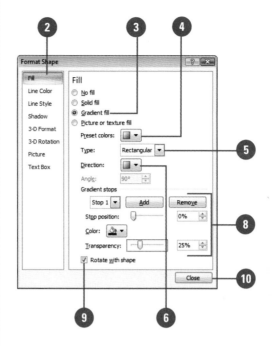

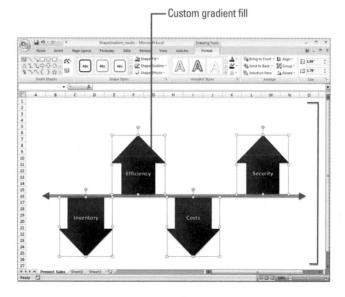

Custom gradient fill

Applying Shape Effects

You can change the look of a shape by applying effects (**New!**), like shadows, reflections, glow, soft edges, bevels, and 3-D rotations. Apply effects to a shape by using the Shape Effects gallery for quick results, or by using the Format Shape dialog box for custom results. From the Shape Effects gallery you can apply a built-in combination of 3-D effects or individual effects to a shape. To quickly see if you like a shape effect, point to a thumbnail in the Shape Effects gallery to display a live preview (**New!**) of it in the selected shape. If you like it, you can apply it. If you no longer want to apply a shape effect to an object, you can remove it. Simply select the shape, point to the effect type in the Shape Effects gallery, and then select the No effect type option.

Add a Preset Effect to a Shape

1. Select the shape you want to modify.

2. Click the **Format** tab under Drawing Tools.

3. Click the **Shape Effects** button, and then point to **Preset**.

   The current effect appears highlighted in the gallery.

4. Point to an effect.

   A live preview (**New!**) of the style appears in the current shape.

5. Click the effect you want from the gallery to apply it to the selected shape.

6. To remove the preset effect, click the **Shape Effects** button, point to **Preset**, and then click **No Preset**.

Did You Know?

3-D effects take precedence. If you add a 3-D effect, such a bevel or 3-D rotation, to a shape and then add soft edges, the soft edge effect doesn't appear in the shape until you delete the 3-D effect.

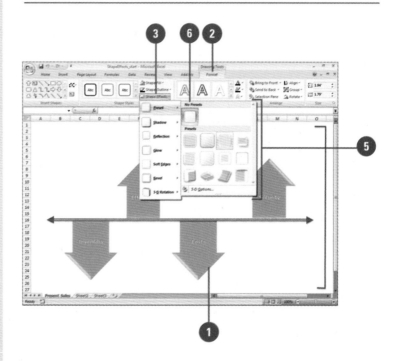

Add Individual Effects to a Shape

1. Select the shape you want to modify.

2. Click the **Format** tab under Drawing Tools.

3. Click the **Shape Effects** button, and then point to one of the following:

    ◆ **Shadow** to select No Shadow, one of the shadow types (Outer, Inner, or Perspective), or More Shadows.

    ◆ **Reflection** to select No Reflection or one of the Reflection Variations.

    ◆ **Glow** to select No Glow, one of the Glow Variations, or More Glow Colors.

    ◆ **Soft Edges** to select No Soft Edges, or a point size to determine the soft edge amount.

    ◆ **Bevel** to select No Bevel, one of the bevel variations, or More 3-D Settings.

    ◆ **3-D Rotation** to select No Rotation, one of the rotation types (Parallel, Perspective, or Oblique), or More 3-D Settings.

    When you point to an effect, a live preview (**New!**) of the style appears in the current shape.

4. Click the effect you want from the gallery to apply it to the selected shape.

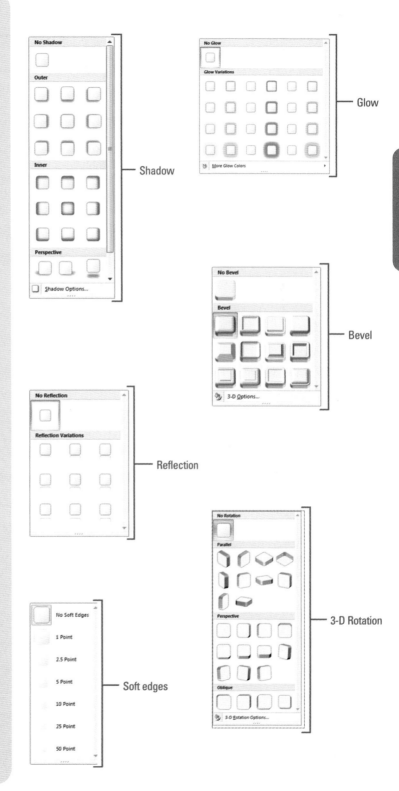

Shadow

Reflection

Soft edges

Glow

Bevel

3-D Rotation

Adding 3-D Effects to a Shape

You can add the illusion of depth to your worksheets by adding a 3-D effect to a shape. Create a 3-D effect by using one of the preset 3-D styles, or use the 3-D format tools to customize your own 3-D style (**New!**). The settings you can control with the customization tools include the bevel (a 3-D top or bottom edge effect), the shape depth (distance of shape from its surface), the contour (raised border), the surface material and lighting. You can apply interesting surfaces—matte, plastic, metal, wire frame, soft or dark edges, flat, translucent, and clear (**New!**)—to a 3-D shape. In addition, you can change the type of lighting—neutral, warm, cool, flat, glow, and bright room (**New!**)—applied to a 3-D shape. Each lighting type defines one or more lights that illuminate a 3-D scene, not just for the shape. Each light contains a position, intensity, and color.

Add a 3-D Effect to a Shape

1. Select the shape you want to modify.

2. Click the **Format** tab under Drawing Tools.

3. Click the **Shape Effects** button, and then point to **Preset** or **Bevel**.

   The current effect appears highlighted in the gallery.

4. Point to an effect.

   A live preview (**New!**) of the style appears in the current shape.

5. Click the effect you want from the gallery to apply it to the selected shape.

6. To remove the 3-D effect, click the **Shape Effects** button, point to **Preset** or **Bevel**, and then click **No Preset** or **No Bevel**.

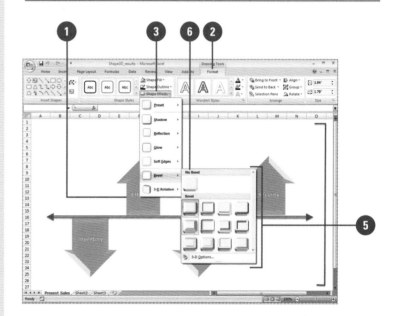

Add a Custom 3-D Effect to a Shape

① Select the shape you want to modify.

② Click the **Format** tab under Drawing Tools.

③ Click the **Shape Effects** button, point to **Preset** or **Bevel**, and then click **3-D Options**.

④ Specify the following custom options:

◆ **Bevel.** Click Top or Bottom to apply a raised edge to the top or bottom of a shape. The corresponding width and height numbers appear.

◆ **Depth.** Click the Color button to select a depth color, and then enter a depth number.

◆ **Contour.** Click the Color button to select a contour color, and then enter a size.

◆ **Surface.** Click Material to select a surface, and then click Lighting to specify the way light illuminates the 3-D shape.

To rotate all of the lights around the front face of a shape, enter an angle.

All your changes are instantly applied to the shape.

⑤ To remove 3-D formatting and restore default setting, click **Reset**.

⑥ Click **Close**.

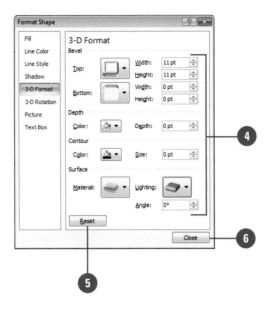

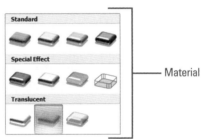

Material

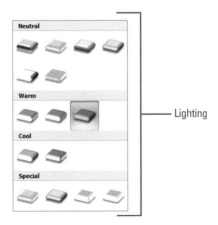

Lighting

Adding 3-D Rotation Effects to a Shape

After you create a 3-D or even a 2-D shape, you can use 3-D rotation options to change the orientation and perspective of the shape. You can also create a 3-D rotation effect using one of the preset 3-D rotation styles, or you can use the 3-D rotation tools to create your own 3-D effect (**New!**). The settings control with the customization tools include the 3-D rotation (x, y, and z axis), text rotation, and object position (distance from ground).

Add a 3-D Rotation Effect to a Shape

① Select the shape you want to modify.

② Click the **Format** tab under Drawing Tools.

③ Click the **Shape Effects** button, and then point to **3-D Rotation**.

The current effect appears highlighted in the gallery.

④ Point to an effect.

A live preview (**New!**) of the style appears in the current shape.

⑤ Click the effect you want from the gallery to apply it to the selected shape.

⑥ To remove the 3-D rotation effect, click the **Shape Effects** button, point to **3-D Rotation**, and then click **No Rotation**.

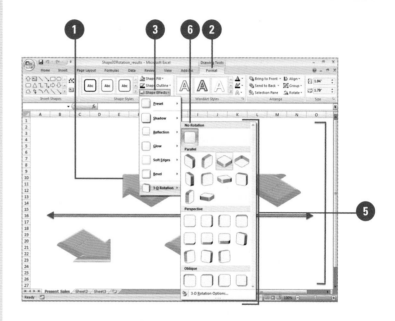

> **Did You Know?**
>
> ***You can add a custom 3-D rotation effect to a shape.*** Click the shape you want to modify, click the Format tab, click the Shape Effects button, point to 3-D Rotation, click 3-D Rotation Options, select the rotation x and y, rotation z, rotation perspective, text and object position options you want, and then click Close.

Creating Shadows

You can give objects on your worksheets the illusion of depth by adding shadows. Excel provides several preset shadowing options, or you can create your own by specifying color, transparency, size, blur, angle, and distance (**New!**). You can change all these shadow options at the same time in the Format Shape dialog box. Instead of starting from scratch, you can select a preset shadow in the Format Shape dialog box, and then customize it.

Add a Preset Shadow to a Shape

1. Select the shape you want to modify.

2. Click the **Format** tab under Drawing Tools.

3. Click the **Shape Effects** button, and then point to **Shadow**.

   The current effect appears highlighted in the gallery.

4. Point to an effect.

   A live preview (**New!**) of the style appears in the current shape.

5. Click the effect you want from the gallery to apply it to the selected shape.

6. To remove the shadow, click the **Shape Effects** button, point to **Shadow**, and then click **No Shadow**.

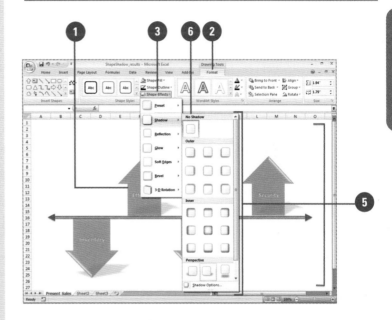

Did You Know?

You can add a custom shadow to a shape. Click the shape you want to modify, click the Format tab, click the Shape Effects button, point to Shadow, click More Shadows, click the Presets button, select a shadow, select the color, transparency, size, blur, angle, and distance options you want, and then click Close.

Aligning and Distributing Objects

In addition to using grids and guides to align objects to a specific point, you can align a group of objects to each other. The Align commands make it easy to align two or more objects relative to each other vertically to the left, center, or right, or horizontally from the top, middle, or bottom. To evenly align several objects to each other across the worksheet, either horizontally or vertically, select them and then choose a distribution option. Before you select an align command, specify how you want Excel to align the objects. You can align the objects in relation to the worksheet or to the selected objects.

Distribute Objects

1 Select the objects you want to distribute.

2 Click the **Format** tab under Drawing Tools.

3 Click the **Align** button.

4 On the Align menu, click the alignment method you want.

◆ Click **Snap to Grid** if you want the objects to align relative to the worksheet grid.

◆ Click **Snap to Shape** if you want the objects to align relative to each other.

5 On the Align submenu, click the distribution command you want.

◆ Click **Distribute Horizontally** to evenly distribute the objects horizontally.

◆ Click **Distribute Vertically** to evenly distribute the objects vertically.

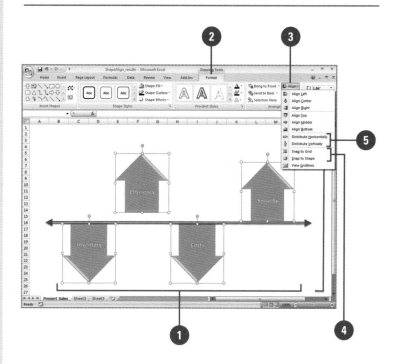

Align Objects with Other Objects

1. Select the objects you want to align.

2. Click the **Format** tab under Drawing Tools.

3. Click the **Align** button.

4. On the Align menu, click the alignment method you want.

   ◆ Click **Snap to Grid** if you want the objects to align relative to the worksheet grid.

   ◆ Click **Snap to Shape** if you want the objects to align relative to each other.

5. On the Align menu, click the alignment command you want.

   ◆ Click **Align Left** to line up the objects with the left edge of the selection or worksheet.

   ◆ Click **Align Center** to line up the objects with the center of the selection or worksheet.

   ◆ Click **Align Right** to line up the objects with the right edge of the selection or worksheet.

   ◆ Click **Align Top** to line up the objects with the top edge of the selection or worksheet.

   ◆ Click **Align Middle** to line up the objects vertically with the middle of the selection or worksheet.

   ◆ Click **Align Bottom** to line up the objects with the bottom of the selection or worksheet.

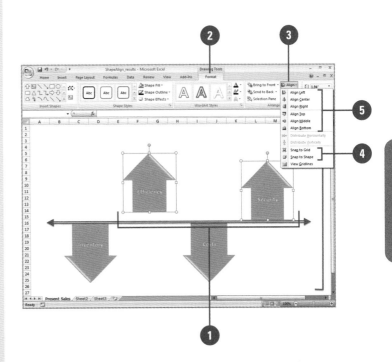

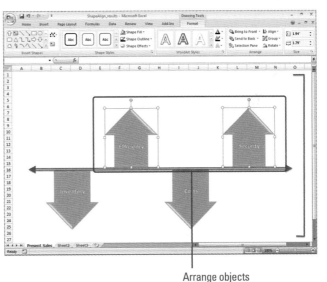

Arrange objects

Connecting Shapes

Excel makes it easy to draw and modify flow charts and diagrams. Flow charts and diagrams consist of shapes connected together to indicate a sequence of events. With Excel, you can join two objects with a connecting line. There are three types of connector lines: straight, elbow, and curved. Once two objects are joined, the connecting line moves when you move either object. The connecting line touches special connection points on the objects. When you position the pointer over an object, small red handles, known as **connection sites**, appear, and the pointer changes to a small box, called the connection pointer. You can drag a connection end point to another connection point to change the line or drag the adjustment handle (yellow diamond) to change the shape of the connection line. After you're done connecting shapes, you can format connector lines in the same way you format others lines in Excel, including the use of Shape Quick Styles (**New!**).

Connect Two Objects

1. Click the **Insert** tab.

2. Click the **Shapes** button, and then click a connector (located in the Lines category) in the Shapes gallery.

   ◆ To draw multiple connector lines, right-click the connector in the Shapes gallery, and then click Lock Drawing Mode.

   TIMESAVER *In the Shapes gallery, point to shapes in the Lines category to display ScreenTips to locate a connector.*

3. Position the pointer over an object handle (turns red).

4. Drag the connector to the object handle (turns red) on another object.

   TIMESAVER *To constrain the line at 15-degree angles from its starting point, hold down Shift while you drag.*

   An attached connector point appears as red circles, while an unattached connector point appears as light blue (almost transparent).

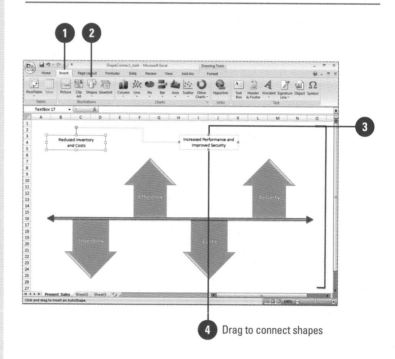

Drag to connect shapes

Selecting Objects Using the Selection Pane

Sometimes it's hard to select an object when it is behind another one. With the Selection task pane (**New!**), you can now select individual objects and change their order and visibility. When you open the Selection task pane, Excel lists each shape on the current worksheet by name (in terms of object type). You can click a shape title to select a "hard-to-select" object on the worksheet, use the Re-order buttons to change the stacking order on the worksheet, or click the eye icon next to a shape title to show or hide "hard-to-see" individual objects.

Select Objects Using the Selection Pane

1. Display the worksheets with the objects you want to select.

2. Click the **Format** tab under Drawing or Picture Tools.

3. Click the **Selection Pane** button.

   Titles for all the shapes on the current worksheet appear in the task pane.

4. To select an object, click the title in the task pane.

   To select more than one object, hold down the Ctrl key while you click object titles.

5. To change the order of the objects, select an object, and then click the **Move Up** or **Move Down** buttons in the task pane.

6. To show or hide individual objects, click the eye icon in the task pane.

7. When you're done, click the **Close** button on the task pane.

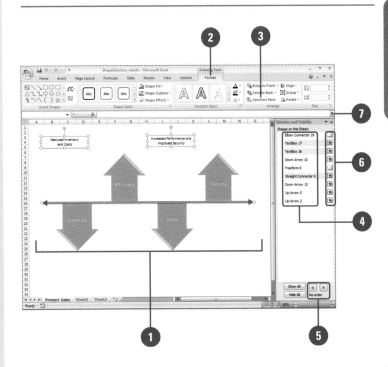

Changing Stacking Order

Multiple objects on a worksheet appear in a stacking order, like layers of transparencies. Stacking is the placement of objects one on top of another. In other words, the first object that you draw is on the bottom and the last object that you draw is on top. You can change the order of this stack of objects by using Bring to Front, Send to Back, Bring Forward, and Send Backward commands on the Format tab under Drawing or Picture Tools.

Arrange a Stack of Objects

1. Select the objects you want to arrange.

2. Click the **Format** tab under Drawing or Picture Tools.

3. Click the stacking option you want.

   ◆ Click the **Bring to Front** button arrow, and then click **Bring to Front** or **Bring Forward** to move a drawing to the top of the stack or up one location in the stack.

   ◆ Click the **Send to Back** button arrow, and then click **Send to Back** or **Send Backward** to move a drawing to the bottom of the stack or back one location in the stack.

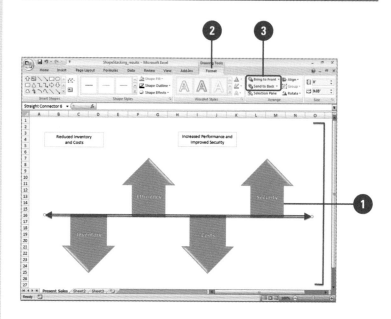

> ### Did You Know?
>
> **You can view a hidden object in a stack.** Press the Tab key or Shift+Tab to cycle forward or backward through the objects until you select the object you want.

Rotating and Flipping a Shape

After you create an object, you can change its orientation on the worksheet by rotating or flipping it. Rotating turns an object 90 degrees to the right or left; flipping turns an object 180 degrees horizontally or vertically. For a more freeform rotation, which you cannot achieve in 90 or 180 degree increments, drag the green rotate lever at the top of an object. You can also rotate and flip any type of picture—including bitmaps—in a workbook. This is useful when you want to change the orientation of an object or image, such as changing the direction of an

Rotate an Object to any Angle

1. Select the object you want to rotate.

2. Position the pointer (which changes to the Free Rotate pointer) over the green rotate lever at the top of the object, and then drag to rotate the object.

3. Click outside the object to set the rotation.

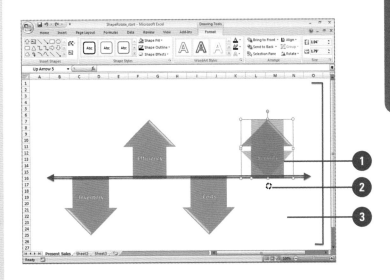

Rotate or Flip an Object Using Preset Increments

1. Select the object you want to rotate or flip.

2. Click the **Format** tab under Drawing or Picture Tools.

3. Click the **Rotate** button, and then click the option you want.

   ◆ **Rotate.** Click Rotate Right 90° or Rotate Left 90°.

   ◆ **Flip.** Click Flip Vertical or Flip Horizontal.

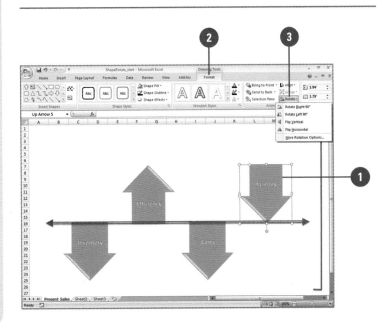

Grouping and Ungrouping Shapes

Objects can be grouped, ungrouped, and regrouped to make editing and moving them easier. Rather than moving several objects one at a time, you can group the objects and move them all together. Grouped objects appear as one object, but each object in the group maintains its individual attributes. You can change an individual object within a group without ungrouping. This is useful when you need to make only a small change to a group, such as changing the color of a single shape in the group. You can also format specific shapes, drawings, or pictures within a group without ungrouping. Simply select the object within the group, change the object or edit text within the object, and then deselect the object. However, if you need to move an object in a group, you need to first ungroup the objects, move it, and then group the objects together again. After you ungroup a set of objects, Excel remembers each object in the group and regroups those objects in one step when you use the Regroup command. Before you regroup a set of objects, make sure that at least one of the grouped objects is selected.

Group Objects Together

1. Select the objects you want to group together.

2. Click the **Format** tab under Drawing or Picture Tools.

3. Click the **Group** button, and then click **Group**.

Did You Know?

You can use the Tab key to select objects in order. Move between the drawing objects on your worksheet (even those hidden behind other objects) by pressing the Tab key.

You can use the shortcut menu to select Group related commands. Right-click the objects you want to group, point to Group, and then make your selections.

You can no longer ungroup tables. Due to the increased table size and theme functionality, tables can no longer be ungrouped.

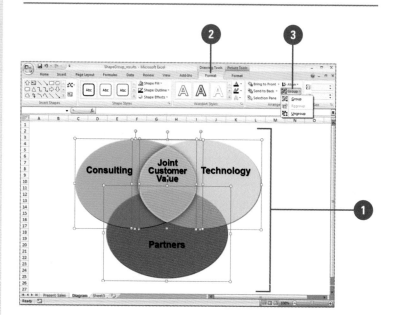

Ungroup a Drawing

1. Select the grouped object you want to ungroup.

2. Click the **Format** tab under Drawing or Picture Tools.

3. Click the **Group** button, and then click **Ungroup**.

See Also

See "Selecting Objects Using the Selection Pane" on page 251 for information on selecting "hard-to-select" objects.

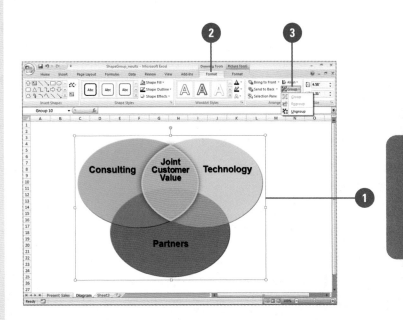

Regroup a Drawing

1. Select one of the objects in the group of objects you want to regroup.

2. Click the **Format** tab under Drawing or Picture Tools.

3. Click the **Group** button, and then click **Regroup**.

Did You Know?

You can troubleshoot the arrangement of objects. If you have trouble selecting an object because another object is in the way, you can use the Selection pane to help you select it.

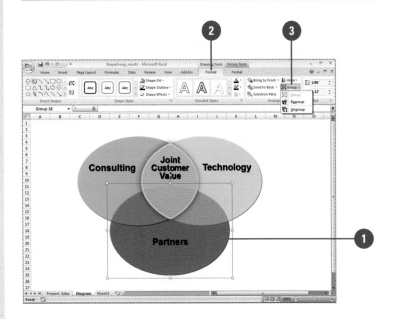

Adding a Shape to the Clip Organizer

After spending time creating an object, you might want to save it for use in future workbooks. You can add any object you create to the Microsoft Clip Organizer—an organized collection of clip art, pictures, videos, and sounds that comes with Excel. You can also find a picture in the Clip Organizer and use it as the basis for the logo for your home business. For example, you could use the basket of bread image for a home bakery.

Add Your Own Shape to the Clip Organizer

1. Select the shape you want to add to the Clip Organizer.

2. Click the **Copy** button on the Home tab.

3. Click the **Insert** tab, and then click the **Clip Art** button.

4. Click **Organize clips** at the bottom of the Clip Art task pane.

5. Click the collection folder you want to add the clip to.

6. Click the **Edit** menu in the Clip Organizer, and then click **Paste**.

7. Click the **Close** button to close the Microsoft Clip Organizer.

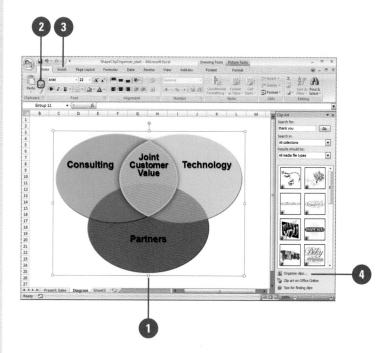

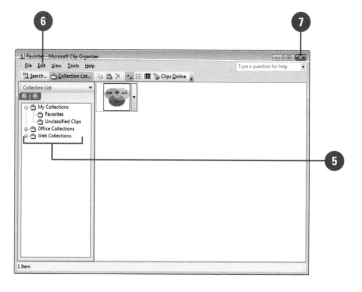

Did You Know?

The AutoImport dialog box doesn't automatically open on first run. When Clip Organizer runs for the first time, it no longer calls the AutoImport dialog box (**New!**). However, you can click the File menu, point to Add Clips to Organizer, and then click Automatically to run it.

Creating and Modifying Charts

9

Introduction

When you're ready to share data with others, a worksheet might not be the most effective way to present the information. A page full of numbers, even if attractively formatted, can be hard to understand and perhaps a little boring. Microsoft Office Excel makes it easy to create and modify charts so that you can effectively present your information. A **chart** is a visual representation of selected data in your worksheet. Whether you turn numbers into a bar, line, pie, surface, or bubble chart, patterns become more apparent. For example, the trend of annual rising profits becomes powerful in a line chart. A second line showing diminishing annual expenses creates an instant map of the success of a business.

A well-designed chart draws the reader's attention to important data by illustrating trends and highlighting significant relationships between numbers. Excel generates charts based on data and chart type you select. Excel makes it easy to select the best chart type, design elements, and formatting enhancements for any type of information.

Once you create a chart, you may want to change your chart type to see how your data displays in a different style. You can move and resize your chart, and even draw on your chart to highlight achievements. Other formatting elements are available to assure a well-designed chart.

Understanding Chart Terminology

Handles
Small white circles that appear
around the perimeter of a selected
object, indicating that you can
move, resize, copy, or delete the
object

Title
Optional text that
identifies the purpose
of a chart

Data Marker
A chart object, such as
a circle, dot, or square,
that denotes a data
point

Gridlines
Vertical and horizontal
guidelines that appear
behind a chart to make
the chart easier to read

Legend
A key that explains the
colors, patterns, or
symbols in a chart

Y-axis
The vertical axis of a
chart–default, a
value axis

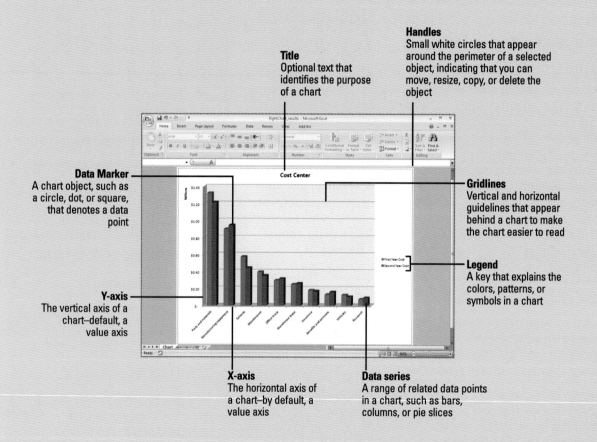

X-axis
The horizontal axis of
a chart–by default, a
value axis

Data series
A range of related data points
in a chart, such as bars,
columns, or pie slices

Choosing the Right Type of Chart

When you create a chart in Excel, you can choose from a variety of chart types. Each type interprets data in a slightly different way. For example, a pie chart is great for comparing parts of a whole, such as regional percentages of a sales total, while a column chart is better for showing how different sales regions performed throughout a year. Although there is some overlap, each chart type is best suited for conveying a different type of information.

When you generate a chart, you need to evaluate whether the chart type suits the data being plotted, and whether the formatting choices clarify or overshadow the information. Sometimes a colorful 3-D chart is just what you need to draw attention to an important shift; other times, special visual effects might be a distraction.

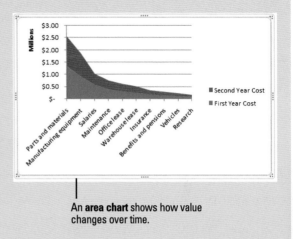

An **area chart** shows how value changes over time.

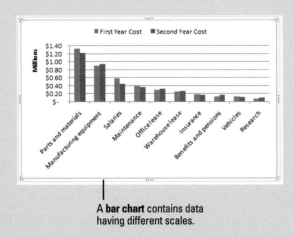

A **bar chart** contains data having different scales.

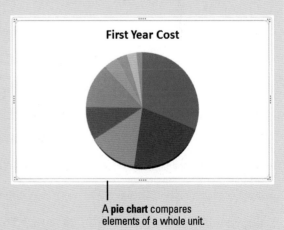

A **pie chart** compares elements of a whole unit.

Creating a Chart

Microsoft
Certified
Application
Specialist

EX07S-4.1.1, EX07S-4.1.2,
EX07S-4.2.2

A **chart** provides a visual, graphical representation of numerical data. Charts add visual interest and useful information represented by lines, bars, pie slices, or other markers. A group of data values from a worksheet row or column of data makes up a **data series**. Each data series has a unique color or pattern on the chart. Titles on the chart, horizontal (x-axis), and vertical (y-axis) identify the data. Gridlines are horizontal and vertical lines to help the reader determine data values in a chart. When you choose to place the chart on an existing sheet, rather than on a new sheet, the chart is called an **embedded object**. You can then resize or move it just as you would any graphic object.

Insert and Create a Chart

1. Select the data you want to use to create a chart.

2. Click the **Insert** tab.

3. Use one of the following methods:

   ◆ **Basic Chart Types**. Click a chart button (Column, Line, Pie, Bar, Area, Scatter, Other Charts) in the Charts group, and then click the chart type you want.

   ◆ **All Chart Types**. Click the **Charts Dialog Box Launcher**, click a category in the left pane, click a chart, and then click **OK**.

   A chart appears on the worksheet as an embedded chart.

Did You Know?

Embedded charts are beneficial. A chart sheet is beneficial when you want to view or print a chart or PivotChart report separately from worksheet data or a PivotTable report.

Charts Dialog Box Launcher

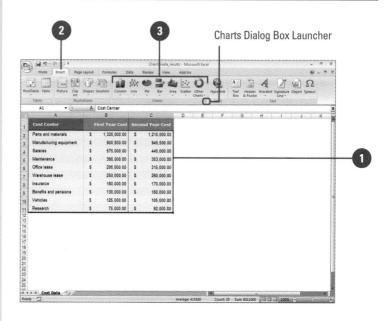

Select a Chart Category

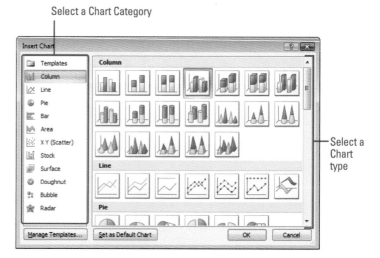

Select a Chart type

Move a Chart to Another Worksheet

1. Click the chart you want to modify.

2. Click the **Design** tab under Chart Tools.

3. Click the **Move Chart** button.

4. Use one of the following methods:

   ◆ To move the chart to a chart sheet, click the **New sheet** option, and then type a new name for the chart tab.

   ◆ To move the chart to another worksheet as an embedded object, click the **Object in** option, and then select the worksheet you want.

5. Click **OK**.

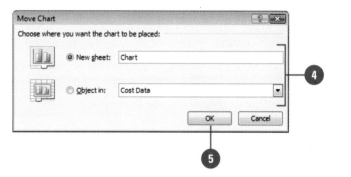

Did You Know?

You can quickly create a default chart. Select the data you want to use for the chart, and then press F11 to create a chart on a new sheet, or press Alt+F1 to create an embedded chart on the active worksheet.

You can set the default chart. In the Insert Chart dialog box, select the chart type and chart subtype you want to set as the default, and then click Set as Default Chart.

You can edit the contents of chart text. To edit the contents of a title, click the chart or axis title. To edit the contents of a data label, double-click the data label. Click to place the insertion, and then make changes.

Editing a Chart

Editing a chart means altering any of its features, from data selection to formatting elements. For example, you might want to use more effective colors or patterns in a data series. To change a chart's type or any element within it, you must select the chart or element. When a chart is selected, handles are displayed around the window's perimeter, and chart tools become available, the Design, Layout, and Format tabs. As the figure below illustrates, you can point to any object or area on a chart to see what it is called. When you select an object, its name appears in the Chart Objects list box on the Ribbon, and you can then edit it. A chart consists of the following elements.

◆ **Data markers**. A graphical representation of a data point in a single cell in the datasheet. Typical data markers include bars, dots, or pie slices. Related data markers constitute a data series.

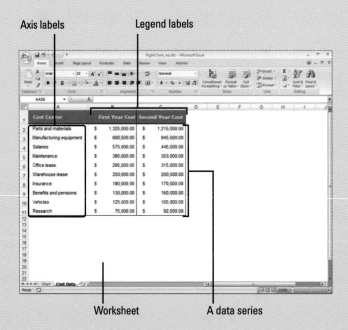

Axis labels   Legend labels

Worksheet   A data series

◆ **Legend**. A pattern or color that identifies each data series.

◆ **X-axis**. A reference line for the horizontal data values.

◆ **Y-axis**. A reference line for the vertical data values.

◆ **Tick marks**. Marks that identify data increments.

Editing a chart has no effect on the data used to create it. You don't need to worry about updating a chart if you change worksheet data because Excel automatically does it for you. The only chart element you might need to edit is a data range. If you decide you want to plot more or less data in a range, you can select the data series on the worksheet, as shown in the figure below, and then drag the outline to include the range you want in the chart.

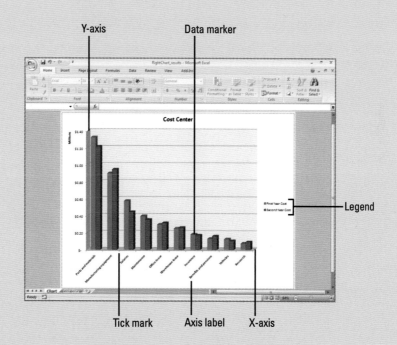

Moving and Resizing a Chart

You can move or resize an embedded chart after you select it. If you've created a chart as a new sheet instead of an embedded object on an existing worksheet, the chart's size and location are fixed by the sheet's margins. You can change the margins to resize or reposition the chart. If you don't like the location, you can move the embedded chart off the original worksheet and onto another worksheet. When resizing a chart downward, be sure to watch out for legends and axis titles.

Move an Embedded Chart

1. Select a chart you want to move.

2. Position the mouse pointer over a blank area of the chart, and then drag the pointer to move the outline of the chart to a new location.

3. Release the mouse button.

Resize an Embedded Chart

1. Select a chart you want to resize.

2. Position the mouse pointer over one of the handles.

3. Drag the handle to the new chart size.

4. Release the mouse button.

See Also

See "Modifying Picture Size" on page 198 for information on how to size a chart using different methods.

Selecting Chart Elements

Chart elements are the individual objects that make up a chart, such as an axis, the legend, or a data series. The **plot area** is the bordered area where the data are plotted. The **chart area** is the area between the plot area and the chart elements selection box. Before you can change or format a chart element, you need to select it first. You can select a chart element directly on the chart or use the Chart Elements list arrow on the Ribbon. When you select a chart, handles (small white circles) display around the window's perimeter, and chart tools become available on the Design, Layout, and Format tabs. When you select an element in a chart, the name of the object appears in the Chart Elements list, which indicates that you can now edit it.

Select a Chart Element

1. Select the chart you want to change.

2. Click the **Format** or **Layout** tab under Chart Tools.

3. Click the **Chart Elements** list arrow.

4. Click the chart element you want to select.

   When a chart object is selected, selection handles appear.

   TIMESAVER *To select a chart object, click a chart element directly in the chart.*

Did You Know?

You can enlarge a chart object to select it. Increase the zoom percentage to enlarge your view before using the mouse pointer to select chart objects.

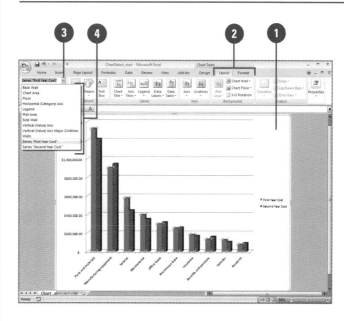

Changing a Chart Type

Microsoft
Certified
Application
Specialist

EX07S-4.2.3

Your chart is what your audience sees, so make sure to take advantage of Excel's pre-built chart layouts and styles (**New!**) to make the chart appealing and visually informative. Start by choosing the chart type that is best suited for presenting your data. There are a wide variety chart types, available in 2-D and 3-D formats, from which to choose. For each chart type, you can select a predefined chart layout and style to apply the formatting you want. If you want to format your chart beyond the provided formats, you can customize a chart. Save your customized settings so that you can apply that chart formatting to any chart you create. You can change the chart type for the entire chart, or you can change the chart type for a selected data series to create a combination chart.

Change a Chart Type for an Entire Chart

1. Select the chart you want to change.

2. Click the **Design** tab under Chart Tools.

3. Click the **Change Chart Type** button.

4. Click the chart type you want.

5. Click **OK**.

Did You Know?

You can reset chart formatting. Click the chart you want to reset, click the Format tab under Chart Tools, and then click the Reset to Match Style button.

You can delete a chart. Click the chart object, and then press Delete.

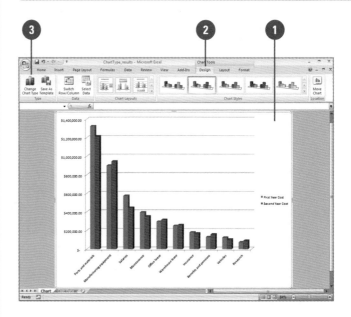

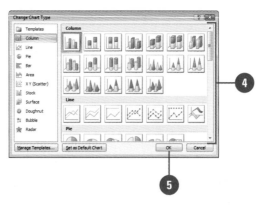

Change a Chart Type of a Single Data Series

1. Select the data series in a chart you want to change.

   You can only change the chart type of one data series at a time.

2. Click the **Design** tab under Chart Tools.

3. Click the **Change Chart Type** button.

4. Click the chart type you want.

5. Click **OK**.

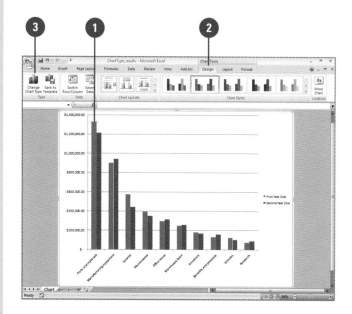

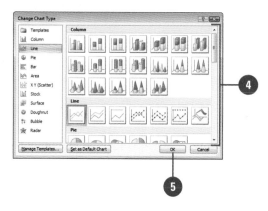

Changing a Chart Layout and Style

Microsoft
Certified
Application
Specialist

EX07S-4.1.3

Your chart is what your audience sees, so make sure to take advantage of Excel's pre-built chart layouts and styles (**New!**) to make the chart appealing and visually informative. Start by choosing the chart type that is best suited for presenting your data. There are a wide variety chart types, available in 2-D and 3-D formats, from which to choose. For each chart type, you can select a predefined chart layout and style to apply the formatting you want. If you want to format your chart beyond the provided formats, you can customize a chart. Save your customized settings so that you can apply that chart formatting to any chart you create.

Apply a Chart Layout

1. Select the chart you want to change.

2. Click the **Design** tab under Chart Tools.

3. Click the scroll up or down arrow, or click the **More** list arrow in the Chart Layouts group to see variations of the chart type.

4. Click the chart layout you want.

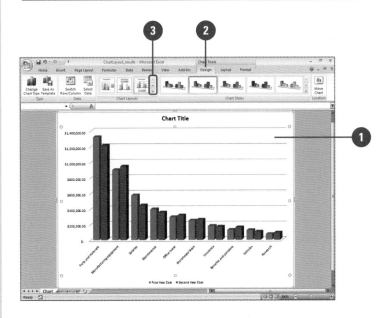

Apply a Chart Style

① Select the chart you want to change.

② Click the **Design** tab under Chart Tools.

③ Click the scroll up or down arrow, or click the **More** list arrow in the Chart Styles group to see color variations of the chart layout.

④ Click the chart style you want.

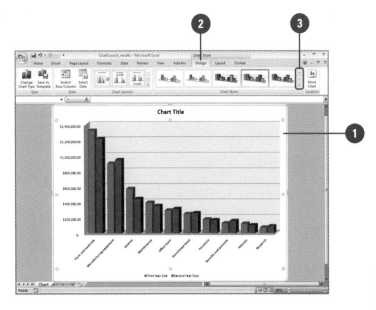

Formatting Chart Elements

Before you can format a chart element, you need to select it first. You can select a chart element directly on the chart or use the Chart Elements list arrow on the Ribbon. After you select a chart element, you can use the Format Selection button to open the Format dialog box, where you can change formatting options, including number, fill, border color and styles, shadow, 3-D format, and alignment. Formatting options vary depending on the selected chart element. In the same way you can apply shape fills, outlines, and effects to a shape, you can also apply them to elements and shapes in a chart (**New!**).

Format a Chart Object

1. Select the chart element you want to modify.

2. Click the **Format** tab under Chart Tools.

3. Click the **Format Selection** button.

4. Select the options you want. The available options vary depending on the chart.

   Some common formatting option categories in the left pane include the following:

   ◆ **Number** to change number formats.

   ◆ **Fill** to remove or change the fill color, either solid, gradient, picture, or texture.

   ◆ **Border Color** or **Styles** to remove or change the border color and styles, either solid or gradient line.

   ◆ **Shadow** to change shadow options, including color, transparency, size, blur, angle, and distance.

   ◆ **3-D Format** to change 3-D format options, including bevel, depth, contour, and surface.

   ◆ **Alignment** to change text alignment, direction, and angle.

5. Click **Close**.

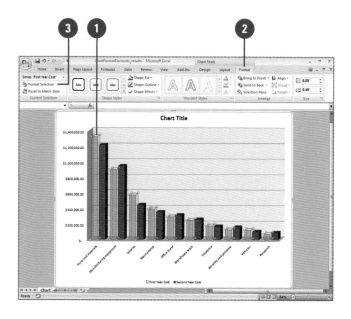

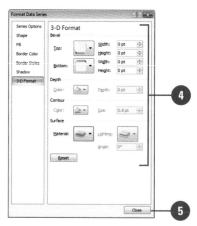

Apply a Shape Style to a Chart Object

1. Select the chart element you want to modify.

2. Click the **Format** tab under Chart Tools.

3. Click the **Shape Fill**, **Shape Outline**, or **Shape Effects** button, and then click or point to an option.

   ◆ **Fill.** Click a color, No Fill, or Picture to select an image, or point to Gradient, or Texture, and then select a style.

   ◆ **Outline.** Click a color or No Outline, or point to Weight, or Dashes, and then select a style.

   ◆ **Effects.** Point to an effect category (Preset, Shadow, Reflection, Glow, Soft Edges, Bevel, or 3-D Rotations), and then select an option.

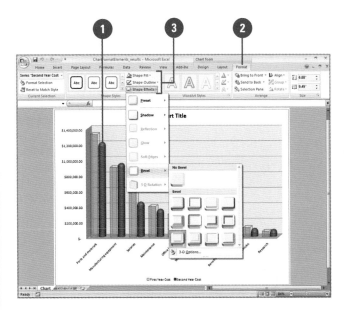

Changing Chart Gridlines and Axes

You can change the chart display by showing axis or gridlines with different measurements. An **axis** is a line bordering the chart plot area used as a reference for measurement. Chart axes are typically x (vertical or value), y (horizontal or category), and z (only for 3-D charts). If axis titles or scales are too long and unreadable, you might want to change the angle to make titles fit better in a small space, or change the interval between tick marks and axis labels to display with a better scale. **Tick marks** are small lines of measurement similar to divisions on a ruler on an axis. **Gridlines** are horizontal and vertical lines you can add to help the reader determine data point values in a chart. There are two types of gridlines: major and minor. Major gridlines occur at each value on an axis, while minor gridlines occur between values on an axis. Use gridlines sparingly and only when they improve the readability of a chart.

Change Chart Gridlines

 Select the chart element you want to modify.

 Click the **Layout** tab under Chart Tools.

 Click the **Gridlines** button, point to **Primary Horizontal Gridlines, Primary Vertical Gridlines**, or **Depth Gridlines** (3-D charts) and then click any of the following options:

- ◆ None
- ◆ Major Gridlines
- ◆ Minor Gridlines
- ◆ Major & Minor Gridlines

 To select custom chart gridlines options, click the **Gridlines** button, and then do one of the following:

- ◆ Point to **Primary Horizontal Gridlines**, and then click **More Primary Horizontal Gridlines Options**.

- ◆ Point to **Primary Vertical Gridlines**, and then click **More Primary Vertical Gridlines Options**.

- ◆ Point to **Depth Gridlines**, and then click **More Depth Gridlines Options**.

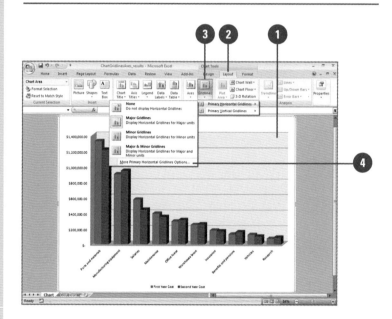

Change Chart Axes

1. Select the chart element you want to modify.

2. Click the **Layout** tab under Chart Tools.

3. Click the **Axes** button, point to **Primary Horizontal Axis**, and then click any of the following options:

   - None
   - Show Left to Right Axis
   - Show Axis without labeling
   - Show Right to Left Axis

4. Click the **Axes** button, point to **Primary Vertical Axis**, and then click any of the following options:

   - None
   - Show Default Axis
   - Show Axis in Thousands
   - Show Axis in Millions
   - Show Axis in Billions
   - Show Axis with Log Scale

5. Click the **Axes** button, point to **Depth Axis** (3-D charts), and then click any of the following options:

   - None
   - Show Default Axis
   - Show Axis without labeling
   - Show Reverse Axis

6. To select custom chart axes options, click the **Axes** button, and then do one of the following:

   - Point to **Primary Horizontal Axis**, and then click **More Primary Horizontal Axis Options**.

   - Point to **Primary Vertical Axis**, and then click **More Primary Vertical Axis Options**.

   - Point to **Depth Axis**, and then click **More Depth Axis Options**.

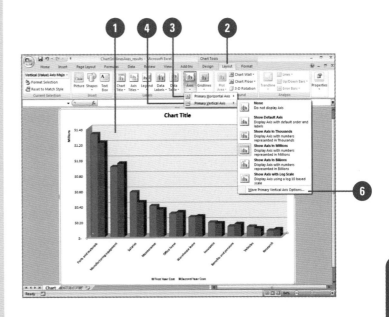

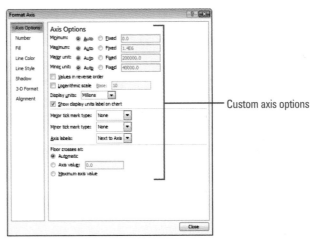

Custom axis options

Changing Chart Titles

Microsoft Certified Application Specialist

EX07S-4.2.1

The layout of a chart typically comes with a chart title, axis titles, and a legend. However, you can also include other elements, such as data labels, and a data table. You can show, hide, or change the positions of these elements to achieve the look you want. The chart title typically appears at the top of the chart. However, you can change the title position to appear as an overlap text object on top of the chart. When you position the chart title as an overlay, the chart is resized to the maximum allowable size. In the same way, you can also reposition horizontal and vertical axis titles to achieve the best fit in a chart. If you want a more custom look, you can set individual options using the Format dialog box.

Change Chart Title

1. Select the chart you want to modify.

2. Click the **Layout** tab under Chart Tools.

3. Click **Chart Titles** button, and then click one of the following:

   ◆ **None** to hide the chart title.

   ◆ **Centered Overlay Title** to insert a title on the chart without resizing it.

   ◆ **Above Chart** to position the chart title at the top of the chart and resize it.

   ◆ **More Title Options** to set custom chart title options.

4. Double-click the text box to place the insertion point, and then modify the text.

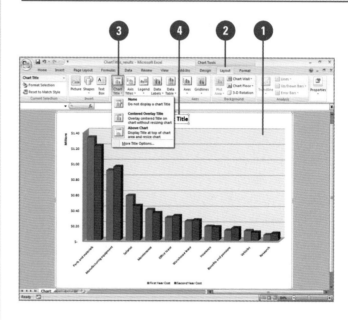

Did You Know?

You can link a chart or axis title to a worksheet cell. On the chart, click the chart or axis title you want to link, click in the formula bar, type equal sign (=), select the worksheet cell that contains the data or text you want to display in the chart, and then press Enter.

Change Chart Axis Titles

1. Select the chart you want to modify.

2. Click the **Layout** tab under Chart Tools.

3. Click the **Axis Titles** button, point to **Primary Horizontal Axis Title**, and then click any of the following options:

   ◆ **None** to hide the axis title.

   ◆ **Title Below Axis** to display the title below the axis.

4. Click the **Axis Titles** button, point to **Primary Vertical Axis Title**, and then click any of the following options (to show or hide):

   ◆ **None** to hide the axis title.

   ◆ **Rotated Title** to display the axis title rotated.

   ◆ **Vertical Title** to display the axis title vertical.

   ◆ **Horizontal Title** to display the axis title horizontal.

5. To select custom chart axis titles options, click the **Axis Titles** button, and then do one of the following:

   ◆ Point to **Primary Horizontal Axis Title**, and then click **More Primary Horizontal Axis Title Options**.

   ◆ Point to **Primary Vertical Axis Title**, and then click **More Primary Vertical Axis Title Options**.

6. To change title text, double-click the text box to place the insertion point, and then modify the text.

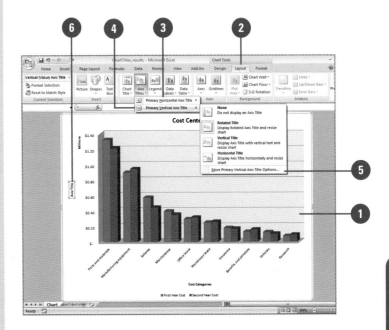

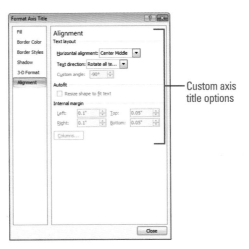

Custom axis title options

Changing Chart Labels

A **legend** is a set of text labels that helps the reader connect the colors and patterns in a chart with the data they represent. Legend text is derived from the data series plotted within a chart. You can rename an item within a legend by changing the text in the data series. If the legend chart location doesn't work with the chart type, you can reposition the legend at the right, left, top or bottom of the chart or overlay the legend on top of the chart on the right or left side. **Data labels** show data values in the chart to make it easier for the reader to see, while a Data table shows the data values in an associated table next to the chart. If you want a customized look, you can set individual options using the Format dialog box.

Change the Chart Legend

1. Select the chart you want to modify.

2. Click the **Layout** tab under Chart Tools.

3. Click the **Legend** button, and then click one of the following:

   ◆ **None** to hide the legend.

   ◆ **Show Legend at Right** to display and align the legend on the right.

   ◆ **Show Legend at Top** to display and align the legend at the top.

   ◆ **Show Legend at Left** to display and align the legend on the left.

   ◆ **Show Legend at Bottom** to display and align the legend at the bottom.

   ◆ **Overlay Legend at Right** to position the legend on the chart on the right.

   ◆ **Overlay Legend at Left** to position the legend on the chart on the left.

   ◆ **More Legend Options** to set custom legend options.

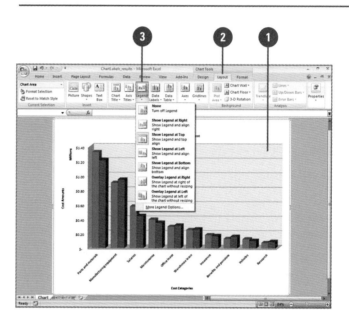

Change Chart Data Labels

1. Select the chart you want to modify.

2. Click the **Layout** tab under Chart Tools.

3. Click the **Data Labels** button, and then click one of the following:

   ◆ **None** to hide data labels.

   ◆ **Show** to display data labels centered on the data points.

   ◆ **More Data Label Options** to set custom data label options.

   The available options vary depending on the select chart.

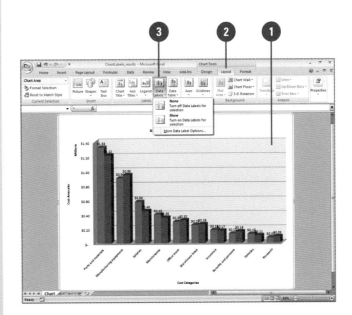

Show or Hide a Chart Data Table

1. Select the chart you want to modify.

2. Click the **Layout** tab under Chart Tools.

3. Click the **Data Table** button, and then click one of the following:

   ◆ **None** to hide a data table.

   ◆ **Show Data Table** to show the data table below the chart.

   ◆ **Show Data Table with Legend Keys** to show the data table below the chart with legend keys.

   ◆ **More Data Table Options** to set custom data table options.

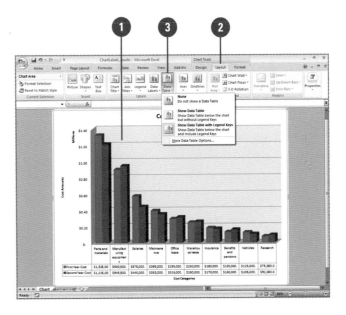

Pulling Out a Pie Slice

A pie chart is an effective and easily understood chart type for comparing parts that make up a whole entity, such as departmental percentages of a company budget. You can call attention to individual pie slices that are particularly significant by moving them away from the other pieces, or **exploding** the pie. Not only will this make a visual impact, it will also restate the values you are graphing.

Explode a Pie Slice

1. Select a pie chart.

2. To explode a single slice, double-click to select the pie slice you want to explode.

3. Drag the slice away from the pie.

4. Release the mouse button.

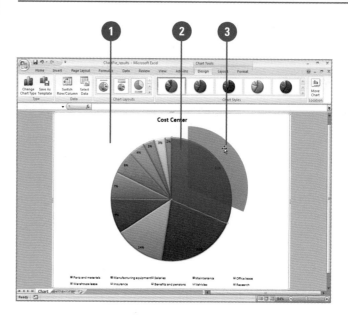

> ### Did You Know?
>
> *You can select a pie slice to make it stand out.* Because a pie chart has only one data series, clicking any slice selects the entire data series. Click a second time to select a specific slice.

Undo a Pie Explosion

1. Select a pie chart.

2. Drag a slice toward the center of the pie.

3. Release the mouse button.

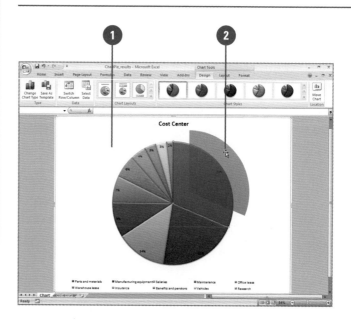

Formatting Chart Data Series

If you want to further enhance a chart, you can insert a picture in a chart so that its image occupies a bar or column. You can use the Format Selection button to open the Format dialog box and change Fill options to format a chart data series with a solid, gradient, picture, or texture fill. In addition, you can also change a chart data series with a border color, border style, shadow, and 3-D formats, which include bevel, depth, contour, and surface styles.

Format a Chart Data Series

1. Select the chart series you want to modify.

2. Click the **Format** tab under Chart Tools.

3. Click the **Format Selection** button.

4. Select the options you want:

   ◆ **Series Options** to change the gap width and depth (for 3-D charts), or series overlap (for 2-D charts).

   ◆ **Shape** to change the shape to a box, pyramid, cone, or cylinder (for 3-D charts).

   ◆ **Fill** to remove or change the fill, either solid color, gradient, picture, or texture.

   ◆ **Border Color** or **Styles** to remove or change the border color and styles, either solid or gradient line.

   ◆ **Shadow** to change shadow options, including color, transparency, size, blur, angle, and distance.

   ◆ **3-D Format** to change 3-D format options, including bevel, depth, contour, and surface.

5. Click **Close**.

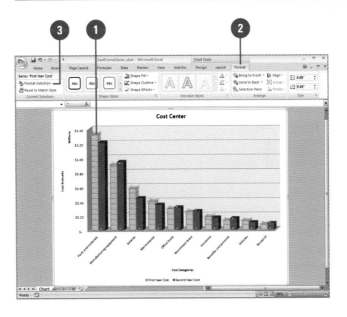

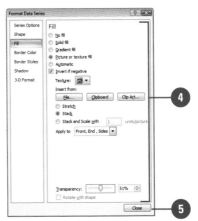

Formatting Chart Text

Objects such as chart and axis titles, data labels, and annotated text are referred to as chart text. To make chart text more readable, you can use formatting tools on the Home or Format tabs to change the text font, style, and size. For example, you might decide to change your chart title size and alignment, or change your axis text color. If you want to change the way text appears, you can also rotate text to a diagonal angle or vertical orientation. On the Format tab under Chart Tools, you can apply WordArt (New!) and Shape Styles (New!) to chart text.

Format Chart Text

1. Select the chart that contains the text you want to change.

2. Select the text object in the chart you want to format.

    If you want to select only a portion of the text, click the text object again to place the insertion point, and then select the part of the text you want to format.

3. Click the **Format** tab under Chart Tools, and then click the WordArt or Shape Style you want.

4. Click the **Home** tab.

5. In the Font group, select any combination of options: Font, Font Size, Increase Font Size, Decrease Font Size, Bold, Italic, Underline, Fill Color, or Font Color.

6. In the Alignment group, select any combination of alignment options.

    TIMESAVER *To quickly format chart text, right-click the text, and then click a formatting button on the Mini-Toolbar.*

7. To set custom text formatting options, click the **Font** or **Alignment Dialog Box Launcher**.

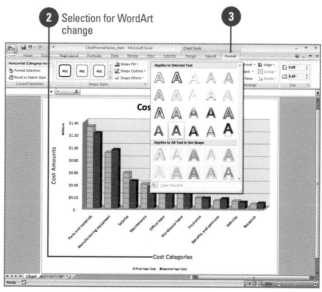

Selection for axis label change

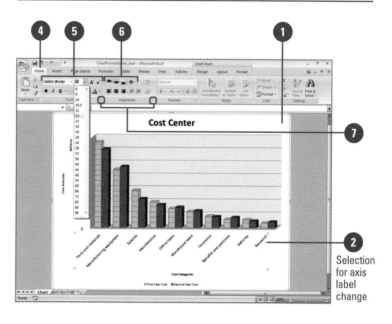

Selection for WordArt change

280

Formatting Line and Bar Charts

If you're using a line or bar chart, you can add trendlines, series lines, drop lines, high-low lines, up/down bars, or error bars with different options to make the chart easier to read. **Trendlines** are graphical representations of trends in data that you can use to analyze problems of prediction. For example, you can add a trendline to forecast a trend toward rising revenue. **Series lines** connect data series in 2-D stacked bar and column charts. **Drop lines** extend a data point to a category in a line or area chart, which makes it easy to see where data markers begin and end. **High-low lines** display the highest to the lowest value in each category in 2-D charts. Stock charts are examples of high-low lines and up/down bars. **Error bars** show potential error amounts graphically relative to each data marker in a data series. Error bars are usually used in statistical or scientific data.

Format Line and Bar Charts

1 Select the line or bar chart you want to modify.

2 Click the **Layout** tab under Chart Tools.

3 In the Analysis group, click any of the following:

◆ **Trendline** to remove or add different types of trendlines: Linear, Exponential, Linear Forecast, and Two Period Moving Average.

◆ **Lines** to hide Drop Lines, High-Low Lines or Series Lines, or show series lines on a 2-D stacked Bar/Column Pie or Pie or Bar of Pie chart.

◆ **Up/Down Bars** to hide Up/Down Bars, or show Up/Down Bars on a line chart.

◆ **Error Bars** to hide error bars or show error bars with using Standard Error, Percentage, or Standard Deviation.

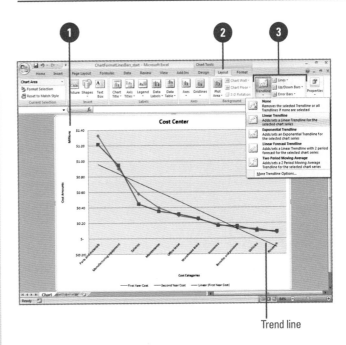

Trend line

Changing the Chart Background

Format the background of a chart by showing or hiding the chart wall or floor with a default color fill, or by changing the 3-D view of a chart. The **plot area** is bounded by the axes, which includes all data series. The **chart wall** is the background, and the **chart floor** is the bottom in a 3-D chart. The 3-D view allows you to change the rotation of a 3-D chart using the x-, y-, or z-axis, and apply a 3-D perspective to the chart.

Change the Chart Background

1. Select the chart element you want to modify.

2. Click the **Layout** tab under Chart Tools.

3. Click any of the following buttons:

   ◆ **Plot Area** to show or hide the plot area.

   ◆ **Chart Wall** to show or hide the chart wall with the default color fill.

   ◆ **Chart Floor** to show or hide the chart floor with the default color fill.

   ◆ **3-D Rotation** to change the 3-D viewpoint of the chart.

   In the Format Chart Area dialog box, click 3-D Rotation or 3-D Format in the left pane, select the 3-D options you want, and then click Close.

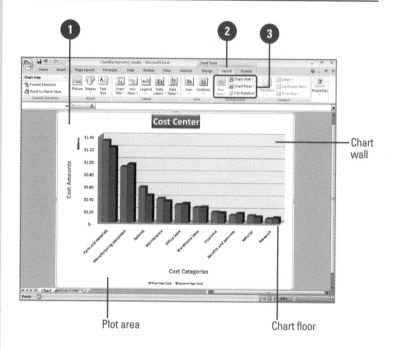

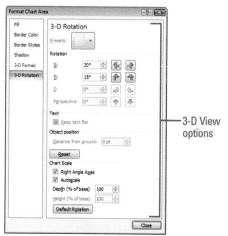

Enhancing a Chart

If you want to further enhance a chart, you can insert a picture, shape or text annotation to add visual appeal. In the same way you insert a picture, shape, or text box into a worksheet, you can insert them into a chart. The Picture, Shapes, and Text Box button are available on the Layout tab under Chart Tools.

Insert a Picture, Shape, or Text

1 Select the chart element you want to modify.

2 Click the **Layout** tab under Chart Tools.

3 Use any of the following:

- ◆ **Picture.** Click the Picture button, select a picture, and then click Insert.

- ◆ **Shapes.** Click the Shapes button, click a shape, and then drag to draw the shape.

- ◆ **Text Box.** Click the Text Box button, drag to create a text box, and then type the text you want.

4 Use the Format tab under Drawing Tools to format the shape or text box.

Did You Know?

You can edit shape text. Right-click the shape or text object, click Edit Text, modify the text, and then click outside the object to deselect it.

You can convert a chart to a picture. Select the chart, click the Home tab, click the Copy button, click the Paste button arrow, point to As Picture, and then click Paste as Picture. Instead of using Paste as Picture, you can use Paste Special to paste a chart as a picture with a specific graphic format, such as PNG, JPEG, GIF, Enhanced Metafile, or Bitmap.

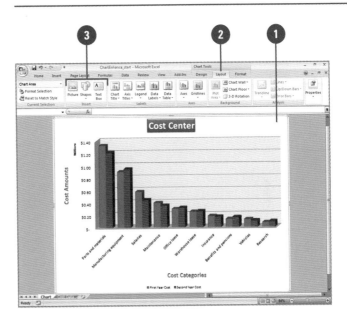

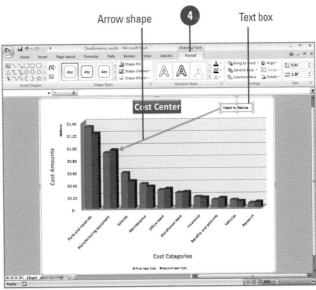

Editing Chart Data

You can edit chart data in an Excel worksheet one cell at a time, or you can manipulate a range of data. If you're not sure what data to change to get the results you want, use the Edit Data Source dialog box (**New!**) to help you. You can work with data ranges by series, either Legend or Horizontal. The Legend series is the data range displayed on the axis with the legend, while the Horizontal series is the data range displayed on the other axis. Use the Collapse Dialog button to temporarily minimize the dialog to select the data range you want. After you select your data, click the Expand Dialog button to return back to the dialog box.

Edit Data in the Worksheet

1. In the worksheet, use any of the following methods to edit cell contents:

   ◆ To replace the cell contents, click the cell, type the data you want to enter in the cell. It replaces the previous entry.

   ◆ To edit the cell content, double-click the selected cell where you want to edit.

   Press Delete or Backspace to delete one character at a time, and then type the new data.

2. Press Enter to move the insertion point down one row or press Tab to move the insertion point right to the next cell.

Did You Know?

You can plot data series from rows or columns. Select the chart, click the Design tab under Chart Tools, and then click the Switch Row/Column button. This switches between plotting the data series in a chart from worksheet rows or from columns.

Edit the Data Source

1 Click the chart you want to modify.

2 Click the **Design** tab.

3 Click the **Select Data** button on the Design tab under Chart Tools.

4 In the Select Data Source dialog box, use any of the following:

> **IMPORTANT** *Click the* ***Collapse Dialog*** *button to minimize the dialog, so you can select a range in the worksheet. Click the* ***Expand Dialog*** *button to maximize it again.*

◆ **Chart data range.** Displays the data range in the worksheet of the plotted chart.

◆ **Switch Row/Column.** Click to switch plotting the data series in the chart from rows or columns.

◆ **Add.** Click to add a new Legend data series to the chart.

◆ **Edit.** Click to make changes to a Legend or Horizontal series.

◆ **Remove.** Click to remove the selected Legend data series.

◆ **Move Up and Move Down.** Click to move a Legend data series up or down in the list.

◆ **Hidden and Empty Cells.** Click to plot hidden worksheet data in the chart and determine what to do with empty cells.

5 Click **OK**.

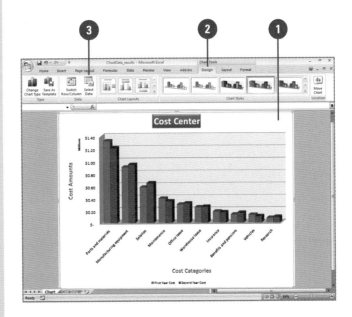

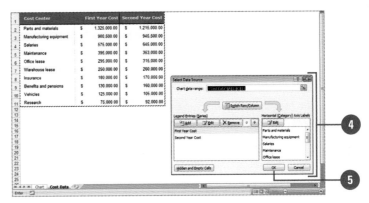

For Your Information

Displaying Hidden Data and Empty Cells in Charts

Hidden data in rows and columns of a worksheet is not displayed in a chart and empty cells are displayed as gaps. In the Select Data Source dialog box, you can click the Hidden and Empty Cells button to change the way Excel displays hidden data and empty cells in a chart. You can set options to show data in hidden rows and columns and show empty cells as a zero or connect data points with a line.

Adding and Deleting a Data Series

Many components make up a chart. Each range of data that comprises a bar, column, or pie slice is called a **data series**; each value in a data series is called a **data point**. The data series is defined when you select a range on a worksheet and then open the Chart Wizard. But what if you want to add a data series once a chart is complete? Using Excel, you can add a data series by using the Design tab under Chart Tools, or using the mouse. As you create and modify more charts, you might also find it necessary to delete or change the order of one or more data series. You can delete a data series without re-creating the chart.

Add a Data Series Quickly

1. Click the chart you want to modify.

2. Click the **Design** tab under Chart Tools, and then click the **Select Data** button.

3. Click **Add**.

4. Enter a data series name, and then specify the data series range, and then click **OK**.

5. Click **OK**.

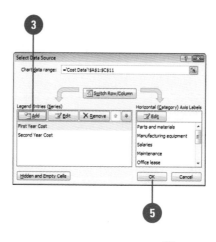

Delete a Data Series

1. Click the chart you want to modify.

2. Click the **Design** tab under Chart Tools, and then click the **Select Data** button.

3. Click the data series you want to delete.

4. Click **Remove**.

5. Click **OK**.

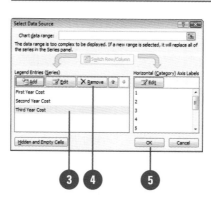

Change a Data Series

1. Click the chart you want to modify.

2. Click the **Design** tab under Chart Tools, and then click the **Select Data** button.

3. Click the series name you want to change.

4. Click **Edit**.

5. Click the **Collapse Dialog** button to change the series name or values, make the change, and then click the **Expand Dialog** button.

6. Click **OK**.

7. Click **OK**.

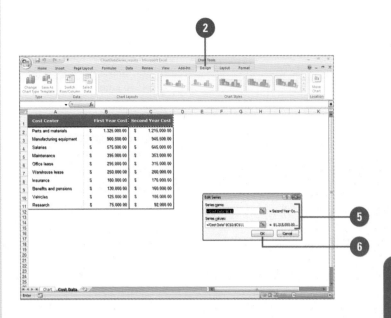

Change Data Series Order

1. Click the chart you want to modify.

2. Click the **Design** tab under Chart Tools, and then click the **Select Data** button.

3. Click the series name you want to change.

4. To switch data series position, click the **Switch Row/Column** button.

5. To reorder the data series, click the **Move Up** or **Move Down** button.

6. Click **OK**.

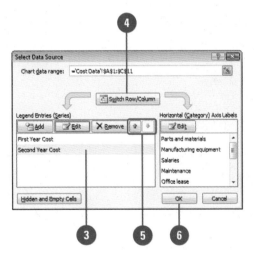

Saving a Chart Template

A chart template file (.crtx) (**New!**) saves all the customization you made to a chart for use in other workbooks. You can save any chart in a workbook as a chart template file and use it to form the basis of your next workbook chart, which is useful for standard company financial reporting. Although you can store your template anywhere you want, you may find it handy to store it in the Templates/Charts folder that Excel and Microsoft Office uses to store its templates. If you store your design templates in the Templates/Charts folder, those templates appear as options when you insert or change a chart type using My Templates (**New!**). When you create a new chart or want to change the chart type of an existing chart, you can apply a chart template instead of re-creating it.

Create a Custom Chart Template

1. Click the chart you want to save as a template.

2. Click the **Design** tab under Chart Tools.

3. Click the **Save As Template** button.

4. Make sure the Charts folder appears in the Save in box.

    Microsoft Office templates are typically stored in the following location:

    Windows Vista. C:/Users/*your name*/AppData/Microsoft /Roaming/Templates/Charts

    Windows XP. C:/Documents and Settings/*your name*/Application Data/Microsoft/Templates/Charts

5. Type a name for the chart template.

6. Click **Save**.

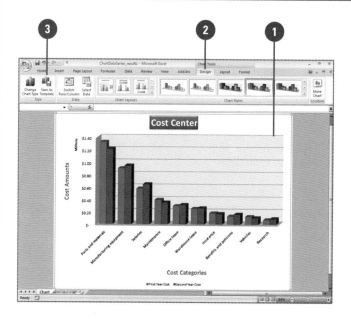

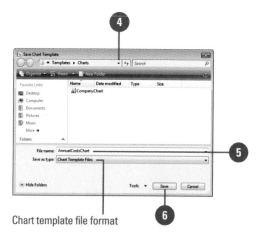

Chart template file format

Apply a Chart Template

1 Use one of the following methods:

◆ **New chart.** Click the **Insert** tab, and then click the **Charts Dialog Box Launcher**.

◆ **Change chart.** Select the chart you want to change, click the **Design** tab under Chart Tools, and then click the **Change Chart Type** button.

2 In the left pane, click **Templates**.

3 Click the custom chart type you want.

4 Click **OK**.

> ### Did You Know?
>
> ***You can set a chart as the default.*** If you use the same chart template over and over again, you can set a chart as the default when creating a new chart. In the Chart Type dialog box, click Template in the left pane, select the chart you want to use, click Set as Default Chart, and then click Cancel.

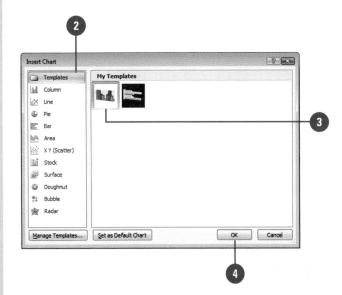

Managing Chart Templates

If you no longer need a chart template, you can use the Chart Type dialog box to access and manage chart templates files (.crtx). You can click the Manage Templates button to open the Charts folder and move, copy, or delete chart templates. Microsoft Office stores chart template files in the Charts folder, so all Office programs can use them. When you store templates in the Charts folder, those templates appear as options when you insert or change a chart type using My Templates. So, if you no longer need a chart template, you can move it from the Charts template folder for later use or you can permanently delete it from your computer.

Move or Delete a Custom Chart Template

1. Select a chart.

2. Click the **Design** tab under Chart Tools.

3. Click the **Change Chart Type** button.

   TIMESAVER *To open the Chart Types dialog box, you can click the Charts Dialog Box Launcher on the Insert tab.*

4. Click **Manage Templates**.

   The Charts folder opens.

   Windows Vista. C:/Users/*your name*/AppData/Microsoft /Roaming/Templates/Charts

   Windows XP. C:/Documents and Settings/*your name*/Application Data/Microsoft/Templates/Charts

5. To move a chart template file from the Charts folder, drag it to the folder where you want to store it, or right-click the file and use the Cut and Paste commands.

6. To delete a chart template file, right-click it, and then click **Delete**.

7. When you're done, click the **Close** button.

8. Click **Cancel** in the Chart Type dialog box.

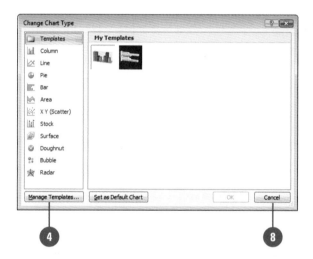

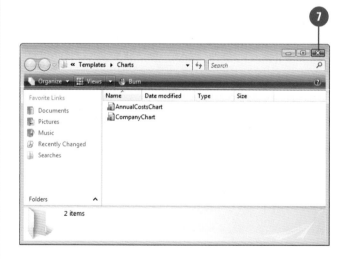

Analyzing Worksheet Data

10

Introduction

In addition to using a worksheet to calculate values, you can also use it to manage and analyze a table of information. For example, you can create an inventory list, a school grade book, or a customer database. You can quickly turn a range of cells into a table (previously referred to as an Excel list), and then format the data using Quick Styles. Additionally, you can insert and delete rows and columns, create a calculation column, display and calculate data totals, and reference a table by name instead of by cells.

Controlling how data is entered decreases errors and makes a worksheet more reliable. Data entry in a table is enhanced by features such as a pick list to ensure restricted field entry, and adding data validation rules which will restrict the entry of data into certain fields. You can also create a drop-down list of entries you define to help provide consistent, accurate data entry.

Sorting data in your list can be accomplished a few ways: one with the sort ascending or descending buttons, the other by using Excel's AutoFilter option. By typing in a set field to sort by, you can pull all the records in your list that contain a matching field. PivotTables are also available to pull your data together for easier viewing and reporting. Excel has some designed reports that contain layout formatting to give that extra touch to your reports.

If you have access to a Microsoft Office SharePoint Services site, you can export table data to a SharePoint list, so others can view, edit, and update it.

What You'll Do

Understand Tables

Create and Format a Table

Create or Modify a Table Style

Format Table Elements

Create Calculations in a Table

Work with Tables

Remove Table Rows and Columns

Enter Data in a Table Using a Drop-Down List

Sort Data in a Table

Display Parts of a Table with AutoFilter

Create Custom Searches

Analyze Data Using a PivotTable

Update a PivotTable and PivotChart

Modify a PivotTable and PivotChart

Chart a PivotTable

Create Groups and Outlines

Convert Text to Columns

Add Data Validation to a Worksheet

Export a Table to a SharePoint List

Understanding Tables

A **table** is a series of rows and columns with data you manage separately from other data in a worksheet. Examples of tables are an address book, a list of customers or products, and a telephone directory. In Excel 2007, you can turn a range of cells into a table (previously referred to as an Excel list) to make it easier to manage and analyze a group of data (New!). You can create more than one table in the same worksheet. However, you cannot create a table in a shared workbook.

When you create a table, Excel adds filtering in the header row where you can sort data by order or color, and filter data by criteria. After you create a table, you can easily format table data using Quick Styles. Additionally, you can insert and delete table rows and columns, create a calculation column, display and calculate data totals, reference the table by name instead of by cells, use built-in data validation to ensure data integrity, and export a table to a SharePoint list.

Record
One set of related fields, such as all the fields pertaining to one customer or product. In a worksheet, each row represents a unique record.

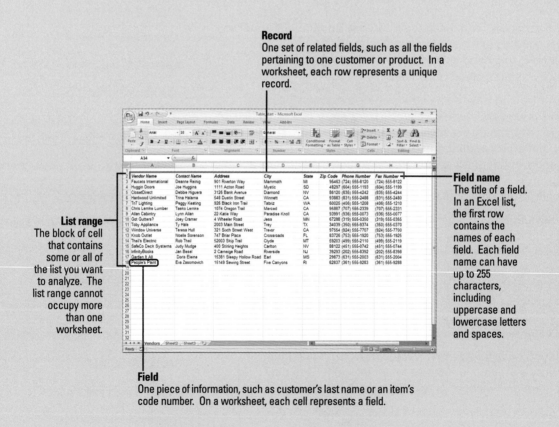

List range
The block of cell that contains some or all of the list you want to analyze. The list range cannot occupy more than one worksheet.

Field name
The title of a field. In an Excel list, the first row contains the names of each field. Each field name can have up to 255 characters, including uppercase and lowercase letters and spaces.

Field
One piece of information, such as customer's last name or an item's code number. On a worksheet, each cell represents a field.

Creating a Table

To create a table in Excel, you can enter data on worksheet cells, just as you do on any other worksheet data, but the placement of the field names and range must follow these rules: (1) Enter field names in a single row that is the first row in the list (2) Enter each record in a single row (3) Do not include any blank rows within the range (4) Do not use more than one worksheet for a single range. You can enter data directly in the table. Don't worry about entering records in any particular order; Excel tools can organize an existing list alphabetically, by date, or in almost any order you can imagine.

Create a Table

1. Open a blank worksheet, or use a worksheet that has enough empty columns and rows for your table.

2. Enter a label for each field in adjacent columns across the first row of the table.

3. Enter field information for each record in its own row; start with the row directly below the field names.

4. Select the range of cells for the table, including labels.

5. Do any of the following (**New!**):

   ◆ Click the **Insert** tab, and then click the **Table** button.

   ◆ Click the **Home** tab, click the **Format as Table** button, and then select a table style.

6. If necessary, adjust the table size, and select the **My table has headers** check box.

7. Click **OK**.

Did You Know?

You can delete or clear a data table. Select the table, and then press Delete to delete the entire table. Select the table, click the Home tab, click the Clear button, and then click Clear Contents.

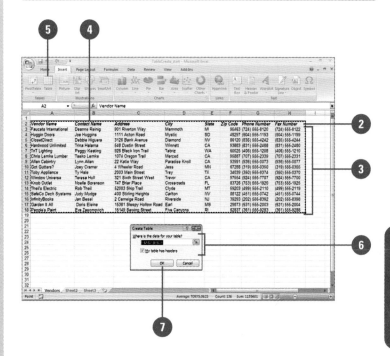

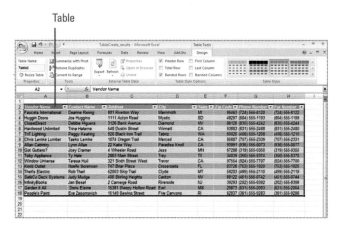

Table

Formatting a Table

Microsoft
Certified
Application
Specialist

EX07S-2.4.1

Formatting worksheet table data can be quick and easy with Table Quick Styles (New!). To make formatting data more efficient, Excel has a gallery of table styles based on the current theme. A table style includes preset combinations of fill colors and patterns, font attributes, borders, and font colors that are professionally designed to enhance your worksheets. You can apply a Table Quick Style using the Home or Design tab under Table Tools.

Apply a Quick Style to a Table

1. Select a cell or range in the table to which you want to apply a Quick Style.

2. Do any of the following:

   ◆ Click the **Design** tab under Table Tools, click the **More** arrow under Table Styles, and then select a table style.

   ◆ Click the **Home** tab, click the **Format as Table** button, and then select a table style.

Did You Know?

You can copy cell formats with Format Painter. Select the cell or range whose formatting you want to copy, double-click the Format Painter button on the Home tab, select the cells you want to format, and then click the Format Painter button.

You can remove or clear a table style. Click a cell in the table, click the Design tab under Table Tools, click the More arrow under Table Styles, and then click Clear.

You can print an Excel table. Click a cell within the table, click the Office button, click Print, click the Table option, and then click OK.

Table styles

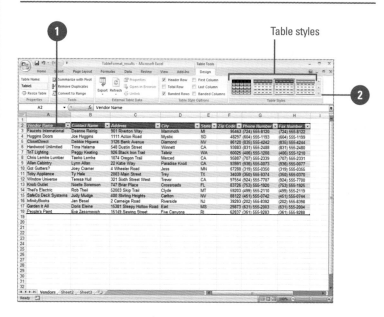

Table styles gallery

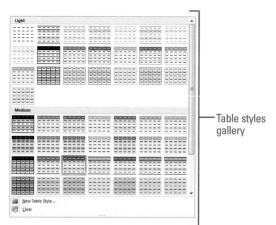

Creating or Modifying a Table Style

Excel Table Quick Styles give any worksheet a professional look, but you may need to modify a Quick Style to better suit the needs of a particular project. For example, the Quick Style you applied might be perfect except that the font or color used should be different—to match the rest of your report. You can modify an existing Table Quick Style or create a new one from scratch (**New!**). When you create or modify a Table Quick Style, you have the option to set the table style as the default when you create a new table.

Create or Modify a Table Style

1. Click the **Home** tab.

2. Click the **Format as Table** button.

3. Do any of the following:

   - **Create.** Click **New Table Style**.

   - **Modify.** Right-click the style you want to change, and then click **Modify**.

4. Type a name for the Quick Style.

5. Select a table element.

6. Click **Format**.

7. Use the Font, Border, and Fill tabs to set formatting options you want, and then click OK.

8. Repeat steps 5 through 7 to complete the formatting you want.

9. Select or clear the **Set as default table quick style for this document** check box.

10. When you're done, click **OK**.

> ### Did You Know?
>
> ***You can delete a custom table style.***
> Click the Home tab, click the Format as Table button, right-click the custom style you want to delete, and then click Delete.

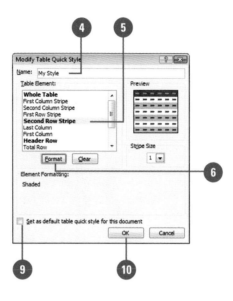

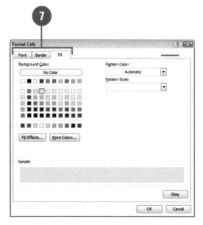

Formatting Table Elements

Microsoft Certified Application Specialist

EX07S-2.4.1

When you create a table in a worksheet, Excel displays a standard set of elements, including headings, columns, and rows. You can select options on the Design tab under Table Tools to quickly format a table (**New!**). These options allow you to format the header row, and first and last column as special. You can also format even columns or rows differently than odd columns or rows. If you want to total numbers in a column, you can format the bottom row of a table for column totals. If you no longer want these formatting elements, you can hide them. If you hide the header row, the table header AutoFilters and any applied filters are removed from the table.

Show or Hide Table Formatting Elements

1. Select a cell or range in the table you want to modify.

2. Click the **Design** tab under Table Tools.

3. Select or clear the check box for the element you want to show or hide:

   ◆ **Header Row** to format the top row of the table as special.

   ◆ **Totals Row** to format the bottom row of the table for column totals.

   ◆ **First Column** to format the first column of the table as special.

   ◆ **Last Column** to format the last column of the table as special.

   ◆ **Banded Column** to format even columns differently than odd columns.

   ◆ **Banded Rows** to format even rows differently than odd rows.

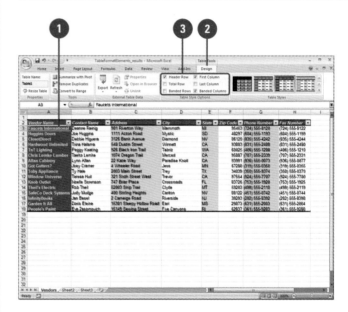

Creating Calculations in a Table

Microsoft Certified Application Specialist

EX07S-4.5.2

Total the Data in a Table

1 Click a cell in a table.

2 Click the **Design** tab under Table Tools.

3 Select the **Total Row** check box.

The total row appears as the last row in the table and displays the word *Total* in the leftmost cell.

4 Click the cell in the column for which you want to calculate a total, and then click the drop-down list arrow.

5 From the drop-down list, select the function you want to use to calculate the total.

TIMESAVER *Enter a formula in the row directly below a table without a total row to create a total row without the word Total.*

Did You Know?

You can create a calculated column. A calculated column uses a single formula that adjusts for each row in a table. To create a calculated column, click a cell in a blank table column, and then type a formula. The formula is automatically filled into all cells of the column. Not every cell in a calculated column needs to be the same. You can enter a different formula or data to create an exception.

You can quickly total data in a table using the Total Row option (**New!**). When you display a total row at the end of the table, a drop-down list appears for each total cell along with the word *Total* in the leftmost cell. The drop-down list allows you to select a function to perform a calculation. If the function you want is not available in the drop-down list, you can enter any formula you want in a total row cell. If you're not using a total function, you can delete the word *Total*.

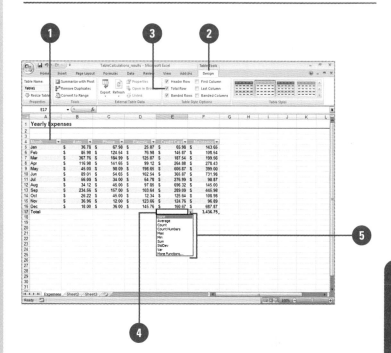

Working with Tables

EX07S-2.4.2,
EX07S-2.4.3

After you create a table, you can sort the entries, add new entries, and display totals. You can insert rows anywhere in a table or add rows at the bottom of the table. To add a blank row at the end of the table, select any cell in the last row of the table, and then press Enter, or press Tab in the last cell of the last row. If you no longer need the data in table form, you can convert the list back to normal Excel data. Selecting table rows and columns is different than selecting worksheet rows and columns. Selecting cells is the same.

Insert a Row or Column

1. Click a cell in the table where you want to insert a row or column. To insert multiple rows or columns, select more than one row or column.

2. Click the **Home** tab.

3. Click the **Insert** button arrow, and then do one of the following:

   ◆ **Rows**. Click **Insert Table Rows Above** or **Insert Table Rows Below**.

   ◆ **Columns**. Click **Insert Table Columns to the Left** or **Insert Table Columns to the Right**.

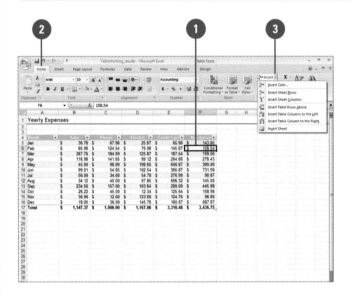

Select Rows and Columns

◆ **Column**. Click the top edge of the column header or the column in the table to select column data (press Ctrl+Spacebar). Double-click the top edge to select the entire column (press Ctrl+Spacebar twice).

◆ **Row**. Click the left border of the row.

◆ **Entire Table**. Click the upper-left corner of the table to select table data (press Ctrl+A). Double-click the upper-left corner to select the entire table (press Ctrl+A twice).

Selection cursor

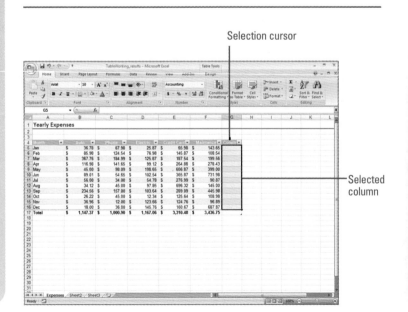

Selected column

Resize a Table

1. Click a cell in the table.

2. Click the **Design** tab under Table Tools.

3. Click the **Resize Table** button.

4. Type the range you want to use for the table.

   You can click the **Collapse Dialog** button, select the range you want, and then click the **Expand Dialog** button.

   TIMESAVER *To resize the table using the mouse, drag the triangular resize handle at the lower-right corner of the table to select the range you want.*

5. Click **OK**.

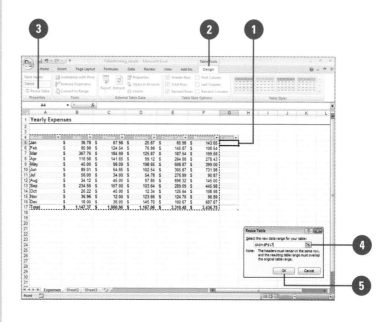

Convert a Table to a Range

1. Click a cell in the table.

2. Click the **Design** tab under Table Tools.

3. Click the **Convert to Range** button.

4. Click **Yes** to confirm the change.

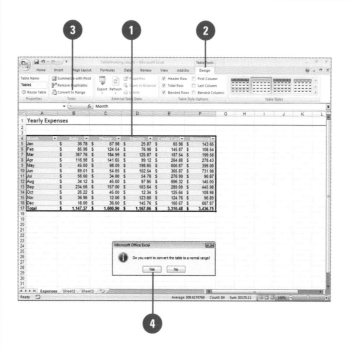

Removing Table Rows and Columns

Microsoft Certified Application Specialist

EX07S-1.2.2,
EX07S-2.4.3

If you no longer need a row or column in a table, you can quickly remove it using Delete commands on the Home tab. You delete rows and columns in a table the same way you delete rows and columns in a worksheet. As you enter data in a table, sometimes you accidentally enter the same data more than once. Instead of searching for duplicates manually, Excel can search for duplicates and then remove them for you.

Delete Rows or Columns from a Table

1. Click a cell in the table where you want to delete a row or column.

2. Click the **Home** tab.

3. Click the **Delete** button arrow, and then click **Delete Table Rows or Delete Table Columns**.

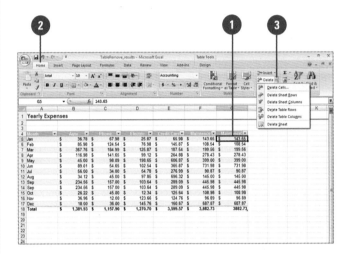

Remove Duplicate Rows from a Table

1. Click a cell in the table.

2. Click the **Design** tab under Table Tools.

3. Click the **Remove Duplicates** button.

4. Select the columns with duplicates you want to remove. You can click **Select All** or **Unselect All**.

5. Click **OK**.

6. Click **OK** to remove duplicates.

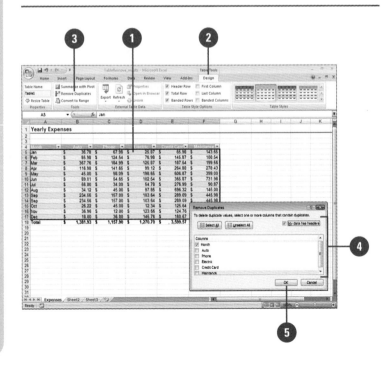

Entering Data in a Table Using a Drop-Down List

Entering data in a list can be tedious and repetitive. You can enter data using the PickList or List AutoFill feature to make the job easier. **PickList** is activated once you have entered at least one record in the list; it uses your previous entries to save you the trouble of typing repetitive information. PickList displays previous entries made in the current field in a list format. **List AutoFill** automatically extends the list's formatting and formulas to adjacent cells. As data is added to a list, AutoFill looks at the preceding cells to determine what formatting and formulas should be extended.

Enter Data in a List Using Pick From Drop-Down List

1. Right-click the cell in which you want to use PickList, and then click **Pick From Drop-Down List**.

2. Click a selection in the list.

3. Press Enter or Tab to accept the entry, or press Esc to cancel the entry.

See Also

See "Creating a Drop-Down List" on page 315 for information on creating a drop-down list using data validation.

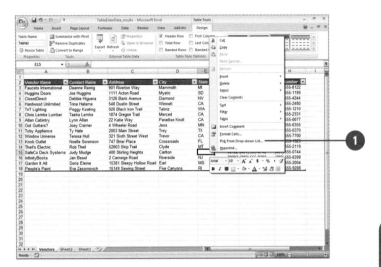

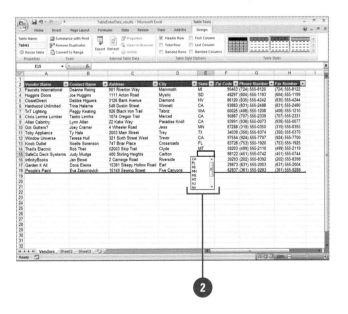

Sorting Data in a Table

Microsoft Certified Application Specialist

EX07S-4.6.1, EX07S-4.6.3, EX07S-4.6.4

After you enter records in a list, you can reorganize the information by sorting the records. For example, you might want to sort records in a client list alphabetically by last name or numerically by their last invoice date. **Ascending order** lists records from A to Z, earliest to latest, or lowest to highest. **Descending order** lists records from Z to A, latest to earliest, or highest to lowest. You can sort the entire list or use AutoFilter to select the part of the list you want to display in the column. You can also sort a list based on one or more **sort fields**—fields you select to sort the list. A sort, for example, might be the telephone directory numerically by area code and then alphabetically by last name. If you have manually or conditionally formatted a range or table column by cell or font color or by an icon set (**New!**), you can sort by these cell attributes using the Sort button.

Sort Data Quickly

1. Click the table cell with the field name by which you want to sort.

2. Click the **Data** tab.

3. Click the **Sort Ascending** or the **Sort Descending** button.

   The list arrow displays an icon indicating the field is sorted.

4. To clear or reapply a data sort, do the following:

   ◆ To clear all filters in a worksheet and redisplay all rows, click the **Clear** button.

   ◆ To reapply a filter, click the **Reapply** button.

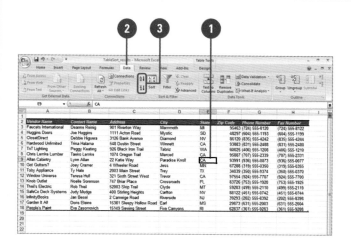

Did You Know?

You can sort data in rows. If the data you want to sort is listed across a row instead of down a column, click the table cell you want to sort by, click the Data tab, click the Sort button, click the Sort left to right option, and then click OK.

Sort a Table Using Multiple Fields and Attributes

1. Click anywhere within the table range.

2. Click the **Data** tab.

3. Click the **Sort** button.

4. Click the **Column** list arrow, and then select a sort field.

5. Click the **Sort on** list arrow, and then select a sort field (**New!**): **Values**, **Cell Color**, **Font Color**, or **Cell Icon**.

6. Click the **Order list** list arrow, and then select a sort field: **A to Z**, **Z to A**, or **Custom List**.

7. To add another level of sorting, click **Add Level**, and then repeat steps 4 through 6.

8. To change the sort order, select a sort, and then click the **Move Up** or **Move Down** buttons.

9. To delete or copy a sort level, select a sort, and then click the **Delete Level** or **Copy Level**.

10. Click **OK**.

   The list arrow displays an icon indicating the field is sorted.

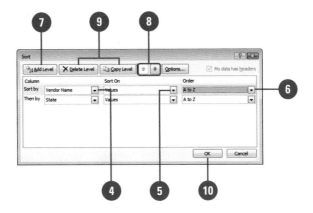

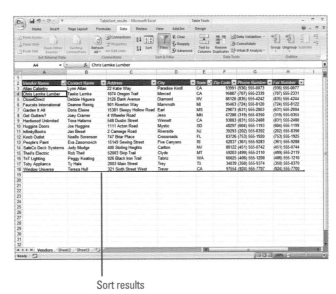

Sort results

Did You Know?

You can sort data with the case sensitive option. Click the table cell you want to sort by, click the Data tab, click the Sort button, click Options, and then select the Case sensitive check box, and then click OK.

Displaying Parts of a Table with AutoFilter

Working with a list that contains numerous records can be difficult—unless you can narrow your view of the list when necessary. For example, rather than looking through an entire inventory list, you might want to see records that come from one distributor. The **AutoFilter** feature creates a list of the items found in each field (**New!**), which is useful in PivotTables. You select the items that you want to display in the column (that is, the records that meet certain criteria). Then you can work with a limited number of records.

Display Specific Records Using AutoFilter

1. Click anywhere within the table range.

2. Click the **Data** tab.

3. If necessary, click the **Filter** button to highlight and turn it on.

4. Click the list arrow of the field for which you want to specify search criteria.

5. Select the item that records must match in order to be included in the table.

6. To use built-in filters, point to **<Column Name> Filters**, and then select a filter option, such as Equals, Begins With, or Contains.

7. Repeat steps 4 through 6, as necessary, to filter out more records using additional fields.

   The list arrow displays an icon indicating the field is filtered.

8. To clear a filter, click the list arrow of the field, and then click **Clear Filter From <Column Name>**.

   ◆ To clear all filters in a worksheet and redisplay all rows, click the **Clear** button.

   ◆ To reapply a filter, click the **Reapply** button.

9. To turn off AutoFilter, click the **Filter** button to deselect it.

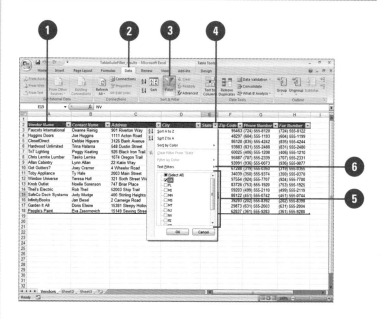

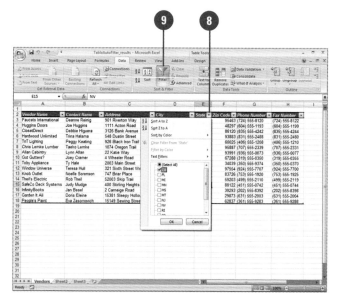

Creating Custom Searches

Microsoft Certified Application Specialist

EX07S-4.6.2

There are many times you'll want to search for records that meet multiple criteria. For example, you might want to see out-of-stock records of those orders purchased from a particular distributor. Using the AutoFilter feature and the Custom command, you can create complex searches. You can use **logical operators** to measure whether an item in a record qualifies as a match with the selected criteria. You can also use the **logical conditions** AND and OR to join multiple criteria within a single search. The result of any search is either true or false; if a field matches the criteria, the result is true. The OR condition requires that only one criterion be true in order for a record to qualify. The AND condition, on the other hand, requires that both criteria in the statement be true in order for the record to qualify.

Create a Custom Search Using AutoFilter

1. Click anywhere within the table range.

2. Click the **Data** tab.

3. Click the list arrow next to the first field you want to include in the search.

4. Point to **<type> Filter**, and then click **Custom Filter** to enable the command (a check mark appears).

5. Click the **Field** list arrow (on the left), and then select a logical operator.

6. Click the list arrow (on the right), and then select a field choice.

7. If you want, click the **And** or **Or** option.

8. If you want, click the list arrow (on the left), and then select a logical operator.

9. If you want, click the list arrow (on the right), and then select a field choice.

10. Click **OK**.

   The list arrow displays an icon indicating the field is filtered.

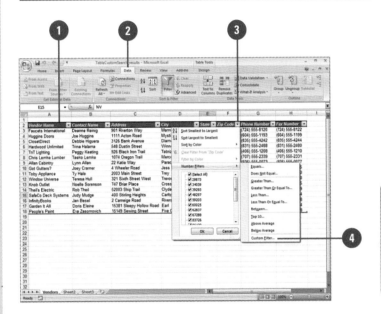

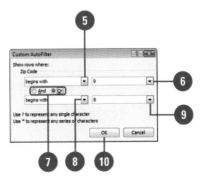

Analyzing Data Using a PivotTable or PivotChart

When you want to summarize information in a lengthy list using complex criteria, use the **PivotTable** to simplify your task. Without the PivotTable, you would have to manually count or create a formula to calculate which records met certain criteria, and then create a table to display that information. You can use the PivotTable layout to determine what fields and criteria you want to use to summarize the data and how you want the resulting table to look (**New!**). Sometimes a PivotTable is hard to read. To help you present PivotTable data, you can create a chart. A chart of a PivotTable is called a **PivotChart**.

Create a PivotTable or PivotChart Report

1. Click anywhere within the table range, or select a range of cells.

2. Click the **Insert** tab.

3. Click the **PivotTable** button arrow, and then click **PivotTable**, or **PivotChart**.

4. Click the **Select a table or range** option, or click the **Use an external data source** option, click **Choose Connection**, and then select a connection.

5. Click the **New worksheet** option or **Existing worksheet** option, and specify a cell range.

6. Click **OK**.

   The Options and Design tab under PivotTable Tools appears.

7. Select the check boxes next to the fields you want to use to add them to the empty PivotTable. As you create or modify a PivotTable, Excel updates the PivotChart.

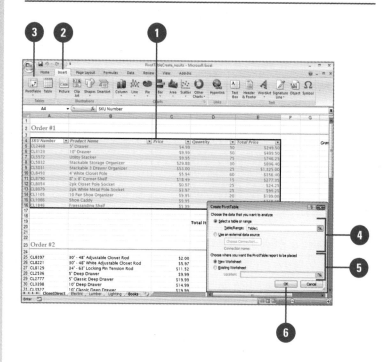

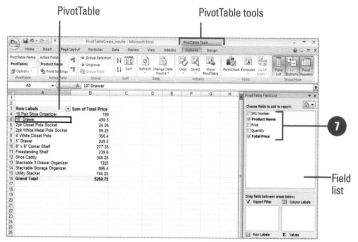

PivotTable

PivotTable tools

Field list

Did You Know?

You can delete a PivotTable. Click the PivotTable report, click the Options tab, click the Select button, click Entire PivotTable, and then press Delete.

Updating a PivotTable or PivotChart

You can quickly update a PivotTable report using the PivotTable Field List or the Options tab under PivotTable Tools (**New!**), which appears whenever a PivotTable is active. This saves you from having to recreate a PivotTable every time you add new data to a list. When you do want to add or remove data to and from a PivotTable or PivotChart, Excel makes it easy by allowing you to select or clear field check boxes.

Add or Remove a Field in a PivotTable or PivotChart Report

1 Click any field in the PivotTable report.

2 Select or clear the check boxes next to the fields you want to include or exclude from the PivotTable and PivotChart.

3 To change the position of a field, drag the field in the Field list to another one of the following boxes:

- **Values.** Use to display summary numeric data.

- **Row Labels.** Use to display fields as rows on the side of the report. Axis field in a PivotChart.

- **Column Labels.** Use to display fields as columns at the top of the report. Legend field in a PivotChart.

- **Report Filter.** Use to filter the entire report based on the selected item in the report filter.

TIMESAVER *Right-click a field in the Field list to access move and other related field commands.*

Each time you make a change in the PivotTable Field List, the report layout is automatically updated.

4 To enable manual layout updating, select the **Defer layout update** check box. Click **Update** to manually update the report layout.

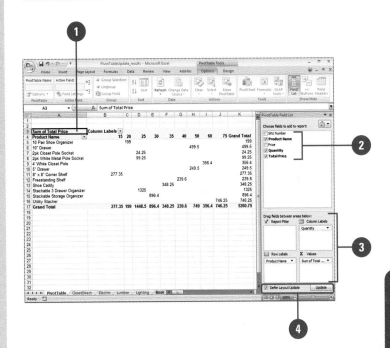

Modifying a PivotTable

You can use the Options tab (**New!**) under PivotTable Tools to modify a PivotTable to summarize, organize, and display the information you want to present. Many of the options—Group, Sort, Clear, Select, or Move—are similar to the ones available for Excel tables and charts. You can use the Options button to change PivotTable layout, format, totals, filter, display, printing and data settings. Use the Field Setting button to change field layout, print, subtotals, and filter settings.

Modify a PivotTable Report

① Click any field in the PivotTable report.

② Click the **Options** tab under PivotTable Tools.

③ To change PivotTable options, click the **Options** button, make the changes you want, and then click **OK**.

④ To change field settings, select the field you want to change, click the **Field Settings** button, make the changes you want, and then click **OK**.

⑤ Use any of the following options to change the PivotTable:

◆ **Group Selection, Ungroup,** or **Group Field.** Use to group, ungroup PivotTable elements or fields.

◆ **Sort.** Use to sort fields in a PivotTable.

◆ **Clear.** Use to clear filters, labels, values, and formatting.

◆ **Select.** Use to select PivotTable elements.

◆ **Formula.** Use to insert calculated fields and items, change solve order, and list formulas.

◆ **Field List.** Show or hide the Field List.

◆ **Buttons.** Show or hide group +/- buttons.

◆ **Field Headers.** Show or hide field headers for columns and rows.

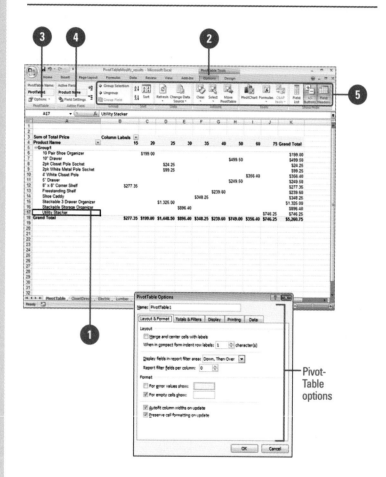

Pivot-Table options

Field Settings

Formatting a PivotTable

After you create a PivotTable, you can use formatting tools on the Design tab under PivotTable Tools to modify the look and feel of a PivotTable. Formatting a PivotTable can be quick and easy with PivotTable Quick Styles (**New!**). When you create a PivotTable, Excel displays a standard set of elements, including headings, columns, and rows. You can select or clear options on the Design tab to quickly format a PivotTable (**New!**) the way you want. Layout buttons, such as Subtotals, Grand Totals, Report Layout, and Blank Row, give you additional options to show or hide PivotTable elements.

Format a PivotTable Report

1. Click any field in the PivotTable report.

2. Click the **Design** tab under PivotTable Tools.

3. Click the **More** list arrow under PivotTable Styles, and then click the PivotTable style you want.

4. Select or clear the PivotTable format options you want to turn on or off:

   ◆ **Row Headers.**

   ◆ **Column Headers.**

   ◆ **Banded Rows.**

   ◆ **Banded Columns.**

5. Click any of the following layout buttons to select options to show or hide PivotTable elements:

   ◆ **Subtotals.** Show or hide subtotals.

   ◆ **Grand Totals.** Turn on or off grand totals for columns or rows.

   ◆ **Report Layout.** Set to compact, outline, or tabular form.

   ◆ **Blank Row.** Insert or remove a blank line after each item.

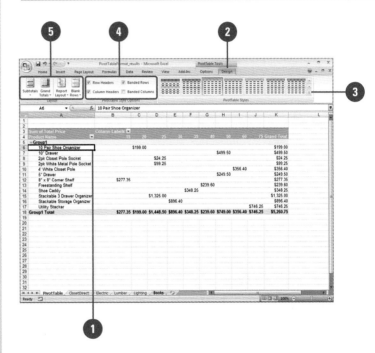

Charting a PivotTable

Data summarized in a PivotTable is an ideal candidate for a chart, since the table itself represents an overwhelming amount of data. A chart of a PivotTable is called a **PivotChart**. Once you select data within the PivotTable, you can chart it like any other worksheet data using similar tabs under PivotChart Tools (New!). The additional Analyze tab provides options to collapse or expand fields, refresh or clear data, and show or hide the Field List and PivotChart Filter Pane.

Create a PivotChart Report from a PivotTable Report

1. Click any data field in the PivotTable.

2. Click the **Options** tab under PivotTable Tools.

3. Click the **PivotChart** button.

4. Click the chart type you want.

5. Click **OK**.

   The PivotChart appears on the existing worksheet along with the PivotChart Filter Pane.

Did You Know?

You can delete a PivotChart. Click the PivotChart report, and then press Delete.

You can rename a PivotTable or PivotChart. Click the PivotTable report, click the Options tab, click the PivotTable Name box, type a new name and then press Enter. Click the PivotChart report, click the Layout tab, click the PivotChart Name box, type a new name and then press Enter.

You can rename a field in a PivotTable or PivotChart. Click the PivotTable report, click the Options tab, click the Active Field Name box, type a new name and then press Enter. Click the PivotChart report, click the Analyze tab, click the Active Field Name box, type a new name and then press Enter.

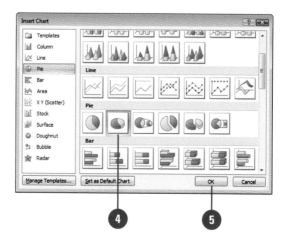

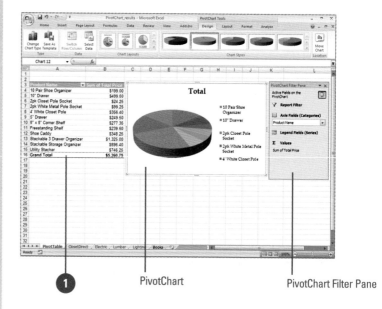

PivotChart

PivotChart Filter Pane

Modify a PivotChart Report

1. Click the PivotChart in the worksheet.

2. To filter fields, click the **Axis Fields (Categories)** or **Legends Fields (Series)** list arrow on the PivotTable Filter pane, and then select the filter options you want.

   Filters vary depending of field type.

3. Click the **Analyze** tab.

4. To modify the field display, select a field, and then click the **Expand Entire Field** or **Collapse Entire Field** button.

5. Use any of the tabs under PivotChart Tools to modify and format the PivotChart report:

   ◆ **Design.** Use to change chart styles, layouts, and type.

   ◆ **Layout.** Use to change chart labels, axes, and background.

   ◆ **Format.** Use to format chart elements using Shape and WordArt styles.

Did You Know?

You can select a different data source for a PivotTable. Click the PivotTable report, click the Options tab, click the Change Data Source button, click the Select a table or range option and specify a range, or click the Use an external data source option and specify a connection, and then click OK.

You can refresh PivotTable or PivotChart data. Click the PivotTable report, click the Options tab, and then click the Refresh button. Click the PivotChart report, click the Analyze tab, and then click the Refresh button.

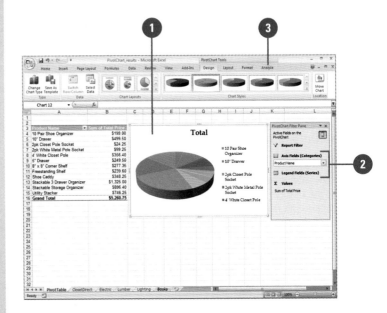

Creating Groups and Outlines

Microsoft Certified Application Specialist

EX07S-4.5.1

A sales report that displays daily, weekly, and monthly totals in a hierarchical format, such as an outline, helps your reader to sift through and interpret the pertinent information. In outline format, a single item can have several topics or levels of information within it. An outline in Excel indicates multiple layers of content by displaying a plus sign (+) on its left side. A minus sign (-) indicates that the item has no contents, is fully expanded, or both.

Create an Outline or Group

1. Organize data in a hierarchical fashion—place summary rows below detail rows and summary columns to the right of detail columns.

2. Select the data that you want to outline.

3. To create an outline, click the **Data** tab, click the **Group** button arrow, and then click **AutoOutline**.

4. To create a group, click the **Data** tab, click the **Group** button arrow, and then click **Group**. Click the **Rows** or **Columns** option, and then click **OK**.

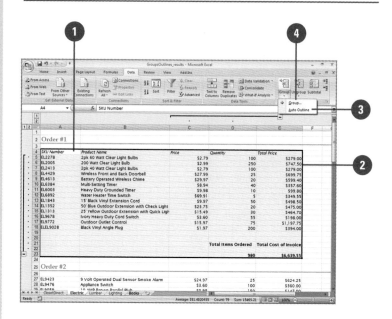

Work an Outline or Group

◆ Click a plus sign (+) to expand an outline level; click a minus sign (-) to collapse an outline level.

Did You Know?

You can ungroup outline data. Select the data group, click the Data tab, click the Ungroup button arrow, and then click Ungroup, click the Rows or Columns option, and then click OK.

You can clear an outline. Select the outline, click the Data tab, click the Group button arrow, and then click Clear Outline.

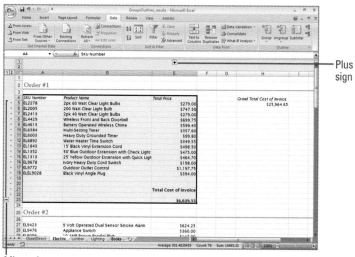

Plus sign

Minus sign

Converting Text to Columns

The Convert to Columns Wizard helps you separate simple cell contents into different columns. For example, if a cell contains first and last names, you can use the Convert to Columns Wizard to separate first and last name into different columns. The wizard uses the delimiter—such as a tab, semicolon, comma, space, or custom—to determine where to separate the cell contents into different columns; the wizard options vary depending on the delimiter type. For example, the cell contents *Julie, Kenney* uses the comma delimiter.

Convert Text to Columns

1. Select the range you want to covert to columns.

2. Click the **Data** tab.

3. Click the **Text to Columns** button.

4. In Step 1, click **Delimited**.

5. Click **Next**.

6. In Step 2, select the delimiter type you want to use, and then clear the other check boxes.

   The wizard options vary depending on the selected delimiter.

7. Click **Next**.

8. In Step 3, click a column in the Data preview box, and then click the **Text** option, and then repeat this for each column you want.

9. Click the **Collapse Dialog** button, select a new destination for the separated data, and then click the **Expand Dialog** button.

10. Click **Finish**.

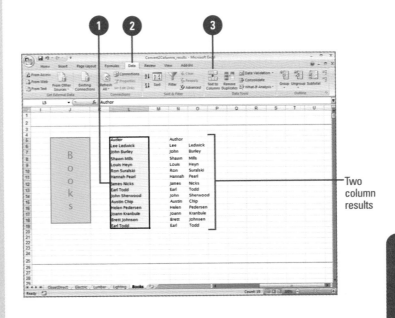

Two column results

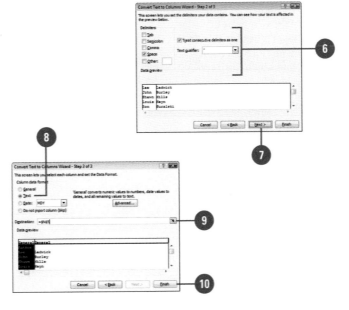

Adding Data Validation to a Worksheet

Microsoft
Certified
Application
Specialist

EX07S-1.2.1

Worksheet cells can be adjusted so that only certain values can be entered. Controlling how data is entered decreases errors and makes a worksheet more reliable. You might, for example, want it to be possible to enter only specific dates in a range of cells. You can use **logical operators** (such as equal to, not equal to, less than, or greater than) to set validation rules. When invalid entries are made, a message—developed and written by you—appears indicating that the entry is in violation of the validation rules. The rule set will not allow data to flow into the cell.

Create Validation Rules

1. Select the range you want covered in the validation rules.

2. Click the **Data** tab.

3. Click the **Data Validation** button.

4. Click the **Settings** tab.

5. Click the **Allow** list arrow, and then select a value type.

   Options vary depending on the Allow value type you select.

6. Click the **Data** list arrow, and then select a logical operator.

7. Enter values or use the **Collapse Dialog** button to select a range for the minimum and maximum criteria.

8. Click the **Input Message** tab, and then type a title and the input message that should be displayed when invalid entries are made.

9. Click the **Error Alert** tab, and then select an alert style, type a title, and error message.

10. Click **OK**.

11. To view invalid data, click the **Data Validation** button arrow, and then click **Circle Invalid Data**. To clear the circles, click the **Data Validation** button arrow, and then click **Clear Validation Circles**.

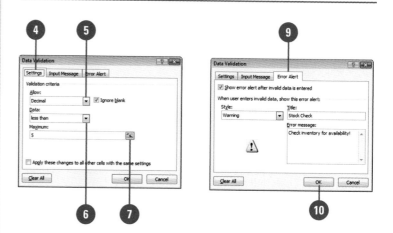

Validation circles

Creating a Drop-Down List

Microsoft
Certified
Application
Specialist   EX07S-1.2.1

Entering data in a table can be tedious and repetitive. To make the job easier, you can create a drop-down list of entries you define. This way you get consistent, accurate data. To create a drop-down list, create a list of valid entries in a single column or row without blanks, define a name, and then use the List option in the Data Validation dialog box. To enter data using a drop-down list, click the cell with the defined drop-down list, click the list arrow, and then click the entry you want.

Create a Drop-Down List

1. Type entries in a single column or row without blanks in the order you want.

2. Select the cell range, click the **Name** box, type a name, and then press Enter.

3. Select the cell where you want the drop-down list.

4. Click the **Data** tab.

5. Click the **Data Validation** button.

6. Click the **Settings** tab.

7. Click the **Allow** list arrow, and then click **List**.

8. Enter values or use the **Collapse Dialog** button to select a range of valid entries.

9. Click the **Input Message** tab, and then type a title and the input message that should be displayed when invalid entries are made.

10. Click the **Error Alert** tab, and then select an alert style, type a title, and error message.

11. Click **OK**.

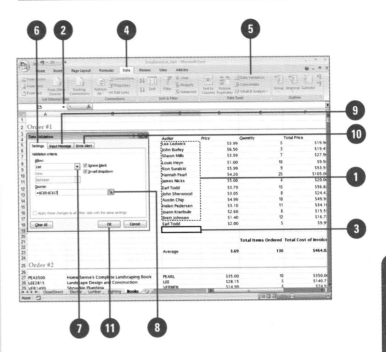

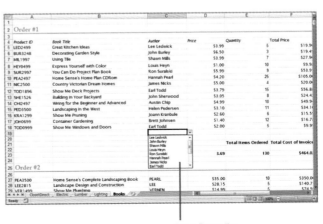

Drop-Down list

Exporting a Table to a SharePoint List

If you have access to a Microsoft Office SharePoint Services site, you can export table data to a SharePoint list (**New!**), for others to view, edit, and update. A SharePoint Services site is a server application that uses Web site templates to create, organize, and share information. To access a SharePoint Services site, you might need access privileges. See your network administrator for a user name and password. You can access a SharePoint Services site from Excel or a Web browser. When others make changes to the table in the SharePoint list, you can synchronize the changes to keep your Excel table up-to-date.

Export a Table to a SharePoint List

1. Select a cell in the table.

2. Click the **Design** tab under Table Tools.

3. Click the **Export** button, and then click **Export Table to SharePoint List**.

4. Enter a SharePoint address.

5. Type a name and description.

6. Click **Next**.

   If asked, enter a user name and password, and then click **OK**.

7. Click **Finish**.

8. Click **OK** to the alert.

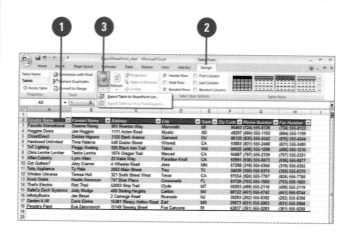

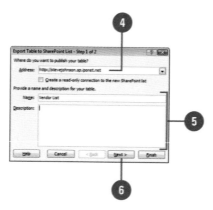

See Also

See "Working with a Shared Workspace" on page 479 for information on working with a SharePoint Services site from Excel.

Building More Powerful Worksheets

11

Introduction

Excel also includes a variety of add-ins—programs that provide added functionality—to increase your efficiency. Some of these supplemental programs—including Conditional Sum Wizard, Lookup Wizard, and Solver—are useful to almost anyone using Excel. Others, such as the Analysis ToolPak, add customized features, functions, or commands specific to use in financial, statistical, and other highly specialized fields. The purpose of each of these customization features is the same—to make Excel even easier to use and to enable you to accomplish more with less effort.

Before you can use an Excel or a third-party add-in, you need to load it first. When you load an add-in, the feature may also add a command to a Ribbon tab or toolbar. You can load one or more add-ins. If you no longer need an add-in, you should unload it to save memory and reduce the number of commands on a Ribbon tab. When you unload an add-in, you may also need to restart Excel to remove an add-in command from a Ribbon tab.

If your worksheet or workbook needs to go beyond simple calculations, Microsoft Office Excel offers several tools to help you create more specialized projects. With Excel, you can perform "what if" analysis using several different methods to get the results you want.

Use Data Analysis Tools

Create Conditional Sums

Look at Alternatives with Data Tables

Ask "What If" with Goal Seek

Create Scenarios

Use Solver

Use Lookup and Reference Functions

Use Text Functions

Summarize Data Using Subtotals

Summarize Data Using Functions

Determine Specific Dates

Using Data Analysis Tools

Excel provides a collection of statistical functions and macros to analyze data in the **Analysis ToolPak**. The Analysis Toolpak is an add-in program, which may need to be loaded using the Add-In pane in Excel Options. The tools can be used for a variety of scientific and engineering purposes and for general statistical analysis. You provide the data, and the tools use the appropriate functions to determine the result. To effectively use these tools, you need to be familiar with the area of statistics or engineering for which you want to develop an analysis. You can view a list of all the tools in the Data Analysis dialog box. For additional information about each tool, see the online Help.

Use Data Analysis Tools

1. Click the **Data** tab.

2. Click the **Data Analysis** button. If not available, load the add-in.

3. Click the analysis tool you want to use.

4. To get help about each tool, click **Help**.

5. Click **OK**.

6. Select or enter the input range (a single row or column). You can use the **Collapse Dialog** button to select a range and the **Expand Dialog** button to return.

7. Select or enter the output range. You can use the **Collapse Dialog** button to select a range and the **Expand Dialog** button to return.

8. Specify any additional tool-specific options you want.

9. Click **OK**.

See Also

See "Loading and Unloading Add-ins" on page 432 for information on loading the Analysis ToolPak and other pre-installed Excel add-ins.

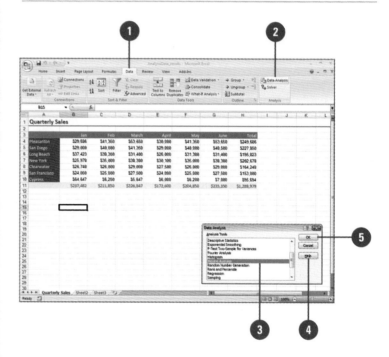

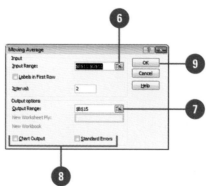

Creating Conditional Sums

The Conditional Sum Wizard helps you write formulas that sum specific values in a column based on other values in a list. Excel provides this feature as an add-in program, which may need to be loaded using the Add-In pane in Excel Options. The wizard guides you through the process to create the desired results you want. All you need to do is specify the sum conditions you want to use and select data, and the wizard does the rest.

Create a Conditional Sum

1. Click the **Formulas** tab.

2. Click the **Conditional Sum** button. If not available, load the add-in.

3. Specify the list that contains the values to sum, including the column labels.

   You can use the **Collapse Dialog** button to select a range and the **Expand Dialog** button to return.

4. Click **Next**.

5. Click the **Column to sum** list arrow, and then select the column label.

6. Select the column you want to evaluate, and then type or select a value to compare with the data.

7. Click **Add Condition**.

   You can repeat steps 5 through 7 to enter more than one condition.

8. Click **Next**.

9. Click the **Copy just the formula to a single cell** or **Copy the formula and conditional values** option.

10. Click **Next**.

11. Select the cell where you want to copy the conditional sum formula.

12. Click **Finish**.

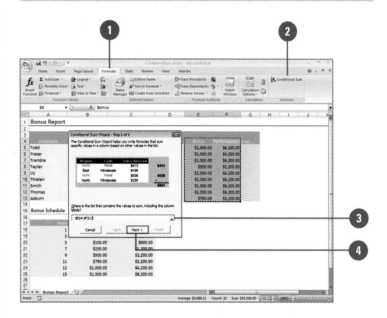

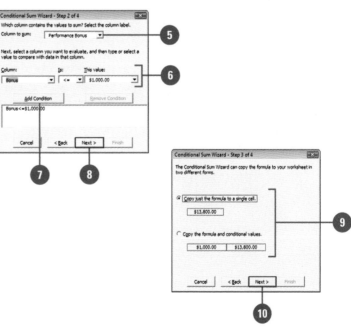

Looking at Alternatives with Data Tables

Data tables provide a shortcut by calculating all of the values in one operation. A **data table** is a range of cells that shows the results of substituting different values in one or more formulas. For example, you can compare loan payments for different interest rates. There are two types of data tables: one-input and two-input. With a **one-input table**, you enter different values for one variable and see the effect on one or more formulas. With a **two-input table**, you enter values for two variables and see the effect on one formula.

Create a One-Input Data Table

1. Enter the formula you want to use.

   If the input values are listed down a column, specify the new formula in a blank cell to the right of an existing formula in the top row of the table. If the input values are listed across a row, enter the new formula in a blank cell below an existing formula in the first column of the table.

2. Select the data table, including the column or row that contains the new formula.

3. Click the **Data** tab.

4. Click the **What-If Analysis** button, and then click **Data Table**.

5. Enter the input cell.

   If the input values are in a column, enter the reference for the input cell in the Column Input Cell box. If the input values are in a row, enter the reference for the input cell in the Row Input Cell box.

6. Click **OK**.

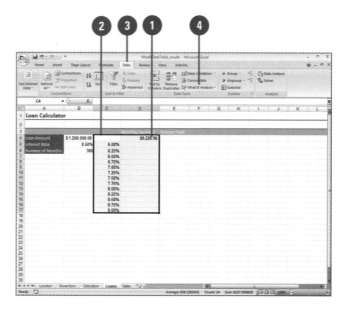

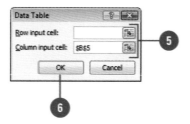

Asking "What If" with Goal Seek

Excel functions make it easy to create powerful formulas, such as calculating payments over time. Sometimes, however, being able to make these calculations is only half the battle. Your formula might tell you that a monthly payment amount is $2,000, while you might only be able to manage a $1,750 payment. **Goal Seek** enables you to work backwards to a desired result, or goal, by adjusting the input values.

Create a "What-If" Scenario with Goal Seek

1. Click any cell within the list range.

2. Click the **Data** tab.

3. Click the **What-If Analysis** button, and then click **Goal Seek**.

4. Click the **Set Cell** box, and then type the cell address you want to change.

    You can also click the **Collapse Dialog** button, use your mouse to select the cells, and then click the **Expand Dialog** button.

5. Click the **To Value** box, and then type the result value.

6. Click the **By Changing Cell** box, and then type the cell address you want Excel to change.

    You can also click the **Collapse Dialog** button, use your mouse to select the cells, and then click the **Expand Dialog** button.

7. Click **OK**.

    The Goal Seek Status dialog box, opens displaying the goal seek results.

8. Click **OK**.

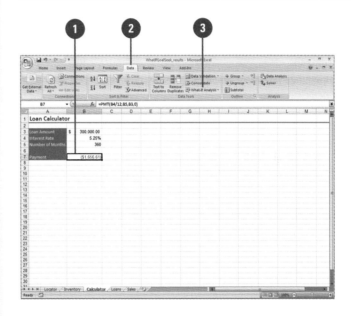

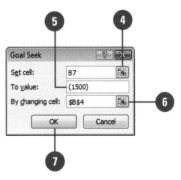

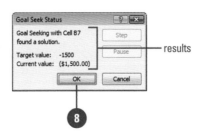

results

Creating Scenarios

Because some worksheet data is constantly evolving, the ability to create multiple scenarios lets you speculate on a variety of outcomes. For example, the marketing department might want to see how its budget would be affected if sales decreased by 25 percent. Although it's easy enough to plug in different numbers in formulas, Excel allows you to save these values and then recall them at a later time.

Create and Show a Scenario

1. Click the **Data** tab.

2. Click the **What-If Analysis** button, and then click **Scenario Manager**.

3. Click **Add**.

4. Type a name that identifies the scenario.

5. Type the cells you want to modify in the scenario, or click the **Collapse Dialog** button, use your mouse to select the cells, and then click the **Expand Dialog** button.

6. If you want, type a comment.

7. If you want, select the **Prevent changes** check box to protect the cell.

8. Click **OK**.

9. Type values for each of the displayed changing cells.

10. Click **OK**.

11. Click **Close**.

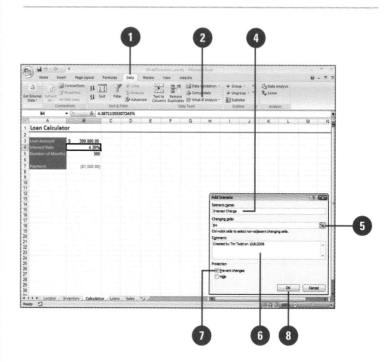

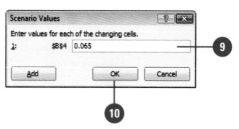

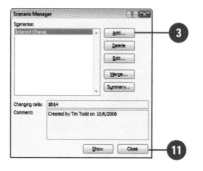

Show a Scenario

1. Click the **Data** tab.

2. Click the **What-If Analysis** button, and then click **Scenario Manager**.

3. Select the scenario you want to see.

4. Click **Show**.

5. Click **Close**.

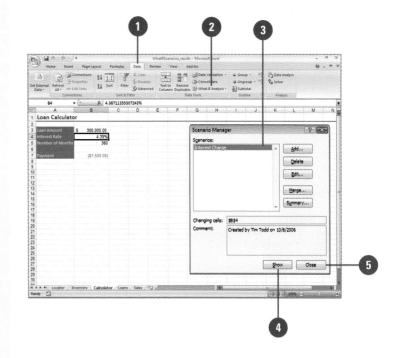

Create a Scenario Summary or PivotTable Report

1. Click the **Data** tab.

2. Click the **What-If Analysis** button, and then click **Scenario Manager**.

3. Select the scenario you want to see.

4. Click **Summary**.

5. Click the **Scenario summary** or **Scenario PivotTable report** option.

6. Click **OK**.

   A scenario summary worksheet tab appears with the report.

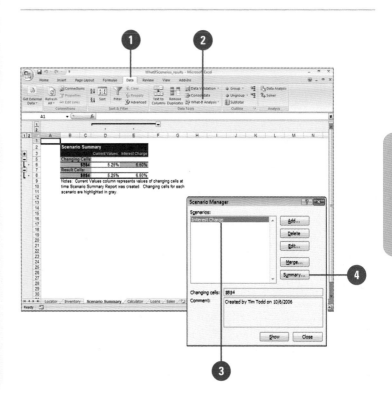

Using Solver

The Solver is similar to Goal Seek and scenarios, but provides more options to restrict the allowable range of values for different cells that can affect the goal. The **Solver** is an add-in program, which may need to be loaded using the Add-In pane in Excel Options. The Solver is useful for predicting how results might change over time based on different assumptions. For example, suppose you have sales goals and quotas for the next three months. The Solver can take the expectations and the current quotas for each month, and determine how sales quotas for all three amounts be adjusted to achieve the goal.

Use Solver

1 Click the **Data** tab.

2 Click the **Solver** button.

3 Select the target cell.

4 Click an Equal To option, and then, if necessary, enter a value.

5 Select the range of cells the solver uses to compare against the target cell.

6 Click **Add**.

7 Enter specific cell reference and constraint, and then click **Add**. You can specify several cell constraints.

8 Click **OK**.

9 Click **Solve**.

If the Solver finds a solution, the Solver Results dialog box opens.

Target cell

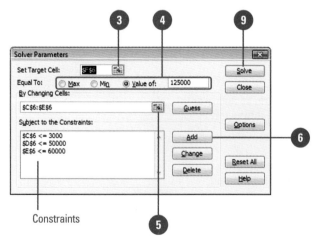

Constraints

324

10 Click the **Keep Solver Solution** option.

11 Click a report type.

12 Click **OK**.

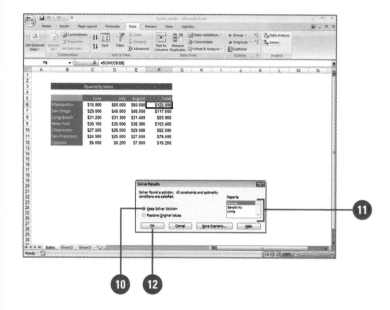

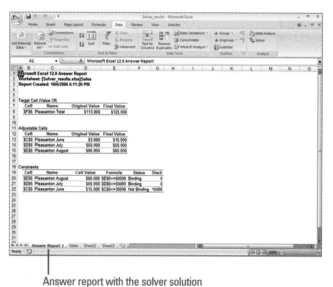

Answer report with the solver solution

Using Lookup and Reference Functions

You can use lookup and reference functions in Excel to easily retrieve information from a data list. The lookup functions (VLOOKUP and HLOOKUP) allow you to search for and insert a value in a cell that is stored in another place in the worksheet. The HLOOKUP function looks in rows (a horizontal lookup) and the VLOOKUP function looks in columns (a vertical lookup). Each function uses four arguments (pieces of data) as shown in the following definition: =VLOOKUP (lookup_value, table_array, col_index_num, range_lookup). The VLOOKUP function finds a value in the left-most column of a named range and returns the value from the specified cell to the right of the cell with the found value, while the HLOOKUP function does the same to rows. In the example, =VLOOKUP(12,Salary,2,TRUE), the function looks for the value 12 in the named range Salary and finds the closest (next lower) value, and returns the value in column 2 of the same row and places the value in the active cell. In the example, =HLOOKUP ("Years",Salary,4,FALSE), the function looks for the value "Years" in the named range Salary and finds the exact text string value, and then returns the value in row 4 of the column.

Use the VLOOKUP Function

1. Create a data range in which the left-most column contains a unique value in each row.

2. Click the cell where you want to place the function.

3. Type **=VLOOKUP(**value, named range, column, **TRUE** or **FALSE),** and then press Enter.

   Or click the **Formulas** tab, click the **Look & Reference** button, click **VLOOKUP**, specify the function arguments, and then click **OK**.

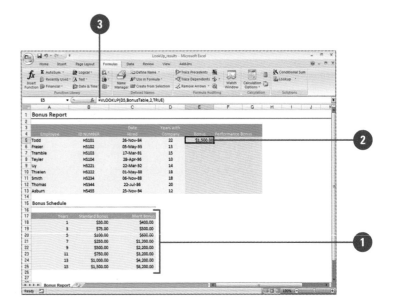

Use the HLOOKUP Function

① Create a data range in which the uppermost row contains a unique value in each row.

② Click the cell where you want to place the function.

③ Type **=HLOOKUP**(*value, named range, row,* **TRUE** *or* **FALSE**), and then press Enter.

Or click the **Formulas** tab, click the **Look & Reference** button, click **HLOOKUP**, specify the function arguments, and then click **OK**.

Did You Know?

You can also use the Lookup Wizard add-in. Excel also includes a Lookup Wizard to help you lookup information step-by-step. Use the Add-In pane in Excel Options to load the Lookup Wizard add-in, click the Formulas tab, click the LookUp button, and then follow the wizard instructions.

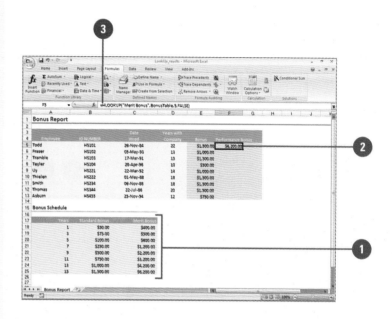

Lookup Function Arguments

Argument	Description
lookup_value	The value found in the row or the column of the named range. You can use a value, cell reference or a text string (enclosed in quotation marks).
table_array	The named range of information in which Excel looks up data.
col_index_num	The numeric position of the column in the named range (counting from the left) for the value to be returned (use only for VLOOKUP).
row_index_num	The numeric position of the row in the named range (counting from the top) for the value to be returned (use only for HLOOKUP).
range_lookup	The value returned when the function is to find the nearest value (TRUE) or an exact match (FALSE) for the lookup_value. The default value is TRUE.

Using Text Functions

Microsoft Certified Application Specialist

EX07S-3.7.1

You can use text functions to help you work with text in a workbook. If you need to count the number of characters in a cell or the number of occurrences of a specific text string in a cell, you can use the LEN and SUBSTITUTE functions. If you want to narrow the count to only upper or lower case text, you can use the UPPER and LOWER functions. If you need to capitalize a list of names or titles, you can use the PROPER function. The function capitalizes the first letter in a text string and converts all other letters to lowercase.

Use Text Functions

1. Create a data range in which the left-most column contains a unique value in each row.

2. Click the cell where you want to place the function.

3. Type = (equal sign), type a text function, specify the argument for the selected function, and then press Enter.

    Some examples include:

    ◆ =LEFT(A4,FIND(" ",A4)-1)

    ◆ =RIGHT(A4,LEN(A4-FIND("*",SUBSTITUTE(A4," ","*",LEN(A4)-LEN(SUBSTITUTE(A4," ","")))))

    ◆ =UPPER(A4)

    ◆ =LOWER(A4)

    ◆ =PROPER(A4)

    Or click the **Formulas** tab, click the **Text** button, click text function, specify the function arguments, and then click **OK**.

Did You Know?

You can use wildcard characters in a criteria. A question mark (?) matches any single character. An asterisk (*) matches any sequence of characters. If you want to find an actual question mark or asterisk, type a tilde (~) before the character.

Summarizing Data Using Subtotals

EX07S-3.3.1

If you have a column list with similar facts and no blanks, you can automatically calculate subtotals and grand totals in a list. Subtotals are calculated with a summary function, such as Sum, Count, or Average, while Grand totals are created from detailed data instead of subtotal values. **Detailed data** is typically adjacent to and either above or below or to the left of the summary data. When you summarize data using subtotals, the data list is also outlined to display and hide the detailed rows for each subtotal.

Subtotal Data in a List

1. Organize data in a hierarchical fashion—place summary rows below detail rows and summary columns to the right of detail columns.

2. Select the data that you want to subtotal.

3. Click the **Data** tab.

4. Use sort buttons to sort the column.

5. Click the **Subtotal** button.

6. Click the column to subtotal.

7. Click the summary function you want to use to calculate the subtotals.

8. Select the check box for each column that contains values you want to subtotal.

9. To set automatic page breaks following each subtotal, select the **Page break between groups** check box.

10. To show or hide a summary row above the detail row, select or clear the **Summary below data** check box.

11. To remove subtotals, click **Remove All**.

12. Click **OK**.

13. To add more subtotals, use the **Subtotals** button again.

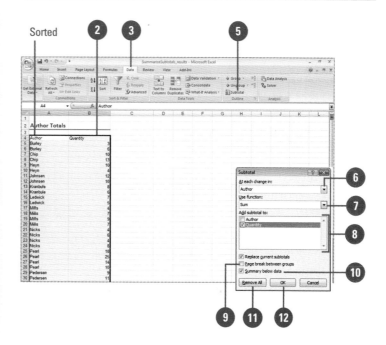

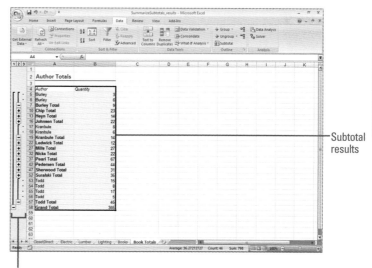

Subtotal results

Use +/- button to expand/collapse subtotals.

Summarizing Data Using Functions

Microsoft
Certified
Application
Specialist

EX07S-3.3.1,
EX07S-3.4.1

You can use conditional functions, such as SUMIF, COUNTIF, and AVERAGEIF to summarize data in a workbook. These functions allow you to calculate a total, count the number of items, and average a set of numbers based on a specific criteria. You can use the SUMIF function to add up interest payment for accounts over $100, or use the COUNTIF function to find the number of people who live in CA from an address list. If you need to perform these functions based on multiple criteria, you can use the SUMIFS, COUNTIFS, and AVERAGEIFS functions.

Use Summarize Data Functions

1. Click the cell where you want to place the function.

2. Type = (equal sign), type a text function, specify the argument for the selected function, and then press Enter.

Some examples include:

- =AVERAGE(D6:D19)

- ={=SUM(1/COUNTIF(C6:C19, C6:19))}

- =SUMIF(C6:C19,"Todd", Quantity_Order1)

- =SUM(Quantity_Order1)

Or click the **Formulas** tab, click the **Text** button, click text function, specify the function arguments, and then click **OK**.

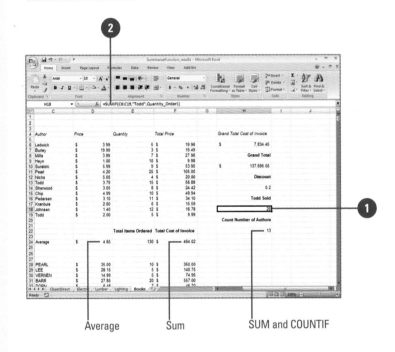

Average   Sum   SUM and COUNTIF

Summarize Data Function Examples

Formula	Result	Descriptions
SUM(num1,num2,...)	SUM(A1:A10)	Add the cells within a range.
SUMIF(range, criteria,sum_range)	SUMIF(A1:A10,">100",B1:B10)	Add the cells within a range that meets specific criteria. The sum_range are the cells to add that corresponds to cells in the range that match the criteria. Blanks and text values are ignored. Criteria is 10, "10", "<10", or B3.
COUNT(value1,value2,...)	COUNT(A1:A10)	Counts the number of cells that contain numbers within the list of arguments.
COUNTA(value1,value2,...)	COUNTA(A1:A10)	Counts the number of cells that are not empty and the values within the list of arguments.
SUMIFS(sum_range,criteria_range1, criteria1, criteria_range2, criteria2...)	SUMIF(B1:B10,">100",A1:A10, "<1000,C1:C10)	Add the cells within a range that meets multiple criteria. The sum_range are the cells to add that corresponds to cells in the range that match the criteria. Blanks and text values are ignored. Criteria is 10, "10", "<10", or B3.
COUNTIF (range, criteria)	COUNTIF(A1:A10,"CA")	Counts the number of cells within a range that meets specific criteria. Blanks and text values are ignored. Criteria is 10, "10", "<10", or B3.
COUNTIFS(range1, criteria1, range2, criteria2...)	COUNTIFS(A1:A10,"CA", B1:B10,"94588")	Counts the number of cells within a range that meets multiple criteria. Blanks and text values are ignored. Criteria is 10, "10", "<10", or B3.
AVERAGE(range)	AVERAGE(A1:A10)	Adds a group of numbers and then divides by the count of those numbers.
AVERAGEIF(range, criteria, average_range)	AVERAGE(A1:A10,"<1000" B1:B10)	Returns the average of all the cell in a range that meets specific criteria. TRUE or FALSE are ignored. Criteria is 10, "10", "<10", or B3.
AVERAGEIFS(average_range, range1, criteria1,range2, criteria2...)	AVERAGE(B1:B10,"<1000" A1:A10,">500")	Returns the average of all the cell in a range that meets multiple criteria. TRUE or FALSE are ignored. Criteria is 10, "10", "<10", or B3.
MIN(num1,num2,...)	MIN(A1:A10)	Returns the largest number in a set of values.
MAX(num1,num2,...)	MAX(A1:A10)	Returns the largest number in a set of values.

Determining Specific Dates

Calculating Dates

You can use different formulas to return a specific date. Here are some common examples you can use.

Calculate a Specific Day

You can use the Date function to quickly calculate a specific day, such as New Year's (January 1st), US Independence Day (July 4th), or Christmas (December 25th).

=Date(A1,1,1)
=Date(A1,7,4)
=Date(A1,12,25)

Calculate a Changing Day

You can use the DATE and WEEKDAY function to calculate a holiday that changes each year, such as Thanksgiving, which is celebrated on the fourth Thursday in November.

=Date(A1,11,1)+IF(5<WEEKDAY (DATE(A1,11,1)),
7-WEEKDAY(DATE(A1,11,1))+5,
5-WEEKDAY(DATE(A1,11,1)))+((4-1)*7)

Calculate the Day of the Year

You can calculate the day of the year for a specific date in the A1 cell. This function returns an integer between 1 and 365.

=A1-DATE(YEAR(A1),1,0)

Calculate the Day of the Week

You can use the WEEKDAY function to calculate the day of the week for a specific date in a cell. The function returns an integer between 1 and 7. This example returns 1 for Sunday, October 7, 2007.

=WEEKDAY(DATE(2007, 10,7))

Calculate a Person's Age

You can use the DATEIF function to calculate the age of a person. The function returns an integer. For this example, A1 is birth date, A2 is the current date, and "y" indicates years ("md" indicates days and "ym" indicates months). If you loaded the Analysis ToolPak, you can also use the INT function.

=DATEIF(A1, A2,"y") or INT(YEARFRAC(A1,A2))

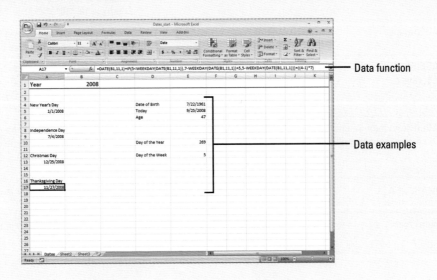

Data function

Data examples

Protecting and Securing a Workbook

12

Introduction

When you've developed content in your workbook and want feedback, you can electronically send an Excel workbook to reviewers so that they can read, revise, and comment on the workbook without having to print it. Instead of reading handwritten text or sticky notes on your printout, you can get clear and concise feedback.

Adding a password to protect your workbook is not only a good idea for security purposes, it's an added feature to make sure that changes to your workbook aren't made by unauthorized people. You can protect all or part of a worksheet or an entire workbook. In each case, you'll be asked to supply a password, and then enter it again when you want to work on the file. Not only can you guard who sees your workbook, you can set rights on who can add changes and comments to your workbook. You can also add restricted access known as Information Rights Access (IRM). IRM is a tool that is available with all Microsoft Office applications that restricts a file being sent through e-mail to other users. If you need to validate the authenticity of a document, you can add an invisible digital signature, an electronic secure stamp of authentication on a document, or a visible signature line. A signature line allows you to create a paperless signature process for documents, such as contracts.

The Trust Center (**New!**) is a place where you set security options and find the latest technology information as it relates to document privacy, safety, and security from Microsoft. The Trust Center allows you to set security and privacy settings and provides links to Microsoft privacy statements, a customer improvement program, and trustworthy computing practices.

Inspecting Documents

Microsoft Certified Application Specialist

EX07S-5.3.1

While you work on your workbook, Excel automatically saves and manages personal information and hidden data to enable you to create and develop a workbook with other people. The personal information and hidden data includes comments, revision marks, versions, ink annotations, document properties, invisible content, header and footer information, rows and columns, worksheets, document server properties, and custom XML data. The **Document Inspector** (New!) uses inspector modules to find and remove any hidden data and personal information specific to each of these modules that you might not want to share with others. If you remove hidden content from your workbook, you might not be able to restore it by using the Undo command, so it's important to make a copy of your workbook before you remove any information.

Inspect a Document

1. Click the **Office** button, click **Save As**, type a name to save a copy of the original, specify a folder location, and then click **Save**.

2. Click the **Office** button, point to **Prepare**, and then click **Inspect Document**.

3. Select the check boxes with the content you want to find and remove:

   ◆ **Comments and Annotations.** Includes comments and ink annotations.

   ◆ **Document Properties and Personal Information.** Includes metadata document properties (Summary, Statistics, and Custom tabs), the file path for publishing Web pages, document server properties, and content type information.

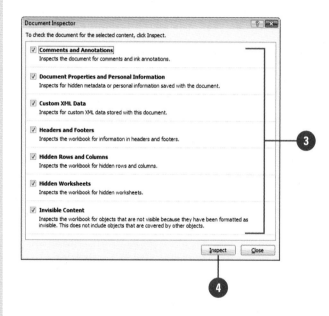

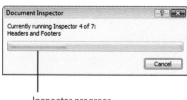

Inspector progress

- ◆ **Custom XML Data.** Includes any custom XML data.

- ◆ **Headers and Footers.** Includes information in headers and footers.

- ◆ **Hidden Rows and Columns.** Includes information in hidden rows and columns.

- ◆ **Hidden Worksheets.** Includes information in hidden worksheets.

- ◆ **Invisible Content.** Includes objects formatted as invisible. Doesn't include objects covered by other objects.

4 Click **Inspect**.

5 Review the results of the inspection.

6 Click **Remove All** for each inspector module in which you want to remove hidden data and personal information.

TROUBLE? *Before you click Remove All, be sure you want to remove the information. You might not be able to restore it.*

7 Click **Close**.

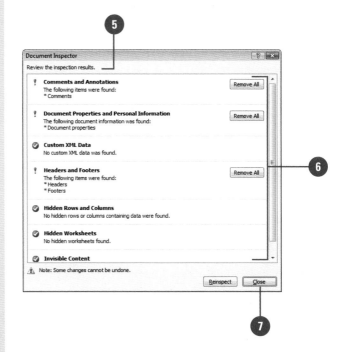

Protecting a Worksheet

Microsoft Certified Application Specialist

EX07S-5.2.1

To preserve all your hard work—particularly if others use your files—protect it with a password. You can protect a sheet or an entire workbook. In each case, you'll be asked to supply a password, and then enter it again when you want to work on the file. Passwords are case sensitive, so be sure to supply your password as it was first entered. If you forget a password, there is no way to open the file, so it's very important to remember or write down your password(s). Keep your password in a safe place. Avoid obvious passwords such as your name, your company, or your favorite pet.

Apply a Password to a Worksheet

1. Click the **Review** tab.

2. Click the **Protect Sheet** button.

3. Select the check boxes for the options you want protected in the sheet.

4. Type a password.

5. Click **OK**.

6. Retype the password.

7. Click **OK**.

Did You Know?

You can protect workbook elements.
Click the Review tab, click the Protect Workbook button, and then select or clear the Structure or Windows check boxes. Select the Structure check box to prevent users from viewing, copying, moving, or inserting worksheets. It also prevents users from recording new macros, displaying data from PivotTable reports, using analysis tools, or creating scenario summary reports. Select the Windows check box to prevent users from moving, resizing, or closing windows.

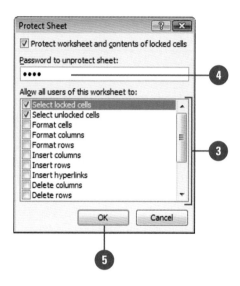

Apply a Password to Edit Parts of a Worksheet

1. Select the range in which you want to apply a password.

2. Click the **Review** tab.

3. Click the **Allow Users to Edit Ranges** button.

4. Click **New**.

5. Type a range password.

6. Click **OK**.

7. Retype the password.

8. Click **OK**.

9. To modify or delete a range, click a range, and then click **Modify** or **Delete**.

10. Click **OK**.

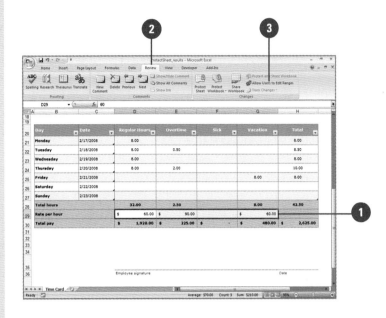

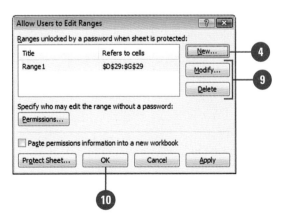

Did You Know?

You can quickly unprotect a worksheet or workbook. Click the Review tab, Unprotect Worksheet or Unprotect Workbook, type the password, and then click OK.

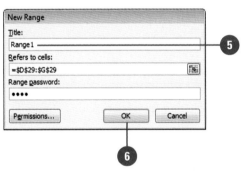

See Also

See "Hiding and Unhiding Worksheets and Workbooks" on page 114 for information on hiding data in selected worksheets or workbooks without deleting it.

Locking or Unlocking Worksheet Cells

To prevent accidental changes to your data, you can lock worksheet cells. When you lock selected cells, you cannot make changes to them until you unlock them. When you lock cells, users can unlock the data and make changes unless you add password protection to the worksheet. For security or confidentiality reasons, you might want to hide formulas from view. If so, you can hide or unhide them using the Protection tab in the Format Cells dialog box.

Lock or Unlock Worksheet Cells

1. Select the cell or range you want to lock or unlock.

2. Click the **Home** tab.

3. Click the **Format** button, and then click **Lock Cell** to lock or unlock the current selection.

    This toggle command turns on or off the Locked check box on the Protection tab in the Format Cells dialog box.

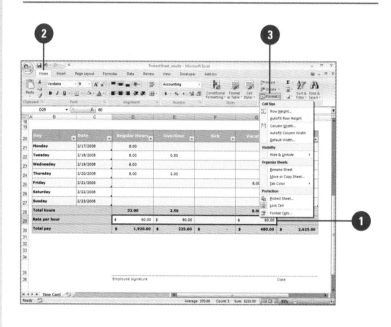

Hide or Show Formulas

1. Select the cell or range with the formulas you want to hide or show.

2. Click the **Home** tab.

3. Click the **Format** button, and then click **Format Cells**.

4. Click the **Protection** tab.

5. Select the **Hidden** check box to hide formulas or clear it to show formulas.

6. Click **OK**.

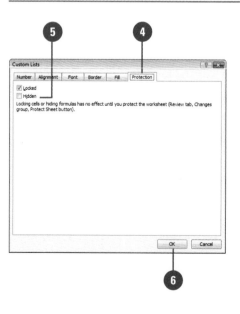

Adding Security Encryption to a Workbook

Microsoft
Certified
Application
Specialist   EX07S-5.2.1

File encryption is additional security you can apply to a workbook. File encryption scrambles your password to protect your workbook from unauthorized people from breaking into the file. You don't have to worry about the encryption, Excel handles everything. All you need to do is remember the password. If you forget it, you can't open the file. Password protection takes effect the next time you open the workbook. To set password protection using file encryption, select the Office button, point to Prepare, select Encrypt Document, enter a password, write it down for safekeeping, and then reenter the password again.

Apply File Encryption

1. Click the **Office** button, point to **Prepare**, and then click **Encrypt Document**.

2. Type a password.

3. Click **OK**.

4. Retype the password.

5. Click **OK**.

Did You Know?

You can remove file encryption. Click the Office button point to Prepare, click Encrypt Document, delete the file encryption password, and then click OK.

Adding Password
Protection to
a Workbook

EX07S-5.2.1

You can assign a password and other security options so that only those who know the password can open the workbook, or to protect the integrity of your workbook as it moves from person to person. At times, you will want the information to be used but not changed; at other times, you will want only specific people to be able to view the workbook. Setting a workbook as read-only is useful when you want a workbook, such as a company-wide bulletin, to be distributed and read, but not changed. Password protection takes effect the next time you open the workbook.

Add Password Protection to a Workbook

1. Open the workbook you want to protect.

2. Click the **Office** button, and then click **Save As**.

3. Click **Tools**, and then click **General Options**.

4. Type a password in the Password to open box or the Password to modify box.

   IMPORTANT *It's critical that you remember your password. If you forget your password, Microsoft can't retrieve it.*

5. Select or clear the **Always create backup** check box.

6. Select or clear the **Read-only recommended** check box.

7. Click **OK**.

8. Type your password again.

9. Click **OK**.

10. If you entered passwords for Open and Modify, type your password again, and then click **OK**.

11. Click **Save**, and then click **Yes** to replace existing workbook.

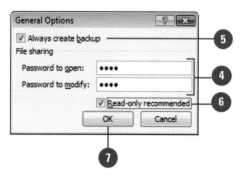

For Your Information

Using a Strong Password

Hackers identify passwords as strong or weak. A strong password is a combination of uppercase and lowercase letters, numbers, and symbols, such as Grea8t!, while a weak one doesn't use different character types, such as Hannah1. Be sure to write down your passwords and place them in a secure location.

Open a Workbook with Password Protection

1. Click the **Office** button, click **Open**, navigate to a workbook with password protection, and then click **Open**.

2. Click **Read Only** if you do not wish to modify the workbook, or type the password in the Password dialog box.

3. Click **OK**.

Change or Remove the Password Protection

1. Click the **Office** button, click **Open**, navigate to a workbook with password protection, and then click **Open**.

2. Type the password in the Password dialog box.

3. Click **OK**.

4. Click the **Office** button, click **Save As**, click **Tools**, and then click **General Options**.

5. Select the contents in the Password to modify box or the Password to open box, and then choose the option you want:

   ◆ **Change password.** Type a new password, click **OK**, and then retype your password.

   ◆ **Delete password.** Press Delete.

6. Click **OK**.

7. Click **Save**, and then click **Yes** to replace existing workbook.

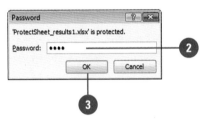

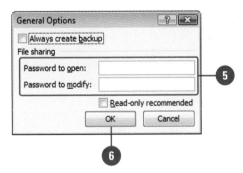

Restricting Workbook Access

Microsoft Certified Application Specialist

EX07S-5.3.2

Information Rights Management (IRM) in Office 2007 programs provides restricted access to Office documents. In Outlook, you can use IRM to restrict permission to content in workbooks from being forwarded, printed, copied, faxed, or edited by unauthorized people. You can also enforce corporate polices and set file expirations. IRM uses a server to authenticate the credentials of people who create or receive workbooks or e-mail with restricted permission. For Microsoft Office users without access to one of these servers, Microsoft provides a free trial IRM service, which requires a .NET Passport. If you want to view or change the permissions for a workbook, click Change Permission in the Message Bar or click the IRM icon button in the Status bar (**New!**). If someone tries to access a restricted workbook, a message appears with the author's address or Web site address so the individual can request permission.

Set Up Information Rights Management

1. Click the **Office** button, point to **Prepare**, point to **Restrict Permission**, and then click **Manage Credentials**.

2. Click **Yes** to download and install IRM. Follow the wizard instructions to install IRM software.

   Upon completion, the Service Sign-Up Wizard opens.

3. Click the **Yes, I Want To Sign Up For This Free Trial Service From Microsoft** option.

4. Click **Next**, and then follow the remaining instructions to create a .NET Passport and complete the service sign-up. You'll need to select a certificate type, either Standard or Temporary.

5. Click **Finish**.

6. Select a user account with the credentials you want to use.

7. Select or clear the **Always use this account** check box.

8. Click **Cancel** or **OK** to restrict permission.

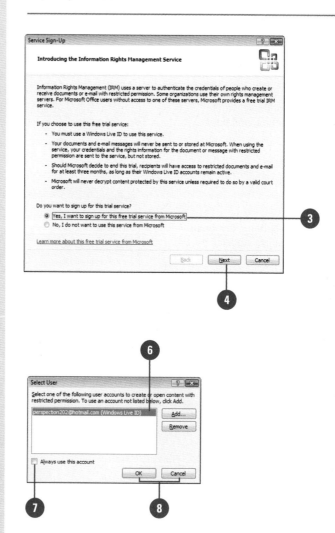

Create a Workbook with Restricted Permission

① Open the workbook you want to restrict permission.

② Click the **Office** button, point to **Prepare**, point to **Restrict Permission**, and then click **Restrict Access**.

TIMESAVER *Click the Protect Workbook button on the Review tab to access the same commands.*

③ If necessary, click the user with the permissions to create or open restricted content, and then click **OK**. If expired, click **OK**, and then click **Add** to renew it.

④ Select the **Restrict permission to this workbook** check box.

⑤ Enter e-mail addresses or click the **Read** or **Change** button to select users from your Address Book.

⑥ Click **More Options**.

⑦ Select the check boxes with the specific permissions you want.

⑧ Click **OK**, and click **OK**, if needed.

The Message Bar appears with the current rights management, along with a **Change Permission** button, which you can use to change workbook permissions.

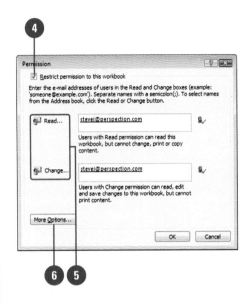

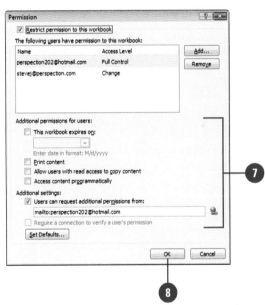

Did You Know?

You can unrestrict access to a workbook. Click the Office button, point to Prepare, point to Restrict Permission, and then click Unrestricted Access.

You can change permission. Click Change Permission in the Message Bar, or click the IRM icon on the Status bar.

Adding a Digital Signature

Microsoft Certified Application Specialist

EX07S-5.3.4

After you've finished a workbook, you might consider adding an invisible digital signature—an electronic, secure stamp of authentication on a document. Before you can add a digital signature, you need to get a **digital ID**, or **digital certificate**, which provides an electronic way to prove your identity. A digital certificate checks a public key to validate a private key associated with a digital signature. To assure a digital signature is authentic, it must have a valid (non expired or revoked) certificate issued by a reputable certification authority (CA), and the signing person must be from a trusted publisher. If you need a verified authenticate digital certificate, you can obtain one from a trusted Microsoft partner CA. If you don't need a verified digital certificate, you can create one of your own. If someone modifies the file, the digital signature is removed and revoked. If you're not sure if a workbook is digitally signed, you can use the Signatures task pane to view or remove valid signatures.

Create an Digital ID

1. Click the **Office** button, point to **Prepare**, and then click **Add a Digital Signature**.

2. If an alert message appears, click **Signature Services from the Office Marketplace** to open an informational Web site where you can sign up for a digital certificate, or click **OK** to create your own.

   If you don't want to see this dialog box again, select the **Don't show this message again** check box.

3. If necessary, click **OK** and verify your Rights Management account credentials using your .NET password.

4. If you don't have a digital ID, click the option to get an ID from a Microsoft Partner or create your own, and then click **OK**.

5. Enter your name, e-mail address, organization name, and geographic location.

6. Click **Create**.

   You can sign a document, or click **Cancel**.

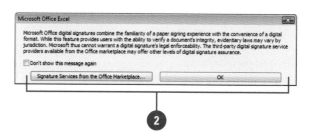

Add a Digital Signature to a Document

1. Click the **Office** button, point to **Prepare**, and then click **Add a Digital Signature**.

2. To change the digital signature, click **Change**, select the one you want, and then click **OK**.

3. Enter the purpose for signing this document.

4. Click **Sign**.

5. If necessary, click **OK**.

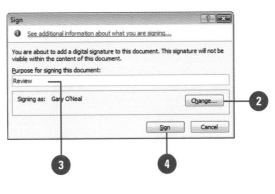

View or Remove Signatures

1. Click the **Signature** icon on the Status bar.

   The Signatures task pane appears, displaying valid signatures in the workbook. Invalid signatures are no longer automatically removed (**New!**).

2. Point to a signature, and then click the list arrow.

3. To see signature details, click **Signature Details**, select a signature, click **View**, click **OK** when you're done, and then click **Close**.

4. To remove a signature, point to a signature, click the list arrow, click **Remove Signature**, click **Yes**, and then if necessary click **OK**.

5. Click the **Close** button on the task pane.

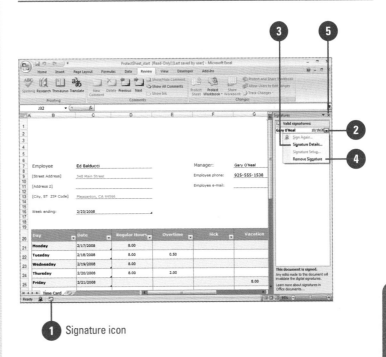

Signature icon

Adding a Signature Line

Microsoft
Certified
Application
Specialist

EX07S-5.3.4

If you prefer a visible signature line instead of an invisible digital signature, you can insert a visible signature line along with a digital certificate of authenticity. Signature lines allow you to create a paperless signature process for documents, such as contracts. A visible signature line looks like a typical signature line with a name, a date and a line for a signature. When you send a document out with a signature request, the signer sees a signature line and a notification request with instructions. The signer can type—or ink with a Tablet PC—a signature next to the *X*, or select a signature image. To add a signature line and digital signature at the same time, first you insert a signature line into your document, and then you sign it.

Add a Signature Line

1. Click the **Insert** tab.

2. Click the **Signature Line** button arrow, and then click **Microsoft Office Signature Line**.

3. If an alert message appears, click **Signature Services from the Office Marketplace** to open an informational Web site where you can sign up for a digital certificate, or click **OK** to create your own.

4. Type information about the person who will be signing on this signature line.

5. If you want, type any instructions for the signer.

6. To show the signature date, select the **Allow the signer to add comments in the Sign dialog box** check box.

7. To show the signature date, select the **Show sign data in signature line** check box.

8. Click **OK**.

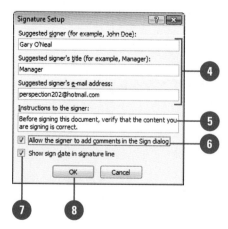

Sign the Signature Line

1. Double-click the signature line that needs a signature.

2. To add a printed version of your signature, type your name.

   If you have a Tablet PC, you can sign your name.

3. To select an image of your written signature, click Select Image, navigate to the signature image, and then click Select.

4. Click **Sign**.

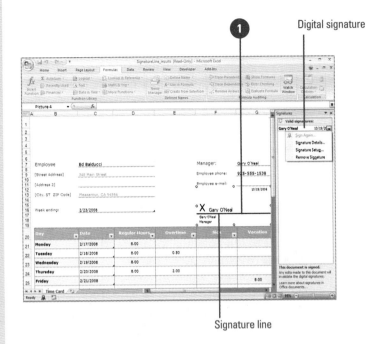

Digital signature

Signature line

Avoiding Harmful Attacks

Spreading Harmful Infections

Many viruses and other harmful attacks spread through file downloads, attachments in e-mail messages, and data files that have macros, ActiveX controls, add-ins, or Visual Basic for Applications (VBA) code attached to them. Virus writers capitalize on people's curiosity and willingness to accept files from people they know or work with, in order to transmit malicious files disguised as or attached to benign files. When you start downloading files to your computer, you must be aware of the potential for catching a computer virus, worm, or Trojan Horse. Typically, you can't catch one from just reading a mail message or downloading a file, but you can catch one from installing, opening, or running an infected program or attached code.

Understanding Harmful Attacks

Phishing is a scam that tries to steal your identity by sending deceptive e-mail asking you for bank and credit card information online. Phishers spoof the domain names of banks and other companies in order to deceive consumers into thinking that they are visiting a familiar Web site.

Phishers create a Web address that looks like a familiar Web address but is actually altered. This is known as a **homograph**. The domain name is created using alphabet characters from different languages, not just English. For example, the Web site address "www.microsoft.com" looks legitimate, but what you can't see is that the "i" is a Cyrillic character from the Russian alphabet.

Don't be fooled by spoofed Web sites that looks like the official site. Never respond to requests for personal information via e-mail; most companies have policies that do not ask for your personal information through e-mail. If you get a suspicious e-mail, call the institution to investigate and report it.

Spam is unsolicited e-mail, which is often annoying and time-consuming to get rid of. Spammers harvest e-mail addresses from Web pages and unsolicited e-mail. To avoid spam, use multiple e-mail addresses (one for Web forms and another for private e-mail), opt-out and remove yourself from e-mail lists. See the Microsoft Windows and Microsoft Outlook Help system for specific details.

Spyware is software that collects personal information without your knowledge or permission. Typically, spyware is downloaded and installed on your computer along with free software, such as freeware, games, or music file-sharing programs. Spyware is often associated with **Adware** software that displays advertisements, such as a pop-up ad. Examples of spyware and unauthorized adware include programs that change your home page or search page without your permission. To avoid spyware and adware, read the fine print in license agreements when you install software, scan your computer for spyware and adware with detection and removal software (such as Ad-aware from Lavasoft), and turn on Pop-up Blocker. See the Microsoft Windows Help system for specific details.

Avoiding Harmful Attacks Using Office

There are a few things you can do within any Office 2007 program to keep your system safe from the infiltration of harmful attacks.

1) Make sure you activate macro, ActiveX, add-in, and VBA code detection and notification. You can use the Trust Center to help protect you from attached code attacks. The Trust Center checks for trusted publisher and code locations on your computer and provides security options for add-ins, ActiveX controls, and macros to ensure the best possible protection. The Trust Center displays a security alert in the Message Bar when it detects a potentially harmful attack.

2) Make sure you activate Web site spoofing detection and notification. You can use the Trust Center to help protect you from homograph attacks. The *Check Office documents that are from or link to suspicious Web sites* check box under Privacy Options in the Trust Center is on by default and continually checks for potentially spoofed domain names. The Trust Center displays a security alert in the Message Bar when you have a document open and click a link to a Web site with an address that has a potentially spoofed domain name, or you open a file from a Web site with an address that has a potentially spoofed domain name.

3) Be very careful of file attachments in e-mail you open. As you receive e-mail, don't open or run an attached file unless you know who sent it and what it contains. If you're not sure, you should delete it. The Attachment Manager provides security information to help you understand more about the file you're opening. See the Microsoft Outlook Help system for specific details.

Avoiding Harmful Attacks Using Windows

There are a few things you can do within Microsoft Windows to keep your system safe from the infiltration of harmful attacks.

1) Make sure Windows Firewall is turned on. Windows Firewall helps block viruses and worms from reaching your computer, but it doesn't detect or disable them if they are already on your computer or come through e-mail. Windows Firewall doesn't block unsolicited e-mail or stop you from opening e-mail with harmful attachments.

2) Make sure Automatic Updates is turned on. Windows Automatic Updates regularly checks the Windows Update Web site for important updates that your computer needs, such as security updates, critical updates, and service packs. Each file that you download using Automatic Update has a digital signature from Microsoft to ensure its authenticity and security.

3) Make sure you are using the most up-to-date antivirus software. New viruses and more virulent strains of existing viruses are discovered every day. Unless you update your virus-checking software, new viruses can easily bypass outdated virus checking software. Companies such as McAfee and Symantec offer shareware virus checking programs available for download directly from their Web sites. These programs monitor your system, checking each time a file is added to your computer to make sure it's not in some way trying to change or damage valuable system files.

4) Be very careful of the sites from which you download files. Major file repository sites, such as FileZ, Download.com, or TuCows, regularly check the files they receive for viruses before posting them to their Web sites. Don't download files from Web sites unless you are certain that the sites check their files for viruses. Internet Explorer monitors downloads and warns you about potentially harmful files and gives you the option to block them.

Using the Trust Center

The **Trust Center (New!)** is a place where you set security options and find the latest technology information as it relates to document privacy, safety, and security from Microsoft. The Trust Center allows you to set security and privacy settings—Trusted Publishers, Trusted Locations, Add-ins, ActiveX Settings, Macro Settings, Message Bar, and Privacy Options—and provides links to Microsoft privacy statements, a customer improvement program, and trustworthy computing practices. The Trust Center also provides a link to open the Windows Security Center on your computer.

View the Trust Center

1. Click the **Office** button, and then click **Excel Options**.

2. In the left pane, click **Trust Center**.

3. Click the links in which you want online information at the Microsoft Online Web site.

   ◆ **Show the Microsoft Office Excel privacy statement.** Opens a Microsoft Web site detailing privacy practices.

   ◆ **Microsoft Office Online privacy statement.** Opens a Microsoft Web site detailing privacy practices.

   ◆ **Customer Experience Improvement Program.** Opens the Microsoft Customer Experience Improvement Program (CEIP) Web site.

   ◆ **Microsoft Windows Security Center.** Opens Windows Security Center on your computer.

   ◆ **Microsoft Trustworthy Computing.** Opens a Microsoft Web site detailing security and reliability practices.

4. When you're done, close your Web browser or dialog box, and return to Excel.

5. Click **OK**.

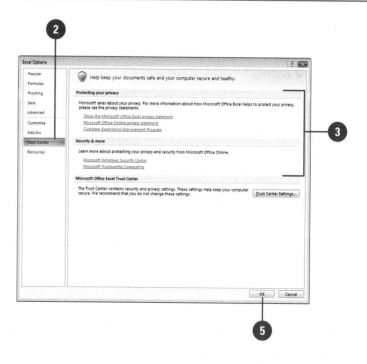

Selecting Trusted Publishers and Locations

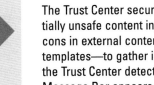

The Trust Center security system continually checks for external potentially unsafe content in your documents. Hackers can hide Web beacons in external content—images, linked media, data connections and templates—to gather information about you or cause problems. When the Trust Center detects potentially harmful external content, the Message Bar appears with a security alert and options to enable or block the content. Trusted publishers are reputable developers who create application extensions, such as a macro, ActiveX control, or add-in. The Trust Center uses a set of criteria—valid and current digital signature, and reputable certificate—to make sure publishers' code and source locations are safe and secure. If you are sure that the external content is trustworthy, you can add the content publisher and location to your trusted lists (**New!**), which allows it to run without being checked by the Trust Center.

Modify Trusted Publishers and Locations

1. Click the **Office** button, and then click **Excel Options**.

2. In the left pane, click **Trust Center**.

3. Click **Trust Center Settings**.

4. In the left pane, click **Trusted Publishers**.

5. Select a publisher, and then use the **View** and **Remove** buttons to make the changes you want.

6. In the left pane, click **Trusted Locations**.

7. Select a location, and then use the **Add new location**, **Remove**, and **Modify** buttons to make the changes you want.

8. Select or clear the **Allow trusted locations on my network (not recommended)** check box.

9. Select or clear the **Disable all Trusted Locations, only files signed by Trusted Publishers will be trusted** check box.

10. Click **OK**.

11. Click **OK**.

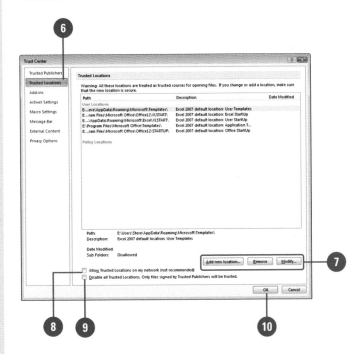

Setting Add-in Security Options

An add-in, such as smart tags, extends functionality to Microsoft Office programs (**New!**). An add-in can add buttons and custom commands to the Ribbon. When an add-in is installed, it appears on the Add-Ins tab of an Office program and includes a special ScreenTip that identifies the developer. Since add-ins are software code added to Microsoft Office programs, hackers can use them to do malicious harm, such as spreading a virus. The Trust Center uses a set of criteria—valid and current digital signature, reputable certificate and a trusted publisher—to make sure add-ins are safe and secure. If it discovers a potentially unsafe add-in, it disables the code and notifies you in the Message Bar. If the add-in security options are not set to the level you need, you can change them in the Trust Center.

Set Add-in Security Options

1. Click the **Office** button, and then click **Excel Options**.

2. In the left pane, click **Trust Center**.

3. Click **Trust Center Settings**.

4. In the left pane, click **Add-ins**.

5. Select or clear the check boxes you do or don't want.

   ◆ **Require Application Add-ins to be signed by Trusted Publisher.** Select to check for a digital signature on the .dll file.

   ◆ **Disable notification for unsigned add-ins (code will remain disabled).** Only available if the above check box is selected. Select to disable unsigned add-ins without notification.

   ◆ **Disable all Application Add-ins (may impair functionality).** Select to disable all add-ins without any notifications.

6. Click **OK**.

7. Click **OK**.

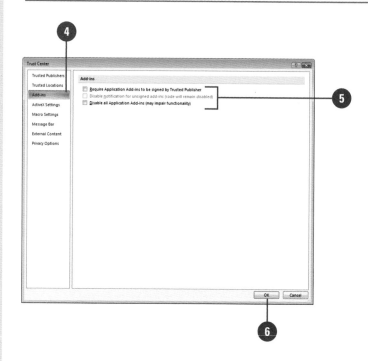

Setting ActiveX Security Options

An ActiveX control (**New!**) provides additional functionality, such as a text box, button, dialog box, or small utility program. ActiveX controls are software code, so hackers can use them to do malicious harm, such as spreading a virus. You can use the Trust Center to prevent ActiveX controls from harming your computer. If the ActiveX security options are not set to the level you want, you can change them in the Trust Center. If you change ActiveX control settings in one Office program, it effects all Microsoft Office programs. The Trust Center uses a set of criteria—checks the kill bit and Safe for Initialization (SFI) settings—to make sure ActiveX controls run safely.

Change ActiveX Security Settings

1. Click the **Office** button, and then click **Excel Options**.

2. In the left pane, click **Trust Center**.

3. Click **Trust Center Settings**.

4. In the left pane, click **ActiveX Settings**.

5. Click the option you want for ActiveX in documents not in a trusted location.

   ◆ Disable all controls without notification.

   ◆ Prompt me before enabling Unsafe for Initialization controls with additional restrictions and Save for Initialization (SFI) controls with minimal restrictions (default).

   ◆ Prompt me before enabling all controls with minimal restrictions.

   ◆ Enable all controls with restrictions and without prompting (not recommended, potentially dangerous controls can run).

6. Click **OK**.

7. Click **OK**.

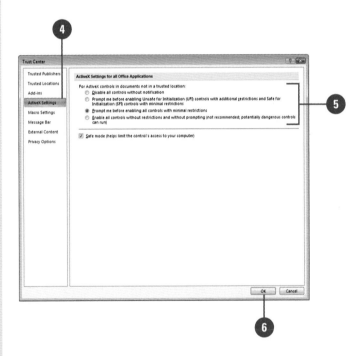

Setting Macro
Security Options

A macro allows you to automate frequently used steps or tasks to save time and work more efficiently. Macros are written using VBA (Visual Basic for Applications) code, which opens the door to hackers to do malicious harm, such as spreading a virus. The Trust Center uses a set of criteria—valid and current digital signature, reputable certificate and a trusted publisher—to make sure macros are safe and secure. If the Trust Center discovers a potentially unsafe macro, it disables the code and notifies you in the Message Bar. You can click Options on the Message Bar to enable it or set other security options. If the macro security options are not set to the level you need, you can change them in the Trust Center (**New!**).

Change Macro Security Settings

1. Click the **Office** button, and then click **Excel Options**.

2. In the left pane, click **Trust Center**.

3. Click **Trust Center Settings**.

4. In the left pane, click **Macro Settings**.

5. Click the option you want for macros in documents not in a trusted location.

   ◆ Disable all macros without notification.

   ◆ Disable all macros with notification (default).

   ◆ Disable all macros except digitally signed macros.

   ◆ Enable all macros (not recommended, potentially dangerous code can run).

6. If you're a developer, select the **Trust access to the VBA project object model** check box.

7. Click **OK**.

8. Click **OK**.

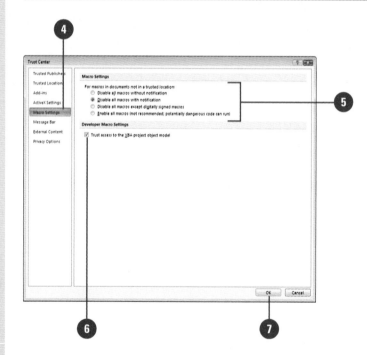

Changing Message Bar Security Options

The Message Bar (**New!**) displays security alerts when Office detects potentially unsafe content in an open document. The Message Bar appears below the Ribbon when a potential problem arises. The Message Bar provides a security warning and options to enable external content or leave it blocked. If you don't want to receive alerts about security issues, you can disable the Message Bar.

Modify Message Bar Security Options

1. Click the **Office** button, and then click **Excel Options**.

2. In the left pane, click **Trust Center**.

3. Click **Trust Center Settings**.

4. In the left pane, click **Message Bar**.

5. Click the option you want for showing the Message bar.

   ◆ Show the Message Bar in all applications when content has been blocked (default).

      This option is not selected if you selected the Disable all macros without notification check box in the Macros pane of the Trust Center.

   ◆ Never show information about blocked content.

6. Click **OK**.

7. Click **OK**.

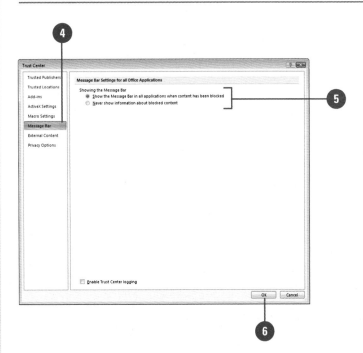

Setting Privacy Options

Privacy options in the Trust Center allow you to set security settings that protect your personal privacy online. For example, the *Check Office documents that are from or link to suspicious Web sites* option checks for spoofed Web sites and protects you from phishing schemes (**New!**). If your kids are doing research online using the Research task pane, you can set Privacy Options to enable parental controls and a password to block sites with offensive content.

Set Privacy Options

1. Click the **Office** button, and then click **Excel Options**.

2. In the left pane, click **Trust Center**.

3. Click **Trust Center Settings**.

4. In the left pane, click **Privacy Options**.

5. Select or clear the check boxes you do or don't want.

   ◆ **Search Microsoft Office Online for Help content when I'm connected to the Internet.** Select to get up-to-date Help content.

   ◆ **Update featured links from Microsoft Office Online.** Select to get up-to-date headlines and featured templates.

   ◆ **Download a file periodically that helps determine system problems.** Select to have Microsoft request error reports, update trouble-shooting help, and accept downloads from Office Online.

   ◆ **Sign up for the Customer Experience Improvement Program.** Select to sign-up.

   ◆ **Check Microsoft Office documents that are from or link to suspicious Web sites.** Select to check for spoofed Web sites.

6. Click **OK**.

7. Click **OK**.

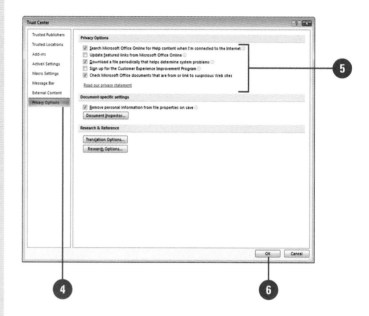

Set Parental Controls for Online Research

1 Click the **Office** button, and then click **Excel Options**.

2 In the left pane, click **Trust Center**.

3 Click **Trust Center Settings**.

4 In the left pane, click **Privacy Options**.

5 Click **Research Options**.

6 Click **Parental Control**.

7 Select the **Turn on content filtering to make services block offensive results** check box.

8 Select the **Allow users to search only the services that can block offensive results** check box, if necessary.

9 Enter a password, so users cannot change these settings.

10 Click **OK**, retype the password, and then click **OK**.

11 Click **OK**.

12 Click **OK**.

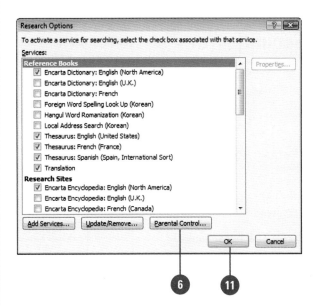

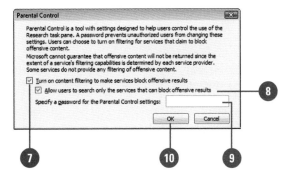

Setting External Content Security Options

External content is any content that is connected or linked to a workbook from a potentially unsafe external source, such as images, linked media, hyperlinks, data connections, or templates. Excel allows you to connect to external data from databases and other workbooks. Blocking external content prevents hackers from hiding malicious code in it that might do harm to your files and computer. You can set security options for data connections and workbook links to enable or disable the external content or display a security warning (**New!**).

Set Security Settings for Data Connections

① Click the **Office** button, and then click **Excel Options**.

② In the left pane, click **Trust Center**.

③ Click **Trust Center Settings**.

④ In the left pane, click **External Content**.

⑤ Click the option you want for data connections security.

- ◆ **Enable all Data Connections (not recommended).** Select to open workbooks with external data connections or to create external data connections without security warnings.

- ◆ **Prompt user about Data Connections.** Select to receive a security warning when you open or create workbooks with external data connections.

- ◆ **Disable all Data Connections.** Select to not allow any external data connections.

⑥ Click **OK**.

⑦ Click **OK**.

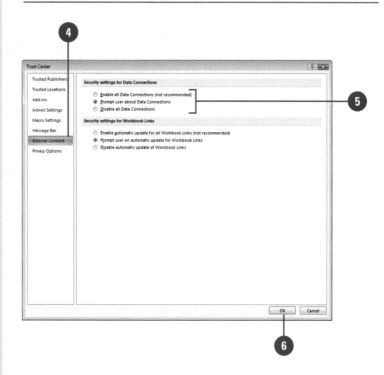

Set Security Settings for Workbook Links

1 Click the **Office** button, and then click **Excel Options**.

2 In the left pane, click **Trust Center**.

3 Click **Trust Center Settings**.

4 In the left pane, click **External Content**.

5 Click the option you want for workbook links security.

◆ **Enable automatic update for all Workbook Links (not recommended).** Select to automatically update links to data in another workbook without security warnings.

◆ **Prompt user on automatic update for Workbook Links.** Select to receive a security warning when you run automatic updates for links to data in another workbook.

◆ **Disable automatic update of Workbook Links.** Select to not allow any automatic updates for links to data in another workbook.

6 Click **OK**.

7 Click **OK**.

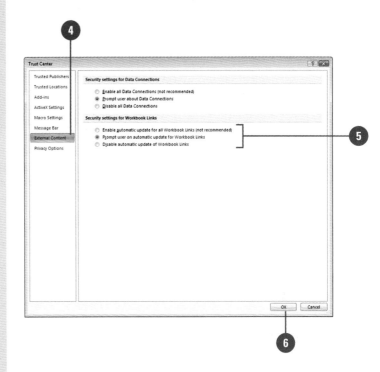

Working with Office Safe Modes

Microsoft Office 2007 uses two types of safe modes—Automated and User-Initiated (**New!**)—when it encounters a program problem. When you start an Office 2007 program, it automatically checks for problems, such as an extension not properly loading. If the program is not able to start the next time you try, the programs starts in **Automated Safe mode**, which disables extensions—macros, ActiveX controls, and add-ins—and other possible problem areas. If you're having problems and the Office program doesn't start in Automated Safe mode, you can start the program in **User-Initiated Safe mode**. When you start an Office program in Office Safe mode, not all features are available. For instance, templates can't be saved, AutoCorrect list is not loaded, Smart tags are not loaded, preferences cannot be saved, restricted permission (IRM) can't be used, and all command-line options are ignored except /a and /n. Before you can use Office Safe mode, you need to enable it in the Trust Center. When you're in safe mode, you can use the Trust Center to find out the disabled items and enable them one at a time to help you pin point the problem.

Enable Safe Mode

1. Click the **Office** button, and then click **Excel Options**.

2. In the left pane, click **Trust Center**.

3. Click **Trust Center Settings**.

4. In the left pane, click **ActiveX Settings**.

5. Select the **Safe Mode (Helps limit the control's access to your computer)** check box.

6. Click **OK**.

7. Click **OK**.

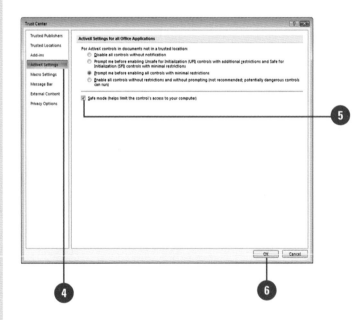

See Also

See "Diagnosing and Repairing Problems" on page 32 for information on fixing problems with a Microsoft Office 2007 program.

Start User-Initiated Safe Mode

1. Click the **Start** button on the taskbar, point to **All Programs**, and then click **Microsoft Office**.

2. Press and hold Ctrl, and then click **Microsoft Office Excel 2007**.

Did You Know?

You can use the Run dialog box to work in Safe mode. At the command prompt, you can use the */safe* parameter at the end of the command-line to start the program.

View Disabled Items

1. Click the **Office** button, and then click **Excel Options**.

2. In the left pane, click **Add-Ins**.

3. Click the **Manage** list arrow, and then click **Disabled Items**.

4. Click **Go**.

5. In the dialog box, you can select an item, click **Enable** to activate and reload the add-in, and then click **Close**.

6. Click **OK**.

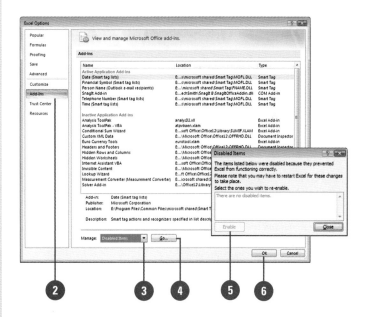

Marking a Workbook as Read-Only

**Microsoft
Certified
Application
Specialist**

EX07S-5.3.5

As a precaution to prevent readers and reviews from making accidental changes, you can use the Mark as Final command (**New!**) to make a Excel 2007 workbook read-only. The Mark as Final command disables or turns off typing, editing commands, and proofing marks, and sets the *Status property* field in the Document Information Panel to Final. The Mark as Final command is not a security option; it only prevents changes to the workbook while it's turned on and it can be turned off by anyone at any time.

Mark a Workbook as Final

1 Click the **Office** button, point to **Prepare**, and then click **Mark as Final**.

2 Click **OK**, and then click **OK** again, if necessary.

The workbook is marked as final and then saved.

3 If necessary, click **OK** and verify your Right Management account credentials using your .NET password.

The Mark as Final icon appears in the Status bar to indicate the workbook is currently marked as final.

IMPORTANT *An Excel 2007 workbook marked as final is not read-only when opened in an earlier version of Microsoft Excel.*

Did You Know?

You can enable editing for a workbook marked as final. Click the Office button, point to Prepare, and then click Mark as Final again to toggle off the Mark as Final feature.

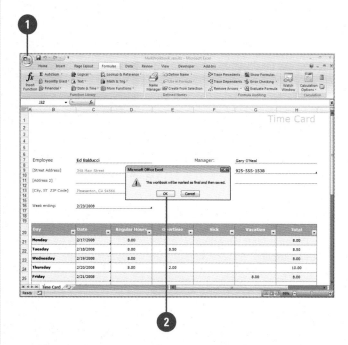

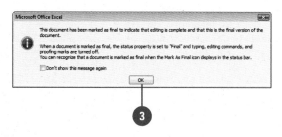

Reviewing and Sharing Workbook Data

13

Introduction

Creating successful workbooks is not always a solitary venture; you may need to share a workbook with others or get data from other programs before a project is complete. In Microsoft Office Excel, you have several methods that you can use to create a joint effort. In many offices, your co-workers (and their computers) are located across the country or the world. They are joined through networks that permit users to share information by opening each other's files and to simultaneously modify data.

Microsoft Office Excel makes it easy for you to communicate with your teammates. Instead of writing on yellow sticky notes and attaching them to a printout, you can insert electronic comments within worksheet cells. You can also track changes within a workbook made by you and others. After you finish making changes to your workbook, you can quickly send it to another person for review using e-mail or an Internet Fax service.

XML (Extensible Markup Language) is a universal language that enables you to create documents in which data is stored independently of the format so you can use the data more seamlessly in other forms. When you work with XML, you can attach an XML Schema—a set of rules that defines the elements and content used in an XML document. XML schemas are created by developers who understand XML.

By using a variety of techniques, you can link, embed, hyperlink, export, or convert data to create one seamless workbook that is a group effort by many co-workers. You can also use Excel to create and edit connections to external data sources, such as Microsoft Access, to create more permanent links to data.

Sharing Workbooks

Microsoft
Certified
Application
Specialist

EX07S-5.2.2

When you're working with others in a networked environment, you may want to share workbooks you have created. You may also want to share the responsibilities of entering and maintaining data. **Sharing** means users can add columns and rows, enter data, and change formatting, while allowing you to review their changes. When sharing is enabled, "[Shared]" appears in the title bar of the shared workbook. This type of work arrangement is particularly effective in team situations where multiple users have joint responsibility for data within a single workbook. In cases where multiple users modify the same cells, Excel can keep track of changes, and you can accept or reject them at a later date.

Enable Workbook Sharing

1. Open the workbook you want to share.

2. Click the **Review** tab.

3. Click the **Share Workbook** button.

4. Click the **Editing** tab.

5. Select the **Allow changes by more than one user at the same time** check box.

6. Click **OK**.

7. Click **OK** again to save your workbook.

Did You Know?

You can set file options to prompt to open as read-only. To prevent accidental changes to a workbook, you can display an alert requesting (not requiring) the user open the file as read-only. A read-only file can be read or copied. If the user makes changes to the file, the modifications can only be saved with a new name.

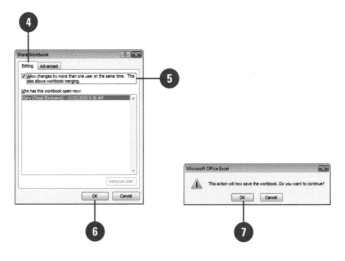

Change Sharing Options

① Open the workbook you want to share.

② Click the **Review** tab.

③ Click the **Share Workbook** button.

④ Click the **Advanced** tab.

⑤ To indicate how long to keep changes, select one of the Track changes options, and then set the number of days, if necessary.

⑥ To indicate when changes should be saved, select one of the Update changes options, and then set a time internal, if necessary.

⑦ To resolve conflicting changes, select one of the Conflicting Changes Between Users options.

⑧ Select one or both of the Include In Personal View check boxes.

⑨ Click **OK**.

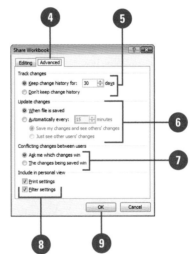

Creating and Reading a Cell Comment

Microsoft
Certified
Application
Specialist   EX07S-5.1.2

Any cell on a worksheet can contain a **comment**—information you might want to share with co-workers or include as a reminder to yourself without making it a part of the worksheet. (Think of a comment as a nonprinting sticky note attached to an individual cell.) A cell containing a comment displays a red triangle in the upper-right corner of the cell. By default, comments are hidden and are displayed only when the mouse pointer is held over a cell with a red triangle.

Add a Comment

1. Click the cell to which you want to add a comment.

2. Click the **Review** tab.

3. Click the **New Comment** button.

4. Type the comment in the comment box.

5. Click outside the comment box when you are finished, or press Esc twice to close the comment box.

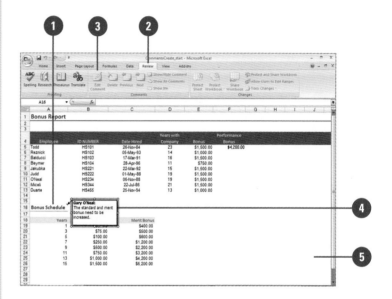

Read a Comment

1. Position the mouse pointer over a cell with a red triangle to read its comment.

2. Move the mouse pointer off the cell to hide the comment.

3. Click the **Review** tab.

4. Do any of the following navigation buttons:

   ◆ Click the **Previous Comment** or **Next Comment** button to move from comment to comment.

   ◆ Select a cell, and then click the **Show/Hide Comment** button to show or hide comments.

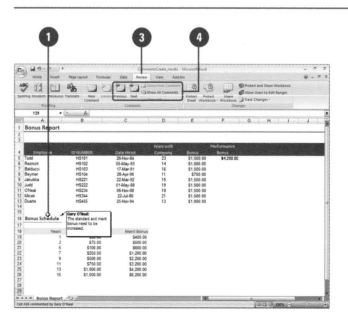

Editing and Deleting a Cell Comment

You can edit, delete, and even format cell comments just as you do other text on a worksheet. If you are working with others online, they may want to delete a comment after reading it. You might want to format certain comments to add emphasis. You can use formatting buttons—such as Bold, Italic, Underline, Font Style, Font Color, or Font Size—on the Home tab. When you no longer need a comment, you can quickly delete it.

Edit a Comment

1. Click the cell with the comment you want to edit.

2. Click the **Review** tab.

3. Click the **Edit Comment** button.

4. Make your changes using common editing tools, such as the Backspace and Delete keys, as well as the Formatting toolbar buttons.

5. Press Esc twice to close the comment box.

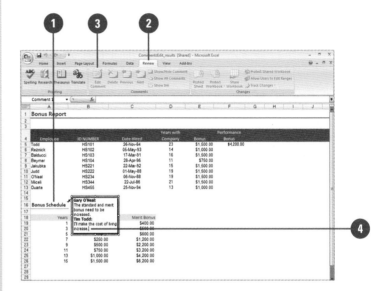

Delete a Comment

1. Click the cell with the comment you want to delete.

2. Click the **Review** tab.

3. Click the **Delete Comment** button.

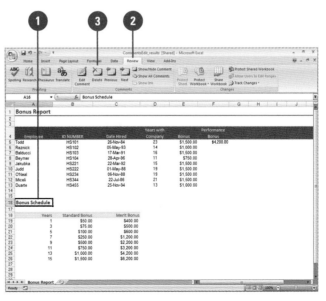

Tracking Changes

Microsoft
Certified
Application
Specialist

EX07S-5.1.1

As you build and fine-tune a workbook—particularly if you are sharing workbooks with co-workers—you can keep track of all the changes that are made at each stage in the process. The Track Changes feature makes it easy to see who made what changes and when, and to accept or reject each change, even if you are the only user of a worksheet. When you or another user applies the Track Changes command to a workbook, the message "[Shared]" appears in the title bar of the workbook to alert you that this feature is active. To take full advantage of this feature, turn it on the first time you or a co-worker edits a workbook. Then, when it's time to review the workbook, all the changes will be recorded. You can review tracked changes in a workbook at any point. Cells containing changes are surrounded by a blue border, and the changes made can be viewed instantly by moving your mouse pointer over any outlined cell. When you're ready to finalize the workbook, you can review each change and either accept or reject it.

Turn On Track Changes

1. Click the **Review** tab.

2. Click the **Track Changes** button, and then click **Highlight Changes**.

3. Select the **Track changes while editing** check box.

4. Select the **When, Who**, and/or **Where** check box. Click an associated list arrow, and then select the option you want.

5. Select or clear the **Highlight changes on screen** or **List changes on a new sheet** check boxes.

6. Click **OK**, and then click **OK** again, if necessary.

7. Make changes in worksheet cells.

   Column and row indicators for changed cells appear in red. The cell containing the changes has a blue outline.

8. To view tracked changes, position the mouse pointer over an edited cell.

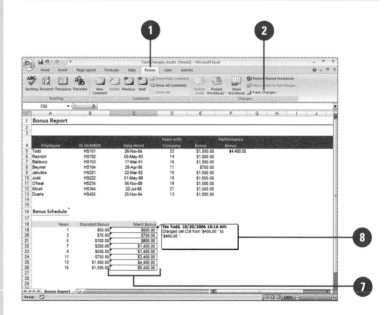

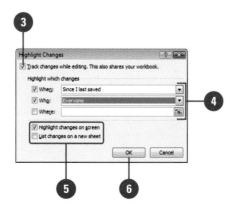

Accept or Reject Tracked Changes

1 Click the **Review** tab.

2 Click the **Track Changes** button, and then click **Accept/Reject Changes**. If necessary, click **OK** in the message box.

3 If you want, change tracking, and then click **OK** to begin reviewing changes.

4 If necessary, scroll to review all the changes, and then click one of the following buttons:

- ◆ Click **Accept** to make the selected change to the worksheet.

- ◆ Click **Reject** to remove the selected change from the worksheet.

- ◆ Click **Accept All** to make all of the changes to the worksheet after you have reviewed them.

- ◆ Click **Reject All** to remove all of the changes to the worksheet after you have reviewed them.

5 Click **Close**.

Did You Know?

You can protect a shared workbook.
Open the shared workbook you want to protect. Click the Review tab, click the Protect Shared Workbook button, select the Shared with track changes check box, type a password if you want, and then click OK. You can only add a password if the workbook is unshared.

Sending a Workbook for Review Using E-Mail

After you finish making changes to a workbook, you can quickly send it to another person for review using e-mail. Excel allows you to send workbooks out for review as an attachment, either a workbook, PDF, or XPS document, using e-mail from within the program so that you do not have to open your e-mail program. An e-mail program, such as Microsoft Outlook, needs to be installed on your computer before you begin. When you send your workbook out for review, reviewers can add comments and then send it back to you.

Send a Workbook for Review Using E-Mail

1. Click the **Office** button, point to **Send**, and then click **E-mail**, **E-mail as PDF Attachment**, or **E-mail as XPS Attachment**.

2. If the Compatibility Checker appears, click **Continue** or **Cancel** to stop the operation.

   IMPORTANT *To complete the following steps, you need to have an e-mail program installed on your computer and an e-mail account set-up.*

   An e-mail message opens in Microsoft Outlook with your workbook attached. The subject line contains the file name of the workbook that you are sending.

3. Enter your recipients and subject (appears with workbook name by default).

   ◆ To add recipients from your address book or contacts list, click **To**, click the recipient names, click **To**, **Cc**, or **Bcc** until you're done, and then click **OK**.

4. Enter a message for your reviewer with instructions.

5. Click the **Send** button.

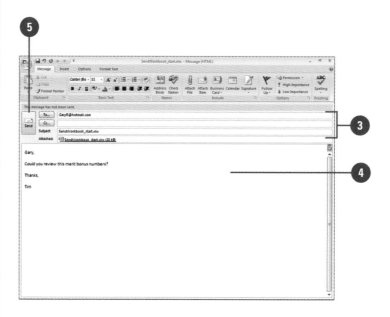

Sending a Workbook by Internet Fax ▶

If you are a member of an online fax service—such as eFax, InterFAX, MyFax, or Send2Fax—you can use Excel to send and receive faxes over the Internet directly from within your Microsoft Office program. If you're not a member, a Web site can help you sign up. You also need to have Microsoft Outlook and Word installed to use the fax service and Outlook must be open to send your fax. If Outlook is not open and you send the fax, it will be stored in your Outbox and not sent until you open Outlook again.

Send a Workbook by Internet Fax

1. Click the **Office** button, point to **Send**, and then click **Internet Fax**.

2. If you're not signed up with an Internet Fax service, click **OK** to open a Web page and sign up for one. When you're done, return to Excel, and then repeat Step 1.

3. If the Compatibility Checker appears, click **Continue** or **Cancel** to stop the operation.

   An e-mail message opens in Microsoft Outlook with your workbook attached as a .tif (image) file.

4. Enter a Fax Recipient, Fax Number and Subject (appears with workbook name by default).

   ◆ You can enter a fax number from your address book. Country codes in your address book must begin with a plus sign (+).

   ◆ To send your fax to multiple recipients, click Add More, and then enter fax information.

5. In the Fax Service pane, choose the options you want.

6. Complete the cover sheet in the body of the e-mail message.

7. Click the **Send** button.

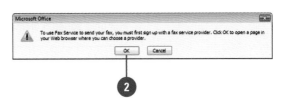

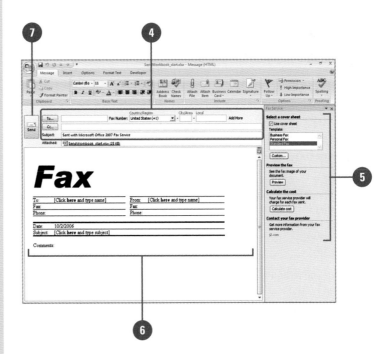

Working with XML

XML (Extensible Markup Language) is a universal language that enables you to create documents in which data is stored independently of the format so you can use the data more seamlessly in other forms. XML is supported in Office 2007 through Word, Excel, and Access. XML allows you to work with the familiar Office interface and create and save documents as XML, without ever knowing the XML language. When you work with XML, you can attach an XML Schema—a set of rules that defines the elements and content used in an XML document. XML schemas are created by developers who understand XML. After you attach a schema, you should change XML map properties before you map schema elements to cells in your worksheet.

Attach a Schema

① Click the **Developer** tab.

② Click the **Source** button.

③ In the task pane, click **XML Maps**.

④ Click **Add**.

⑤ Locate and select the XML schema file you want to attach, and then click **Open**.

⑥ If necessary, click **OK** to create a schema based on the XML source data.

⑦ To delete or rename an XML schema, select the schema, and then click **Delete** or **Rename**.

⑧ Click **OK**.

⑨ When you're done, click the **Close** button on the task pane.

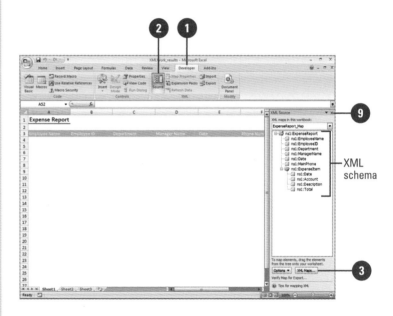

—XML schema

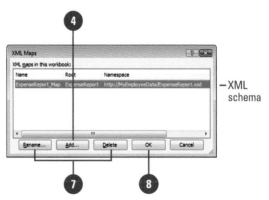

—XML schema

> ### Did You Know?
>
> *You can change XML view options.* In the XML Source task pane, click Options to turn on or off options to preview data in the task pane, hide help text in the task pane, automatically merge elements when mapping, include data heading, and hide border of inactive lists.

Change XML Data Map Properties

1. Open the worksheet in which you want to map the XML data.

2. Click the **Developer** tab.

3. Click the **Source** button.

4. Click the **Map Properties** button.

5. If you want, change the name of the XML Map.

6. Select or clear the following options:

   ◆ **Validate data against schema for import and export.**

   ◆ **Save data source definition in workbook.**

   ◆ **Adjust column width.**

   ◆ **Preserve column filter.**

   ◆ **Preserve number formatting.**

7. Select the refreshing or importing data option you want.

8. Click **OK**.

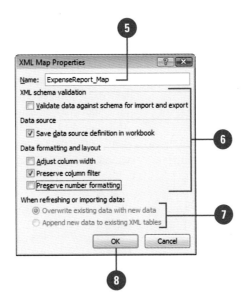

Creating an XML Data Map

Using XML data in Excel follows the same basic process: (1) Add an XML schema file (.xsd) to a workbook, (2) map XML schema elements to individual cells, (3) Import an XML data file (.xml), (4) enter data, and (5) export revised data from mapped cells to an XML data file. You can use the XML Source task pane to create and manage XML maps. The task pane displays a hierarchical list of XML elements in the current XML map that you use to map to worksheet cells. After you create an XML data map, you can import XML data to fill in the information you want from a data source.

Create an XML Data Map

1. Open the worksheet in which you want to map the XML data.

2. Click the **Developer** tab.

3. Click the **Source** button.

4. Click the **Map name** list arrow, and then click the XML schema you want to use.

5. Drag the named elements from the XML Source task pane to the corresponding cells in the worksheet.

6. Click the **Header Options** button, and then click the header option you want.

7. When you're done, click the **Close** button on the task pane.

Drag XML element

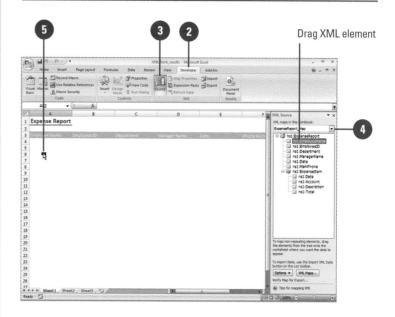

Did You Know?

You can change the list of XML elements in the XML Source task pane. In the XML Source task pane, click the Options button, and then click the display option you want.

An XML data map is a potential security risk. From a security perspective, Excel saves an XML map and its data source with a workbook, which any user can view using VBA.

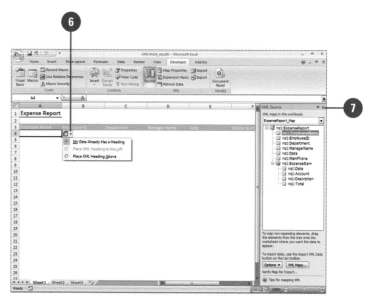

Import XML Data

① Open the worksheet in which you want to map the XML data.

② Click the **Developer** tab.

③ Click the **Import** button.

④ Click the **Files of type** list arrow, and then click **XML Files**.

⑤ Locate, and then select the XML data file you want to import.

⑥ Click **Open**.

Did You Know?

You can add XML expansion packs. Click the Developer tab, click the Expansion Packs button, click Add, locate and select an expansion pack, and then click Open. You can also attach, update, or delete XML expansion packs.

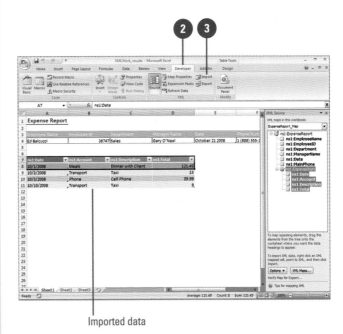

Imported data

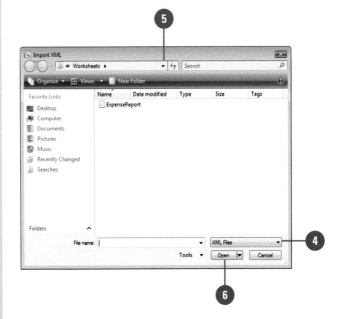

Exporting and Saving Data in XML

After you finish working with your XML document, you can export or save the data for use in other XML compatible documents and applications. You can save the contents of a mapped range with the XML Data format or XML Spreadsheet format. The XML Data format is an independent XML industry standard that uses a separate XML schema, while the XML Spreadsheet format is a specialized Excel XML file that uses its own XML schema to store information, such as file properties.

Export XML Data

1. Open the worksheet with the XML data.

2. Click the **Developer** tab.

3. Click the **Export** button.

4. If necessary, click the XML map you want to use, and then click **OK**.

5. Select a location where you want to export the XML data.

6. Type a name for the XML file.

7. Click **Export**.

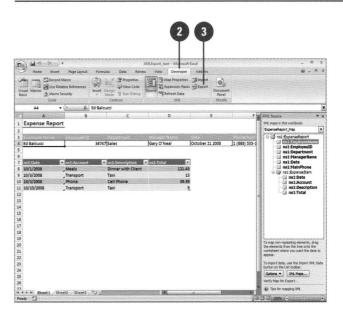

Did You Know?

You can quickly verify a data map before you export the data. Click the Developer tab, click the Source button, click the Verify Map for Export link at the bottom of the task pane, and then click OK when it's done.

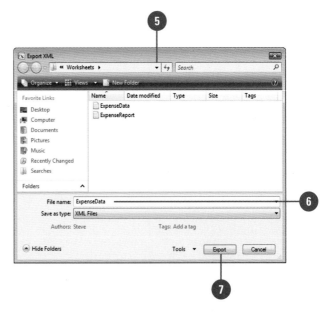

Save XML Data

① Open the worksheet with the XML data.

② Click the **Office** button, click **Save As**, and then click **Other Formats**.

③ Click the **Save as type** list arrow, and then click **XML Data** or **XML Spreadsheet 2003**.

④ Select a location where you want to save the XML data.

⑤ Type a name for the XML file.

⑥ Click **Save**.

⑦ If necessary, click **Continue**, click the XML map you want to use, and then click **OK**.

IMPORTANT *When you save with the XML Data format, the active worksheet is now the XML data. To work with the original worksheet, you need to re-open it.*

Did You Know?

You can also open an XML data file. Click the Office button, click Open, click the Files of type list arrow, click XML Files, select the XML data file, click Open, click the As an XML table, As a read-only workbook, or Use The XML Source task pane option, and then click OK.

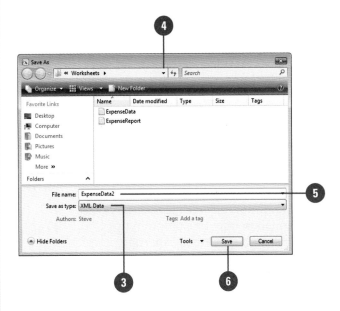

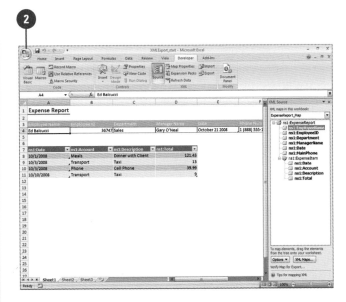

Sharing Information Between Programs

Office can convert data or text from one format to another using a technology known as **object linking and embedding (OLE)**. OLE allows you to move text or data between programs in much the same way as you move them within a program. The familiar cut and paste or drag and drop methods work between programs and documents just as they do within a document. In addition, Excel and all Office programs have special ways to move information from one program to another, including importing, exporting, embedding, linking, and hyperlinking.

Importing and Exporting

Importing and exporting information are two sides of the same coin. **Importing** copies a file created with the same or another program into your open file. The information becomes part of your open file, just as if you created it in that format. Some formatting and program-specific information such as formulas may be lost. **Exporting** converts a copy of your open file into the file type of another program. In other words, importing brings information into your open document, while exporting moves information from your open document into another program file.

Embedding

Embedding inserts a copy of a file created in one program into a file created in another program. Unlike imported files, you can edit the information in embedded files with the same commands and toolbar buttons used to create the original file. The original file is called the **source file**, while the file in which it is embedded is called the **destination file**. Any

changes you make to an embedded object appear only in the destination file; the source file remains unchanged.

For example, if you place an Excel chart into a PowerPoint presentation, Excel is the source program, and PowerPoint is the destination program. The chart is the source file; the workbook is the destination file.

Linking

Linking displays information from one file (the source file) in a file created in another program (the destination file). You can view and edit the linked object from either the source file or the destination file. The changes are stored in the source file but also appear in the destination file. As you work, Office updates the linked object to ensure you always have the most current information. Office keeps track of all the drive, folder, and file name information for a source file. However, if you move or rename the source file, the link between files will break.

Embedding and Linking

Term	Definition
Source program	The program that created the original object
Source file	The file that contains the original object
Destination program	The program that created the document into which you are inserting the object
Destination file	The file into which you are inserting the object

Once the link is broken, the information in the destination file becomes embedded rather than linked. In other words, changes to one copy of the file will no longer affect the other.

Hyperlinking

The newest way to share information between programs is hyperlinks—a term borrowed from World Wide Web technology. A **hyperlink** is an object (either colored, underlined text or a graphic) that you can click to jump to a different location in the same document or a different document.

Deciding Which Method to Use

With all these different methods for sharing information between programs to choose from, sometimes it is hard to decide which method to use. To decide which method is best for your situation, answer the following questions:

1. Do you want the contents of another file displayed in the open document?

    ◆ **No**. Create a hyperlink. See "Creating a Hyperlink" on page 398.

    ◆ **Yes**. Go to question 2.

2. Do you want to edit the content of the file from within the open document?

    ◆ **No**. Embed the file as a picture. See "Linking and Embedding Files" on page 382.

    ◆ **Yes**. Go to question 3.

3. Is the source program (the program used to create the file) available on your computer?

    ◆ **No**. Import the file. See "Exporting and Importing Data" on page 380.

    ◆ **Yes**. Go to question 4.

4. Do you want to use the source program commands to edit the file?

    ◆ **No**. Import the file. See "Exporting and Importing Data" on page 380.

    ◆ **Yes**. Go to question 5.

5. Do you want changes you make to the file to appear in the source file (the original copy of the file)?

    ◆ **No**. Embed the file. See "Exporting and Importing Data" on page 380.

    ◆ **Yes**. Link the file. See "Linking and Embedding Files" on page 382.

Exporting and Importing Data

In cases where you don't need the data you are using from another source to be automatically updated if the source data changes, the most expedient way to get the data is to copy and paste it. In cases where you want to copy data from one program to another, you can convert the data to a format that the other program accepts. If you have text you want to include on your worksheet, you can **import**, or open, a text file in a workbook.

Export Excel Data Using Copy and Paste

1. Select the cell or range that you want to copy.

2. Click the **Home** tab.

3. Click the **Copy** button.

4. Open the destination file, or click the program's taskbar button if the program is already open.

5. Select the cell where you want the data to be copied.

6. Click the **Paste** button.

7. Click the **Paste Options** button, and then click the option you want.

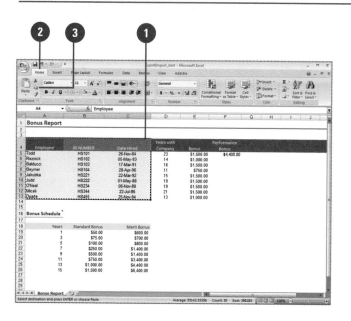

Did You Know?

Excel can save a file to a format only with an installed converter. If the format you want to save a file in does not appear in the Save as type list, you'll need to install it by running Setup from the Microsoft Office 2007 CD.

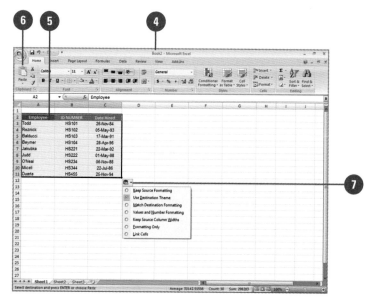

Export an Excel File to Another Program Format

1. Open the file from which you want to export data.

2. Click the **Office** button, click **Save As**, and then click **Other Formats**.

3. Click the **Save in** list arrow, and then click the drive or folder where you want to save the file.

4. Click the **Save as type** list arrow, and then click the format you want.

5. If you want, change the file name.

6. Click **Save**.

See Also

See "Saving a Workbook with Different Formats" on page 24 for information on Excel file formats.

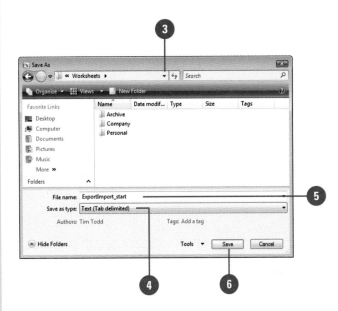

Import a Text File

1. Click the **Office** button, and then click **Open**.

2. Click the **Files of type** list arrow, and then click **Text Files**.

3. Click the **Look in** list arrow, and then select the folder where the text file is located.

4. Click the text file you want to import.

5. Click **Open**.

6. If the file is a text file (.txt), Excel starts the Import Text Wizard.

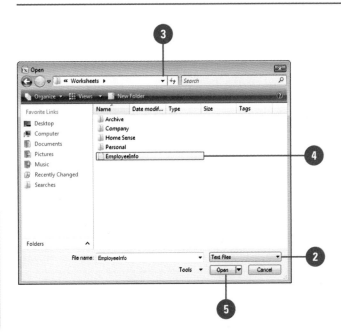

Linking and Embedding Files

Information created using other Office programs can be shared among them. This means that data created in an Excel workbook, and can be included in a Word document without being retyped. This makes projects such as annual or departmental reports simple to create. Information can be either **linked** or **embedded**. Data that is linked has the advantage of always being accurate because it is automatically updated when the linked document is modified.

Create a Link to Another File

1. Open the source file and any files containing information you want to link.

2. Select the information in the source file.

3. Click the **Home** tab.

4. Click the **Copy** button.

5. Click the insertion point in the file containing the link.

6. Click the **Paste** button arrow, and then click **Paste Link**.

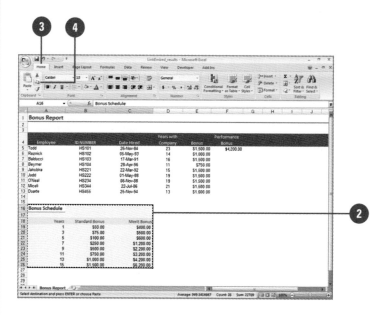

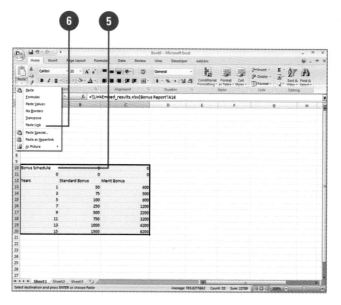

Did You Know?

You can edit an embedded object. Edit an embedded object only if the program that created it is installed on your computer.

Embed a New Object

1. Click the **Insert** tab.

2. Click **Insert Object** button.

3. Click the **Create New** tab.

4. Click the object type you want to insert.

5. Click **OK**.

6. Follow the necessary steps to insert the object.

   The steps will vary depending on the object type.

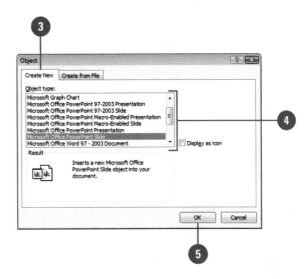

Embed or Link to an Existing Object

1. Click the **Insert** tab.

2. Click **Insert Object** button.

3. Click the **Create from File** tab.

4. Click **Browse**, locate and select the file that you want to link, and then click **Open**.

5. To create a link to the object, select the **Link to file** check box.

6. Click **OK**.

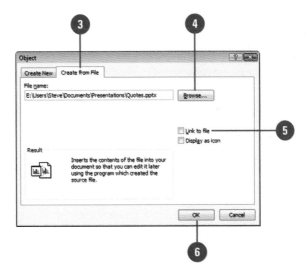

Did You Know?

You can update links each time you open a linked document. When you open a workbook that contains links, a warning dialog box opens asking you if you want to update all linked information (click Yes) or to keep the existing information (click No).

Consolidating Data

In some cases, you'll want to consolidate data from different worksheets or workbooks into one workbook, rather than simply linking the source data. For instance, if each division in your company creates a budget, you can pull together, or **consolidate**, the totals for each line item into one company-wide budget. If each divisional budget is laid out in the same way, with the budgeted amounts for each line item in the same cell addresses, then you can very easily consolidate the information without any retyping. If data in individual workbooks change, the consolidated worksheet or workbook will always be correct.

Consolidate Data from Other Worksheets or Workbooks

1. Open all the workbooks that contain the data you want to consolidate.

2. Open or create the workbook that will contain the consolidated data.

3. Select the destination range.

4. Click the **Data** tab.

5. Click the **Consolidate** button.

6. Click the **Function** list arrow, and then select the function you want to use to consolidate the data.

7. Type the location of the data to be consolidated, or click the **Collapse Dialog** button, and then select the cells to be consolidated.

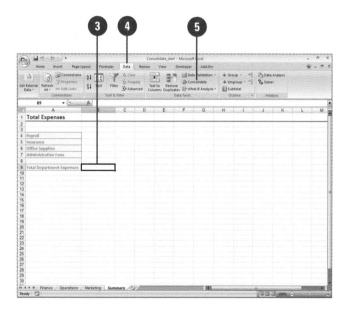

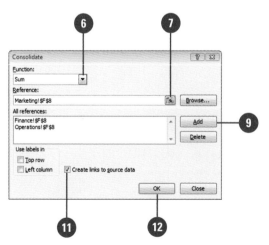

Did You Know?

You can include all labels. Make sure you select enough cells to accommodate any labels that might be included in the data you are consolidating.

8 Click the **Expand Dialog** button.

9 Click **Add** to add the reference to the list of consolidated ranges.

10 Repeat steps 7 through 9 until you have listed all references to consolidate.

11 Select the **Create links to source data** check box.

12 Click **OK**.

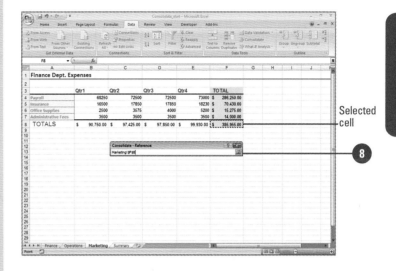

Selected cell

8

Did You Know?

You can consolidate worksheets even if they are not laid out identically. If the worksheets you want to consolidate aren't laid out with exactly the same cell addresses, but they do contain identical types of information, select the Top Row and Left Column check boxes in the Consolidate dialog box so that Excel uses labels to match up the correct data.

You can arrange multiple workbooks. Use the Window group on the View tab to move between workbooks or to arrange them so they are visible at the same time.

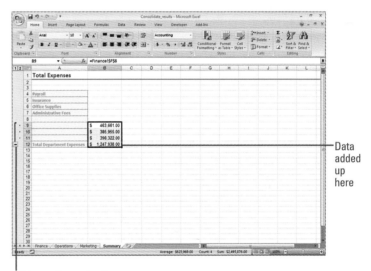

Data added up here

Click to collapse the data

Linking Data

A link can be as simple as a reference to a cell on another worksheet, or it can be part of a formula. You can link cells between sheets within one workbook or between different workbooks. Cell data to be linked is called the source data. The cell or range linked to the source data is called the destination cell or destination range. If you no longer want linked data to be updated, you can easily break a link. Create links instead of making multiple identical entries; it saves time and ensures your entries are correct.

Create a Link Between Worksheets or Workbooks

1. Select the cell or range that contains the source data.

2. Click the **Home** tab.

3. Click the **Copy** button.

4. Click the sheet tab where you want to link the data.

5. Select the destination cell or destination range.

6. Click the **Paste** button.

7. Click the **Paste Options** button, and then click **Link Cells**.

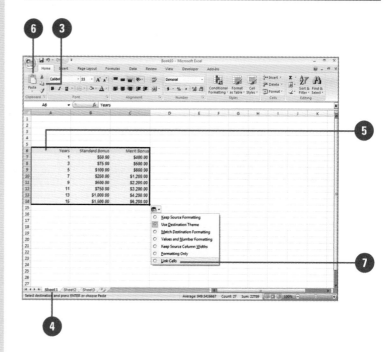

Did You Know?

You can include a link in a formula and treat the linked cell as one argument in a larger calculation. Enter the formula on the formula bar, and then select a cell in the worksheet or workbook you want to link. A cell address reference to a worksheet is =tab name!cell address (=Orders!A6). A cell reference to a workbook is ='[workbook name.xls]tab name'!cell address (='[Product Orders.xls]Orders'!A6).

You can arrange worksheet windows to make linking easier. To arrange open windows, click the View tab, and then click the Arrange All button.

Getting External Data

Introduction

If you need to temporarily exchange data between programs, copying and pasting or linking works the best. However, if you need to permanently exchange data, creating a connection to the data source is the best solution. A **data source** is a stored set of information that allows Excel to connect to an external database. A cell range, table, PivotTable report, or PivotChart report in Excel can be connected to an external data source.

External Data Sources

Microsoft allows you to retrieve data from several types of databases, including Microsoft Office Access, Microsoft Office Excel, Microsoft SQL Server, Microsoft SQL Server OLAP services, dBASE, Microsoft FoxPro, Oracle, Paradox, and text file databases. You can also use ODBC (Open Database Connectivity) drivers or data source drivers from other manufactures to retrieve information from other data sources. You can use the Data Connection Wizard to connect to an external data source that has already been

established. To open the Data Connection Wizard, click the Data tab, click the From Other Sources button, and then click From Data Connection Wizard. The Data tab also includes buttons to access Microsoft Access, Web, and Text data.

You retrieve data from a database by creating a query, which is data selection criteria to retrieve the data you want. Microsoft Query makes connections to external data sources and shows you what data is available. The **Query Wizard** helps you select data from different tables and fields in the data source, such as a database. During the wizard process you can sort and filter the data to retrieve only the information you want. After you create a query and import the data in a workbook, Microsoft Query provides Excel with query and data source information that you can use for other purposes.

After you connect to an external data source in an Excel workbook, all you need to do is refresh the data to update it from the source. You can refresh external data automatically when you open a workbook or at regular time intervals, or you can manually refresh external data using the Refresh button on the Data tab.

Security

When you open a workbook that connects to external data, the connection to the data source might be disabled if Excel detects a possible security risk. To connect to data when you open a workbook, you need to enable data connections by using the Trust Center, or by putting the workbook in a trusted location.

Managing Connections

You can use Excel to create and edit connections to external data sources (New!). When you create a connection, Excel stores the connection in the workbook or a connection file, such as Office Data Connection (ODC) file or a Universal Data Connection (UDC) file. A connection file is useful for sharing connections with other users. When you use a connection file, Excel copies the connection information into your Excel workbook. However, if you change connection information, the connection file is not updated. You can manage one or more connections to external data sources using the Workbook Connections dialog box. You can use the Connection Properties dialog to set options for connections to external data sources, and to use, reuse, or switch connection files.

Connect to External Data Using an Existing Connection

1. Click the **Data** tab.

2. Click the **Existing Connections** button.

   The Existing Connections dialog box opens.

3. Click the **Show** list arrow, and then click **All Connections** or the specific connection type you want to display.

4. Select the connection you want to use. If you don't see the connection you want, click **Browse for More**, and then click **New Source** to start the Data Connection Wizard.

5. Click **Open**.

6. If requested, click the table you want, and then click **OK**.

   The Import Data dialog box opens.

7. Click the **Table, PivotTable Report** or **PivotChart and PivotTable Report** option.

8. Click the **Existing worksheet** option, and then specify a cell location, or click the **New worksheet** option.

9. Click **OK**.

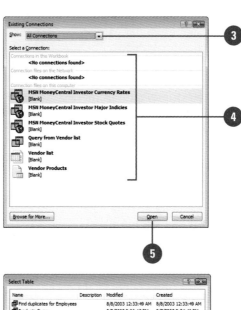

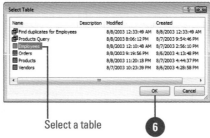

Select a table

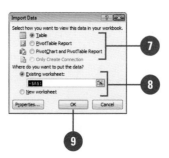

Change Connection Properties

1 Click the **Data** tab.

2 Click the **Connections** button.

3 To manage connections, do any of the following:

♦ **Add.** Click **Add**, click **OK** (if necessary for the security alert), and then connect to external data using the Existing Connections dialog box.

♦ **Remove.** Select the connection you want to remove, click **Remove**, and then click **OK**.

♦ **Properties.** Select the connection you want to change, click **Properties**, set refresh, formatting, and layout options, and then click **OK**.

♦ **Refresh.** Select a connection, click the **Refresh** button arrow, and then click a refresh option.

4 Click **Close**.

Did You Know?

You can refresh data in Excel from the data source. Click the Data tab, and then click the Refresh button arrow, and then click Refresh All to refresh multiple external data ranges. To refresh imported text, click the Refresh button arrow, click Refresh, select the text file, and then click Import.

You can remove the data connection from external data range. Click the Name box arrow, click the name of the external data range you want to remove the data connection, click the Tools tab, and then click the Unlink button.

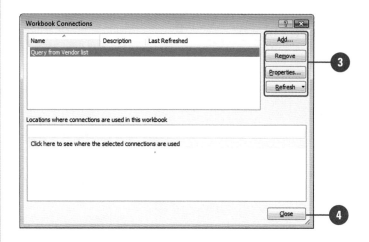

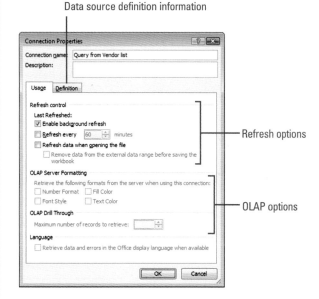

Data source definition information

Refresh options

OLAP options

Getting Query Data from a Database

If you have data in a database, you can use functions in Excel to retrieve data from a table in a database. To retrieve the data, you can select or create a data source, build a query to create a link to the data, and optionally, create a filter to limit the information. When you select or create a data source, you need to identify the database type and then connect to it. To build a query, you can use the Query wizard to step you through the process, or you can manually create a query the same way you do in Microsoft Access. You can also retrieve data from other sources. If you use the same table in a database for data, you can define and save the data source for use later.

Define a New Data Source

1. Click the **Data** tab.

2. Click the **From Other Source** button, and then click **From Microsoft Query**.

3. Click the **Databases** tab.

4. Click **<New Data Source>**.

5. Click **OK**.

6. Type the name of the source.

7. Click the second box list arrow, and then select a driver for the type of database, such as Driver do Microsoft Access Driver (*.mdb).

8. Click **Connect**.

9. Click **Select**.

10. Navigate to the folder with the database you want to use, and then click **OK**.

11. Click **OK** again.

12. Click the fourth box list arrow, and then click the default table for the data source.

13. Click **OK**.

    Follow the steps to create a query on the next page, starting with step 6.

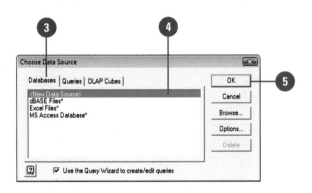

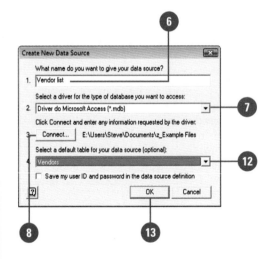

Create a Database Query

1. Click the **Data** tab.
2. Click the **From Other Source** button, and then click **From Microsoft Query**.
3. Click the **Databases** tab.
4. Click the name of the data sources you want to use.
5. Click **OK**.
6. Click a table column name, and then click **Add** to add it to your query. Add the columns you want.
7. Click **Next** to continue.
8. Click the name of the column by which you want to filter the results.
9. Click the first comparison operator list arrow, and then click the operator you want to use.
10. Type the first value to use in the comparison
11. If necessary, type a second value in the second value box.
12. Click **Next** to continue.
13. Click the **Sort by** list arrow, and then click the name of the column by which to sort the query results.
14. Click **Next** to continue.
15. Click **Save Query**, type a name for the query, and then click **Save**.
16. Click **Finish**.
17. Select the import options you want.
18. Click **OK**.

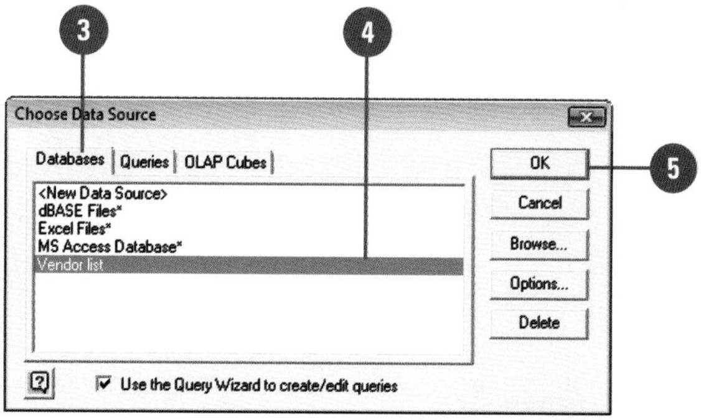

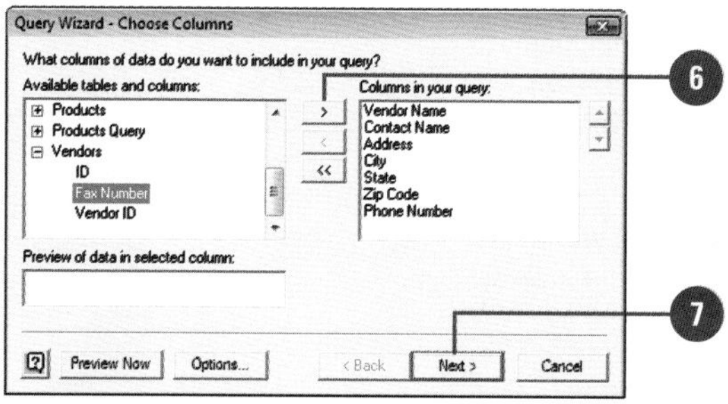

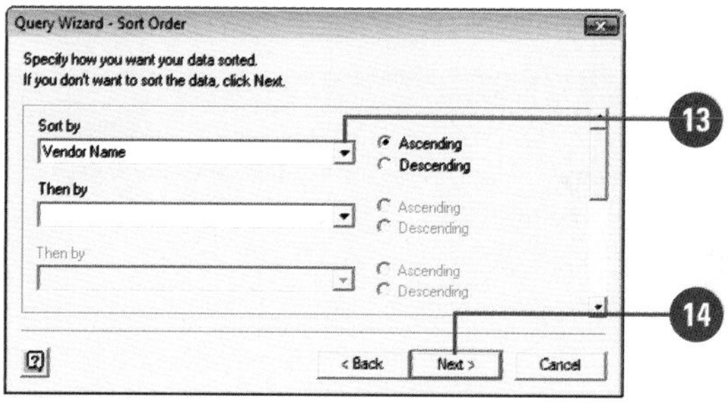

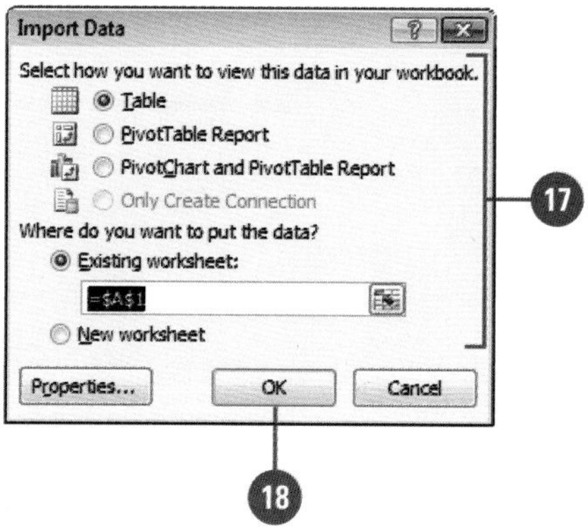

Getting Data from Microsoft Access

Information you want to analyze may not always exist in an Excel workbook; you might have to retrieve it from another Office program, such as Access. Access table data can be easily converted into Excel worksheet data. Before you can analyze Access data in a workbook, you must convert it to an Excel file. You can either use the Excel command in Access to export data as an Excel table file, or use the PivotTable or PivotChart and PivotTable Report option in Excel to use the Access data as a PivotTable, a table you can use to perform calculations with or rearrange large amounts of data.

Export an Access Database Table into an Excel Workbook

1 Click **Start** on the taskbar, point to **All Programs**, click **Microsoft Office**, and then click **Microsoft Office Access 2007**.

2 Open the database you want, and then display Tables in the task pane.

3 Click the table you want to analyze.

4 Click the **External Data** tab.

5 Click the **Excel** button in the Export group.

6 Specify the destination file name and format.

7 Specify the export options you want.

8 Click **OK**, and then click **Close**.

9 Use Excel tools to edit and analyze the data.

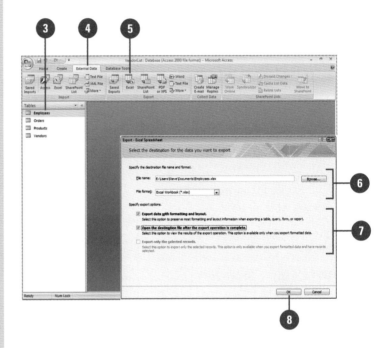

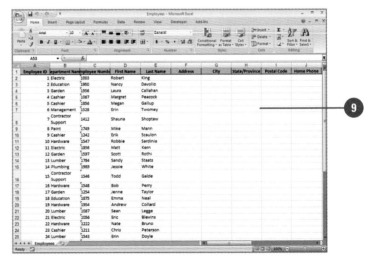

Create an Excel Workbook PivotTable from an Access Database

1 Click the **Data** tab.

2 Click the **From Access** button.

3 Click the table from Access you want to use.

4 Click **OK**.

5 Click the **PivotTable Report** or **PivotChart and PivotTable Report** option.

6 Click the **Existing worksheet** option, and then specify a cell location, or click the **New worksheet** option.

7 To set refresh, formatting, and layout options for the imported data, click **Properties**, make the changes you want, and then click **OK**.

8 Click **OK**.

9 Use tabs under PivotChart Tools to create and format the PivotChart.

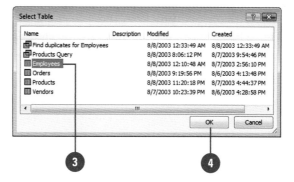

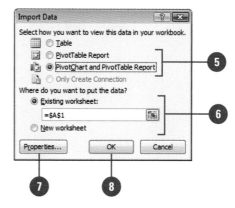

Getting Text Data

If you have data in a text file, you can either open the file using the Open command on the Office menu, or you can import the text file as an external data range using the From Text button on the Data tab. There are two commonly used text file formats to store data that you can import in Excel: Tab delimited text (.txt) and Comma separated values text (.csv). When you open a .txt file, Excel starts the Import Text Wizard. When you open a .csv file, Excel opens the file using current default data format settings.

Import a Text File

1. Open the workbook in which you want to insert text data.

2. Click the **Data** tab.

3. Click the **From Text** button.

4. Click the **Files of type** list arrow, and then click **Text Files**.

5. Click the **Look in** list arrow, and then select the folder where the text file is located.

6. Click the text file you want to import.

7. Click **Import**.

8. If the file is a text file (.txt), Excel starts the Import Text Wizard. Step through the wizard (3 steps), and then click **Finish**.

9. Click the **Existing worksheet** option, and then specify a cell location, or click the **New worksheet** option.

10. Click **OK**.

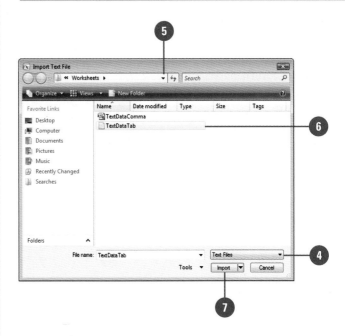

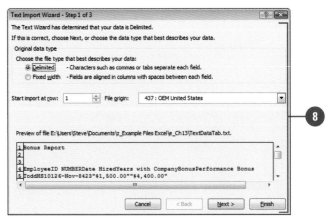

Publishing Data on the Web

14

Introduction

Microsoft Office Excel provides you with the tools you need to create and save your workbook as a Web page and to publish it on the Web. The Save As command allows you to format your workbook in **Hypertext Markup Language (HTML)**, a simple coding system used to format documents for an intranet or the Internet. Saving your workbook in HTML format means you can use most Web browsers to view your workbook. Any workbook can easily be saved as a Web document and viewed in a Web browser. By saving your Excel workbooks as Web pages, you can share your data with others via the Internet.

Incorporating hyperlinks within your Microsoft Office Excel worksheet adds an element of connectivity to your work. You can create a worksheet and then have a hyperlink with supporting research to add to the content of your data. Or, you can copy data from a Web page and incorporate it into your Excel workbook. Either way, using the Web to publish Excel data or incorporate research into your workbook, is a great resource.

Opening a Workbook as a Web Page

After saving a workbook as a Web page, you can open the Web page, an HTML file, in Excel. This allows you to quickly and easily switch from HTML to the standard Excel format and back again without losing any formatting or functionality. For example, if you create a formatted chart in an Excel workbook, save the workbook file as a Web page, and then reopen the Web page in Excel, the chart will look the same as the original chart in Excel. Excel preserves the original formatting and functionality of the workbook.

Open a Workbook as a Web Page in Excel

1. Click the **Office** button, and then click **Open**.

2. Click the **Files of type** list arrow, and then click **All Web Pages**.

3. Click the **Look in** list arrow, and then select the folder where the file is located.

4. Click the Web workbook file.

5. Click **Open**.

   ◆ To open the Web page in your browser, click the **Open** button arrow, and then click **Open in Browser**.

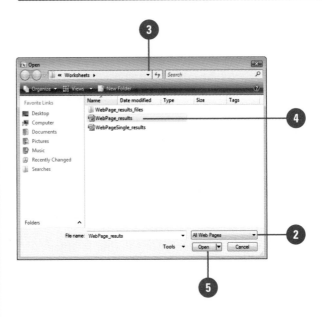

Did You Know?

You can change the appearance of Web pages and Help Viewer window. In the Internet Options dialog box for Windows, click Accessibility on the General tab, select the Ignore colors specified on Web pages check box, and then click OK. In the Internet Properties dialog box, click Colors to select text and background colors or Fonts to change text style.

Previewing a Web Page

You can view any Excel worksheet as if it were already on the Web by previewing the Web page. By previewing a file you want to post to the Web, you can see if there are any errors that need to be corrected, formatting that needs to be added, or additions that need to be made. Just as you should always preview a worksheet before you print it, you should preview a Web page before you post it. Previewing the Web page is similar to using the Print Preview feature before you print a worksheet. This view shows you what the page will look like once it's posted on the Internet. You do not have to be connected to the Internet to preview a worksheet as a Web page.

View the Web Page

1. Open the workbook file you want to view as a Web page.

2. Click the **Web Page Preview** button on the Quick Access Toolbar.

   If necessary, use the Customize pane in Excel Options to add the button to the Quick Access Toolbar.

   Your default Web browser starts and displays the Web page.

3. Click the **Close** button to quit your Web browser, and then return to Excel.

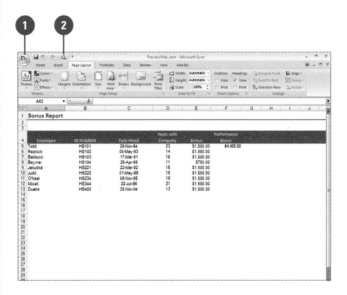

Workbook Web Page

Did You Know?

Web addresses and URLs mean the same thing. Every Web page has a Uniform Resource Locator (URL), or Web address. Each URL contains specific parts that identify where a Web page is located. For example, the URL for Perspection's Web page is: *http://www.perspection.com/index.htm* where "http://" shows the address is on the Web, "www.perspection.com" shows the computer that stores the Web site, and "index.htm" is a Web page on the Web site.

Creating a Hyperlink

Microsoft
Certified
Application
Specialist

EX07S-2.3.8

With instant access to the Internet, your worksheet can contain links to specific sites so you and anyone else using your worksheet can access Web information. An Internet link that is embedded on a worksheet is called a **hyperlink**—because when it is clicked, you are instantly connected to the link's defined address on the Web. If your worksheet contains a hyperlink, the link appears in a worksheet cell as blue text. When you point to hyperlinked text or an object, the cursor changes to a pointing hand to indicate it's a hyperlink. To connect to the linked location, such as a Web site, just click the hyperlink.

Create or Edit a Hyperlink

1. Select a cell or object, such as a picture, where you want to create or edit a hyperlink.

2. Click the **Insert** tab.

3. Click the **Hyperlink** button.

   TIMESAVER Press Ctrl+K.

4. Click one of the icons on the Link To bar for quick access to frequently used files, Web pages, and links.

   ◆ **Existing File or Web Page.** Click to link to a workbook or other file.

   ◆ **Place in This Document.** Click to link to another location in the current workbook. Select or type a cell reference, or select a defined name.

   ◆ **Create New Document.** Click to link to a new document.

   ◆ **E-mail Address.** Click to create a link to an e-mail address. When you click the e-mail address, your e-mail program automatically opens with the address.

5. Type or select the name and location of the file or Web page you want to link to.

6. Click **OK**.

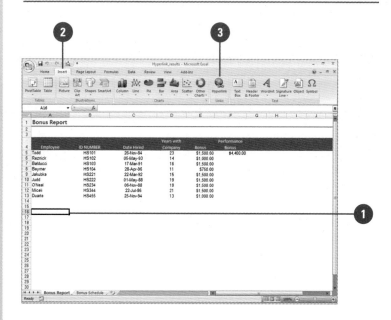

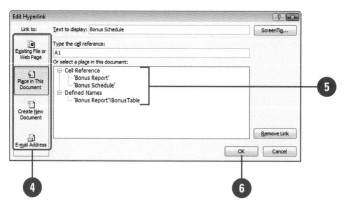

Jump to a Hyperlink

1. Click the hyperlink on your worksheet.

   Excel opens the linked location. For Web addresses, Excel opens your Web browser, displaying the Web page associated with the hyperlink..

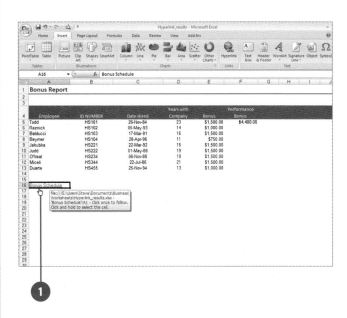

Remove a Hyperlink

1. Right-click the cell containing the hyperlink you want to remove.

2. Do one of the following:

   ◆ **Clear Contents** to delete a hyperlink and the text.

   ◆ **Remove Hyperlink** to remove the hyperlink and keep the text.

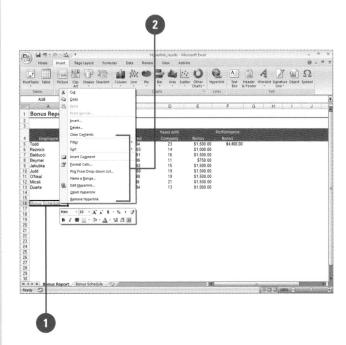

Formatting a Hyperlink

Excel comes with a set of predefined cell styles (**New!**) for various data types, including hyperlinks, in a worksheet. When you create a hyperlink, the default cell style is used to format the text. If you want to change the appearance of hyperlinks in your workbook, you need to change the cell style for hyperlinks.

Change the Hyperlink Cell Style

1. Click the **Home** tab.

2. Click the **Cell Styles** button.

3. Right-click the **Hyperlink** or **Followed Hyperlink**, and then click **Modify**.

4. Click **Format**.

5. Select the formatting options you want on the Font and Fill tabs, and then click **OK**.

6. Select the check boxes with the formatting you want to include in the modified cell style.

7. Click **OK**.

Did You Know?

You can change the text or graphic for a hyperlink. Select the cell with the hyperlink, click in the formula bar, and then edit the text. Right-click the graphic, and then click the option you need to change in the hyperlink.

You can copy or move a hyperlink. Right-click the hyperlink you want to copy or move, click Copy or Cut. Right-click the cell you want to copy or move the hyperlink to, and then click Paste.

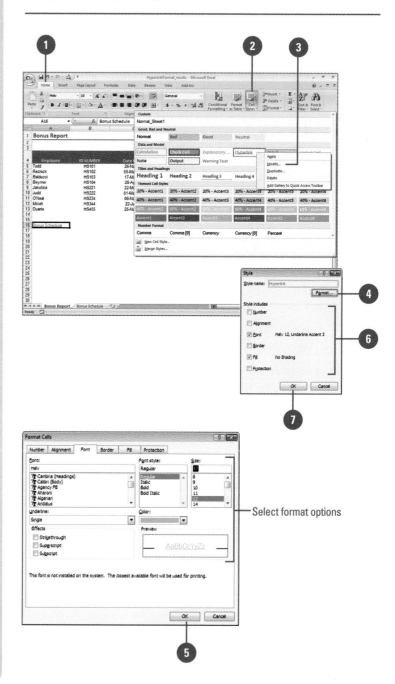

Select format options

Changing Web Page Options

When you save or publish a workbook as a Web page, you can change the appearance of the Web page by changing Excel's Web options. You can set Web options to save any additional hidden data necessary to maintain formulas, allow PNG as a graphic format, rely on CSS for font formatting, reply on VML for displaying graphics in browser, and save new Web pages as Single File Web Pages. Web pages are saved using the appropriate international text encoding so users on any language system are able to view the correct characters.

Change Web Page Options

1. Click the **Office** button, and then click **Excel Options**.

2. In the left pane, click **Advanced**.

3. Click **Web Options**.

4. Click the **General** tab, and then select or clear the Web pages options:

   ◆ **Save any additional hidden data necessary to maintain formulas.**

   ◆ **Load pictures from Web pages not created in Excel.**

5. Click the **Browsers** tab.

6. Click the **Target Browsers** list arrow, and then select the version you want to support.

7. Select or clear the Web page options:

   ◆ **Allow PNG as a graphic format.**

   ◆ **Rely on CSS for font formatting.** Cascading Style Sheets for Web page formatting.

   ◆ **Reply on VML for displaying graphics in browser.** VML is Vector Markup Language, XML based graphics.

   ◆ **Save new Web pages as Single File Web Pages.**

8. Click **OK**.

9. Click **OK**.

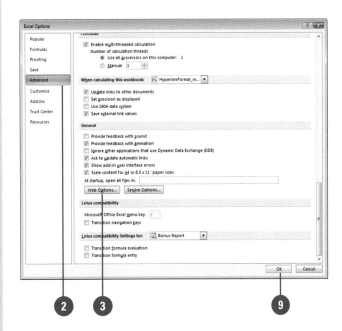

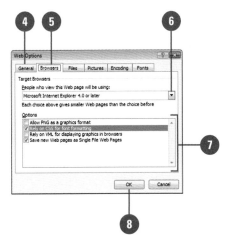

Saving a Worksheet as a Web Page

You can place an existing Excel worksheet on the Internet for others to use. In order for any document to be placed on the Web, it must be in **HTML** (Hypertext Markup Language) format—a simple coding system that specifies the formats a Web browser uses to display the document. This format enables you to post, or submit Excel data on a Web site for others. You don't need any HTML knowledge to save an Excel worksheet as a Web page. When you save a worksheet as a Web page, you can save it using the Web Page or Single File Web Page format. The Web Page format saves the worksheet as an HTML file and a folder that stores supporting files, such as a file for each graphic, worksheet, and so on. Excel selects the appropriate graphic format for you based on the image's content. A single file Web page saves all the elements of a Web site, including text and graphics, into a single file in the MHTML format, which is supported by Internet Explorer 4.0.1 or later.

Save a Workbook or Worksheet as a Web Page

1. Click the **Office** button, and then click **Save As**.

2. Click the **Save as type** list arrow, and then click **Web Page.**

3. Click the **Save in** list arrow, and then select a location for your Web page.

4. Type the name for the Web page.

5. Click the **Entire Workbook** or **Selection: Sheet** option.

6. To change the title of your Web page, click **Change Title**, type the new title in the Set Page Title box, and then click **OK**.

7. To save a thumbnail preview of the Web page, select the **Save Thumbnail** check box.

8. Click **Save**.

9. If necessary, click **Yes** to keep workbook formatting.

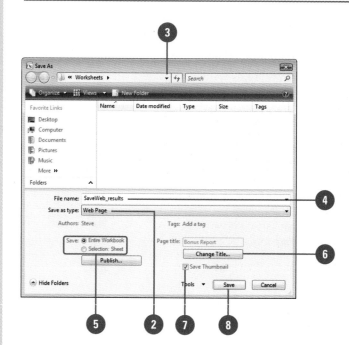

Save a Workbook or Worksheet as a Single File Web Page

1. Click the **Office** button, and then click **Save As**.

2. Click the **Save as type** list arrow, and then click **Single File Web Page**.

3. Click the **Save in** list arrow, and then select a location for your Web page.

4. Type the name for the Web page.

5. Click the **Entire Workbook** or **Selection: Sheet** option.

6. To change the title of your Web page, click **Change Title**, type the new title in the Set Page Title box, and then click **OK**.

7. To save a thumbnail preview of the Web page, select the **Save Thumbnail** check box.

8. Click **Save**.

9. If necessary, click **Yes** to keep workbook formatting.

   The Web page is saved as a single file.

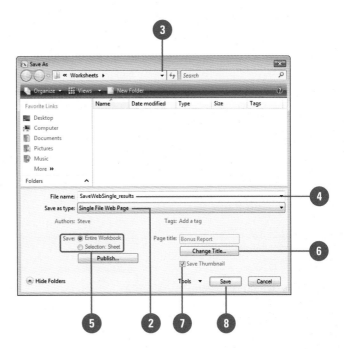

Publishing a Web Page

At times, you'll want to publish a copy of your current workbook in HTML format directly to a **Web server** (a computer on the Internet or intranet that stores Web pages) so others can view and manipulate your data. Publishing to a Web server is as simple as saving a file. You can publish a complete workbook, a single worksheet, or a range of worksheets. A worksheet saved as a Web page retains all its spreadsheet, charting, or PivotTable functionality and formatting properties. This interactivity means that while your worksheet is on the Web, others can manipulate your data. You can elect to let anyone using Internet Explorer 4.01 or later interact with your data from Excel.

Save and Publish a Worksheet as an Interactive Web Page

1. To publish part of a worksheet, select the range you want saved as a Web page.

2. Click the **Office** button, and then click **Save As.**

3. Click the **Save as type** list arrow, and then click **Web Page.**

4. Click the **Save in** list arrow, and then select a location for your Web page.

5. Click the **Selection: Sheet** or **Entire Worksheet** option.

6. Type the name for the Web page or Web address.

7. To change the title of your Web page, click **Change Title**, type the new title in the Set Page Title box, and then click **OK**.

8. Click **Publish**.

9. Click the **Choose** list arrow, and then select the items you want to publish in the Web page.

10. Select or clear the **AutoPublish everytime this workbook is saved** check box.

11. Select or clear the **Open published web page in browser** check box.

12. Click **Publish**.

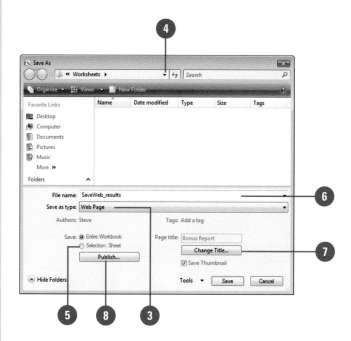

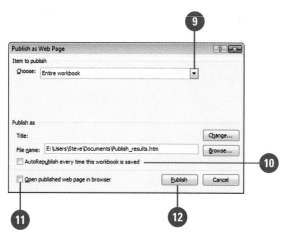

Copying a Web Table to a Worksheet

You can copy tabular information on a Web page and paste or drag the information into an Excel worksheet. It's an easy way to transfer and manipulate Web-based table data using Excel. Excel simplifies access to table data by making it available to anyone with a browser. If you need to make changes to the table, you can use normal editing techniques in Excel.

Copy a Web Table to a Worksheet

1. Open your Web browser.

2. In the Address bar, type the location of the Web page with the table data you want to copy, and then press Enter.

3. Select the table data in the Web page you want to copy.

4. Open the Excel worksheet where you want to paste the table data.

5. Right-click the taskbar, and then click **Show Windows Side by Side** (Vista) or **Tile Windows Vertically** (XP).

6. Drag the table data from the Web browser window to the location on the worksheet where you want the table data, and then release the mouse button.

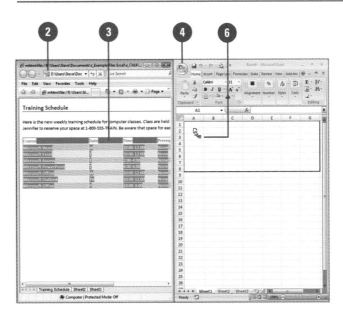

Did You Know?

You can use copy and paste to transfer table data to Excel. In your browser, select the table data you want, copy the data, switch to Excel, click the cell where you want to place the table data, and then click the Paste button on the Home tab.

Creating Refreshable Web Queries

If you need to analyze Web data in a worksheet, you can use the copy and paste commands to bring the data from a Web page into the worksheet. The Paste Options button allows you to specify whether you want the information to keep the data as it is right now or make it refreshable to the current data on the Web. As the data changes on the Web, you can use the Refresh button to quickly update the data in your worksheet. You don't need to copy the information again.

Copy and Paste Refreshable Data from the Web

1. Open the Web page with the information you want to copy into a worksheet, and then select the data.

2. Copy the data.

3. Switch to Excel, and then click the active cell where you want the data.

4. Click the **Paste** button on the Home tab.

5. Click the **Paste Options** button, and then click **Create Refreshable Web Query**.

6. Click the arrow buttons to select the information you want.

7. Click **Import**.

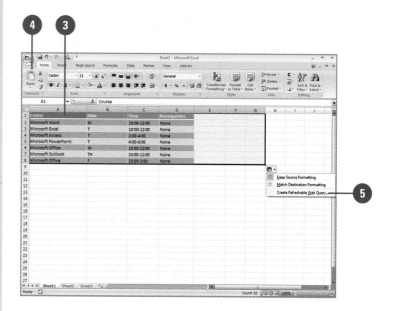

Did You Know?

You can quickly refresh a Web query. Click a cell in the worksheet with the query data, click the Data tab, and then click the Refresh button. A spinning refresh icon appears in the status bar to indicate that the query is running. You can double-click the icon to check the status of the query.

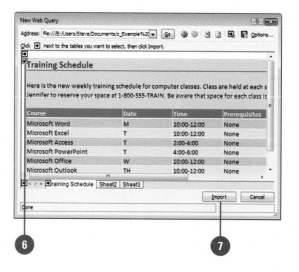

Getting Data from Web Queries

You can import data into Excel through database and Web queries and analyze data with formulas and formatting. You can insert columns within query tables and apply formulas and formatting. When data is refreshed, the formatting and analysis are retained. Excel helps you through the process of bringing data from a Web page to your worksheet. You can create a new Web query as you choose the URL and parameters for how you want to import the Web data. Once you save the query, you can run it again at any time.

Get Data from a New Web Query

① Click the **Data** tab.

② Click the **From Web** button.

③ Type the address for the Web page that contains the data you want.

④ Click the arrow buttons to select the information you want.

⑤ Click **Options** to select the formatting you want your data to keep.

⑥ Click **Import**.

⑦ Click the **Existing worksheet** option and specify a starting cell, or click the **New worksheet** option.

⑧ Click **OK**.

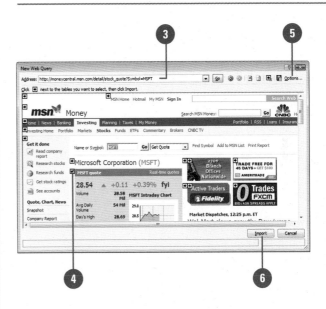

Saving Web Queries

When you create a Web query, it is automatically saved for use in the current workbook. If you need the same query in another workbook, you can save the Web query in a separate file. When you save a query, the file uses the .iqy extension, which you can import into another workbook. After you save a Web query, you can use the Existing Connections button to import the query data into a worksheet.

Save a Web Query

1. Click the **Data** tab.

2. Click the **From Web** button.

3. Display the Web page that contains the data you want.

4. Click the **Save Query** button.

5. Select the drive and folder in which you want to save the query.

6. Type a name for the query.

7. Click **Save**.

8. Click **Cancel**.

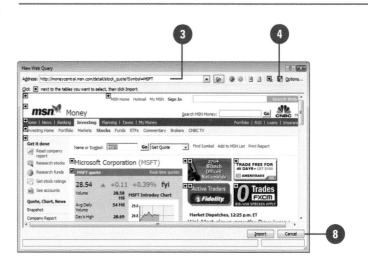

Import a Query

1. Click the **Data** tab.

2. Click the **Existing Connections** button.

3. Click the Web query you want to import.

4. Click **Open**.

5. Click the **Existing worksheet** option and specify a cell location, or click the **New worksheet** option, and then **OK** to insert the query data.

6. To refresh the query data, click the **Refresh All** button arrow, and then click **Refresh**.

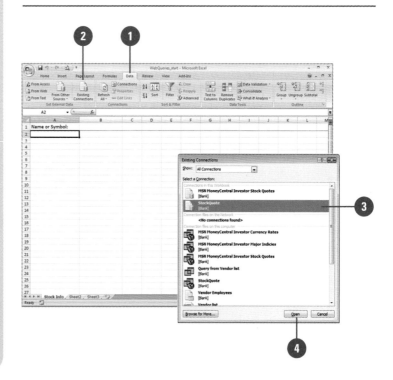

Accessing Office Information on the Web

New information about programs comes out with great frequency. You have access to an abundance of information about Excel and other programs in the Office Suite from Microsoft. This information is constantly being updated. Answers to frequently asked questions, user forums, and update offers are some of the types of information you can find about Microsoft Office. You can also find out about conferences, books, and other products that help you learn just how much you can do with your Office software.

Find Online Office Information

1. Click the **Office** button, and then click **Excel Options**.

2. In the left pane, click **Resources**.

3. Click **Go Online**.

   Your Web browser opens, displaying the Microsoft Office Online Web page.

4. Click a hyperlink of interest.

5. Click the **Close** button to quit the browser and return to Excel.

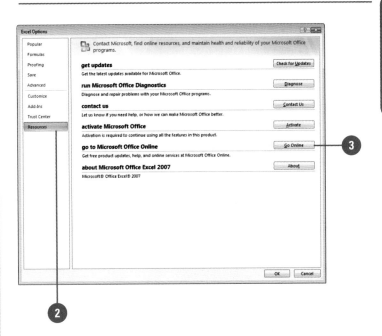

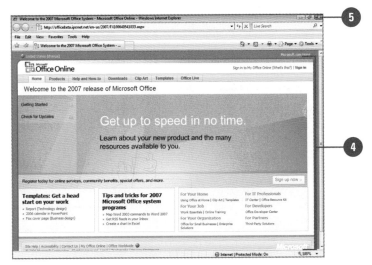

Getting Documents from the Web

File Transfer Protocol (FTP) is an inexpensive and efficient way to transfer files between your computer and others on the Internet. You can download or receive, from another computer, any kind of file, including text, graphics, sound, and video files. To download a file, you need an ID and password to identify who you are. Anonymous FTP sites are open to anyone; they usually use *anonymous* as an ID and your *e-mail address* as a password. You can also save the FTP site address to revisit the site later.

Add or Modify FTP Locations

1. Click the **Office** button, and then click **Open**.

2. Click the **Look in** list arrow, and then click **Add/Modify FTP Locations** (in Windows XP).

3. Type the complete address for an FTP site.

4. Type your e-mail address as the password.

5. Click **Add**.

6. Click **OK**.

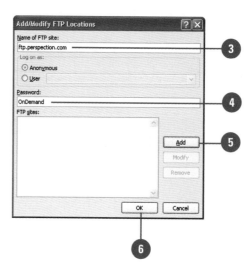

Access an FTP Site

1. Click the **Office** button, and then click **Open**.

2. Click the **Look in** list arrow, and then click **FTP Locations** (in Windows XP).

3. Click the FTP site to which you want to log in.

4. Select a Log on as option.

5. Enter a password (your E-mail address or personal password).

6. Click **OK**.

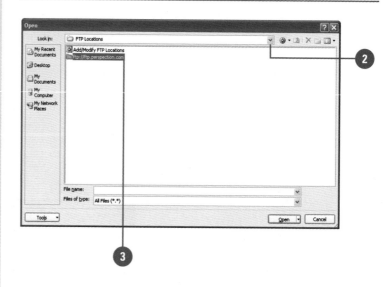

Tools for Working More Efficiently

15

Introduction

Once you've become familiar with Microsoft Office Excel and all its features, you might want to customize the way you work with Excel. You can change your view settings so that your Excel window looks the way you want it to. Excel comes with set defaults—such as opening all documents using a certain view, showing the vertical ruler, or how many files you've recently opened—which you can change to suit your needs.

Some of the other Excel customization features allow you to set a default font and related attributes to use when you are typing text in text boxes. Other defaults might be the color or line style of a shape object that you create. You can change the location of the Ribbon and the configuration of the Quick Access Toolbar to include commands not available on the Ribbon.

When you want to scan one or more documents or faxes and recognize the text using an Optical Character Recognition (OCR), Microsoft Office Document Scanning and Document Imaging gives you the tools you need to quickly and easily scan and recognize text for use in Excel. All you need is scanner hardware.

When you need to manage all the pictures on your computer, Microsoft Office Picture gives you a flexible way to organize, edit, and share your pictures. With Picture Manager, you can view all the pictures on your computer no matter where you store them. If you need to edit a picture, you can use Picture Manager to remove red eye and to change brightness, contrast, and color. You can also crop, rotate and flip, resize, and compress a picture.

Setting Popular Excel Options

You can customize the performance of many Excel features including its editing, saving, spelling, viewing, printing and security procedures. Each person uses Excel in a different way. Excel Options allows you to change popular options to personalize what appears in the Excel window (New!). When you change these options, Excel uses them for all subsequent Excel sessions until you change them again.

Change Popular Options

1. Click the **Office** button, and then click **Excel Options**.

2. In the left pane, click **Popular**.

3. Select the Top options for working with Excel you want:

   ◆ **Show Mini Toolbar on Selection** (New!). Select to show a miniature semi-transparent toolbar that helps you work with selected text.

   ◆ **Enable Live Preview** (New!). Select to show preview changes in a workbook.

   ◆ **Show Developer tab in the Ribbon** (New!). Select to access developer controls, write code, or create macros.

   ◆ **Color Scheme** (New!). Click the list arrow to select a Windows related color scheme.

   ◆ **ScreenTip style** (New!). Click the list arrow to select a screentip option: Show enhanced ScreenTips, Don't show enhanced ScreenTips, or Don't show ScreenTips.

4. Type your name as you want them to appear in Properties, and review comments.

5. Click **OK**.

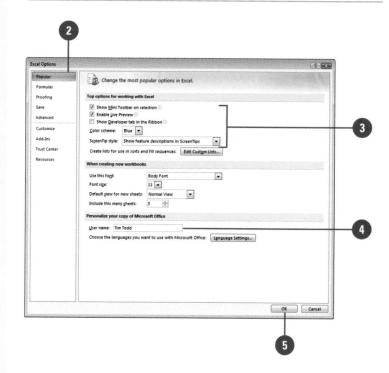

Setting New Workbook Options

You can customize several settings in the Excel work environment to suit the way you like to work. You can make general changes, including the default font and the number of sheets in a new workbook. If your workbooks usually contain five sheets, you could make five the workbook default. Taking a few minutes to change Excel's default setting saves time in the long run.

Change New Workbook Options

1. Click the **Office** button, and then click **Excel Options**.

2. In the left pane, click **Popular**.

3. Click the **Use this font** list arrow, and then select a font.

4. Click the **Font size** list arrow, and then select a font size.

5. Click the **Default view for new sheets** list arrow, and then select a view, either Normal View, Page Break Preview, or Page Layout View.

6. Specify the number of sheets you want to include in this workbook.

7. Click **OK**.

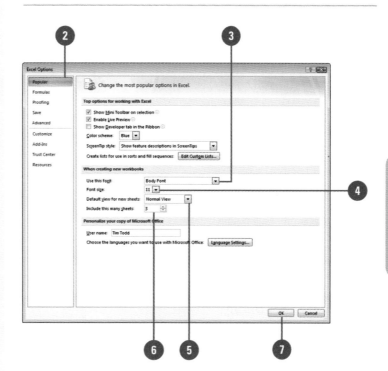

Did You Know?

You can change the appearance of Office programs in Windows. The appearance of the ribbon, toolbars, menus, and dialog boxes in Microsoft Office programs follows the theme or color scheme you set up in the Windows control panel.

Setting Editing Options

If you spend a lot of time modifying worksheets, you can set editing options in Excel to customize the way you work. You can set options to specify the move direction after pressing Enter, allow editing directly in cells, use system number separators or ones you specify, automatically insert a decimal point, or extend data range formats and formulas. Editing options are available on the Advanced pane in the Excel Options dialog box.

Change Edit Options

1. Click the **Office** button, and then click **Excel Options**.

2. In the left pane, click **Advanced**.

3. Select or clear any of the check boxes to change the editing options you want, some options include:

    - **After pressing Enter, move selection Direction.** Specify a direction (Default Down).

    - **Automatically insert a decimal point.** Specify number of decimal places.

    - **Enable fill handle and cell drag-and-drop (New!).** (Default on).

    - **Allow editing directly in cells.** (Default on).

    - **Extend data range formats and formulas.** (Default on).

    - **Enable automatic percent entry.** (Default on).

    - **Enable AutoComplete for cell values.** (Default on).

    - **Alert the user when a potentially time consuming operation occurs (New!).** (Default on).

    - **Use system separators.** Number format separators (Default on).

4. Click **OK**.

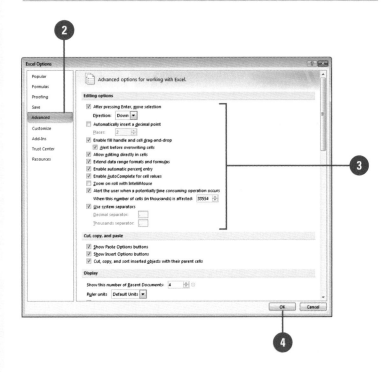

For Your Information

AutoFormatting While You Type

As you work in Excel, you can use AutoCorrect Options to automatically format certain types of text. You can set options to replace Internet and network paths with hyperlinks as you type, include new rows and columns in tables, and automatically fill in formulas in tables to create calculations in columns. To change AutoFormat options, click the Office button, click Excel Options, click Proofing in the left pane, click AutoCorrect Options, click the AutoFormat As You Type tab, select or clear options, and then click OK.

Setting Display View Options

Excel Options allows you to personalize what appears in the Excel window. You can customize the way Excel appears when you work on a worksheet. If you need more room to view another row of data, you can hide the Formula bar or Status bar. You can set chart options to show chart elements and data point values. If you're working with functions to create a formula, you can show function ScreenTips to help decide which function to use and how to use it.

Change Display View Options

1. Click the **Office** button, and then click **Excel Options**.

2. In the left pane, click **Advanced**.

3. Select or clear any of the check boxes to change the display options you want.

   - **Show this number of Recent Documents.** Set to 0 to turn off the recent documents display. (Default is 4).

   - **Ruler units (New!).** Set ruler units to Inches, Centimeters, or Millimeters in Page Layout view. (Default is Default Units).

   - **Show all windows in the Taskbar.** Select to show each workbook window on the taskbar. (Default on).

   - **Show formula bar.** (Default on).

   - **Show function ScreenTips.** (Default on).

   - **Show chart element names on hover.** (Default on).

   - **Show data point values on hover.** (Default on).

   - **For cells with comments, show: No comments or indicators, Indicators only, or comments on hover** (Default), or **Comments and indicators.**

4. Click **OK**.

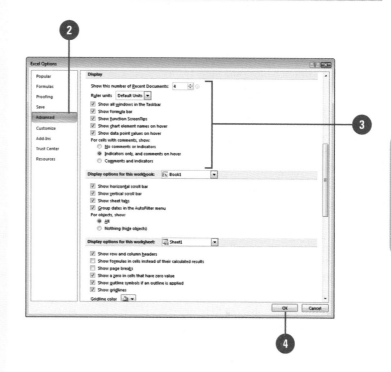

Setting Workbook and Worksheet Display Options

You can customize the way Excel appears when you work on a worksheet. If you don't use scroll bars or sheet tabs, you can hide them to display more data. If you are creating a custom spreadsheet, you can change the color of the gridlines or hide them all together. If you prefer not to see zeroes in cells, you can hide zero values until they change. The Advanced pane in the Excel Options dialog box allows you to change the way you view a worksheet or workbook in Excel to suit your needs (**New!**).

Change Workbook Display Options

1. Click the **Office** button, and then click **Excel Options**.

2. In the left pane, click **Advanced**.

3. Click the **Display options for this workbook** list arrow, and then select the option where you want to apply display options.

4. Select the workbook display options you want:

   ◆ **Show horizontal scroll bar.** Select to display horizontal scroll bars.

   ◆ **Show vertical scroll bar.** Select to display vertical scroll bars.

   ◆ **Show sheet tabs.** Select to display worksheet tab.

   ◆ **Group dates in the AutoFilter menu (New!).** Select to group the list of dates at the bottom of the AutoFilter menu in a date filter. Clear to manually select dates from the list.

   ◆ **For objects, show.** Click All or Nothing (hide objects) option.

5. Click **OK**.

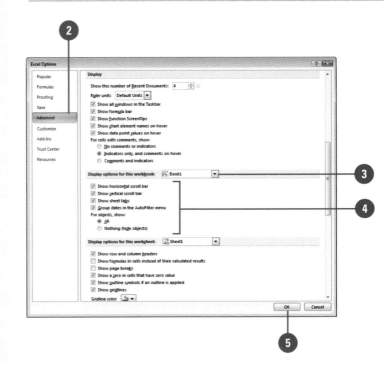

Change Worksheet Display Options

1. Click the **Office** button, and then click **Excel Options**.

2. In the left pane, click **Advanced**.

3. Click the **Display options for this worksheet** list arrow, and then select the option where you want to apply display options.

4. Select the worksheet display options you want:

   ◆ **Show row and column headers**. Select to show row and column headers.

   ◆ **Show formulas in cells instead of their calculated results**. Select to show formulas instead of results.

   ◆ **Show page breaks**. Select to show page breaks.

   ◆ **Show a zero in cells that have zero value**. Select to show 0 in cells with a zero value.

   ◆ **Show outline symbols if an outline is applied**. Click All or Nothing (hide objects) option.

   ◆ **Show gridlines**. Select to show gridlines. Click Gridline color button, and then select a color.

5. Click **OK**.

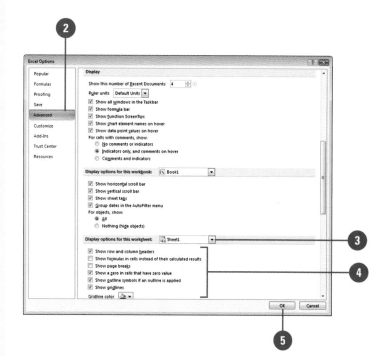

Setting Advanced Options

In addition to display options, the Advanced pane in Excel options also includes options when performing calculations in a workbook and when providing general user feedback. You can set the precision option to permanently change stored values in cells from full precision (15 digits) to the current format, or you can set the feedback options to play sound, show simple cell, row, or column animation, show add-in user interface error, or display alerts to update links.

Change Advanced Options

1. Click the **Office** button, and then click **Excel Options**.

2. In the left pane, click **Advanced**.

3. Click the **When calculating this workbook** list arrow, and then select the option where you want to apply display options.

4. Select the calculating options you want:

   - **Update links to other documents**. (Default on).
   - **Set precision as displayed**.
   - **Use 1904 date system**.
   - **Save external link values**.

5. Select the general options you want:

   - **Provide feedback with sound**. (Default off).
   - **Provide feedback with animation**.
   - **Ignore other applications that use Dynamic Data Exchange (DDE)**. Select to disable embedding and linking. (Default off).
   - **Ask to update automatic links**.
   - **Show add-in user interface errors**.
   - **Scale content for A4 or 8.5 x 11' paper sizes**.

6. Click **OK**.

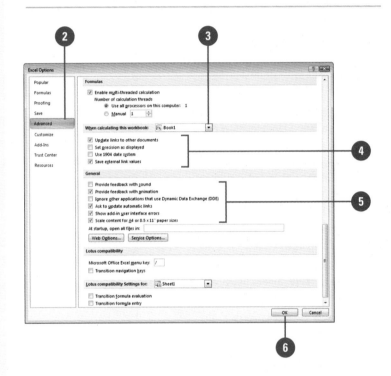

Setting Formula Options

Performing calculations is an important part of working with Excel. To customize the way you work with formulas, you can set options on the Formulas pane in the Excel Options dialog box. If you need to create a nested function (one that references itself), you can set a calculation option to enable iterative calculations. Instead of using the A1 cell reference style, you can use the R1C1 cell reference style, which labels columns and row numerically.

Change Formula Options

1. Click the **Office** button, and then click **Excel Options**.

2. In the left pane, click **Formulas**.

3. Select the calculation options you want:

   ◆ **Workbook Calculation**. Click the Automatic (Default), Automatic except for data tables, or Manual option.

   ◆ **Enable iterative calculation**. Select to allow nested calculations. (Default off). Specify the maximum number of time, and the amount of change to stop it.

4. Select the formula options you want:

   ◆ **R1C1 reference style**. Select to label columns and rows numerically (Default off).

   ◆ **Formula AutoComplete**. (Default on).

   ◆ **Use table name in formulas**. (Default on).

   ◆ **Use GetPivotData functions for PivotTable references**. (Default on).

5. Click **OK**.

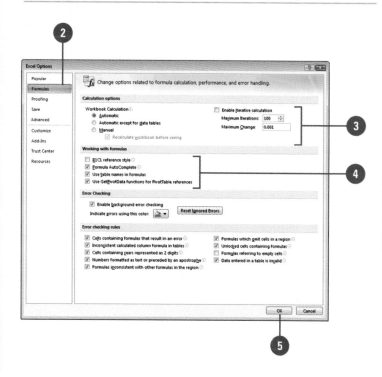

> ### See Also
>
> *See "Correcting Formulas" on page 98 for information on setting error checking options.*

Changing Advanced Document Properties

You can use document properties—also known as metadata—to help you manage and track files. Search tools can use the metadata to find a workbook based-on your search criteria, such as title, subject, author, category, keywords, or comments. You can create advanced custom properties to associate more specific criteria for search tools to use. If you associate a document property to an item in the document, the document property updates when you change the item.

Customize Advanced Properties

1. Click the **Office** button, point to **Prepare**, and then click **Properties**.

2. Click the arrow next to Document Properties, and then click **Advanced Properties**.

3. Click the tabs to view and add information:

   ◆ **General**. To find out file location or size.

   ◆ **Summary**. To add title and author information for the workbook.

   ◆ **Statistics**. To display the number of slides, paragraphs, words and other details about the workbook.

4. Click the **Custom** tab.

5. Type the name for the custom property or select a name from the list.

6. Select the data type for the property you want to add.

7. Type a value for the property.

8. Click **Add**.

9. Click **OK**.

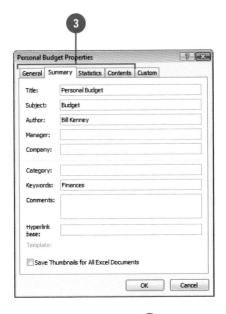

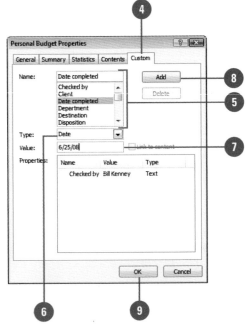

Changing Research Options

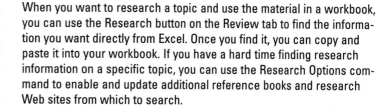

When you want to research a topic and use the material in a workbook, you can use the Research button on the Review tab to find the information you want directly from Excel. Once you find it, you can copy and paste it into your workbook. If you have a hard time finding research information on a specific topic, you can use the Research Options command to enable and update additional reference books and research Web sites from which to search.

Change Research Options

1. Click the **Review** tab.

2. Click the **Research** button.

3. In the task pane, click **Research Options**.

4. Do one or more of the following:

   ◆ **Services.** To activate or remove research services.

   ◆ **Add Services.** To add research services.

   ◆ **Update/Remove.** To update or remove a service provider.

   ◆ **Parental Control.** To turn on parental controls.

5. Click **OK**.

6. When you're done, click the **Close** button on the task pane.

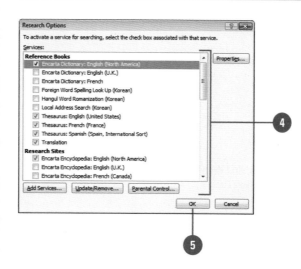

Customizing the Way You Create Objects

When you create a text box, Excel applies a set of default text attributes. Some examples of Excel's font default settings include font style, size, and formatting options, such as bold, italic, and underline. When you draw an object, Excel applies a set of default object attributes. Examples of object default settings include fill color, shadow, and line style. To find out the current default settings for your workbook, you can draw an object, or create a text object and check the object's attributes. If you change a default setting, Excel will use the new setting for all subsequent Excel sessions until you change the setting again.

Customize the Way You Create Text Objects

1 Create a text box.

2 Change the text attributes, including font type, style, and size.

3 Right-click the shape, and then click **Set as Default Text Box**.

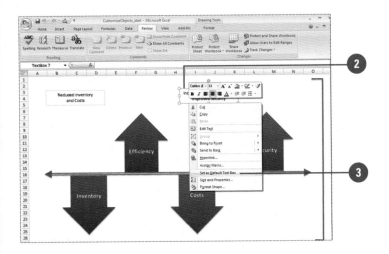

Customize the Way You Create Shape Objects

1 Create a shape.

2 Change the shape attributes, including fill color or effect, text color, outline color and style; and font type, style, and size.

3 Right-click the shape, and then click **Set as Default Shape**.

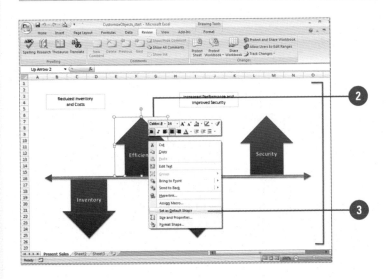

Accessing Commands Not in the Ribbon ▶

If you don't see a command in the Ribbon that was available in an earlier version of Excel, you might think Microsoft removed it from the product. To see if a command is available, check out the Customize section in Excel Options. The Quick Access Toolbar gives access to commands not in the Ribbon (**New!**), which you can add to the toolbar. For example, you can add the following commands: Create Microsoft Office Outlook Task, Replace Fonts, Send to Microsoft Word, and Web Page Preview.

Add Commands Not in the Ribbon to the Quick Access Toolbar

1 Click the **Customize Quick Access Toolbar** list arrow, and then click **More Commands**.

2 Click the **Choose command from** list arrow, and then click **Commands Not in the Ribbon**.

3 Click the **Customize Quick Access Toolbar** list arrow, and then click **For all documents** (Default).

4 Click the command you want to add (left column).

> **TIMESAVER** *Click <Separator>, and then click Add to insert a separator line between buttons.*

5 Click **Add**.

6 Click the **Move Up** and **Move Down** arrow buttons to arrange the commands in the order you want them to appear.

7 Click **OK**.

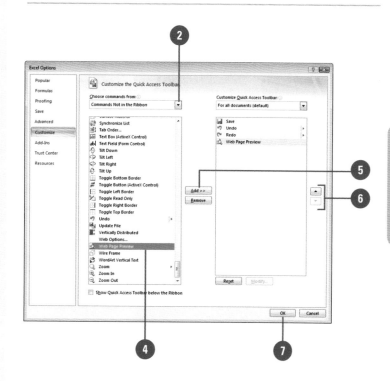

> ### Did You Know?
>
> **You can reset the Quick Access Toolbar to its original state.** In the Excel Options dialog box, click Customize in the left pane, click Reset, and then click OK.

Scanning and Imaging Documents

With Microsoft Office Document Imaging, you can scan and manage multiple page documents using the TIFF file format and recognize text in image documents and faxes as editable text by using Optical Character Recognition (OCR). You can copy scanned text and images into Microsoft Office programs as well as e-mail or fax the document over the Internet. If you need to add information to a document, such as a fax, you can add text as a note or comment, apply highlighting, draw shapes, and insert pictures by using the Annotation toolbar (**New!**).

Scan a Document Image

1. Click the **Start** button, point to **All Programs**, click **Microsoft Office**, click **Microsoft Office Tools**, and then click **Microsoft Office Document Imaging**.

2. Click the **Scan New Document** button on the toolbar.

3. Click **Scanner**, select your scanner hardware, and then click **OK**.

4. Click a preset scanning option.

5. Click the scanner options you want.

6. Click the **Scan** button.

   The document is scanned.

7. Click the **Save** button on the toolbar, specify a name and location, and then click **Save**.

8. When you're done, click **Close**.

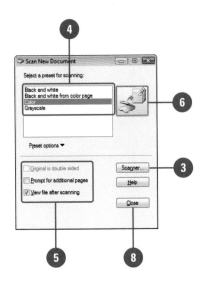

Did You Know?

You can open Microsoft Office Document Scanning program separately. Click the Start button, point to All Programs, click Microsoft Office, click Microsoft Office Tools, and then click Microsoft Office Document Scanning.

Perform OCR on a Document Image

1. Click the **Start** button, point to **All Programs**, click **Microsoft Office**, click **Microsoft Office Tools**, and then click **Microsoft Office Document Imaging**.

2. Click the **Open** button on the toolbar.

3. Click the **Look in** list arrow, and then navigate to the file.

4. Click the document image you want to open, and then click **Open**.

5. Click the **Recognize Text Using OCR** button on the toolbar.

6. To add annotations and comments, use the pen, highlighter, and comments buttons on the Annotation toolbar.

7. Select the text in the document. It appears with a red rectangle around it.

8. Click the **Edit** menu, and then click **Copy**.

9. Save and close the document.

10. Open or switch to Excel, and the place the insertion point where you want to paste the text.

11. Click the **Paste** button on the Home tab.

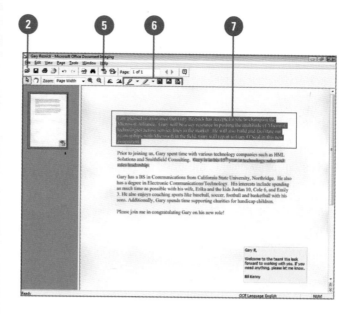

Managing Pictures

With Microsoft Office Picture Manager, you can manage, edit, and share your pictures. You can view all the pictures on your computer and specify which file type you want to open with Picture Manager. If you need to edit a picture, you can use Picture Manager to change brightness, contrast, and color, and to remove red eye. You can also crop, rotate and flip, resize, and compress a picture.

Open Picture Manager and Locate Pictures

1. Click the **Start** button, point to **All Programs**, click **Microsoft Office**, click **Microsoft Office Tools**, and then click **Microsoft Office Picture Manager**.

   The first time you start the program, it asks you to select the file types you want to open with Picture Manager. Select the check boxes with the formats you want, and then click **OK**.

2. If necessary, click **Add Picture Shortcut**.

3. Click **Locate Pictures**.

4. Click the **Look in** list arrow, and then click a drive location.

5. Click **OK**.

6. Use the **View** buttons to view your pictures.

7. When you're done, click the **Close** button.

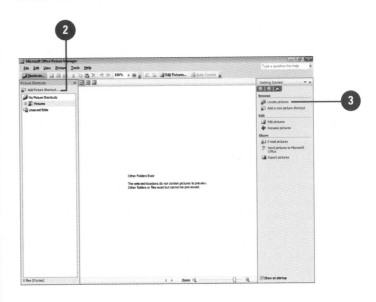

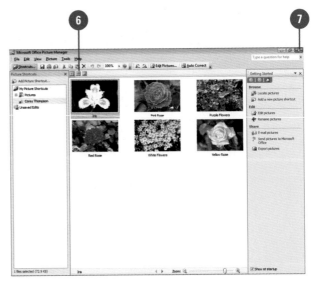

Did You Know?

You can export a folder of files with a new format or size. In Picture Manager, click the File menu, click Export, specify the folder with the pictures you want to change, select an export file format or select a size, and then click OK.

Edit Pictures

① In Picture Manager, select the picture you want to edit.

② Click the **Edit Pictures** button on the Standard toolbar.

③ Use the editing tools on the Edit Pictures task pane to modify the picture.

- ◆ Brightness and Contrast
- ◆ Color
- ◆ Crop
- ◆ Rotate and Flip
- ◆ Red Eye Removal

④ Use the sizing tools on the Edit Pictures task pane to change the picture size.

- ◆ Resize
- ◆ Compress Pictures

⑤ Click the **Save** button on the Standard toolbar.

⑥ When you're done, click the **Close** button.

Did You Know?

You can discard changes to a picture. If you don't like the changes you make to a picture, click the Edit menu, and then click Discard Changes to restore the picture.

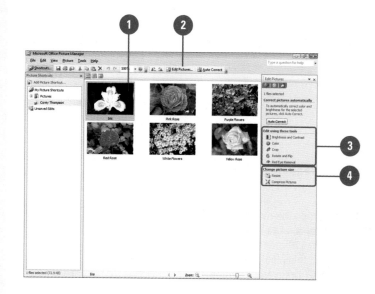

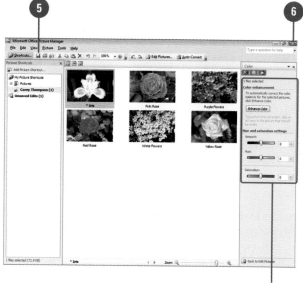

Color enhancing options

Using Multiple Languages

International Microsoft Office users can change the language that appears on their screens by changing the default language settings. Users around the world can enter, display, and edit text in all supported languages—including European languages, Japanese, Chinese, Korean, Hebrew, and Arabic—to name a few. You'll probably be able to use Office programs in your native language. If the text in your document is written in more than one language, you can automatically detect languages or designate the language of selected text so the spelling checker uses the right dictionary.

Add a Language to Office Programs

1. Click **Start** on the taskbar, point to **All Programs**, click **Microsoft Office**, click **Microsoft Office Tools**, and then click **Microsoft Office 2007 Language Settings**.

   TIMESAVER *In Excel, click the Office button, click Excel Options, click Popular, and then click Language Settings.*

2. Select the language you want to enable.

3. Click **Add**.

4. Click **OK**, and then click **Yes** to quit and restart Office.

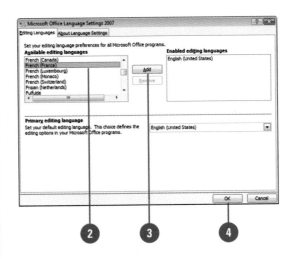

Expanding Excel Functionality

16

Introduction

An add-in extends the functionality of Microsoft Office programs. Excel includes a variety of add-ins—programs that are included with Excel but not essential to its functionality. Some of these supplemental programs—including Analysis ToolPak, Conditional Sum Wizard, Lookup Wizard, and Solver—are useful to almost anyone using Excel. Before you can use an Excel or a third-party add-in, you need to load it first. When you load an add-in, the feature may add a command to a Ribbon tab or toolbar.

If you want to customize Microsoft Office Excel 2007 and create advanced workbooks, you'll need to learn how to work with the Microsoft Office 2007 programming language, **Microsoft Visual Basic for Applications (VBA)**. VBA is powerful and flexible, and you can use it in all major Office applications. To create a VBA application, you have to learn VBA conventions and syntax. Office 2007 makes VBA more user-friendly by providing the Visual Basic Editor, an application that includes several tools to help you write error-free VBA applications. The Visual Basic Editor provides extensive online Help to assist you in this task.

A practical way to use VBA is to create macros. Macros can simplify common repetitive tasks that you regularly use in Excel. Macros can reside on the Quick Access Toolbar for easy access. If a macro has a problem executing a task, the Visual Basic Editor can help you debug, or fix the error in your macro.

An ActiveX control is a software component that adds functionality to an existing program. An ActiveX control supports a customizable, programmatic interface for you to create your own functionality, such as a form. Excel includes several pre-built ActiveX controls—including a label, text box, command button, and check box—to help you create a user interface.

Viewing and Managing Add-ins

An add-in, such as smart tags, extends functionality to Microsoft Office programs (**New!**). An add-in can add buttons and custom commands to the Ribbon. You can get add-ins for Excel on the Microsoft Office Online Web site in the Downloads area, or on third-party vendor Web sites. When you download and install an add-in, it appears on the Add-Ins or other tabs in Office programs depending on functionality, and includes a special ScreenTip that identifies the developer. You can view and manage add-ins from the Add-Ins pane in Excel Options.

View Installed Add-ins

1. Click the **Add-Ins** tab.

   Add-ins with buttons and controls appear on the Ribbon. To display a ScreenTip, point to a button or control.

2. Click the **Office** button, and then click **Excel Options**.

3. In the left pane, click **Add-Ins**.

   The installed add-ins appear in the list by category.

   ◆ **Active Application Add-ins.** Lists the registered and running add-ins. A selected check box for a COM add-in appears here.

   ◆ **Inactive Application Add-ins.** Lists the installed add-ins, but not currently loaded. A cleared check box for a COM add-in appears here.

   ◆ **Document Related Add-ins.** Lists template files currently open in a document.

   ◆ **Disabled Application Add-ins.** Lists automatically disabled add-ins causing Office programs to crash.

4. Click an add-in to display information about it.

5. Click **OK**.

Add-in

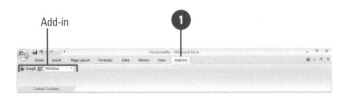

Add-in

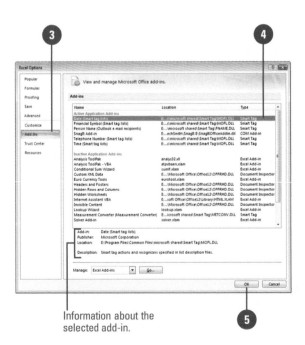

Information about the selected add-in.

Manage Installed Add-ins

1. Click the **Office** button, and then click **Excel Options**.

2. In the left pane, click **Add-Ins**.

3. Click the **Manage** list arrow, and then click the add-in list you want to display:

   ◆ **COM Add-ins.** Opens the COM Add-Ins dialog box and lists the Component Object Model (COM) add-ins.

   ◆ **Excel Add-ins.** Opens the Add-Ins dialog box and lists the currently installed Excel add-ins.

   ◆ **Smart Tags.** Opens the AutoCorrect dialog with the Smart Tags tab and list the installed smart tags.

   ◆ **XML Expansion Pack.** Opens XML Expansion Packs that provide additional XML functionality.

   ◆ **Disabled Items.** Opens the Disabled Items dialog box and lists the disabled items that prevent Excel from working properly. If you want to try and enable an item, select it, click Enable, click Close, and then restart Excel.

4. Click **Go**.

5. Click **OK**.

Add-ins Installed with Excel	
Add-in	**Descriptions**
Analysis ToolPak	Provides data analysis tools for statistical and engineering analysis.
Analysis ToolPak VBA	VBA Functions for Analysis ToolPak.
Conditional Sum Wizard	Helps sum data in lists.
Euro Currency Tools	Conversion and formatting for the euro currency
Internet Assistant VBA	VBA Functions for the Internet.
Lookup Wizard	Helps create formulas to find data in lists.
Solver	Tool for optimization and equation solving.

Loading and Unloading Add-ins

Add-ins are additional programs, designed to run seamlessly within Excel or Office. There are two main types of add-ins: Excel and **Component Object Model (COM)**. Excel add-ins are custom controls designed specifically for Excel, while COM add-ins are designed to run in one or more Office programs and use the file name extension .dll or .exe. Some add-ins are installed when you run the Setup program, while others can be downloaded from Microsoft Office Online or purchased from third-party vendors. To load or unload add-ins, Excel provides commands you can access from an added button on the Quick Access Toolbar or the Add-Ins pane in Excel Options. When you load an add-in, the feature may add a command to a tab or toolbar. You can load one or more add-ins. If you no longer need an add-in, you should unload it to save memory and reduce the number of commands on a tab. When you unload an add-in, you also may need to restart Excel to remove an add-in command from a tab.

Load or Unload a Excel Add-in

1. Click the **Add-Ins** button on the Quick Access Toolbar.

   If necessary, use the Customize pane in Excel Options to add the button to the Quick Access Toolbar.

2. To add an add-in to the list, click **Browse**, locate and select the add-in you want, and then click **OK**.

3. Select a check box to load an add-in or clear a check box to unload an add-in.

4. Click **OK**.

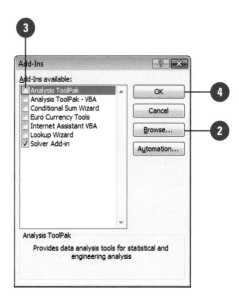

Did You Know?

You can open an add-in dialog box from Excel Options. Click the Office button, click Excel Options, click Add-ins, click the Manage list arrow, click Excel Add-ins or COM Add-ins, and then click Go.

Load or Unload a COM Add-in

①	Click the **COM Add-Ins** button on the Quick Access Toolbar.

	If necessary, use the Customize pane in Excel Options to add the button to the Quick Access Toolbar.

②	Select the check box next to the add-in you want to load, or clear the check box you want to unload.

	TROUBLE? *If the add-in is not available in the list, click Add, locate and select the add-in you want, and then click OK.*

③	To remove the selected add-in, click **Remove**.

④	Click **OK**.

Did You Know?

You can can get more information about COM online. Visit *www.microsoft.com/com.*

See Also

See "Working with Toolbar" on page 6 for information on adding a button to the Quick Access Toolbar.

For Your Information

Dealing with an Add-in Security Alert

When there is a problem with an add-in, Excel disables it to protect the program and your data. When a problem does occur, a security alert dialog box appears, displaying information about the problem and options you can choose to fix or ignore it. You can choose an option to help protect you from unknown content (recommended), enable this add-in for this session only, or enable all code published by this publisher. See "Setting Add-ins Security Options" on page 352 for more information about setting options that trigger the Add-in security alert.

Enhancing a Workbook with VBA

Office 2007 applications like Excel, Access, Word, PowerPoint, and Visio share a common programming language: Visual Basic for Applications (VBA). With VBA, you can develop applications that combine tools from these Office 2007 products, as well as other programs that support VBA. Because of the language's power and flexibility, programmers often prefer to use VBA to customize their Office applications.

Introducing the Structure of VBA

VBA is an object-oriented programming language because, when you develop a VBA application, you manipulate objects. An object can be anything within your workbook, such as a shape, text box, picture, or table. Even Excel itself is considered an object. Objects can have properties that describe the object's characteristics. Text boxes, for example, have the Font property, which describes the font Excel uses to display the text. A text box also has properties that indicate whether the text is bold or italic.

Objects also have methods—actions that can be done to the object. Deleting and inserting are examples of methods available with a record object. Closely related to methods are events. An event is a specific action that occurs on or with an object. Clicking a button initiates the Click event for the button object. VBA also refers to an event associated with an object as an event property. The form button, for example, has the Click event property. You can use VBA to either respond to an event or to initiate an event.

Writing VBA Code

A VBA programmer types the statements, or **code**, that make up the VBA program. Those statements follow a set of rules, called **syntax**, that govern how commands are formulated. For example, to change the property of a particular object, the command follows the general form:

    Object.Property = Expression

Where **Object** is the name of a VBA object, **Property** is the name of a property that object has, and **Expression** is a value that will be assigned to the property. The following statement places text "Expense Report" in cells A1 and A5 on Sheet1:

    Worksheets("Sheet1").Range("A1, A5") =
        "Expense Report"

You can use Office and VBA's online Help to learn about specific object and property names. If you want to apply a method to an object, the syntax is:

    Object.Method arg1, arg2, ...

Where **Object** is the name of a VBA object, **Method** is the name of method that can be applied to that object, and **arg1**, **arg2**, ... are optional **arguments** that provide additional information for the method operation. For example, to set columns A and B on Sheet2 to AutoFit cell contents, you could use the AutoFit method as follows:

    Worksheets("Sheet2").Column(A:B).AutoFit

Working with Procedures

You don't run VBA commands individually. Instead they are organized into groups of commands called **procedures**. A procedure either performs an action or calculates a value. Procedures that perform actions are called **Sub procedures**. You can run a Sub procedure directly, or Office can run it for you in response to an event, such as clicking a button or opening a form. A Sub procedure initiated by an event is also called an **event procedure**. Office provides event procedure templates to help you easily create procedures for common events. Event procedures are displayed in each object's event properties list.

A procedure that calculates a value is called a **function procedure**. By creating function procedures you can create your own function library, supplementing the Office collection of built-in functions. You can access these functions from within the Expression Builder, making it easy for them to be used over and over again.

Working with Modules

Procedures are collected and organized within **modules**. Modules generally belong to two types: class modules and standard modules. A **class module** is associated with a specific object. In more advanced VBA programs, the class module can be associated with an object created by the user. **Standard modules** are not associated with specific objects, and they can be run from anywhere within a database. This is usually not the case with class modules. Standard modules are listed in the Database window on the Modules Object list.

Building VBA Projects

A collection of modules is further organized into a **project**. Usually a project has the same name as a workbook. You can create projects that are not tied into any specific workbook, saving them as Excel add-ins that provide extra functionality to Excel.

Using the Visual Basic Editor

You create VBA commands, procedures, and modules in Office's **Visual Basic Editor**. This is the same editor used by Excel, Word, and other Office programs. Thus, you can apply what you learn about creating programs in Excel to these other applications.

The Project Explorer

One of the fundamental tools in the Visual Basic Editor is the Project Explorer. The **Project Explorer** presents a hierarchical view of all of the projects and modules currently open in Excel, including standard and class modules.

The Modules Window

You write all of your VBA code in the **Modules** window. The Modules window acts as a basic text editor, but it includes several tools to help you write error-free codes. Excel also provides hints as you write your code to help you avoid syntax errors.

The Object Browser

There are hundreds of objects available to you. Each object has a myriad of properties, methods, and events. Trying to keep track of all of them is daunting, but the Visual Basic Editor supplies the **Object Browser**, which helps you examine the complete collection of objects, properties, and methods available for a given object.

Viewing the Visual Basic Editor

The Project Explorer displays a hierarchical list of all open projects and modules.

The Modules window allows you to enter VBA commands.

VBA projects

Currently selected module

The Properties window displays properties for selected objects.

A VBA statement

Method

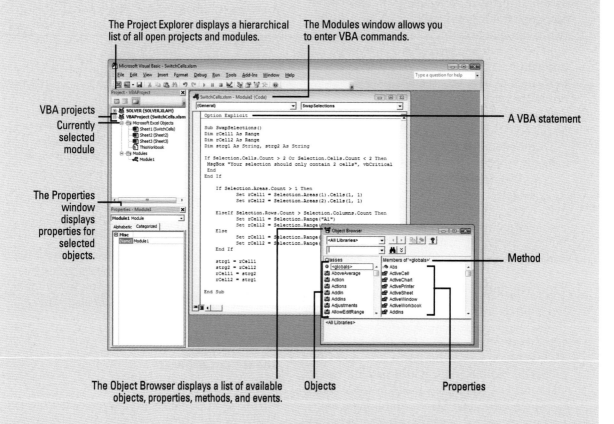

The Object Browser displays a list of available objects, properties, methods, and events.

Objects

Properties

Setting Developer Options

The Developer tab (**New!**) is a specialized Ribbon that you can use to access developer controls, write code, or create macros. You can set an option in the Popular pane in Excel Options to show or hide the Developer tab. As a developer, you can also set an option to show errors in your user interface customization code.

Set Developer Options

1. Click the **Office** button, and then click **Excel Options**.

2. In the left pane, click **Popular**.

3. Select the **Show Developer tab in the Ribbon** check box.

4. In the left pane, click **Advanced**.

5. Select the **Show add-in user interface errors** check box.

6. Click **OK**.

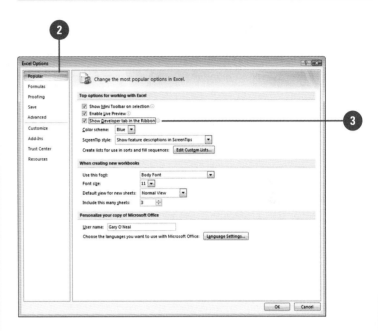

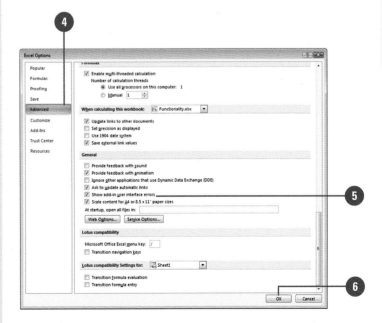

Understanding How Macros Automate Your Work

To complete many tasks in Excel, you need to execute a series of commands and actions. To print two copies of a selected range of Sheet2 of a worksheet, for example, you need to open the workbook, switch to Sheet2, select the print area, open the Print dialog box, and specify that you want to print two copies. If you often need to complete the same task, you'll find yourself repeatedly taking the same series of steps. It can be tiresome to continually repeat the same commands and actions when you can easily create a mini-program, or macro, that accomplishes all of them with a single command.

Creating a **macro** is easy and requires no programming knowledge on your part. Excel simply records the steps you want included in the macro while you use the keyboard and mouse. When you record a macro, Excel stores the list of commands with any name you choose. You can store your macros in the current workbook, in a new workbook, or in Excel's Personal Macro workbook.

Storing your macros in the Personal Macro workbook makes the macros available to you from any location in Excel, even when no workbook is open. When you select the Personal Macro Workbook option to store a macro, Excel creates a hidden personal macro workbook file (Personal.xlsb) and saves the macro in this workbook. The file is stored in the XLStart folder so it will load automatically when Excel starts. The XLStart folder is typically located in the C:\Users\user name\App Data\Roaming\Microsoft\Excel folder for Vista and C:\Documents and Settings\user name\Application Data\Microsoft\Excel folder for XP.

Once a macro is created, you can make modifications to it, add comments so other users will understand its purpose, and test it to make sure it runs correctly.

You can run a macro by choosing the Macro command on the View or Developer tab, or by using a shortcut key or clicking a Quick Access Toolbar button you've assigned to it. From the Macro dialog box, you can run, edit, test, or delete any Excel macro on your system, or create a new one.

If you have problems with a macro, you can step through the macro one command at a time, known as **debugging**. Once you identify any errors in the macro, you can edit it.

Indicates the workbook(s) from which you can access the selected macro

When you create a macro, you can add a description of what the macro does.

Recording a Macro

If you find yourself repeating the same set of steps over and over, you can record a macro. Macros can run several tasks for you at the click of a button. When you turn on the macro recorder, Excel records every mouse click and keystroke action you execute until you turn off the recorder. Then you can "play," or run, the macro whenever you want to repeat that series of actions—but Excel will execute them at a much faster rate. The macro recorder doesn't record in real time, so you can take your time to correctly complete each action.

Record a Macro

1 Click the **Developer** or **View** tab.

2 To record a macro with actions relative to the initially selected cell, click the **Use Relative References** button.

3 Click the **Record Macro** button.

◆ If you use the View tab, click **View Macros** on the menu.

TIMESAVER *To quickly start or stop a macro recording, click the Record icon or Stop Record icon on the Status bar (left side).*

4 Type a name for the macro.

5 Assign a shortcut key to use a keystroke combination to run the macro.

6 Click the **Store macros in** list arrow, and then select a location.

◆ **Personal Macro Workbook**. The macro is available whenever you use Excel.

◆ **New Workbook**. The macro is available in new workbooks.

◆ **This Workbook**. The macro is available only in this workbook.

7 If you want, type a description.

8 Click **OK**.

9 Execute the commands or actions you want to complete the task.

10 Click the **Stop Recording** button.

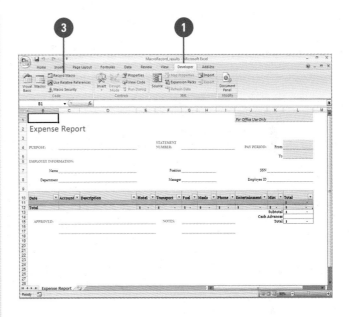

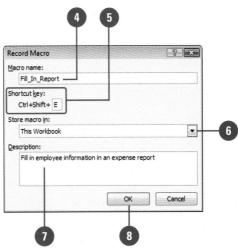

Creating a Macro

If you find yourself repeating the same set of steps over and over, or if you need to add new functionality to Excel, you could create a macro. If you find it difficult to record a macro, you can create one using a programming language called Microsoft Visual Basic for Applications (VBA) (**New!**). With VBA, you create a macro by writing a script to replay the actions you want. The macros for a particular workbook are stored in a macro module, which is a collection of Visual Basic codes.

Create a Macro

1 Click the **Developer** or **View** tab.

2 Click the **Macros** button.

◆ If you use the View tab, click **View Macros** on the menu.

3 Type a name for the macro.

4 Click the **Macros in** list arrow, and then click **All Open Workbooks** or the workbook to which you want the macro stored.

5 Click **Create**.

The Microsoft Visual Basic window opens.

6 Click the Module window (if necessary), and then type new Visual Basic commands, or edit existing ones.

To run the macro, press F5.

7 When you're done, click the **Save** button, click the **File** menu, and then click **Close and Return to Microsoft Excel**.

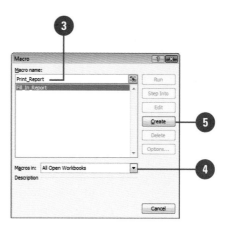

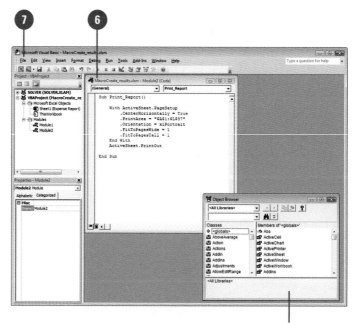

Object Browser helps you insert commands.

Running a Macro

Running a macro is similar to choosing a command in Excel. When you record or edit the macro, you have the choice of making it available through a menu command, a keyboard combination, or even a toolbar button. As with other options in Excel, your choice depends on your personal preferences—and you can choose to make more than one option available. Where you store a macro when you save it determines its availability later. Macros stored in the Personal Macro workbook are always available, and macros stored in any other workbooks are only available when the workbook is open.

Run a Macro

1 Click the **Developer** or **View** tab.

2 Click the **Macros** button.

◆ If you use the View tab, click **View Macros** on the menu.

TIMESAVER *Click the Macros button on the Status bar.*

3 Click the macro you want to run.

4 Click **Run**.

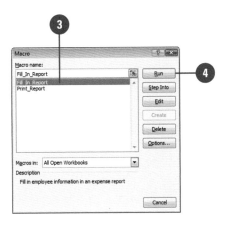

Delete a Macro

1 Click the **Developer** or **View** tab.

2 Click the **Macros** button.

◆ If you use the View tab, click **View Macros** on the menu.

3 Click the macro you want to delete.

4 Click **Delete**, and then click **Delete** again to confirm the deletion.

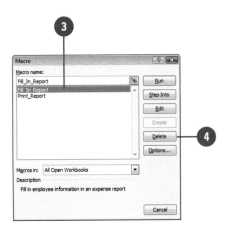

Did You Know?

You can stop a macro. Press Ctrl+Break to stop a macro before it completes its actions.

Controlling a Macro

If a macro doesn't work exactly the way you want it to, you can fix the problem using Microsoft Visual Basic for Applications (VBA). VBA allows you to **debug**, or repair, an existing macro so that you change only the actions that aren't working correctly. All macros for a particular workbook are stored in a macro module, a collection of Visual Basic programming codes that you can copy to other workbook files. You can view and edit your Visual Basic modules using the Visual Basic editor. By learning Visual Basic you can greatly increase the scope and power of your programs.

Debug a Macro Using Step Mode

1. Click the **Developer** or **View** tab.

2. Click the **Macros** button.

   ◆ If you use the View tab, click **View Macros** on the menu.

3. Click the macro you want to debug.

4. Click **Step Into**.

   The Microsoft Visual Basic window opens.

5. Click the **Debug** menu, and then click **Step Into** (or press F8) to proceed through each action.

   ◆ You can also use other commands like **Step Over** and **Step Out** to debug the code.

6. When you're done, click the **Save** button, click the **File** menu, and then click **Close and Return to Microsoft Excel**.

7. Click **OK** to stop the debugger.

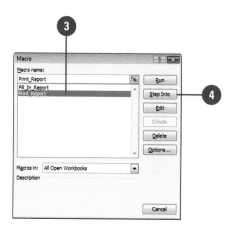

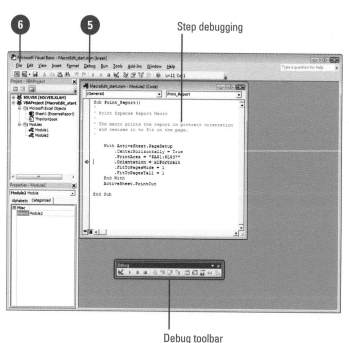

Step debugging

Debug toolbar

Edit a Macro

1. Click the **Developer** or **View** tab.

2. Click the **Macros** button.

   ◆ If you use the View tab, click **View Macros** on the menu.

3. Click the macro you want to edit, and then click **Edit**.

4. Click the Module window containing the Visual Basic code for your macro.

5. Type new Visual Basic commands, or edit the commands already present.

6. Click the **Save** button, click the **File** menu, and then click **Close and Return to Microsoft Excel**.

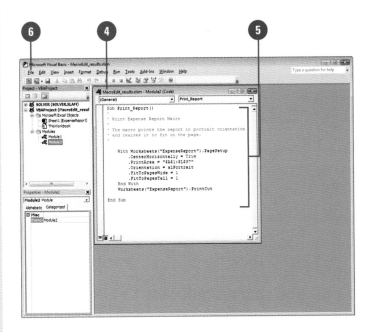

Copy a Macro Module to Another Workbook

1. Open the workbook files you want to copy the macro from and to.

2. Click the **Developer** tab.

3. Click the **Visual Basic** button.

4. Click the **View** menu, and then click **Project Explorer**.

5. Drag the module you want to copy from the source workbook to the destination workbook.

6. Click the **Save** button, click the **File** menu, and then click **Close and Return to Microsoft Excel**.

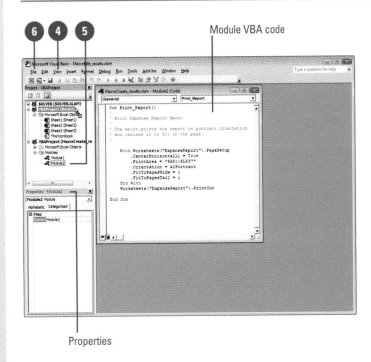

Module VBA code

Properties

Adding a Digital Signature to a Macro Project

If you want to add a digital signature to a workbook with a macro, you need to add it using the Visual Basic editor. If you open a workbook that contains a signed macro project with a problem, the macro is disabled by default and the Message Bar appears to notify you of the potential problem. You can click Options in the Message Bar to view information about it. For more details, you can click Show Signature Details to view certificate and publisher information. If a digital signature has problems—it's expired, not issued by a trusted publisher, or the workbook has been altered—the certificate information image contains a red X. When there's a problem, contact the signer to have them fix it, or save the workbook to a trusted location, where you can run the macro without security checks.

Sign a Macro Project

1. Open the workbook that contains the macro project, and then click the **Developer** tab.

2. Click the **Visual Basic** button to open the Visual Basic window.

3. Click the **Tools** menu, and then click **Digital Signature**.

4. Click **Choose**.

5. Select a certificate in the list.

6. To view a certificate, click **View Certificate**, and then click **OK**.

7. Click **OK**.

8. Click **OK** again.

9. Click the **Save** button, click the **File** menu, and then click **Close and Return to Microsoft Excel**.

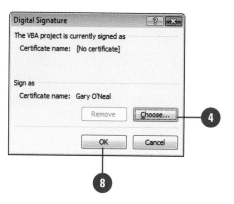

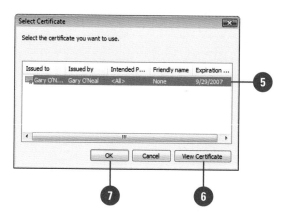

Did You Know?

You can create a self-signing certificate for a macro project. Click the Start button, point to All Programs, click Microsoft Office, click Microsoft Office Tools, click Digital Certificate for VBA Projects, enter a name, and then click OK. Office programs trust a self-signed certificate only on the computer that created it.

Assigning a Macro to a Toolbar

After you create a macro, you can add the macro to the Quick Access Toolbar (**New!**) for easy access. When you create a macro, the macro name appears in the list of available commands when you customize the Quick Access Toolbar in Excel Options. When you point to a macro button on the Quick Access Toolbar, a ScreenTip appears, displaying Macro: *workbook name!macro name.*

Assign a Macro to a Toolbar

1. Click the **Customize Quick Access Toolbar** list arrow, and then click **More Commands**.

2. Click the **Choose command from** list arrow, and then click **Macros**.

3. Click the **Customize Quick Access Toolbar** list arrow, and then click **For all documents** (default).

4. Click the macro you want to add (left column).

5. Click **Add**.

6. Click the **Move Up** and **Move Down** arrow buttons to arrange the commands in the order you want them to appear.

7. Click **Modify**.

8. Type a name for the button.

9. Click an icon in the symbol list.

10. Click **OK**.

11. Click **OK**.

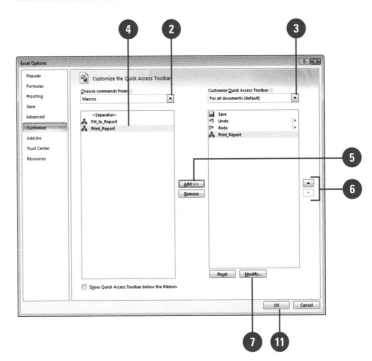

> ### See Also
>
> See "Working with Toolbars" on page 6 and "Accessing Command Not in the Ribbon" on page 423 for information on using the Quick Access Toolbar.

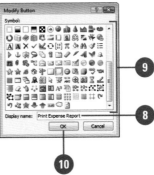

Macro button

Saving a Workbook with Macros

Macros are created using Visual Basic for Applications (VBA) code. If you add a macro to a workbook, you need to save it with a file name extension that ends with an "m" (**New!**), either Excel Macro-Enabled Workbook (.xlsm), or Excel Macro-Enabled Template (.xltm). If you try to save a workbook containing a macro with a file name extension that ends with an "x" (such as .xlsx or .xltx), Excel displays an alert message, restricting the operation. These Excel file types are designated to be VBA code-free.

Save a Workbook with Macros

1. Click the **Office** button, and then click **Save As**.

   TIMESAVER *To select the Excel Macro-Enabled file type, click the Office button, point to Save As, and then click Excel Macro-Enabled Workbook.*

2. Click the **Save in** list arrow, and then click the drive or folder where you want to save the file.

3. Type a workbook file name.

4. If necessary, click the **Save as type** list arrow, and then select the macro format you want:

   ◆ **Excel Macro-Enabled Workbook.** A workbook (.xlsm) that contains VBA code.

   ◆ **Excel Macro-Enabled Template.** A template (.xltm) that includes preapproved macros.

5. Click **Save**.

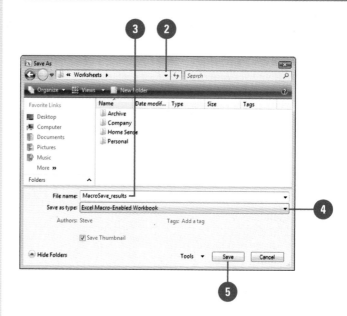

Opening a Workbook with Macros

When you open a workbook with a macro, VBA, or other software code, Excel displays a security warning (**New!**) to let you know the workbook might contain potentially harmful code that may harm your computer. If you know and trust the author of the workbook, you can change security options to enable the macro content and use the workbook normally. If you don't trust the content, you can continue to block and disable the content and use the workbook with limited functionality. If you don't want a security alert to appear, you can change security settings in the Trust Center in Excel Options.

Open a Workbook with Macros

1. Click the **Office** button, and then click **Open**.

2. If necessary, click the **File as type** list arrow, and then the workbook type that contains a macro.

3. If the file is located in another folder, click the **Look in** list arrow, and then navigate to the file.

4. Click the workbook with macros you want to open, and then click **Open**.

5. Click **Options** in the Security Warning.

6. If you trust the workbook content, click the **Enable external content** option or the **Trust all documents from this publisher** option (if available) to open it. If you don't trust it, click the **Help protect me from unknown content** option to block and disable the macros.

7. Click **OK**.

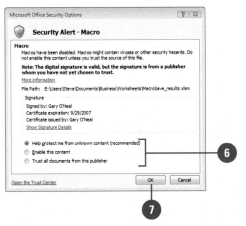

Inserting ActiveX Controls

An ActiveX control is a software component that adds functionality to an existing program. An ActiveX control is really just another term for an OLE (Object Linking and Embedding) object, known as a Component Object Model (COM) object. An ActiveX control supports a customizable, programmatic interface. Excel includes several pre-built ActiveX controls (**New!**) on the Developer tab, including a label, text box, command button, image, scroll bar, check box, option button, combo box, list box, and toggle button. To create an ActiveX control, click the Insert button on the Developer tab, and then click the ActiveX control you want, and then drag to insert it with the size you want. If there is a problem with an ActiveX control, Excel disables it to protect the program and your data. When a problem does occur, a security alert dialog box appears, displaying information about the problem and options you can choose to leave it disabled or enable it.

Insert ActiveX Controls

1. Click the **Developer** tab.

2. Click the **Design Mode** button (highlighted).

3. Click the **Insert** button arrow, and then click the button with the ActiveX control you want to use.

   See the next page for a list and description of each ActiveX control.

4. Display the worksheet where you want to place the ActiveX control.

5. Drag (pointer changes to a plus sign) to draw the ActiveX control the size you want.

6. To resize the control, drag a resize handle (circles) to the size you want.

7. To add Visual Basic code to the ActiveX control, click the **View Code** button, or to change display properties, click the **Properties** button. To exit, click the **Save** and **Close** buttons.

8. Click the **Design Mode** button (not highlighted) to exit.

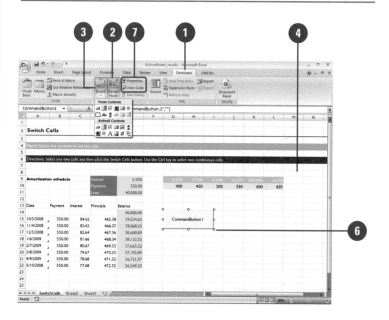

For Your Information

Using Form Controls

Form controls are objects that users can interact with to enter or manipulate data. For example, you can add a Check box control to your worksheet so that users can turn an option on and off. You can select a control from the Developer tab and drag to create the control directly on your worksheet just like an ActiveX control. For an example on using form controls, see Project 2, "Adding a Form Control," on page 485.

Deal with an ActiveX Control Security Alert

1. Click the **Office** button, and then click **Open**.

2. Click the **File as type** list arrow, and then click the workbook type that contains the ActiveX control.

3. If the file is located in another folder, click the **Look in** list arrow, and then navigate to the file.

4. Click the workbook with the ActiveX control you want to open, and then click **Open**.

5. Click **Options** in the Security Warning.

6. If you trust the workbook content, click the **Enable external content** option to open it. If you don't trust it, click the **Help protect me from unknown content** option to block and disable the macros.

7. Click **OK**.

See Also

See "Setting ActiveX Security Options" on page 353 for more information about setting options that trigger the ActiveX security alert.

See "Setting ActiveX Control Properties" on page 451 for more information about setting ActiveX display properties.

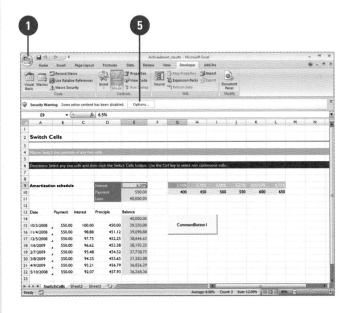

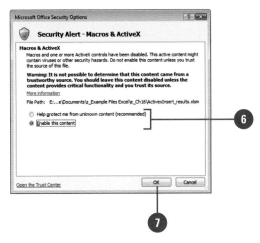

Using ActiveX Controls

ActiveX Controls

Button	Name	Description
A	Label	This button creates a text label. Because the other controls already include a corresponding label, use this button to create labels that are independent of other controls.
abl	Text Box	This button creates a text box in which the user can enter text (or numbers). Use this control for objects assigned to a text or number data type.
↕	Spin Button	This button creates a box in which the user can click arrows to increase or decrease numbers in a box. Use this control assigned to a number data type.
▬	Command Button	This button creates a button that runs a macro or Microsoft Visual Basic function when the user clicks the button in the form.
🖼	Image	This button inserts a frame, in which you can insert a graphic in your form. Use this control when you want to insert a graphic, such as clip art or a logo.
⇳	Scroll Bar	This button creates a scroll bar pane in which the user can enter text (or numbers) in a scrollable text box. Use this control or objects assigned to a text or number data type.
☑	Check Box	This button creates a check box that allows a user to make multiple yes or no selections. Use this control for fields assigned to the yes/no data type.
⦿	Option Button	This button creates an option button (also known as a radio button) that allows the user to make a single selection from at least two choices. Use this control for fields assigned to the yes/no data type.
▤	Combo Box	This button creates a combo box in which the user has the option to enter text or select from a list of options. You can enter your own options in the list, or you can display options stored in another table.
▤	List Box	This button creates a list box that allows a user to select from a list of options. You can enter your own options in the list, or can have another table provide a list of options.
⇴	Toggle Button	This button creates a button that allows the user to make a yes or no selection by clicking the toggle button. Use this control for fields assigned to the yes/no data type.
🛠	More Controls	Click to display other controls, such as Adobe Acrobat Control for ActiveX, Microsoft Forms 2.0, Microsoft Office InfoPath controls, and Microsoft Web Browser.

Setting ActiveX Control Properties

Every ActiveX control has properties, or settings, that determine its appearance and function. You can open a property sheet that displays all the settings for that control in alphabetic or category order directly from Excel (**New!**). The ActiveX controls appear in the Properties window in two columns: the left column displays the name of the control, and the right column displays the current value or setting for the control. When you select either column, a list arrow appears in the right column, allowing you to select the setting you want. After you set properties, you can add VBA code to a module to make it perform.

Set ActiveX Control Properties

1. Click the **Developer** tab.

2. Click the **Design Mode** button (highlighted).

3. Select the control whose properties you want to modify.

4. Click the **Properties** button.

5. To switch controls, click the **Controls** list arrow (at the top), and then select the one you want.

6. Click the **Alphabetic** or **Categorized** tab to display the control properties so you can find the ones you want.

7. Click the property box for the property you want to modify, and then do one of the following.

   ◆ Type the value or information you want to use, such as the control name.

   ◆ If the property box contains a list arrow, click the arrow and then click a value in the list.

   ◆ If a property box contains a dialog button (...), click it to open a dialog box to select options or insert an object, such as a picture.

8. When you're done, click the **Close** button on the Properties window.

9. Click the **Design Mode** button (not highlighted) to exit.

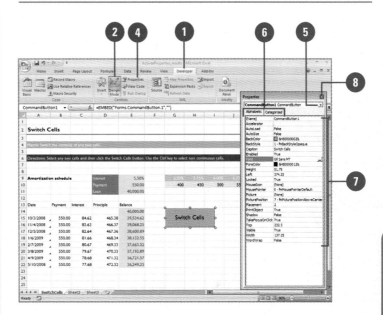

Adding VBA Code to an ActiveX Control

After you add controls and set properties, you can add VBA code to a module to determine how the controls respond to user actions. All controls have a predefined set of events. For example, a command button has a Click event that occurs when the user clicks the button. When you select a control in Design Mode and then click the View Code button, the Visual Basic Editor opens with a Code window, displaying the start of a procedure that runs when the event occurs. The top of the Code window displays the active object and event procedure. The Object list displays the ActiveX control, such as *CommandButton1*, and the Procedure list displays the trigger event, such as *Click*.

Add VBA Code to an ActiveX Control

1. Click the **Developer** tab.

2. Click the **Design Mode** button (highlighted).

3. Select the control to which you want to add VBA code.

4. Click the **View Code** button.

   The Visual Basic Editor window opens.

5. To show the Properties window, click the **Properties window** button.

6. To help with scripting commands, click the **Object Browser** button on the toolbar.

7. Click in the Code window between the beginning and ending line of the procedure, and then type VBA code to perform the task you want.

   The Object list is set to *CommandButton1*, and the Procedure list is set to *Click*.

8. When you're done, click the **Save** button on the toolbar.

9. Click the **Close** button or click the **File** menu, and then click **Close and Return to Microsoft Excel**.

10. Click the **Design Mode** button (not highlighted) to exit.

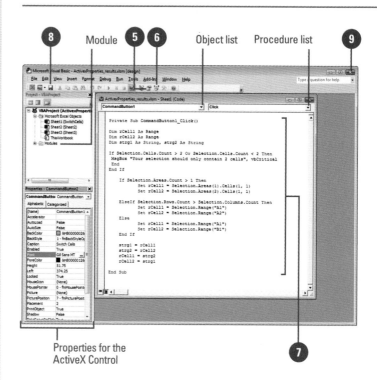

Module — Object list — Procedure list

Properties for the ActiveX Control

Playing a Movie Using an ActiveX Control

Although you cannot insert a Flash movie into an Excel 2007 workbook, you can play one using an ActiveX control and the Flash player (**New!**). Before you can use the control, the ActiveX control and Flash player need to be installed on your computer. You can get the ActiveX control at *http://activex.microsoft.com/activex/activex/*. To play the Flash (.swf) movie, you add the Shockwave Flash Object ActiveX control to the worksheet and create a link to the file. If a movie doesn't play, check ActiveX security options in the Trust Center in Excel Options.

Play a Flash Movie

1. Save the Flash file to a Flash movie file (.swf) using the Flash software.

2. In Excel, click the **Developer** tab.

3. Click the **Design Mode** button (highlighted).

4. Click the **Insert** button arrow, and then click the **More Controls** button.

5. Click **Shockwave Flash Object**.

6. Click **OK**.

7. Drag to draw the movie control.

8. Right-click the Shockwave Flash Object, and then click **Properties**.

9. Click the **Alphabetic** tab.

10. Click the **Movie** property, click in the value column next to Movie, type full path and file name (c:\MyFolder\Movie.swf), or the URL to the Flash movie you want.

11. To set specific options, choose any of the following:

    ◆ To play the file automatically when the worksheet appears, set the Playing property to True.

    ◆ To embed the Flash file, set the EmbedMovie property to True.

12. When you're done, click the **Close** button.

13. Click the **Design Mode** button (not highlighted) to exit.

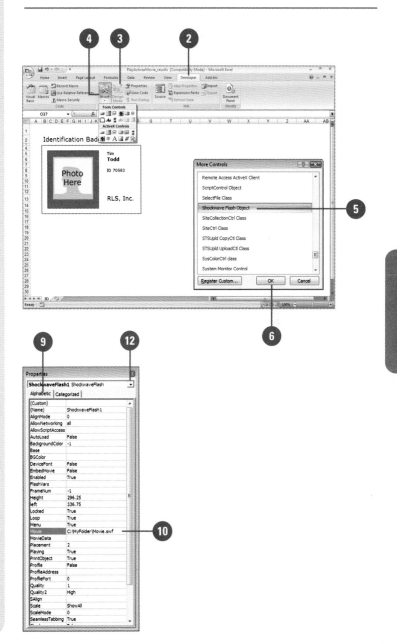

Changing the Document Information Panel

The Document Information Panel (**New!**) helps you manage and track document property information—also known as metadata—such as title, author, subject, keywords, category, and status. The Document Information Panel displays an XML-based mini-form using an InfoPath Form Template (.xsn) file developed in Microsoft InfoPath 2007. By using an XML InfoPath form, you can create your own form templates to edit the document property data and perform data validation.

Select a Document Information Panel Template

1. Click the **Developer** tab.

2. Click the **Document Panel** button.

3. Click **Browse**, locate and select the custom template you want, and then click **Open**.

   ◆ **URL.** Short for Uniform Resource Locator. The address of resources on the Web.

     http://www.perspection.com/index.htm

   ◆ **UNC.** Short for Uniform or Universal Naming Convention. A format for specifying the location of resources on a local-area network (LAN).

     \\server-name\shared-resource-pathname

   ◆ **URN.** Short for Uniform Resource Name.

4. Click the **Display by default** list arrow, and then select the default properties you want.

5. Select the **Always show Document Information Panel on document open and initial save** check box.

6. Click **OK**.

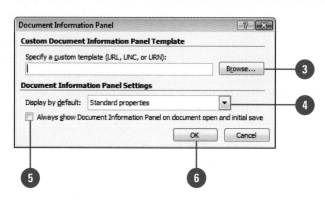

Working Together on Office Documents

17

Introduction

Microsoft Office Groove 2007 is a new addition to the Microsoft Office 2007 Enterprise system that enables teams to set up collaborative workspaces. With Office Groove 2007 (New!), you can bring the team, tools, and information together from any location to work on a project. After creating documents with Microsoft Office programs, you can use Groove for file sharing, document reviews, co-editing and co-reviewing Word documents, and for co-viewing Excel workbooks.

Instead of using a centralized server—like Office SharePoint Server 2007—to store information and manage tasks, Office Groove stores all your workspaces, tools, and data right on your computer. You don't need to connect to a network to access or update information. While you're connected to the Internet, Groove automatically sends the changes you make in a workspace to your team member's computers, and any changes they make get sent to you. Office Groove uses built-in presence awareness, alerts, and unread marks to see who is working online and what team members are doing without having to ask.

Office Groove uses tools and technology from other Microsoft Office system products to help you work together and stay informed. With the Groove SharePoint Files tool, you can check out documents from Microsoft Office SharePoint 2007 into a Groove workspace, collaborate on them, and then check them back in when you're done. With the Groove InfoPath Forms tool, you can import form solutions created in Office InfoPath 2007, or design your own.

If you have access to an Office SharePoint 2007 site, you can use the Document Management task pane directly from Excel to access many Office SharePoint Server 2007 features. For example, you can create a library to work with Excel Services on a SharePoint site to share workbook data (New!).

Configuring Groove

The first time you launch Microsoft Office Groove 2007, the Account Configuration Wizard appears, asking you to create a new Groove account or use an existing one already created on another computer. During the wizard process, you'll enter your Groove Account Configuration Code—for network purposes only—and Groove Account Information, including name, e-mail address, and password. If you want your Groove account to be listed in a Public Groove Directory, you can also select that option during the wizard process.

Start, Configure, and Exit Groove

1. For the first time, click the **Start** button, point to **All Programs**, click **Microsoft Office**, and then click **Microsoft Office Groove 2007**.

2. Click the **Create a new Groove account** option.

3. Click **Next**.

4. Click the Account Configuration Code option you want, and then click **Next**.

5. Enter account information, including name, e-mail address, and password.

6. Click **Next**.

7. Click an option to list your account in the Public Groove Directory, either **No Listing** (default), **Name Only**, and **All Contact Information**.

8. Click **Finish**.

9. Click **Yes or No** to watch a movie about Groove.

10. To exit Groove, click the **Close** button on the title bar.

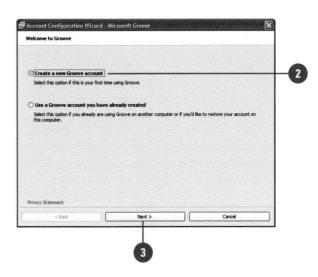

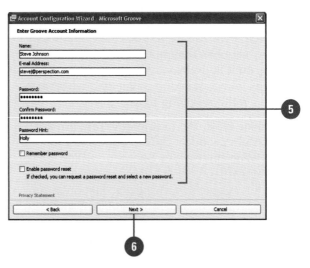

> ## Did You Know?
>
> *You can use your account on another computer.* Click the Options menu, click Invite My Other Computers, click OK, and then copy the account file for use on another computer.

Launching Groove

Microsoft Groove 2007 allows teams to securely work together over the Internet or corporate network as if they were in the same location. Teams using Groove can remotely work with shared files and content, even when they are offline. You can launch Groove 2007 from the Start menu or from the notification area. When you start Groove, the Launchbar window opens, displaying two tabs: one for creating and managing workspaces, and one for adding and managing contacts. If you are having difficulty launching Groove, check to make sure Groove is configured as a Windows Firewall exception.

Launch Groove from the Start Menu and Login

1. Click the **Start** button on the taskbar, point to **All Programs**, click **Microsoft Office**, and then click **Microsoft Office Groove 2007**.

   TIMESAVER *Click the Groove icon in the notification area, and then click Open Groove.*

2. Enter your password, and then click **Login**.

3. To logoff, click the **File** menu, and then click **Log Off Account**.

Add Groove as a Firewall Exception

1. In Windows, click **Start**, and then click **Control Panel**.

2. Double-click the **Windows Firewall** icon.

3. Click the **Exceptions** tab.

4. Click **Add Program**.

5. Click **Browse**, navigate to the Programs Files folder, Microsoft Office folder, Office 12 folder, click **Groove.exe**, and then click **Open**.

6. Click **OK**.

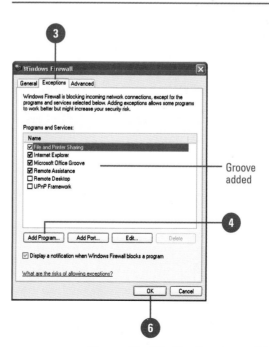

Groove added

Viewing the Groove Window

Workspace   Workspace   Workspace   Launcher
             selector   members

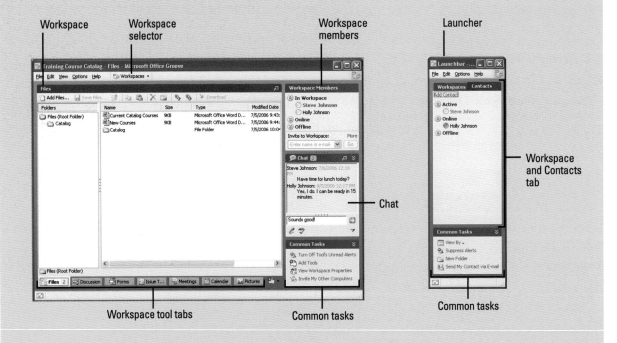

Workspace tool tabs   Common tasks

Chat

Workspace and Contacts tab

Common tasks

Setting General Preferences

Groove makes it easy to set program preferences all in one place by using the Preferences dialog box. You can select from six different tabs —Identities, Account, Security, Alerts, Options, and Synchronization—to specify startup and application settings, alert levels, communication policies, file and workspace restrictions, account privileges, and identity information. The Options tab allows you to set general preferences to startup Groove and related applications, like Launchbar and Workspace Explorer, and scan for viruses.

Set General Preferences

1 In the Launchbar, click the **Options** menu, and then click **Preferences**.

2 Click the **Options** tab.

3 Select or clear the **Launch Groove when Windows starts up** and the **Integrate messenger Contacts** check boxes.

4 Click an application (Launchbar or Workspace Explorer by default), and then click **Settings**, select start up and display options, and then click **OK**.

5 Select or clear the **Discard Groove messages from unknown contacts** check box.

6 Select or clear the **Send e-mail invitations using Microsoft Outlook** check box.

7 Specify the online presence settings you want.

8 Select or clear the **Scan incoming and outgoing files for viruses** check box.

9 Click **OK**.

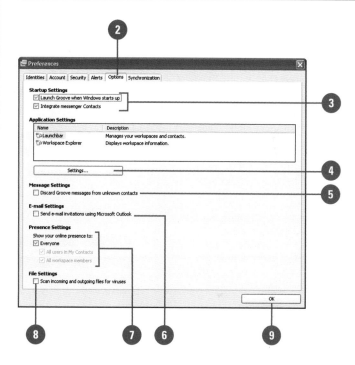

> ### Did You Know?
>
> **You can set workspace properties.** In the workspace, click View Workspace Properties under Command Tasks, click the tab and select the properties you want, and then click OK.

Creating a Groove Workspace

A Groove workspace is a special site template that provides you with tools to share and update documents and to keep people informed about the current status of the documents. After you create a workspace, you can use Files and Discussion Tools to share files, exchange messages, and collaborate with a team. In a Groove workspace, you can point to the Files or Discussion tab to display the contacts currently using a tool.

Create a Workspace

1. In the Launchbar, click the **File** menu, point to **New**, and then click **Workspace**.

2. Click a workspace option:

   ◆ **Standard.** Select to display the Groove Workspace Explorer and initially include the Files and Discussion Tools.

   ◆ **File Sharing.** Select to share the contents of a folder in your Windows system.

   ◆ **Template.** Select to display the Groove Workspace Explorer with the selected tools you want. Click Browse to visit a Groove Web site, where you can download templates.

3. Type a new name for the workspace.

4. Click **OK**.

   The new workspace opens in another window.

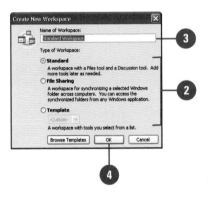

New workspace

Did You Know?

You can delete a workspace. In the workspace, click the File menu, point to Delete Workspace, and then click From This Computer or For All Members.

You can save a workspace as a template or back it up. In the workspace, click the File menu, point to Save Workspace As, and then click Template or Archive.

Inviting Others to a Workspace

Before you can invite someone to a Groove workspace, they need to be a Groove user. Each person you invite to a Groove workspace needs to have a role, either Manager, Participant, or Guest. Each role comes with a set of permissions that allow a user to perform certain tasks. Mangers can invite others, edit existing files, and delete files or the entire workspace. Participants can edit and delete files. Guests can view existing data, but not make changes. After you send an invitation to join a workspace, check for Groove alerts in the notification area to see if the user has accepted your invitation.

Invite Users to a Workspace

1. Open the workspace, click the **Options** menu, and then click **Invite to Workshop**.

2. Click the **To** list arrow, and then select a user.

   If the user you want is not there, click **Add More**, click **Search for User**, type part of the user's name, click **Find**, select the user's name you want, and then click **Add**, and then click **OK**.

3. Click the **Role** list arrow, and then click a role: **Manager**, **Participant**, or **Guest**.

4. Enter a message.

5. Select the **Require acceptance confirmation** check box as a security recommendation.

6. Click **Invite**.

   Monitor your Groove alerts for status and acceptance.

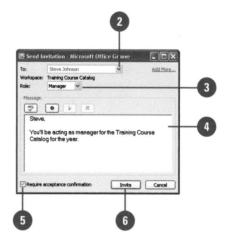

Groove alert with invitation

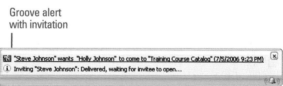

Did You Know?

You can change workspace roles and permissions. In the Launchbar, click Set Roles under Common Tasks. To adjust permissions for a tool, right-click the tool tab, and then click Properties/Permissions.

Dealing with Groove Alerts

Groove alerts appear as blinking messages in the lower right corner of Windows. You can check for Groove alerts by resting the pointer on the Groove icon in the notification area. Groove alerts notify you about updates and work status. For example, Groove sends you an alert when someone accepts an invitation to a workspace, sends a message, changes an existing file or adds a new file. If you're getting more alerts than you want, you can set alert options in the Preferences dialog box.

Check for Groove Alerts

1. Look for a blinking message or Groove icon in the notification area.

2. Point to the **Groove** icon in the notification area to display the alert.

3. Click the alert to open Groove.

Set Alert Options

1. In the Launchbar, click the **Options** menu, and then click **Preferences**.

2. Click the **Alerts** tab.

3. Drag the slider to select an alert level:

   ◆ **Auto.** Similar to the High alert level, but auto-dismissed ignored unread alerts.

   ◆ **High.** Highlight unread content with an icon and display an alert for all unread content.

   ◆ **Medium.** Highlight unread content with an icon.

   ◆ **Off.** Don't display an alert for new or modified content.

4. Specify the number of days you want to keep unread alerts from being removed.

5. Click **OK**.

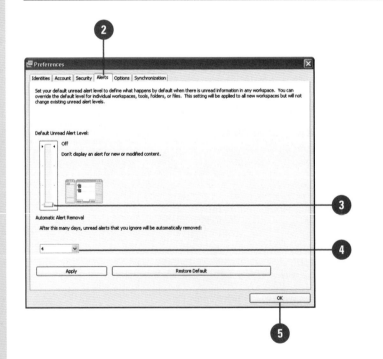

Sharing Files in a Workspace

The Files Tool in Groove allows you to share and collaborate on different types of files, including files from Microsoft Office programs. All team members of a workspace can open files that appear in the Files Tool. When a team member opens, changes, and saves a file to the workspace, Groove automatically updates the file for all other team members. When several team members work on the same file at the same time, the first person to save changes to the workspace updates the original file. If another team member saves changes to the original version, Groove creates a second copy with the editor's name.

Share Files in a Workspace

① In Launchbar, double-click the workspace you want to share.

② Click the **Files** tab.

③ Click the **Add Files** button.

④ Locate and select the files you want to add to the workspace.

⑤ Click **Open**.

The selected files appear in the file list in the workspace.

Manage Tools

◆ **New Files**. Select a folder, click the File menu, point to New, and then click a file type.

◆ **Open Files**. Double-click it, make and save changes, and then click Yes or No to save changes in Groove.

◆ **Delete Files**. Right-click, and then click Delete.

◆ **New Folder**. Select a folder, click the File menu, point to New, click Folder, type a name, and then press Enter.

◆ **Alerts**. Right-click a folder or file, click Properties, click the Alerts tab, drag slider, and then click OK.

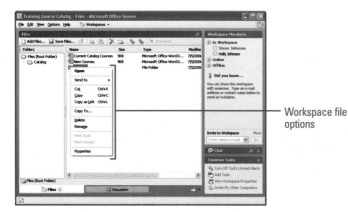

Workspace file options

Holding a Discussion

The Discussion Tool in Groove allows users to post an announcement, news item, or other information for everyone working together in a standard workspace. Team members can add and view discussion items as a threaded conversation. Since the discussions are entered into a different area than the shared document, users can modify the document without affecting the collaborative discussion. Users can add changes to read-only documents and allow multiple users to simultaneously create and edit discussion items.

Start and Participate in a Discussion

1. In Launchbar, double-click the workspace from which you want to hold a discussion.

2. Click the **Discussion** tab.

3. Click the **New** button, and then click **Topic**.

   A new topic opens.

4. Type the Subject.

5. Click the **Category** list arrow, and then select a category.

   If the category you want is not available, click the plus (+) sign, enter a category name, and then click OK.

6. Enter a message in the discussion box.

7. Click **Save** to post the message or click **Save and Create Another** to post and create a new topic.

   The new discussion is displayed in the workspace.

8. To participate in a discussion, double-click the discussion within the workspace in order to respond.

   When you're online, Groove synchronizes the discussion, so all workspace participants can see all new postings and topics.

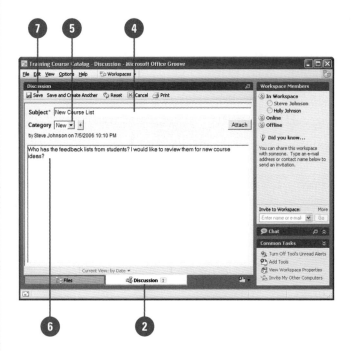

Adding Tools to a Workspace

Like many other Office programs, Groove allows you to add functionality. Groove already comes with the Files and Discussion Tools. You can add other tools, such as InfoPath Forms, Issue Tracking, or SharePoint Files. The InfoPath Tool allows you to collect and view data. The Issue Tracking Tool lets you report on and track the status of issues and incidents. If you have access to an Office or Windows SharePoint Server, the SharePoint Files Tool allows you to synchronize files on a workspace with those on a SharePoint site, document library, or folder.

Add Other Tools to a Workspace

1. In Launchbar, double-click the workspace you want to open.

2. Under Command Tasks, click **Add Tools**.

   TIMESAVER *Click the Add a tool to this workspace button, and then click the tool you want.*

3. Select the check box next to each tool you want to add.

4. Click **OK**.

   A button tab for each tool appears at the bottom of the workspace.

Manage Tools

- **Delete**. Right-click the tool tab, click Delete, and then click Yes.

- **Rename**. Right-click the tool tab, click Rename, enter a new name, and then click OK.

- **Move**. Drag a tool tab name to the left or right.

- **Open in Window**. Right-click the tool tab, and then click Open in New Window.

- **Properties**. Right-click the tool tab, and then click Properties. Click a tab—General, Permissions, Alerts—to view or change properties.

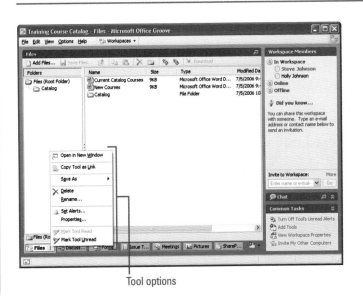

Tool options

Setting Calendar Appointments

Using the Calendar Tool, you can manage your time by doing much more than circling dates. The Calendar collects important information for team members by providing them with critical dates for the completion of a project. Among its many features, the Groove Calendar lets you schedule and manage project appointments and customize the Calendar view to help everyone stay on track.

Add an Appointment

1. In Launchbar, double-click the workspace you want to open, and then click the **Calendar** tab.

2. Click the **New Appointment** button.

   TIMESAVER *To create an appointment with pre-selected dates and times, drag across the range of dates and times you want.*

3. Enter an appointment subject.

4. Fill in the start and end date and a start and end time.

5. Click **OK**.

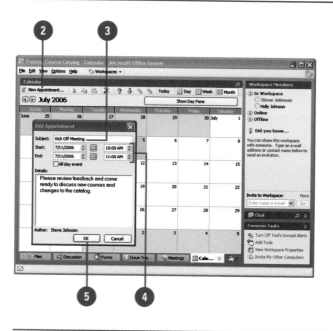

Manage Appointments and the Calendar

- **View**. Point to an appointment to display a text window.

- **Delete**. Select the appointment, and then press Delete.

- **Edit**. Double-click the appointment, make changes, and then click OK.

- **Navigate**. Click Navigate Previous or Next Appointment buttons on the toolbar, or click Navigate Previous or Next Unread buttons on the toolbar.

- **Navigate Calendar Days**. Click the Previous/Next buttons in the Calendar's title bar.

- **Change Calendar Display**. Click the Day, Week, or Month icons.

Navigate days   Change display

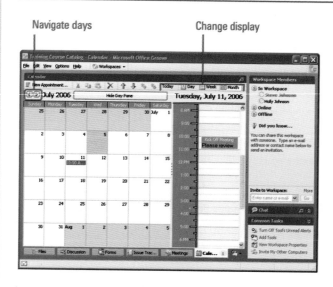

Managing Meetings

The Groove Meetings Tool helps you organize, conduct, and record meetings. Every Groove meeting includes a Meeting profile (start and end times, location, and description), Attendees list, Agenda, Minutes, and Actions, which are displayed as tabs for easy access. You can use a wizard to quickly create a meeting, and then manage all aspects of it.

Create a Meeting

1. In Launchbar, double-click the workspace you want to open, and then click the **Meetings** tab.

2. Click the **New Meeting** button to start the wizard.

3. Enter the subject, start and end times, location and details.

4. Click **OK**.

5. Use the **Attendees** tab to select meeting attendees and appoint a chairperson and minutes-taker.

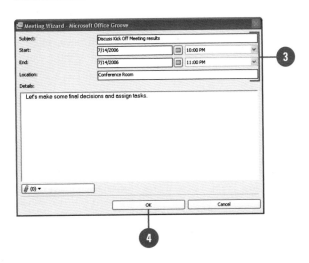

Manage a Meeting

◆ **Agenda**. Click the Agenda tab, click New Topic, fill in the form, and then click OK.

◆ **Action Items**. Click the Actions tab, click New Action Item, fill in the form, and then click OK.

◆ **Record Minutes**. Click the Minutes tab, click Edit, type in text or click Insert Agenda, and then save or discard your work.

◆ **Attendees**. Click the Attendees tab, click Edit, make changes, and then click Save and Close.

◆ **Navigate**. Click the Date of range options button, and then select a range of dates, or click the Previous/Next arrows.

◆ **Attachments**. Select a profile, agenda, or action, click Edit, click Attachments list arrow, and then click Add, Delete, Save all, or file name you want to open.

Meeting options

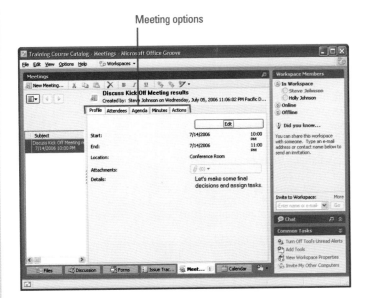

Working with Forms

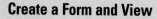

If you need to collect data as part of your project, you can use the Groove Forms Tool to create custom forms in the workspace window, or use the InfoPath Forms Tool to import forms you have already created using Microsoft Office InfoPath 2007. With Designer Access privileges, you can use the Groove Forms Tool to name the form, choose the fields, select the form style, and create a form view to view the data. You create and layout form elements in the design sandbox, which multiple team members can use to help with the design. Like working with files in Groove, your form designs are stored locally until you publish them back to the workspace.

Create a Form and View

1. In Launchbar, double-click the workspace you want to open, and then click the **Forms** tab.

2. Click the **Designer** button, and then click **Create New Form**.
   - ◆ On first run, click **Start Here**.

3. On the Basics tab, enter form name.

4. Select the check boxes with the system fields you want.

5. To create new fields, click **Create New Field** in the left pane, click the field type you want, click **Next**, click a property in the left pane, enter information or select options, and then click **Finish**.

6. Click the **Style Form** button, and then select a style.

7. Click **Column Number** button, and then select a number.

8. Select other options for defining the behavior of the fields and form.

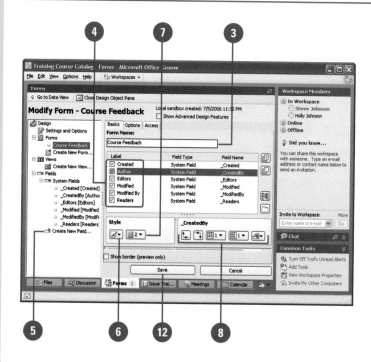

Did You Know?

You can revise a form. In the workspace, click the Forms tab, click the Designer button, point to Modify Form, click a form name, make changes, click Save, and then click Publish Sandbox to update the workspace.

(9) In the left pane, click **Create New View**.

(10) Click the **Basics** tab, and then enter a view name.

(11) Select the check boxes with the fields you want, and other options.

(12) Click **Save**.

(13) Click the **Publish Sandbox** or **Discard Sandbox** button.

Did You Know?

You can change form settings and access. In the workspace, click the Forms tab, click the Designer button, point to Modify Form, click a form name, click the Options or Access tab, select options, click Save, and then click Publish Sandbox.

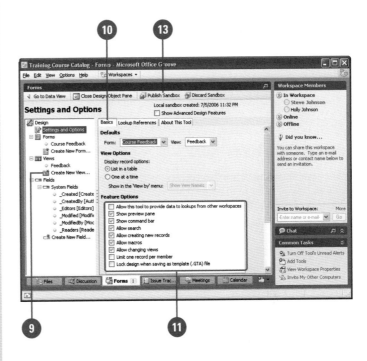

Create and Manage a Form Record

(1) In Launchbar, double-click the workspace you want to open, and then click the **Forms** tab.

(2) Click the **New** button, and then click the form name.

(3) Enter form data.

(4) Click the **Save** or **Save and Create Another** button.

(5) To edit a form record, double-click it, make changes, and then click **Update**.

(6) To delete a form record, click the form record, and then click the **Delete** button.

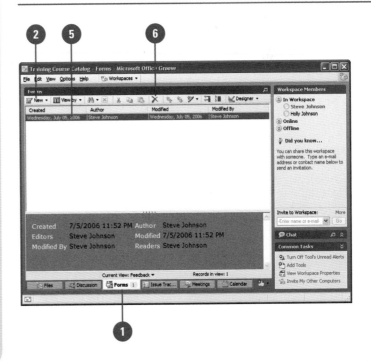

Tracking Issues

Tracking issues is useful for managing all phases of issue reporting and response tracking. Users can create reports, assign ownership, and track status over time. Issue Tracking is a tool designed using the Groove Forms Tool, which includes two basic form types: Issue and Response. The Issue form records issue information, owner assignment, and tracks status. The Response form records a response to an issue record.

Track Issues Using Forms

1. In Launchbar, double-click the workspace you want to open, and then click the **Issue Tracking** tab.

2. Click the **New** button, and then click **Issue**.

3. Click the **Original Report** tab.

4. Enter a title for the issue.

5. Click the list arrow next to each, and then select or add an item.

   ◆ Category.

   ◆ Subcategory.

   ◆ Originated by: Organization.

   ◆ Individual.

6. Enter a description.

7. If you want to attach a file and work with it, use the Attachment buttons.

8. Click the **Current Status** tab.

9. Click the list arrow next to each, and then select or add an item.

   ◆ Status.

   ◆ Priority.

   ◆ Assigned to: Organization.

   ◆ Individual.

10. Enter ongoing remarks.

11. Click the **Save** or **Save and Create Another** button.

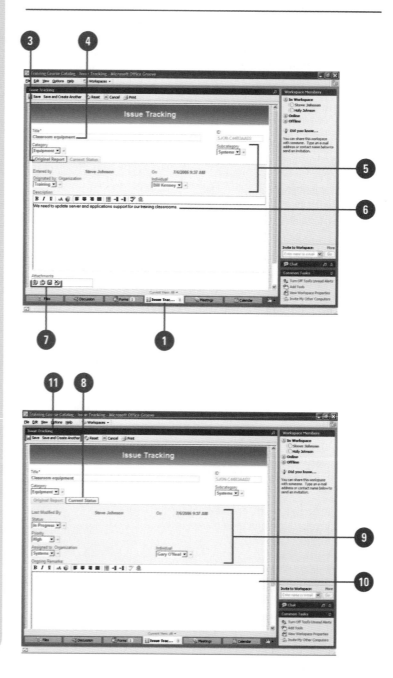

Manage Tools

◆ **Edit**. Double-click the issue, make changes, and then click Update.

◆ **Delete**. Select the issue record, and then click the Delete button on the toolbar.

◆ **Update Assignments**. As a manager, click the Run Macros button on the toolbar, and click Update Assignment - manager only.

◆ **Sort**. Click the column heading you want to sort by.

◆ **View by**. Click the View By button on the toolbar, and then select a view, such as Assignment, Category, Originator, Priority, and Status.

◆ **Search**. Click the Search button on the toolbar, click Search, enter the search criteria you want, and then click Search.

When you're done with the results, click the **Clear Results** button on the toolbar.

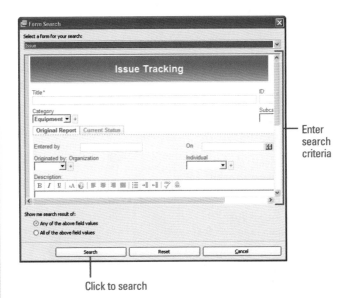

Enter search criteria

Click to search

Did You Know?

You can set alerts for tools. In the workspace, click any tool tab, click Set Tool Alerts under Command Tasks, drag the slider to select an alert level, and then click OK. To turn alerts off, click Turn Off Tool's Unread Alerts under Common Tasks.

Creating a Picture Library

You can add the Groove Pictures Tool to a workspace to display and share picture files in JPEG (.jpg) or bitmap (.bmp) format. You can view a list of picture files that you or other team members have added to the Pictures Tool. The list also includes status information about the picture files, such as type, size, modified date, and last editor. The Pictures Tool automatically scales all pictures you add to fit the current size of the picture viewer window.

Add and View Pictures

1. In Launchbar, double-click the workspace you want to open, and then click the **Pictures** tab.

2. To add pictures, click **Add Pictures**, and then drag and drop files into the list or copy and paste files into the list.

3. To show or hide picture details, click the **Show Pictures Details** or **Hide Picture Details** button.

4. To view pictures, click the **Previous** or **Next** buttons.

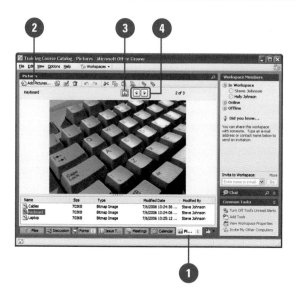

Manage Pictures

◆ **Edit**. Right-click a picture, and then click Open. Your graphics program opens. Edit and save the picture, and then Yes to update in Groove.

◆ **Rename**. Select the picture, click the Rename button on the toolbar, type a new name, and then click OK.

◆ **Export**. Select the picture file, click the Export button on the toolbar, select a location, and then click Save.

◆ **Delete**. Select one or more pictures, and then press Delete.

Toolbar to manage pictures

Adding a Contact

In order to send messages or have a chat with other Groove team members, you need to add them as contacts. In the Launchbar, you can quickly and easily check for the online presence of a contact. By default, each contact appears on the Contacts tab based on status, either Active, Online, or Offline. Each icon next to a contact also indicates whether the member is online, away or offline. In a Groove workspace, you can point to the Files or Discussion tab to display the contacts currently using a tool.

Add a Contact

1 In Launchbar, click the **Contacts** tab.

2 Click the **Add Contact** button.

The Find User window opens.

3 Type part of the user's name.

4 Click **Find**.

5 Select the user's name you want to add as a contact.

6 Click **Add**.

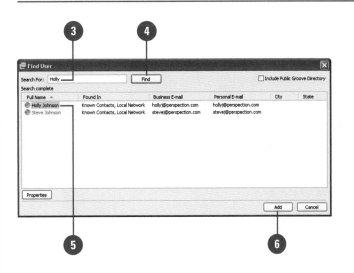

Check the Presence of a Contact

◆ In the Launchbar, click the **Contacts** tab. By default, each contact appears in the Launchbar based on status, either Active, Online, or Offline. Each icon next to a contact also indicates whether the member is online, away or offline.

TIMESAVER *To change order, click the Options menu, point to View Contacts By, and then click a sort method.*

◆ In a Groove workspace, the tabs at the bottom of the workspace display the number of people who are actively using the tool, either Files or Discussion. To see the names of the people using a Tool, point to the tab.

Contacts

Sending a Message

You can send messages to other Groove contacts at any time even if you or your contact are not online. If you or your contact are offline, Groove sends the message and alerts you of delivery, when it's opened, and when your contact replies as soon as you and your contact are online.

Send a Message

1. In Launchbar, click the **Contacts** tab.

2. Right-click a contact, and then click **Send Message**.

   The Send Message window opens.

   TIMESAVER *Press Shift-Shift to open a new instant message window or bring up your next unread instant message from your inbox.*

3. Type a message.

4. Click **Send**.

   An alert appears, indicating your message was sent. Monitor Groove alerts for more message status.

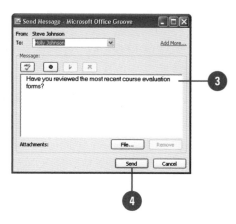

Receive and Reply to a Message

1. When a Groove alert appears, indicating you have received a message, click it.

2. Enter your reply to the message.

3. Click **Send**.

   An alert appears, indicating your message was sent. Monitor Groove alerts for more message status.

   When the original sender received back the message, the sender can Reply, Forward, or Close the message.

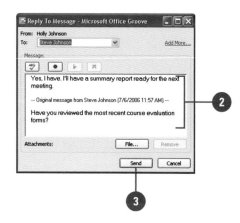

Chatting with Others

A chat is an ongoing conversation you type and send, or post. Each Groove workspace includes a chat tool, where you can communicate with others in real time or offline. The number of team members currently involved in a chat appears on the title bar. When you post a new message in the chat tool, a Groove alert notifies other team members. As each team members post messages in a workspace chat, the ongoing conversation is saved in the workspace for reference until the workspace is deleted.

Chat with Other Workspace Team Members

1. In Launchbar, double-click the workspace you want to open, and then click **Expand Chat** button next to Chart, if necessary.

   IMPORTANT *If you are using Groove on a Tablet PC, the chat window may open by default in Ink mode. To switch to Text mode, click the Options menu (Down Arrow), and then click Switch to Text Mode.*

2. Click in the blank box at the bottom of the chat tool, located on the right side of the workspace, and then type a message.

3. To check spelling, click the **Check Spelling** button, and then correct any mistakes.

4. Click **Go**.

   Your message is added to the ongoing conversation.

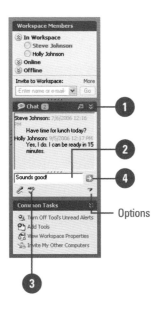

Options

Did You Know?

You can use a microphone. With a microphone installed on your computer, click the Microphone button, and then reply to the Audio Tuner wizard questions.

Sharing Files with SharePoint

If you have access to an Office or Windows SharePoint Server 3.0 site, (workspace collaboration using a Web server), you can synchronize file content between Groove and SharePoint libraries. Groove uses the SharePoint Files Tool as a centralized location to work on SharePoint files and with people outside your workspace. The SharePoint Files Tool synchronizes data with workspace members in the same way as the standard File Tool. The one who sets up the SharePoint connection is the synchronizer, and is typically the workspace Owner. The synchronizer has two options: manual or automatic based on a time interval. Simply double-click a SharePoint file to edit it in its native program. As the synchronizer, you can also check out/in files to avoid conflicts with other SharePoint users while you edit a file.

Set Up a SharePoint Connection

1. In Launchbar, double-click the workspace you want to open, and then click the **SharePoint Files** tab.

2. Click **Setup**.

3. Enter the SharePoint Server Web address, and then press Enter.

    See your Network Administrator for specifics.

4. Click the library in which you want to connect.

5. Click **Select**.

    All the files in the SharePoint library are synchronized with the Groove workspace.

Did You Know?

You can get more information about SharePoint. To download a complete chapter about Office SharePoint, go to *www.perspection.com*.

You can set file permissions for SharePoint files. In the workspace, right-click the SharePoint Files tab, click Properties, click the Permissions tab, select a role, select the permissions you want, and then click OK.

Check Out and In Files to Edit

1. In Launchbar, double-click the workspace you want to open, and then click the **SharePoint Files** tab.

2. Select the file you want to check out.

3. Click the **Check In/Out** button on the toolbar, and then click **Check Out from SharePoint**.

4. To edit a file, double-click the file to open it in its native program, make changes, save and close it.

5. In Groove, click **Yes** to save changes.

6. Click the **Check In/Out** button on the toolbar, and then click **Check In from SharePoint**.

7. Describe your changes, and then click **OK**.

Synchronize Files

1. In Launchbar, double-click the workspace you want to open, and then click the **SharePoint Files** tab.

2. To set synchronization options, click the **Calendar** icon, click the **Manually** or **Automatically** option, and then if necessary, specify an interval, and then click **OK**.

3. To manually synchronize files, click **Synchronize Now**.

   The Preview Synchronization dialog box opens.

4. Click **Synchronize Now**.

   Resolve any conflicts that arise. If necessary, click Resolve, select another file version, and then click OK.

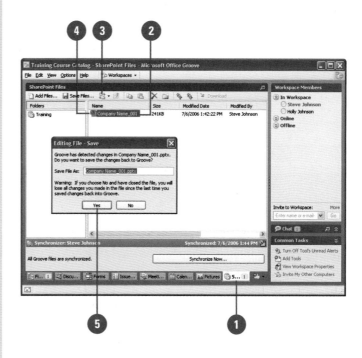

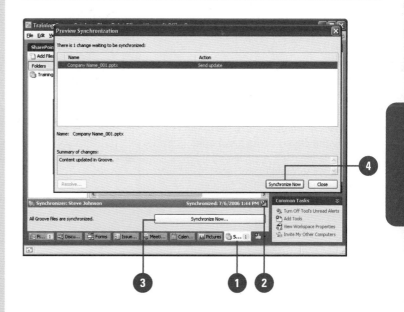

Sharing Files with Synchronizing Folders ▶

Instead of using the File Tool in Groove, you can use Groove Folder Synchronization (GFS) in Windows to make sure all changes within a folder are shared between users and kept up-to-date. You create GFS folders in your Windows file system using Windows Explorer. GFS folders are separate from workspaces and currently have a 2 gigabyte size limit. Files shared in Groove workspaces are stored in an encrypted format, while files in a GFS folder are only encrypted during transmission between computers. Any new files added to a synchronized folder are automatically shared with other team members to ensure a secure environment. In Windows Explorer, you can use the Groove Folder Synchronization pane to view the details of the file sharing workspace, view members of the workspace, send workspace invitations, and set workspace and folder properties.

Synchronize Local Folders

① In Windows Explorer, click the folder you want to share as a GFS folder.

② Click the **Folder Sync** button.

The Groove Folder Synchronization pane replaces the Windows Folder pane.

③ Click **Start synchronizing** *foldername*.

④ Click **Synchronize Now**, if necessary, to continue from the preview synchronization.

⑤ Click **Yes** to confirm the folder share.

⑥ Use commands in the Groove Folder Synchronization pane to view the details of the file sharing workspace, view members of the workspace, send workspace invitations, mark folders read or unread, and set workspace and folder properties.

⑦ In Groove, click the **Workspace** tab to access the GFS folder, and view read and unread files.

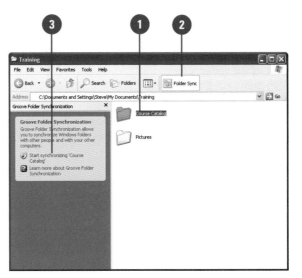

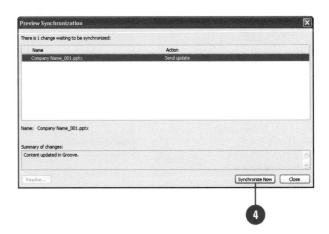

Working with a Shared Workspace

A **Document Workspace** is an Office SharePoint site template that provides you with tools to share and update documents and to keep people informed about the current status of the documents. Using icons on the Document Management task pane, you can connect to an Office SharePoint Server directly from Excel. Each icon displays different information relating to your document: Status, Members, Tasks, Document, and Links. Users can show current tasks, view the status of a document, see the availability of a document, display properties of a document, and list additional resources, folders, and privileges.

Work with a Shared Workspace

1 In Excel, open the workbook you want to share.

2 Click the **Office** button, point to **Publish** (to create) and then click **Create Document Server**, or point to **Server** (to modify), and then click **Document Management Server**.

3 To create a workspace, type a name for the site, type the URL or network location, and then click **Create**.

4 Use the Document Management task pane tools.

◆ **Status**. Displays the checked-in/checked-out status of your current document.

◆ **Members**. Shows you who is online from your Team Members Group. You can add new members and send e-mail message to members.

◆ **Tasks**. Shows you the tasks assigned for this document and the completion status. You can add new tasks, create alerts, and view workflow tasks.

◆ **Documents**. Displays the name and workspace of the selected document. You can add new documents and folders, and alert me about documents.

◆ **Links**. Displays links to files, folders, and resources. You can add new links and alerts.

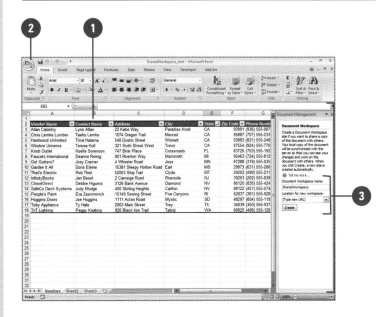

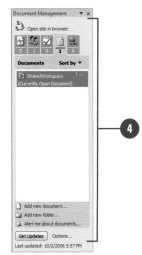

Working with Excel Services

Excel Services (**New!**) is a Microsoft Office SharePoint Server 2007 component that you can use to share, secure, and manage Excel 2007 workbooks as interactive reports. Excel Services consists of three parts: **Excel Calculation Services** (ECS), **Excel Web Access** (EWA), and **Excel Web Services** (EWS). ECS loads the workbook, calculates and refreshes data and maintains sessions. EWA displays data and charts from a workbook in report form as a Web page, known as a Web Part. EWS provides developer support for custom applications. To use Excel Service, create a workbook in Excel and save it to a Document Library in Excel Services. Excel is the authoring tool and Excel Services in the reporting tool. When you publish worksheets to a Document Library to a SharePoint Server, team members can refresh data, sort and filter data, and create reports.

Access Excel Services on a SharePoint Site

1. Open the workbook you want to save to a Document Management Server.

2. Click the **Office** button, point to **Publish**, and then click **Excel Services**.

3. Navigate to the network folder location on the SharePoint server where you want to save the file.

4. Type a workbook file name.

5. If necessary, click the **Save as type** list arrow, and then click **Excel Workbook.**

6. Select the **Open in Excel Services** check box.

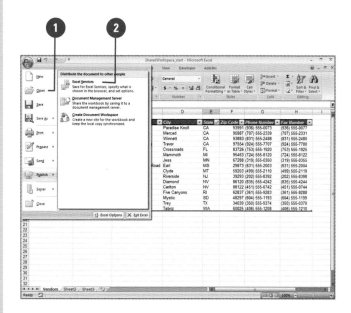

Did You Know?

You can set shared workspace options in Excel. Click the Office button, click Excel Options, click Advanced, click Service Options, click Document Management, select the Shared Workspace options and updates you want, and then click OK twice.

7 Click **Excel Services Options**.

8 Click the **Show** tab.

9 Click the list arrow, and then select the items you want shown by Excel Services in a Web browser.

10 Click the **Parameters** tab.

Determine which parameters you want to edit using Excel Services by adding or deleting them.

11 To add a parameter, click **Add,** select the single cell named ranges (blank or value) you want to view using Excel Services., and then click **OK**.

12 To delete a parameter, select the item, click **Delete** or **Delete All,** and then click **Yes** to confirm.

13 Click **OK**.

14 Click **Save**.

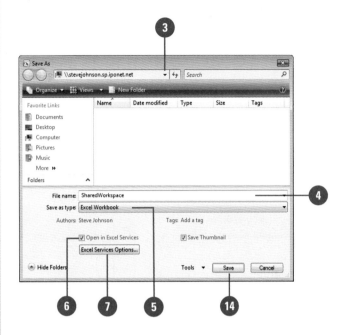

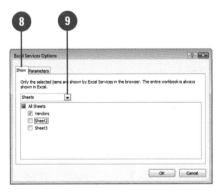

Did You Know?

You can create a snapshot in Excel Services. A snapshot is a static, read-only copy of a workbook that is created at a point in time. Open the document library with the workbook, point to the workbook item, click the arrow next to it, click Open Snapshot in Excel, and then save the workbook snapshot to a folder or document library.

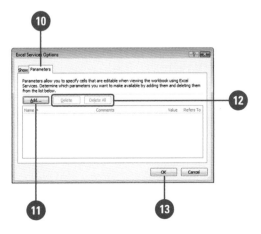

Saving a Workbook to a Document Management Server

You can save workbooks to a Document Management Server (**New!**), such as a Document Library on an Office SharePoint site, in a similar way that you save workbooks on your hard disk. After you save the workbook for the first time using the Document Management Server command, you can click the Save button on the Quick Access Toolbar as you do for any workbook to update the document on the site. If you save a file to a library that requires you to check documents in and out, the SharePoint site checks it out for you. However, you need to check the document in when you're done with it. If the site stores multiple content types, you might be asked to specify the content type.

Save a Workbook to a Document Management Server

1. Open the workbook you want to save to a Document Management Server.

2. Click the **Office** button, point to **Publish**, and then click **Document Management Server**.

3. Navigate to the network folder location on the SharePoint server where you want to save the file.

4. Type a workbook file name.

5. If necessary, click the **Save as type** list arrow, and then click **Excel Workbook.**

6. Click **Save**.

Point to access online SharePoint document resources

SharePoint server location

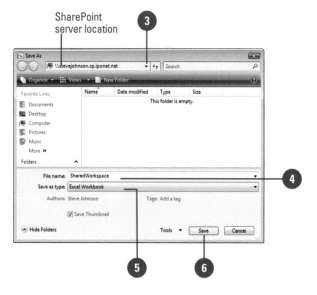

Did You Know?

You can access SharePoint resources from Excel. After you save or publish a workbook to a SharePoint Server site, you can click the Office button, and then point to Server to access other server related commands: View Version History, View Workflow Tasks, and Document Management Information.

Workshop

Introduction

The Workshop is all about being creative and thinking outside of the box. These workshops will help your right-brain soar, while making your left-brain happy; by explaining why things work the way they do. Exploring possibilities is great fun; however, always stay grounded with knowledge of how things work.

Getting and Using the Project Files

Each project in The Workshop includes a start file to help you get started with the project, and a final file to provide you with the results of the project so you can see how well you accomplished the task.

Before you can use the project files, you need to download them from the Web. You can access the files at *www.perspection.com* in the software downloads area. After you download the files from the Web, uncompress the files into a folder on your hard drive to which you have easy access from your Microsoft Office program.

Project 1: Creating a Drop-Down List

Skills and Tools: Create a drop-down list

Entering data in a worksheet can be tedious and repetitive. To make the job easier and get consistent accurate data, you can create a drop-down list of entries you define. To create a drop-down list, you create a list of valid entries in a single column or row without blanks, define a name, and then use the List option in the Data Validation dialog box. To enter data using a drop-down list, click the cell with the defined drop-down list, click the list arrow, and then click the entry you want.

The Project

In this project, you'll learn how to create a drop-down list from a named range of cells for use in conditional formatting.

The Process

1. Open Excel 2007, open **DropDown_start.xlsm**, and then save it as **DropDown.xlsm**.

2. Click the **Numbers** tab.

3 Select the cell range of numbers in column A, (A1:A50).

To create a drop-down list, you need a single column or row without blanks.

4 Click the **Name** box, type **Numbers**, and then press Enter.

5 Click the **Form Controls** Sheet tab.

6 Select cell B1.

7 Click the **Data** tab.

8 Click the **Data Validation** button.

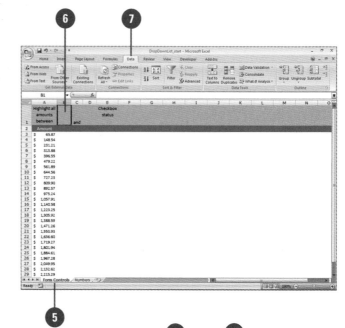

9 Click the **Settings** tab.

10 Click the **Allow** list arrow, and then click **List**.

11 Click the **Source** box, and then type **=Numbers**.

12 Click **OK**.

13 Click the Name box, type **StartNum**, and then press Enter.

14 Select cell D2.

15 Repeat steps 8 through 13, and name the cell **EndNum**.

16 Select cell B1, click the drop-down list, and then select a number.

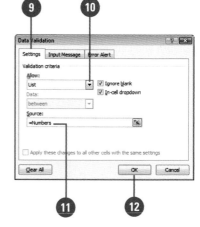

17 Select cell D1, click the drop-down list, and then select a number.

18 Click the **Save** button on the Quick Access Toolbar.

The Results

Finish: Compare your completed project file with the results file **DropDown_results.xlsm**.

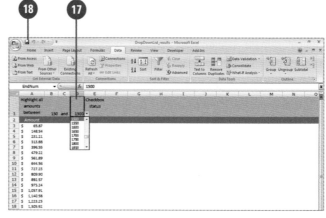

Project 2: Adding a Form Control

Skills and Tools: Insert a Form Control

Form controls are objects that users can interact with to enter or manipulate data. A control is a component on a worksheet used to display information or accept user input. For example, you can add a Checkbox control to your worksheet so that users can turn an option on and off. You can select a control from the Developer tab and drag to create the control directly on your worksheet.

The Project

In this project, you'll learn how to insert a check box form control into a worksheet to control formatting.

The Process

1 Open Excel 2007, open **FormControl_start.xlsm**, and then save it as **FormControl.xlsm**.

2 Click the **Developer** tab.

3 Click the **Design Mode** button (highlighted).

4 Click the **Insert** button, and then click the **Check Box (Form Control)**; located on the the top row.

5 Drag (pointer changes to a plus sign) to draw the form control in a blank area of the worksheet.

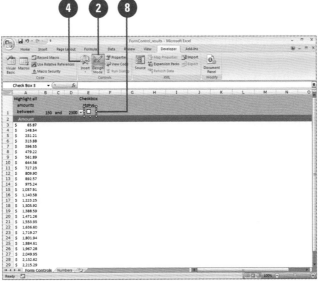

When you point to a control in Excel, you will see the pointer cursor. To select a control, right-click the object, and then click off the menu.

6 Select the check box object (if necessary), select the text to the right of the check box, and the press Delete.

7 Drag the right-middle resize handle (circles) to the size check box control to display only the check box.

8 Drag the check box control to cell E1 below the text *Check box status*.

9 Right-click the check box control, and then click **Format Control**.

Check box

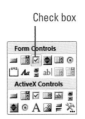

10 Click the **Control** tab.

11 Click the **Checked** option.

12 Click the **Collapse Dialog** button, click cell **E2**, and then click the **Expand Dialog** button.

13 Select the **3-D shading** check box.

14 Click **OK**.

15 Select the check box control (if necessary), click the Name box, type a **CheckBoxSwitch**, and then press Enter.

16 Click the **Design Mode** button (not highlighted), and then click a blank cell to deselect the check box control.

17 Click check box to turn it on and off.

The contents of cell E2 toggles between TRUE and FALSE.

18 Click the **Save** button on the Quick Access Toolbar.

The Results

Finish: Compare your completed project file with the results file **FormControl_results.xlsm**.

Project 3: Adding Conditional Formatting

Skills and Tools: Conditional Formatting

You can make your worksheets more powerful by setting up conditional formatting, which lets the value of a cell determine its formatting. For example, you might want this year's sales total to be displayed in red and italics if it's less than last year's total, but in green and bold if it's more. The formatting is applied to the cell values only if the values meet the condition that you specify. Otherwise, no conditional formatting is applied to the cell values.

The Project

In this project, you'll learn how to add conditional formatting to a named range and include form controls.

The Process

1. Open Excel 2007, open **ConditionalFormat_start.xlsm**, and then save it as **ConditionalFormat.xlsm**.

2. Select the cell range A3:A32.

3. Click the **Home** tab.

4. Click the **Conditional Formatting** button, and then click **New Rules**.

5. Click **New Rules**.

6. Click **Use a formula to determine which cells to format**.

7. Type the formula **=AND($A3>=StartNum,$A3<=EndNum,CheckBoxSwitch)**

8. Click **Format**.

9. Click the **Fill** tab.

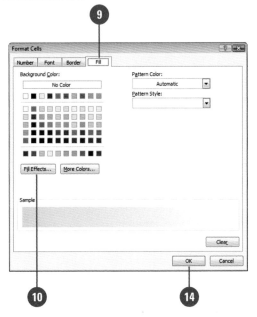

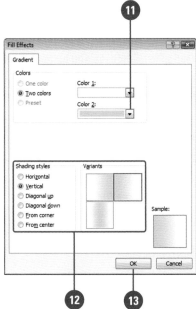

10. Click **Fill Effects**.

11. Click the **Color 2** list arrow, and then select a color.

12. Click a gradient option, and then select a gradient.

13. Click **OK** to close the Fill Effects dialog box.

14. Click **OK** to close the Format dialog box.

15. Click **OK**.

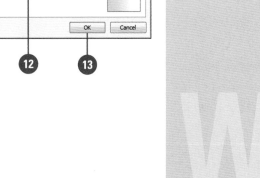

16 Click the **Conditional Formatting** button, and then click **Manage Rules**.

17 Select the **Stop If True** check box to provide compatibility error checking.

18 Click **OK**.

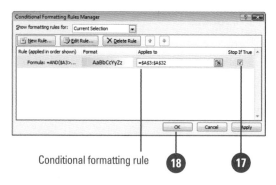

Conditional formatting rule   **18**   **17**

The Results

Finish: Compare your completed project file with the results file **ConditionalFormat_results.xlsm**.

Project 4: Creating a VBA Script

Skills and Tools: Visual Basic for Applications script

Instead of pressing the Caps Lock key every time you want to turn capitalization on and off, you can create a VBA script to change cell contents to upper case. This can be useful when you have column data, such as two-letter US state abbreviations, in a worksheet. You can type the state abbreviation in lower case and let the VBA script change it for you.

The Project

In this project, you'll learn how to create a VBA script to change cell contents in a designated range to uppercase.

The Process

1 Open Excel 2007, open **CAPS_start.xlsm**, and then save it as **CAPS.xlsm**.

2 Click the **Developer** tab.

3 Click the **Visual Basic** button.

4 Double-click the **Sheet1(Vendors)** object.

The Object windows opens.

5 Click the **Object** list arrow, and then click **Worksheet**.

6 Click the **Properties** list arrow, and then click **Change**.

4   **5**   **6**

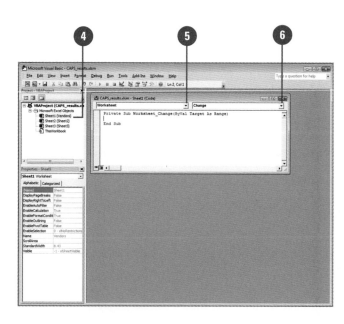

7 Type the VBA code that appears in the following illustration:

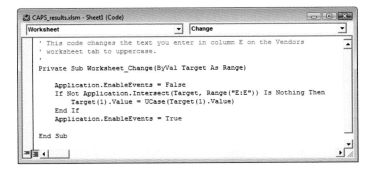

```
CAPS_results.xlsm - Sheet1 (Code)
[Worksheet]                          [Change]

' This code changes the text you enter in column E on the Vendors
' worksheet tab to uppercase.
'
Private Sub Worksheet_Change(ByVal Target As Range)

    Application.EnableEvents = False
    If Not Application.Intersect(Target, Range("E:E")) Is Nothing Then
        Target(1).Value = UCase(Target(1).Value)
    End If
    Application.EnableEvents = True

End Sub
```

Common Cell and Range References

Reference Example	Description
Range("A1")	Cell A1
Range("A1:B5")	Cells A1 through B5
Range("C5:D9,G9:H16")	Cells C5 through D9 and cells G9 through H16
Range("A:A"), Range("A:C")	Column A, Columns A through C
Range("1:1"), Range("1:5")	Row 1, Rows 1 through 5
Range("1:1,3:3,8:8")	Rows 1, 3, and 8
Range("A:A,C:C,F:F)	Columns A, C, and F

8 Click the **Save** button on the Standard toolbar.

9 Click the **Close** button on the Visual Basic Editor window to return to Excel.

10 Type state abbreviations in column E. After you press Enter, cell contents changes to uppercase.

11 Click the **Save** button on the Quick Access Toolbar.

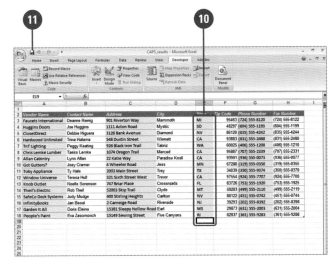

The Results

Finish: Compare your completed project file with the results file **CAPS_results.xlsm**.

Project 5: Creating a VBA Interface

Skills and Tools: ActiveX Controls and Visual Basic for Applications (VBA) form

An ActiveX control is a software component that adds functionality to an existing program. An ActiveX control supports a customizable, programmatic interface using VBA, which you can use to create your own functionality, such as a form. Excel includes several pre-built ActiveX controls—including a label, text box, command button, and check box—to help you create a user interface.

The Project

In this project, you'll learn how to create a form using VBA that allows users to input information using a series of dialogs, like a wizard, and use buttons to clear information and save the worksheet.

The Process

1. Open Excel 2007, open **VBAForm_start.xlsm**, and then save it as **VBAForm.xlsm**.

> ➤ **Insert an ActiveX control.**

2. Click the **Developer** tab.

3. Click the **Design Mode** button (highlighted).

4. Click the **Insert** button, and then click **CommandButton (ActiveX Control)**.

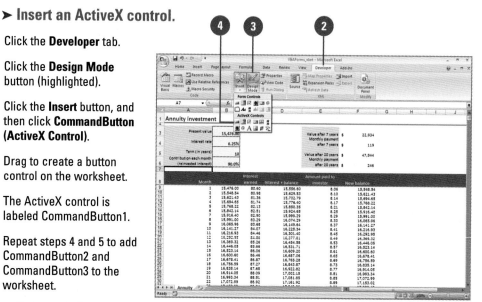

5. Drag to create a button control on the worksheet.

    The ActiveX control is labeled CommandButton1.

6. Repeat steps 4 and 5 to add CommandButton2 and CommandButton3 to the worksheet.

> ➤ **Set control properties.**

1. Click the **CommandButton1** control to select it on the worksheet.

2. Click the **Properties** button.

3. In the Properties window, change the Caption text to **Gather Info**; change the BackColor to **Inactive Title Bar** (click the box next to the property to display a list arrow); change the Height to **24.75**; and change the Width to **81**.

4 Click the CommandButton2 control to select it on the worksheet, change the Caption text to **Clear Results**, and then make the same remaining changes in step 3.

5 Click the CommandButton3 control to select it on the worksheet, change the Caption text to **Save Results**, and then make the same remaining changes in step 3.

6 Click the **Close** button in the Properties window.

7 Click the **Page Layout** tab.

8 Click the **Align** button, and then click **Align Center** to align center the ActiveX control buttons.

9 Click the **Align** button, and then click **Distribute Vertically** to distribute vertically the ActiveX control buttons.

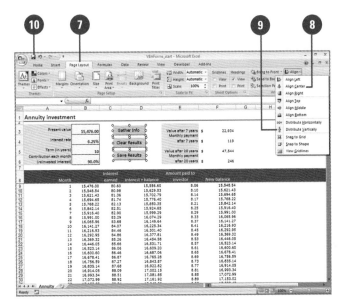

10 Click the **Save** button on the Quick Access Toolbar.

> **Add VBA functionality to the control.**

1 Click the **Developer** tab.

2 Click the **Visual Basic** button.

3 In Project Explorer, double-click the **Sheet(Annuity)** object, if necessary, to open the Code Window.

4 Click the **Object box** list arrow at the top of the Code Window, and then click **CommandButton1**.

5 In the Code window, type the VBA code that appears in the following illustration:

This code clears the current contents of cells B3 through B6, moves the selection out of the way to cell A7, and then assigns named cell values, such as Present_Value, the number entered using the InputBox function. The first argument in the InputBox function is the text you want in the dialog box, and the second argument is the dialog box title.

6 Repeat steps 4 through 6 to add VBA code for CommandButton2 and CommandButton3 to the control that appears in the following illustration:

```
VBAForms_results.xlsm - Sheet1 (Code)
CommandButton2                               ▼  Click                          ▼

  Private Sub CommandButton2_Click()
      Ans = MsgBox("Do You want to save the workbook?", vbYesNo + vbExclamation)
      If Ans = vbYes Then ActiveWorkbook.Save
  End Sub
```

This code creates a Save dialog box. The code uses the MsgBox function to display a dialog box when you click the button (CommandButton2). The first argument in the MsgBox function is the text you want in the dialog box, and the second argument is the type of buttons you want to use (in this case, Yes and No), and the third argument is the type of icon you want to use in the dialog box. See the table at the end of this project for different types of dialog box buttons and icons.

```
VBAForms_results.xlsm - Sheet1 (Code)
CommandButton3                               ▼  Click                          ▼

  Private Sub CommandButton3_Click()
      Ans = MsgBox("Do You want to clear client information?", vbYesNo + vbCritical)
      If Ans = vbYes Then Range("B3:B6").ClearContents
  End Sub
```

This code creates a dialog box to clear the current contents of cells B3 through B6.

7 In Project Explorer, double-click the **ThisWorkbook** object, if necessary, to open the Code Window.

8 Type the VBA code that appears in the following illustration:

```
VBAForms_results.xlsm - ThisWorkbook (Code)
Workbook                                     ▼  Open                           ▼

  Private Sub Workbook_Open()
      MsgBox "This financial information belongs to " & Application.UserName & "."
  End Sub
```

This code creates a dialog box when you open the workbook, displaying text and the username of the workbook (in this case Tim Todd). This code is placed in the ThisWorkbook object and uses the procedure Sub Workbook_Open(), so it gets executed when you open the workbook.

9 Click the **Save** button on the Standard toolbar.

10 Click the **Close** button on the Visual Basic Editor window to return to Excel.

11 Click the **Design Mode** button (not highlighted).

12 Click the **Clear Results** button, and then click **Yes** to clear client information.

13. Click the **Gather Info** button, enter annual salary, click **OK**, enter interest rate, click **OK**, enter the term in years, click **OK**, enter a reinvest percentage, and then click **OK**.

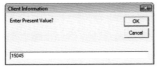
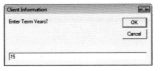

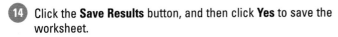

Enter correct values. You'll learn how to add error checking later.

14. Click the **Save Results** button, and then click **Yes** to save the worksheet.

15. Click the **Save** button on the Quick Access Toolbar.

16. Click the **Office** button, and then click **Close**.

17. Click the **Office** button, and then click VBAForm_results on the Recent Documents List.

The message alert dialog box opens.

18. Click **OK**.

19. Click the **Save** button on the Quick Access Toolbar.

➤ **Add VBA conditional functionality to the control.**

1. Click the **Developer** tab.

2. Click the **Visual Basic** button.

3. In Project Explorer, double-click the **Sheet(Annuity)** object, if necessary, to open the Code Window.

4. Click the **Object box** list arrow at the top of the Code Window, and then click **CommandButton1**.

5. In the Code window, change the VBA code to add error checking to the data input that appears in the following illustration:

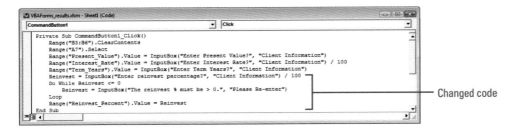

Changed code

Common MsgBox Function Arguments

Constant	Value	Description
vbOKOnly	0	Display OK button only
vbOKCancel	1	Display OK and Cancel buttons
vbAbortRetryIgnore	2	Display Abort, Retry, and Ignore buttons
vbYesNoCancel	3	Display Yes, No, and Cancel buttons
vbYesNo	4	Display Yes and No buttons
vbRetryCancel	5	Display Retry and Cancel buttons
vbCritical	16	Display Critical Message icon
vbQuestion	32	Display Warning Query icon
vbExclamation	48	Display Warning Message icon
vbInformation	64	Display Information Message icon
vbDefaultButton1	0	First button is default
vbDefaultButton2	256	Second button is default
vbDefaultButton3	512	Third button is default
vbDefaultButton4	768	Fourth button is default

⑥ Click the **Save** button on the Standard toolbar.

⑦ Click the **Close** button on the Visual Basic Editor window to return to Excel.

⑧ Click the **Gather Info** button, enter annual salary, click **OK**, enter interest rate, click **OK**, enter the term in years, click **OK**, enter **0** (as a reinvest percentage), re-enter a reinvestment percentage greater than 0, and then click **OK**.

⑨ Click the **Save** button on the Quick Access Toolbar.

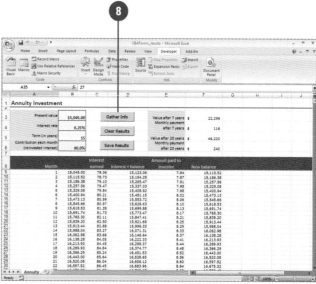

The Results

Finish: Compare your completed project file with the presentation **VBAForm_results.xlsm**.

Want More Projects

You can access and download more workshop projects and related files at *www.perspection.com* in the software downloads area. After you download the files from the Web, uncompress the files into a folder on your hard drive to which you have easy access from your Microsoft Office program.

Get Everything on CD

Instead of downloading everything from the Web, which can take a while depending on your Internet connection speed, you can get all the files used in this book and much more on the Microsoft Office 2007 On Demand CD. The CD contains task and workshop files, tips and tricks, keyboard shortcuts, transition helpers from 2003 to 2007, and other goodies from the author.

To get the Microsoft Office 2007 On Demand CD, go to *www.perspection.com*.

New! Features

Microsoft Office Excel 2007

Microsoft Office Excel 2007 is a spreadsheet program that you can use to track and analyze sales, create budgets, and organize finances—both business and personal. With enhancements to the user interface, and the addition of advanced data tools, enhanced formula writing, page layout, SmartArt graphics, Office themes and Quick Styles for text, shapes, tables, and pictures, you can accomplish a variety of business or personal tasks more easily in Excel 2007.

Only New Features

If you're already familiar with Excel 2003, you can access and download all the tasks in this book with Microsoft Office Excel 2007 New Features to help make your transition to the new version simple and smooth. The Excel 2007 New Features as well as other 2003 to 2007 transition helpers are available on the Web at *www.perspection.com.*

What's New

If you're searching for what's new in Excel 2007, just look for the icon: New!. The new icon appears in the table of contents and throughout this book so you can quickly and easily identify a new or improved feature in Excel 2007. The following is a brief description of each new feature and it's location in this book.

Office 2007

- **Ribbon (p. 4, 423)** The Ribbon is a new look for Excel 2007. It replaces menus, toolbars, and most of the task panes found in Excel 2003. The Ribbon is comprised of tabs with buttons and options that are organized by task.

- **Live Preview (p. 4, 412)** A gallery displays graphical options on the Ribbon. When you point to a gallery on the Ribbon, Office programs display a live preview of the option change so that you can see exactly what your change will look like before committing to it.

- **Office button and menu (p. 5)** The Office button and menu replaces the File menu with a revised list of commands and options, such as the Recent Documents list.

- ◆ **Quick Access Toolbar and Mini-Toolbar (p. 5-7, 134, 412)** Excel includes its most common commands, such as Save and Undo, on the Quick Access Toolbar. The Mini-Toolbar appears above selected text and provides quick access to formatting tools.

- ◆ **Dialog Box Launcher (p. 8)** Dialog Box Launchers are small icons that appear at the bottom corner of some groups on the Ribbon. When you point to a Dialog Box Launcher, a ScreenTip with a thumbnail of the dialog box appears to show you which dialog box opens when you click the Dialog Box Launcher.

- ◆ **Status bar (p. 9)** The Status bar displays the on/off status of features, such as signatures and spelling, and determines what information appears on the bar.

- ◆ **Spotlight (p. 11)** The Spotlight section under the Featured category in the New Workbook dialog box, highlights new Excel content from Microsoft Office Online.

- ◆ **Compatibility mode (p. 12-14)** When you open a workbook from Excel 97-2003, Excel 2007 goes into compatibility mode where it disables new features that cannot be displayed or converted well by previous versions.

- ◆ **Save in XML-based file format (p. 22-25)** Excel 2007 saves files in an XML (Extensible Markup Language) based file format (.xlsx). The XML-based format significantly reduces file sizes, provides enhanced file recovery, and allows for increased compatibility, sharing, reuse, and transportability.

- ◆ **Check compatibility (p. 26)** The Compatibility Checker identifies the potential loss of functionality when you save an Excel 2007 workbook in the Excel 97-2003 Workbook file format.

- ◆ **Document Information Panel (p. 27, 454)** You can view or edit standard document properties or create advanced custom properties by using the Document Information Panel, which is an XML-based Microsoft InfoPath 2007 form hosted in Excel.

- ◆ **Diagnose problems (p. 32-33)** The Diagnose command improves performance by diagnosing and repairing problems, such as missing files from setup, corrupted file by malicious viruses, and registry settings.

- ◆ **Common spell checking and dictionary (p. 62-65)** Microsoft Office 2007 programs share a common spell checker and dictionary, so you only need to make additions and changes once.

- ◆ **English Assistant (p. 69)** The English Assistant is a Microsoft Office Online service that helps people for whom English is a second language write professional English text.

- ◆ **Message Bar (p. 124)** The Message Bar appears based on Trust Center security settings to protect your computer from harmful attacks.

- ◆ **Themes (p. 149, 154-165)** A theme is a set of unified design elements that provides a consistent look for a workbook by using color themes, fonts, and effects, such as shadows, shading, and animations. You can use a standard theme or create one of your own.

- ◆ **Create a PDF or XPS (p. 183-184)** You can now save a workbook as a PDF or XPS file, which is a fixed-layout format that retains the form you intended on a computer monitor or printer.

- ◆ **Picture Quick Styles (p. 194)** The Picture Quick Style gallery provides a variety of different formatting combinations.

- ◆ **Apply a shape to a picture (p. 195)** You can now select a picture and apply one of Excel's shapes to it.

- ◆ **Picture effects (p. 197)** You can now change the look of a picture by applying effects, such as shadows, reflections, glow, soft edges, and 3-D rotations.

- ◆ **Recolor Picture Quick Styles (p. 202-203)** The Recolor Picture Quick Style gallery provides a variety of different formatting combinations.

- ◆ **Text and Shape Quick Styles (p. 206-210, 230, 234-235, 250, 280)** You can quickly add different formatting combinations to text using WordArt Quick Styles or to a shape using Shape Quick Styles. You can also change individual styles by applying shadows, reflections, glow, soft edges, bevels, and 3-D rotations.

- ◆ **SmartArt graphics (p. 212-224)** SmartArt graphics allow you to create diagrams that convey processes or relationships. Excel provides a variety of built-in SmartArt graphic types, including organization charts, graphical lists, process, cycle, hierarchy, relationship, matrix, and pyramid.

- ◆ **Add a gradient to a line (p. 240-241)** You can now add a gradient fill to a line.

- ◆ **3-D Effects (p. 244-246)** You can add the illusion of depth to your worksheets by adding a 3-D effect to a shape. Create a 3-D effect by using one of the preset 3-D styles, or you can use the 3-D format tools to customize your own 3-D style.

- ◆ **Selection pane (p. 251)** With the Selection task pane, you can now select individual objects and change their order and visibility.

- ◆ **Table Quick Styles and effects (p. 292-296)** The Table Quick Style gallery provides a variety of different formatting combinations. You can change the look of a table by applying effects, such as shadows, reflections, glow, soft edges, 3-D rotations, and transformations.

- ◆ **Document Inspector (p. 334-335)** The Document Inspector uses inspector modules to find and remove any hidden data and personal information specific to the modules that you might not want to share with others.

- ◆ **Information Right Management (p. 342-343)** If you want to view or change the permissions for a workbook, you can use the Change Permission button on the Message Bar or the IRM icon button on the Status bar.

- ◆ **Trust Center (p. 350-359)** The Trust Center is a place where you set security options and find the latest technology information as it relates to document privacy, safety, and security from Microsoft. The Trust Center allows you to set security and privacy settings, including Trusted Publishers, Trusted Locations, Add-ins, ActiveX Settings, Macro Settings, Message Bar, and Privacy Options.

- ◆ **Microsoft Office safe mode (p. 360-361)** Microsoft Office 2007 uses two types of safe modes—Automated and User-Initiated—when it encounters a program problem. Safe mode only loads minimal features to help start the Office program.

- ◆ **Mark a workbook as final (p. 362)** The Mark as Final command makes an Excel 2007 workbook read-only and disables or turns off typing, editing commands, and proofing marks.

- ◆ **Microsoft Office Document Imaging (p. 424-425)** With Microsoft Office Document Imaging, you can now add annotations to a scanned document image, such as a fax.

- ◆ **ActiveX controls (p. 437, 448-449, 451)** Excel includes several pre-built ActiveX controls on the Developer tab, including a label, text box, command button, image, scroll bar, check box, option button, combo box, list box, and toggle button that you can insert into your workbooks to add functionality.

- ◆ **Microsoft Office Groove (p. 455-478)** With Office Groove 2007 (an enterprise program), you can bring a team, tools, and information together from any location to work on a project.

Excel 2007

- ◆ **New limits** Excel now supports up to 1 million rows and 16 thousand columns per worksheet. Formatting is now unlimited, and the number of cell references per cell is only limited by available memory. Memory management has increased from 1 GB to 2 GB.

- ◆ **Split worksheet (p. 15, 123)** You can split the worksheet into four panes and two scrollable windows that you can view simultaneously but edit and scroll independently using the Split button.

- ◆ **Excel 2007 Binary file format (p. 22-23)** In addition to the new XML-based file format, Excel also provides a new file format (BIFF12 with the extension .xls) to accommodate large or complex workbooks.

- ◆ **Page Layout view (p. 28, 172-175)** This view allows you to focus on the printed results. You can work with margin settings, headers, and footers directly in the worksheet, and place objects, such as charts or shapes, where you want.

- ◆ **Resizable formula bar (p. 74-75, 84-85)** The formula bar automatically resizes to accommodate long formulas. You can display formulas over multiple lines.

- ◆ **Formula AutoComplete (p. 76-77, 86-87)** You can quickly and correctly write functions with Formula AutoComplete, which detects what you type and tries to fill in the rest.

- ◆ **Name Manager (p. 88-89)** With the Name Manager, you can organize, update, and manage named ranges in one location.

- ◆ **Table references (p. 88)** You can now use table column header names in formulas instead of cell references.

- **Nested functions (p. 106)** A nested function uses a function as one of the arguments. Excel allows you to nest up to 64 levels of functions.

- **Draw a Border (p. 150-151)** You can draw a border outline or grid directly on a worksheet.

- **Cell Style (p. 164-167, 400)** A cell style is a defined collection of formats. You can use one of Excel's built-in cell styles, or create one of your own.

- **Rich conditional formatting (p. 136-143)** You can implement and manage multiple conditional formatting rules that apply rich visual formatting in the form of gradients colors, data bars, and icon sets to data.

- **Added chart types (p. 266-270)** Excel added more built-in chart layouts and styles to make charts more appealing and visually informative.

- **Chart template (p. 288-290)** You can now create a chart template (.crtx) to save a chart style for use in other workbooks.

- **Table header rows (p. 296)** You can turn table headers on or off.

- **Calculated columns (p. 296-297)** A calculated column allows you to use a single formula that automatically expands to include additional rows.

- **Total rows (p. 296-297)** You can now use custom formulas and text entries in a total row.

- **Table AutoFiltering (p. 302-303)** You can sort and filter table data using AutoFilter.

- **Sorting and filtering (p. 302-305)** Improved sorting and filtering allows you to sort data by color and by more than 3 levels, and to filter data by color or dates. With AutoFilter, you can filter multiple items and filter data in PivotTables.

- **PivotTables (p. 306-311)** An improved PivotTable interface makes it easier to add and remove data, and create and style PivotCharts using familiar chart tools. You can apply sorting, filtering, and conditional formatting to a PivotTable. If you make a mistake, you can now Undo most actions.

- **Create two columns (p. 313)** You can now split the contents of a cell into two cells.

- **Connect to external data (p. 388-389)** The Connection Manager makes it easy to access external data from databases and other sources to use in your workbooks.

- **Macros (p. 446-447)** If you add a macro to a workbook, you need to save it with a file name extension that ends with an "m", either Excel Macro-Enabled Workbook (.xlsm), or Excel Macro-Enabled Template (.xltm).

- **Excel Services (p. 480-481)** Excel Services is a Microsoft Office SharePoint Server 2007 component that you can use to share, secure, and manage Excel 2007 workbooks as interactive reports.

- ◆ **Document Management Server and SharePoint (p. 316, 480-482)** You can save your workbooks to a Document Management Server, such as a Document Library on an Office SharePoint site that provides you with tools to share and update documents and to keep people informed about the current status of the documents using a workflow and validation process.

What Happened To . . .

- ◆ **Detect and Repair** The Detect and Repair command has been replaced by Microsoft Office Diagnostics, which provides additional detection and repair capabilities.

  ➤ Click the **Office** button, click **Excel Options**, click **Resources**, and then click **Diagnose**.

- ◆ **File menu** The File menu has been replaced by the Office button and menu with a revised list of commands and options.

- ◆ **Lists** The Excel List feature has been renamed to Excel Tables.

  ➤ Select the range you want to turn into a table, click the **Insert** tab, and then click **Table**, or click the **Home** tab, click **Format as Table**, and then select a table format. You can use Ctrl+L (old shortcut) and Ctrl+T to create a table.

- ◆ **NetMeeting** NetMeeting is not available in Excel 2007. Instead you can use Microsoft Office Live Meeting. Check out the Microsoft Web site for details.

- ◆ **PivotTable and PivotChart Report command** Instead of starting a wizard, the PivotTable and PivotChart Report command has been separated into two commands—PivotTable and PivotChart—that each open a dialog box. Both commands are available on the Insert tab. The PivotTable command only creates a PivotTable report, while the PivotChart command creates a PivotChart report with an associated PivotTable report.

- ◆ **Scanner or Camera option** The From Scanner or Camera option for adding pictures to a workbook or photo album is not available in Excel 2007. Instead, you can download the pictures from your camera or scanner, or use the Microsoft Office Document Imaging program that comes with Office 2007, and then insert or paste them into Excel.

- ◆ **Send for Review** The Send for Review command is not available in Excel 2007. Instead, you can attach your workbook file to an e-mail message and send it to a reviewer. The reviewer can add comments and send the marked-up workbook back to you in an e-mail message.

  If you use Excel 2003 or earlier to send your workbook for review, reviewers who use Excel 2007 can view and add comments, but you cannot merge their comments into your workbook.

- ◆ **Web Toolbar** The Web toolbar is not available in Excel 2007, Word 2007, or PowerPoint 2007. However, you can still use some of the commands on the toolbar. You can add the Back and Forward buttons to the Quick Access Toolbar.

Microsoft Certified Applications Specialist

About the MCAS Program

The Microsoft Certified Applications Specialist (MCAS) certification is the globally recognized standard for validating expertise with the Microsoft Office suite of business productivity programs. Earning an MCAS certificate acknowledges you have the expertise to work with Microsoft Office programs. To earn the MCAS certification, you must pass a certification exam for the Microsoft Office desktop applications of Microsoft Office Word, Microsoft Office Excel, Microsoft Office PowerPoint, Microsoft Office Outlook, or Microsoft Office Access. (The availability of Microsoft Certified Applications Specialist certification exams varies by program, program version, and language. Visit *www.microsoft.com* and search on *Microsoft Certified Applications Specialist* for exam availability and more information about the program.) The Microsoft Certified Applications Specialist program is the only Microsoft-approved program in the world for certifying proficiency with Microsoft Office programs.

What Does This Logo Mean?

It means this book has been approved by the Microsoft Certified Applications Specialist program to be certified courseware for learning Microsoft Office Excel 2007 and preparing for the certification exam. This book will prepare you for the Microsoft Certified Applications Specialist exam for Microsoft Office Excel 2007. Each certification level has a set of objectives, which are organized into broader skill sets. Throughout this book, content that pertains to a Microsoft Certified Applications Specialist objective is identified with the following MCAS certification logo and objective number below the title of the topic:

Microsoft Certified Application Specialist EX07S-1.1
EX07S-2.2

Excel 2007 Objectives

Excel 2007 Objectives (continued)

Objective	Skill	Page
EX07S-2.3.2	Create custom cell formats	164-167
EX07S-2.3.3	Apply and modify cell styles	164-167
EX07S-2.3.4	Format text in cells	134-135, 144-145
EX07S-2.3.5	Convert text to columns	313
EX07S-2.3.6	Merge and split cells	146
EX07S-2.3.7	Add and remove cell borders	150-151
EX07S-2.3.8	Insert, modify and remove hyperlinks	398-399
EX07S-2.4	**Format data as a table**	
EX07S-2.4.1	Apply Quick Styles to tables	294, 296
EX07S-2.4.2	Add rows to a table	298-299
EX07S-2.4.3	Insert and delete rows and columns in tables	298-299, 300
EX07S-3	**Creating and Modifying Formulas**	
EX07S-3.1	**Reference data in formulas**	
EX07S-3.1.1	Create formulas that use absolute and relative cell references	80-83
EX07S-3.1.2	Create formulas that reference data from other worksheets or workbooks	80-83
EX07S-3.1.3	Manage named ranges	84-85,88-89
EX07S-3.1.4	Use named ranges in formulas	86-87, 90
EX07S-3.2	**Summarize data using a formula**	
EX07S-3.2.1	Use SUM, COUNT, COUNTA, AVERAGE, MIN, AND MAX	102-105
EX07S-3.3	**Summarize data using subtotals**	
EX07S-3.3.1	Create and modify list ranges	329, 330-331
EX07S-3.4	**Conditionally summarize data using a formula**	
EX07S-3.4.1	Using SUMIF, SUMIFS, COUNTIF, COUNTIFS, AVERAGEIF, AND AVERAGEIFS	330-331
EX07S-3.5	**Look up data using a formula**	
EX07S-3.5.1	Using VLOOKUP and HLOOKUP	326-327
EX07S-3.6	**Use conditional logic in a formula**	
EX07S-3.6.1	Using IF, AND, OR, NOT, IFERROR	106
EX07S-3.A7	**Format or modify text using formulas**	
EX07S-3.7.1	Using PROPER, UPPER, LOWER, SUBSTITUTE	328
EX07S-3.7.2	Convert text to columns	313

Objective	Skill	Page
EX07S-3.8	Display and print formulas	74-75
EX07S-4	**Presenting Data Visually**	
EX07S-4.1	**Create and format charts**	
EX07S-4.1.1	Select appropriate data sources for charts	260-261
EX07S-4.1.2	Select appropriate chart types to represent data sources	260-261, 281
EX07S-4.1.3	Format charts using Quick Styles	268-269
EX07S-4.2	**Modify charts**	
EX07S-4.2.1	Add and remove chart elements	274-275, 276-277
EX07S-4.2.2	Move and size charts	261, 264
EX07S-4.2.3	Change chart types	266-267
EX07S-4.3	**Apply conditional formatting**	
EX07S-4.3.1	Manage conditional formats using the rule manager	140, 141, 142
EX07S-4.3.2	Allow more than one rule to be true	136-139
EX07S-4.3.3	Apply conditional formats	136-139
EX07S-4.4	**Insert and modify illustrations**	
EX07S-4.4.1	Insert and modify pictures from files (not clip art files)	193, 194, 198-199, 201, 202-203
EX07S-4.4.2	Insert and modify SmartArt graphics	212-213, 218-219, 220-221
EX07S-4.4.3	Insert and modify shapes	226-227, 229, 234-235
EX07S-4.5	**Outline data**	
EX07S-4.5.1	Group and ungroup data	312
EX07S-4.5.2	Subtotal data	92-93, 297
EX07S-4.6	**Sort and filter data**	
EX07S-4.6.1	Sort data using single or multiple criteria	302-303
EX07S-4.6.2	Filter data using AutoFilter	304, 305
EX07S-4.6.3	Filter and sort data using conditional formatting	302-303
EX07S-4.6.4	Filter and sort data using cell attributes	302-303
EX07S-5	**Collaborating and Securing Data**	
EX07S-5.1	**Manage changes to workbooks**	
EX07S-5.1.1	Insert, display, modify, and resolve tracked changes	368-369
EX07S-5.1.2	Insert, display, modify, and delete comments	366-367

Excel 2007 Objectives *(continued)*

Objective	Skill	Page
EX07S-5.2	**Protect and share workbooks**	
EX07S-5.2.1	Protect workbooks and worksheets	336-337, 339, 340-341
EX07S-5.2.2	Enable workbooks to be changed by multiple users	364-365
EX07S-5.3	**Prepare workbooks for distribution**	
EX07S-5.3.1	Remove private and other inappropriate data form workbooks	334-335
EX07S-5.3.2	Restrict permissions to a workbook	342-343
EX07S-5.3.3	Add keywords and other information to workbook properties	27, 420
EX07S-5.3.4	Add digital signatures	344-345, 346-347, 444
EX07S-5.3.5	Mark workbooks as final	362
EX07S-5.4	**Save workbooks**	
EX07S-5.4.1	Save workbooks for use in a previous version of Excel	22-23, 26
EX07S-5.4.2	Using the correct format, save a workbook as a template, a Web page, a macro-enabled document, or another appropriate format	22-25, 183, 184, 228-230, 288-289, 402, 403
EX07S-5.5	**Set print options for printing data, worksheets and workbooks**	
EX07S-5.5.1	Define the area of a worksheet to be printed	180
EX07S-5.5.2	Insert and move a page break	176-177
EX07S-5.5.3	Set margins	172-173
EX07S-5.5.4	Add and modify headers and footers	174-175
EX07S-5.5.5	Change the orientation of a worksheet	170-171
EX07S-5.5.6	Scale worksheet content to fit a printed page	178-179

Preparing for a MCAS Exam

Every Microsoft Certified Applications Specialist certification exam is developed from a list of objectives based on how Microsoft Office programs are actually used in the workplace. The list of objectives determine the scope of each exam, so they provide you with the information you need to prepare for MCAS certification. Microsoft Certified Applications Specialist Approved Courseware, including the On Demand series, is reviewed and approved on the basis of its coverage of the objectives. To prepare for the certification exam, you should review and perform each task identified with a MCAS objective to confirm that you can meet the requirements for the exam.

Taking a MCAS Exam

The Microsoft Certified Applications Specialist certification exams are not written exams. Instead, the exams are performance-based examinations that allow you to interact with a "live" Office program as you complete a series of objective-based tasks. All the standard ribbons, tabs, toolbars, and keyboard shortcuts are available during the exam. Microsoft Certified Applications Specialist exams for Office 2007 programs consist of 25 to 35 questions, each of which requires you to complete one or more tasks using the Office program for which you are seeking certification. A typical exam takes from 45 to 60 minutes. Passing percentages range from 70 to 80 percent correct.

The Exam Experience

After you fill out a series of information screens, the testing software starts the exam and the Office program. The test questions appear in the exam dialog box in the lower right corner of the screen.

◆ The timer starts when the first question appears and displays the remaining exam time at the top of the exam dialog box. If the timer and the counter are distracting, you can click the timer to remove the display.

◆ The counter at the top of the exam dialog box tracks how many questions you have completed and how many remain.

◆ If you think you have made a mistake, you can click the Reset button to restart the question. The Reset button does not restart the entire exam or extend the exam time limit.

◆ When you complete a question, click the Next button to move to the next question. It is not possible to move back to a previous question on the exam.

◆ If the exam dialog box gets in your way, you can click the Minimize button in the upper right corner of the exam dialog box to hide it, or you can drag the title bar to another part of the screen to move it.

Tips for Taking an Exam

◆ Carefully read and follow all instructions provided in each question.

◆ Make sure all steps in a task are completed before proceeding to the next exam question.

◆ Enter requested information as it appears in the instructions without formatting unless you are explicitly requested otherwise.

◆ Close all dialog boxes before proceeding to the next exam question unless you are specifically instructed otherwise.

◆ Do not leave tables, boxes, or cells "active" unless instructed otherwise.

◆ Do not cut and paste information from the exam interface into the program.

◆ When you print a document from an Office program during the exam, nothing actually gets printed.

◆ Errant keystrokes or mouse clicks do not count against your score as long as you achieve the correct end result. You are scored based on the end result, not the method you use to achieve it. However, if a specific method is explicitly requested, you need to use it to get credit for the results.

◆ The overall exam is timed, so taking too long on individual questions may leave you without enough time to complete the entire exam.

◆ If you experience computer problems during the exam, immediately notify a testing center administrator to restart your exam where you were interrupted.

Exam Results

At the end of the exam, a score report appears indicating whether you passed or failed the exam. An official certificate is mailed to successful candidates in approximately two to three weeks.

Getting More Information

To learn more about the Microsoft Certified Applications Specialist program, read a list of frequently asked questions, and locate the nearest testing center, visit:

www.microsoft.com

Index

i

D

to pictures, 197
precedence of, 242
to shapes, 243, 244-245
to SmartArt graphics, 221
Solver, 317, 431
using, 324-325
sorting
cell names, 88
data, 291
fields, 302-303
with Groove, 471
tables, data in, 302
sounds
feedback with, 418
inserting, 187
source files, 378
spam, 348
spell-checking, 62
dictionaries, customizing, 64-65
foreign languages, 428
Groove messages, 475
proofing options, changing, 63
Spelling dialog box, 62
Spin button for ActiveX controls, 450
splitters, 15
splitting worksheets into panes, 123
spoofed Web sites, 348-349
Spotlight workbook templates, 11
spyware, 348
squares, drawing, 226
stacking order, changing, 252
standard modules in VBA (Visual Basic for
Applications), 435
standard tabs, 4
starting
Excel, 2
Groove, 456
Start menu, 2
Groove, launching, 457
Status bar
calculations, displaying, 91
controls, 3
using, 9
STDEV functions, 83
step mode, debugging macros with, 442
storing
cell contents, 49
data in Excel 2007, 16

straight connectors, 250
straight lines, drawing, 230
strikethrough text, 134-135
styles. *See also* cell styles; charts; Quick
Styles
ScreenTip styles, selecting, 412
sub procedures in VBA (Visual Basic for
Applications), 435
subscript text, 135
SUBSTITUTE function, 328
subtotals
calculating, 92-93
list, data in, 329
in PivotTable reports, 309
SUM function, 71, 102. *See also* Conditional
Sum Wizard
automatic calculations, 91
subtotals, calculation of, 329
SUMIF function, 330-331
summarize data functions, 330-331
superscript text, 135
surfaces
for data series, 279
shapes, adding to, 244-245
switching
between views, 28
between windows, 19
SYLK files, opening, 13
symbols, inserting, 59
synchronizing. *See also* Groove
scrolling of documents, 19
SharePoint files, 476-477
synonyms, 66
English Assistant finding, 69
syntax for VBA, 434

T

Tab key for selecting objects, 254
tables, 291. *See also* PivotTable
Access table into workbook, exporting,
392
AutoFilter, displaying parts with, 304
banded columns and rows in, 296
calculations in, 297
chart data tables, showing/hiding, 276-
277
clearing, 293
copying cell formats, 294

THIS BOOK IS SAFARI ENABLED

INCLUDES FREE 45-DAY ACCESS TO THE ONLINE EDITION

The Safari® Enabled icon on the cover of your favorite technology book means the book is available through Safari Bookshelf. When you buy this book, you get free access to the online edition for 45 days.

Safari Bookshelf is an electronic reference library that lets you easily search thousands of technical books, find code samples, download chapters, and access technical information whenever and wherever you need it.

TO GAIN 45-DAY SAFARI ENABLED ACCESS TO THIS BOOK:

- Go to **http://www.quepublishing.com/safarienabled**

- Complete the brief registration form

- Enter the coupon code found in the front of this book on page v

If you have difficulty registering on Safari Bookshelf or accessing the online edition, please e-mail customer-service@safaribooksonline.com.